AF687432

Maxon Cinema 4D 2023: A Detailed Guide to Shading, Lighting, and Rendering

IMPROVE YOUR EFFICIENCY WITH CINEMA 4D AND ELEVATE YOUR EXPERTISE AS A CINEMA 4D ARTIST

Pradeep Mamgain

nf

Maxon Cinema 4D 2023: A Detailed Guide to Shading, Lighting, and Rendering

© 2023 Neurons Factory. All rights reserved.

Except for brief excerpts used in critical articles or reviews, no part of this book may be reproduced, stored in a retrieval system, or transmitted in any form or by any means without the publisher's prior written permission.

NOTICE TO THE READER

Electronic Files

This textbook's electronic file in whatever form is licensed only to the original user and may not be transmitted to any other party.

Disclaimer

There is no patent liability assumed in connection with the use of the material included herein. Despite the fact that every precaution was taken in the preparation of this book, neither the author nor Neurons Factory, or its dealers or distributors, will be held accountable for any damages caused or alleged to be caused by this book, directly or indirectly. All terms recognized to be trademarks or service marks in this book have been written correctly. Neurons Factory cannot guarantee the accuracy of this information. The use of a term in this book does not affect the validity of any trademark or service mark.

Book Code: NFB003TD02

Visit our website at *https://neuronsfactory.com* for more information on the books, eBooks, and video courses published by *Neurons Factory*.

Contents

This page is intentionally left blank

Acknowledgments

My gratitude goes out to all those who supported me during the writing of this book. This includes those who provided guidance, shared their comments, and assisted with editing, proofreading, and design.

Thanks to:

Parents, family, and close friends

I extend my appreciation to my mentors and teachers for their valuable insights and guidance, which have been of great advantage to me.

I express my gratitude to all the students I have taught in the different institutions. Their participation has enabled me to learn new things about computer graphics that were previously unknown to me.

Everyone at Maxon [*https://www.maxon.net*].

Finally, thank you for picking up the book.

About the Author

I'll keep it short: I am a digital artist, instructor, and consultant, and the founder of Neurons Factory. My expertise in computer graphics is self-taught, and the Internet, where remarkable artists generously share their knowledge on YouTube, has been my primary learning resource. I enjoy guiding young aspiring 3D artists in their journey towards becoming professionals in the 3D animation and visual effects field. I have assisted my students in securing satisfying careers in these industries.

For nearly fifteen years, I have been involved in CGI. My primary software tools are Maya, 3ds Max, Cinema 4D, Photoshop, Nuke, After Effects, Filmora, and Fusion. In addition to computer graphics, I have an interest in web design/development, digital marketing, and search engine optimization.

You can contact me by sending an e-mail to *pm.nfactory@gmail.com*.

Preface

The book "**Maxon Cinema 4D 2023: A Detailed Guide to Shading, Lighting, and Rendering**" offers a comprehensive walkthrough of every step involved in texturing, lighting, and rendering projects using Cinema 4D. It's a valuable resource for novice and intermediate users of the software, providing insights into important concepts and techniques for rendering that can help you produce high-quality outputs. Whether you're just getting started with texturing, lighting, and rendering in Cinema 4D or looking to enhance your existing skills, this book has got you covered.

This guide takes a systematic and practical approach to teaching you the fundamentals of rendering, followed by real-world examples to improve your texturing and lighting abilities. Each chapter builds upon the previous one, covering all the essential aspects of rendering in Cinema 4D, including sampling, shaders, maps, camera and post effects, and lighting. As you work through the tutorials, you'll acquire a broad range of skills that can be combined to create top-notch renders using the **Standard** and **Physical** renderers. Additionally, you'll gain insight into Cinema 4D's node-based material system for creating material networks using nodes.

With its abundance of tips, tricks, notes, and cautions, this book is a valuable resource for anyone looking to improve their Cinema 4D rendering skills and streamline their workflow. It's a comprehensive guide aimed at teaching the essentials of rendering in Cinema 4D, presented in an accessible manner free of jargon. The tutorials included in the book provide clear step-by-step instructions on how to achieve various tasks using Cinema 4D. By the end of the book, you'll have the knowledge and skills to illuminate and render any scene in Cinema 4D with confidence.

What are the key features of the book?

- Detailed explanation of **Physical** and **Standard** renderers and render settings
- Explanation of post-effects such as **Global Illumination**, **Ambient Occlusion**, and **Color Mapping**
- In-depth coverage of depth-of-field and motion blur effects
- Tutorial on rendering flicker-free animation
- Use of the **Depth** pass to achieve dynamic depth-of-field
- Illuminating a scene using only polygon lights

- Exploration of Cinema 4D lights
- Techniques for product visualization and interior rendering
- Coverage of UV mapping
- Detailed explanation of the **Node Editor** and use of nodes in Cinema 4D
- More than **46** tutorials are included, along with before and after files.
- Explains the process of creating various materials.
- Additional guidance is provided in the form of tips, notes, and cautions.
- Important terms are in bold face so that you never miss them.
- The material presented under the heading "**What just happened?**" provides an explanation of how the instructions are functioning.
- Under the "**What next?**" heading, the content outlines the steps that should be taken after completing a particular step or set of steps.
- The resources for this textbook include an **ePub** file that contains color images of the screenshots and illustrations featured in the book. These images are provided to enhance the learning experience and are included as part of the resources.
- Access to the starting and ending states of each tutorial, as well as the resources used in the tutorials, is available to you.

Who this book is for?

- Beginners and intermediate users of Cinema 4D
- Digital artists
- Motion graphics artists
- Indie game developers
- And anyone who wants to learn Cinema 4D

Prerequisites

- No prior experience is required, beginners friendly
- Cinema 4D software installed on a computer or laptop
- Eagerness to learn and grow
- Willingness to be awesome

How this book is structured?

This book is divided into the following chapters:

- **Chapter 1 - Introduction to UV Mapping:** This chapter provides an overview of UVs, **UV Manager**, and **UV Projection** techniques.

- **Chapter 2 - Standard Renderer:** This chapter covers the basics of the **Standard** renderer, its settings, and various post-effects such as global illumination, ambient occlusion, and more. It also explains the process of creating dynamic depth-of-field effect.
- **Chapter 3 - Physical Renderer:** This chapter focuses on the **Physical** renderer, covering depth-of-field and motion blur effects, and illuminating a scene with polygon lights.
- **Chapter 4 - Material Presets:** This chapter introduces some of the material presets in Cinema 4D and how to create them from scratch.
- **Chapter 5 - Creating Materials:** This chapter explains the material creation process, including creating different materials and understanding the reflectance model of Cinema 4D.
- **Chapter 6 - Node-Based Materials:** This chapter delves into the node-based material system, discussing various nodes and how to use them to create node graphs.
- **Chapter 7 - Lighting:** This chapter covers Cinema 4D lights and various lighting techniques.

Conventions

Icons Used in This Book

Icon	Description
	Tip: A tip provides you with an alternative method to accomplish a task, as well as useful information such as a shortcut or workaround.
	Note: This icon is used to highlight certain points that you may want to keep in mind or remember.
	Caution: If you come across the caution icon in the book, be sure to take note as it indicates any possible adverse consequences that may arise from a particular operation.
	What just happened?: This icon directs your attention to the execution of instructions in a tutorial activity.
	What next?: This icon is used to indicate the steps to be followed in a tutorial activity.

Important Words
Important words such as the name of menu items, tool names, dialog box or window names, button names, and others are emphasized in boldface for better visibility and to highlight their importance. For example:

Select **Options** from the left pane. In the **Options** area, change **Ray Depth** to **6**, **Reflection Depth** to **3**, and **Shadow Depth** to **3**. Clear the **Automatic Size** checkbox and then expand the **Automatic Size** area. Now, change **Bucket Width** and **Bucket Height** to **32** each.

Figure Numbers
Figure numbers are assigned in the following order: Figure 1, Figure 2, and so on. In tutorials, the sequence is reset at the beginning of each tutorial.

Naming Terminology
LMB, MMB, and RMB
These abbreviations stand for the left, middle, and right mouse buttons, respectively.

MEV Menu
This abbreviation stands for Menu in editor view. It depicts the menubar in each Cinema 4D viewport.

Tool
When you click an item in a palette, toolbar, manager, or browser, a command is executed to create/edit an object or do some activity, that item is referred to as a tool. For instance, the **Move** tool, **Rotate** tool, **Loop Selection** tool, and so on.

Right-click Context Menus
Right-click menus (see Figure 1) are contextual menus in Cinema 4D that allow rapid access to commands/functions/tools linked to the presently selected entities.

Hidden Menus
Cinema 4D includes a number of hidden menus. These menus allow you to easily select tools, commands, and functions. The **M** menu, for example, provides easy access to modeling tools. For example, if you wish to launch the **Extrude** tool, hit **MT** (see Figure 2).

Check Box
A small box (labeled 1 in Figure 3) that, when selected by the user, indicates that a certain feature has been enabled or a specific option has been selected.

Drop-down
A drop-down (abbreviated drop-down list; also known as a drop-down menu, drop menu, pull-down list, or picklist) is a graphical control element (labelled as 2 in Figure 3) similar to a list box that allows the user to select one value from a list.

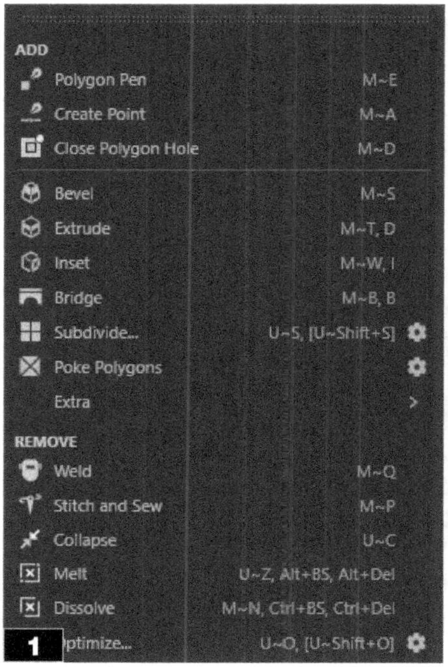

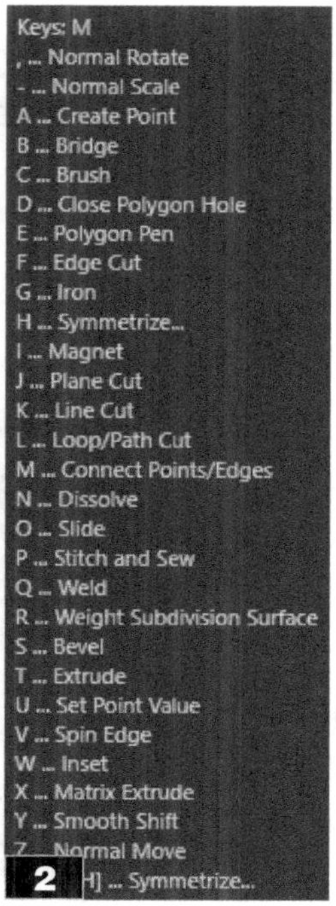

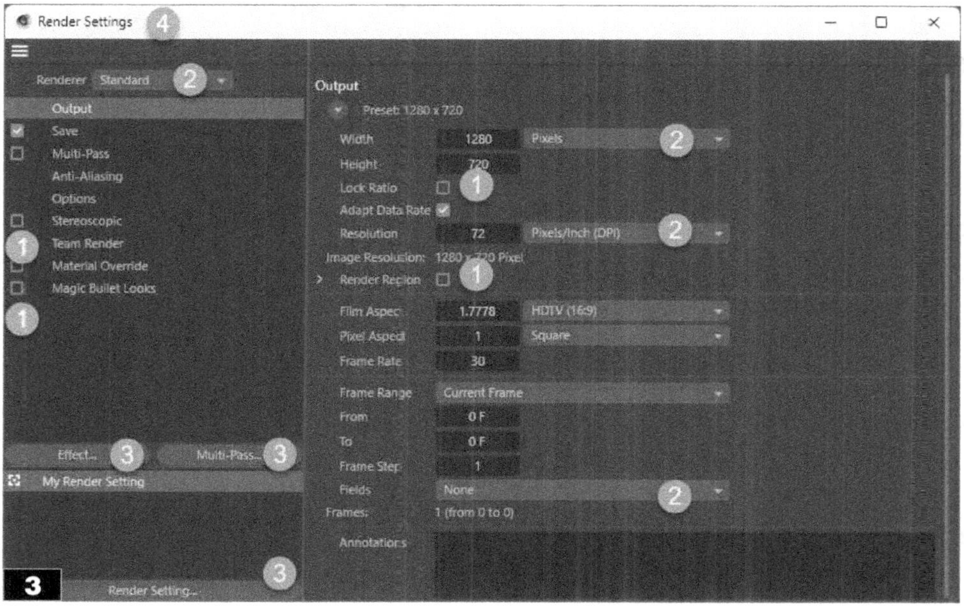

Button

The term button (also known as a command button or push button) refers to any graphical control element (labeled as 3 in Figure 3) that allows the user to easily start an event, such as searching for a query, or interact with dialog boxes, such as confirming an action.

Window
A window (labelled 4 in Figure 3) is a discrete viewing area on a computer display screen in a system that supports numerous viewing areas as part of a graphical user interface (GUI).

Dialog Box or Dialog
An area on screen (see Figure 4) in which the user is prompted to provide information or select commands.

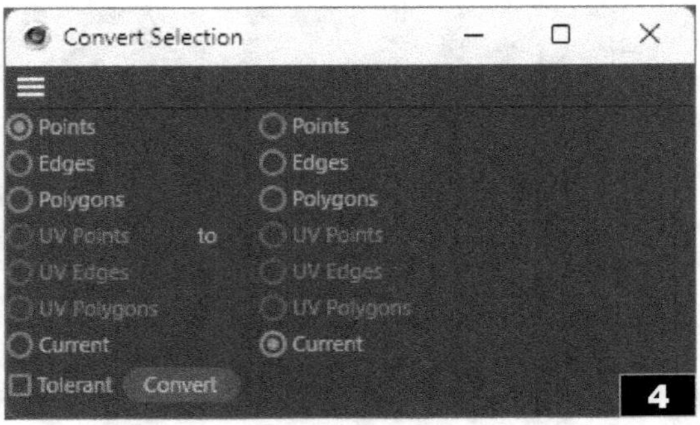

Trademarks
Windows is the registered trademarks of Microsoft Inc. Cinema 4D is the registered trademarks of Maxon Computer.

Access to Resources
This book is available through a variety of distribution platforms. If you do not have access to the resources used in this book, you can request them by visiting the following link: *https://neuronsfactory.com/contact.*

Tech Support
Neurons Factory's technical staff is always accessible to address your technical questions. If you encounter any technical difficulties while using the textbook, please contact the author at the following address: *pm.nfactory@gmail.com*.

Errata
We have made every effort to assure the accuracy of this book and its accompanying content. Please contact us if you see a problem so that we may improve the book's quality. If you find any errors, please report them at *https://neuronsfactory.com/errata*.

This will alleviate the annoyance of other readers. Your errata will appear in the errata section of the book's web page once confirmed.

CHAPTER 1: INTRODUCTION TO UV MAPPING

UV Mapping is a 3D modeling procedure that involves projecting a 2D image onto the surface of a 3D mesh for texture mapping. The letters **U** and **V** denote the axes for the 2D texture in 2D texture space because **X**, **Y**, and **Z** are used by Cinema 4D to represent the position of the mesh in the model space. The UV axes are enough for projecting traditional 2D textures. The third dimension (**W**) is used for 3D shaders and is generated automatically when needed.

TUTORIALS

TEXTURING A CARDBOARD BOX

Let's start by texturing a cardboard box (see Figure 1).

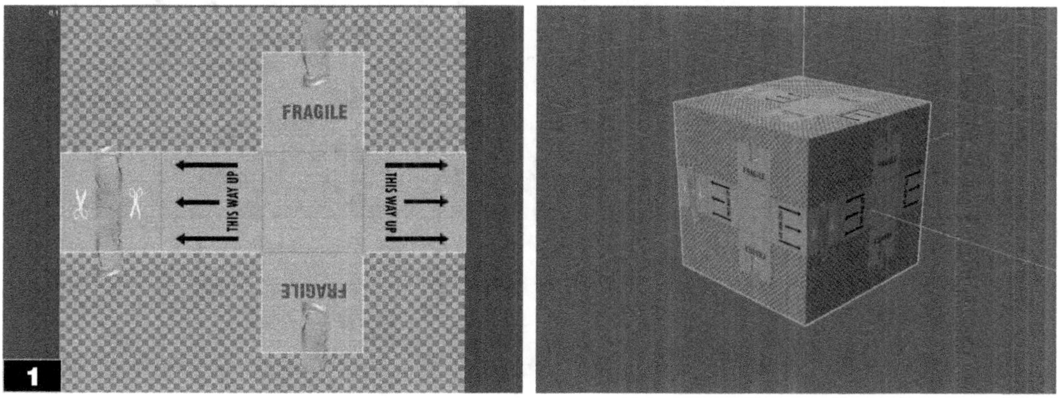

1

Summary	
Topics	Getting Started Texturing the Cardboard Box
Resources folder	**intro-uvmapping**
Final file	**cardboard-finish.c4d**

Getting Started

Start a new scene in Cinema 4D and change units to **Centimeters**.

Texturing the Cardboard Box

Follow these steps:

1. Click **Cube** in the **Objects** palette > **Mesh** command group to create a cube in the editor view. Press **C** to make the cube editable. Double-click on the **Material Manager** to create a new material node. In the **Attribute Manager** > **Mat** > **Color** tab, click on the folder icon and then select the **cardboard_texture.png** file.

> ***WHAT JUST HAPPENED?***
> *I've created a new material and assigned the **cardboard_texture.png** file to it. We will use the UVs of the cube to fit on this pre-made texture.*

2. Drag the **Mat** material to the **Cube** in the viewport. The texture is visible on each face of the cube (see Figure 2). In the **Object Manger**, the **Material Tag "Mat"** is also applied to the **Cube** (see Figure 3).

2

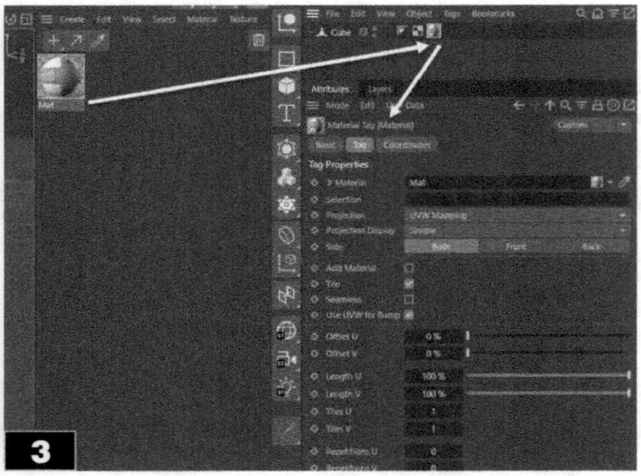

3

> ***WHAT JUST HAPPENED?***
> *When we apply a material to an object, it automatically receives a texture tag. The texture tag specifies how the texture should be mapped or put on the object. The settings are displayed in the **Attribute Manager**.*

3. In the **Attribute Manager** > **Material Tag (Material)** > **Tag** tab, change **Projection** to **Spherical**; notice in the 3D view that the texture is wrapped around the object using the spherical projection. Click **Texture** on the **Standard** palette to view the projection sphere in the 3D view (see Figure 4). You can move the texture on the cube by moving, rotating, or scaling the projection sphere (displayed in wireframe). Experiment with other projection types available in the **Projection** drop-down list.

4. Click **Model** on the **Standard** palette to switch to the **Model** mode. Delete the material tag from the **Object Manager**. **RMB** click on **Cube** in the **Object Manager** and then choose **Material Tags > Material** from the context menu to apply a blank material tag to the object.

5. Drag **Mat** from the **Material Manager** and drop it on the **Material** field in the **Attribute Manager**.

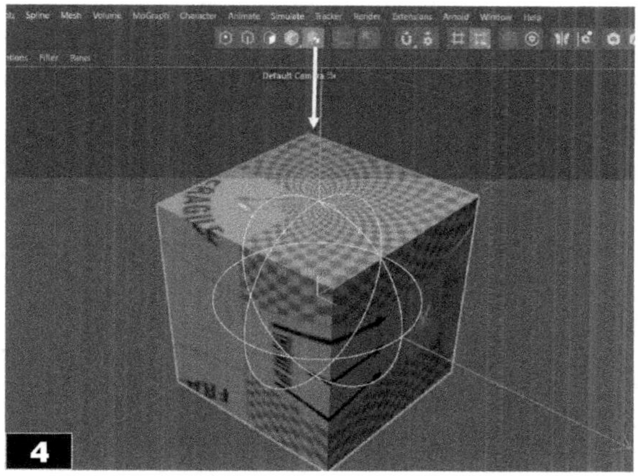

4

Material Tag

As previously stated, whenever a material is applied to an object, a material tag is added to the object in the **Object Manager**. When you select this tag, the **Attribute Manager** displays its attributes. To assign materials to an object, you can use one of the following methods:

- Drag the material from the **Material Manager** to the name of the object in the **Object Manager**.
- Select object in the **Object Manager**, then the material in the **Material Manager**. Next, in the **Material Manager**, click the **Apply** button.
- Drag and drag a new material from the **Material Manager** onto an existing **Material** tag. The new material will replace the old one, but the previous **Material** tag attributes will be carried over.
- To apply a new material to an object in the viewport, drag and drop the material onto the object. If there are multiple objects in the region where you drop the material, hold down the **Ctrl** key while dropping it to display a menu. From the menu, select the object to which you want to apply the material.
- Select the material and then navigate to the **Attribute Manager**'s **Assign** tab. To apply material to an item, drag it from the **Object Manager** to the **Assignment** box on the **Assign** tab.

MATERIAL ATTRIBUTES
*To view the settings for a material, double-click on its **Material** tag. This will open up the corresponding material's settings either in the **Attribute Manager** or the **Material Manager**.*

ANIMATING MATERIALS
*The **Material** field has the capability to be animated in order to morph materials. It allows for seamless blending between two materials without any noticeable steps or transitions.*

Selection

The **Selection** field enables you to apply distinct materials to various parts of an object. To use this feature, you must first create a selection tag and then drag it from the **Object Manager** to the **Selection** field. Alternatively, you can type in the name of the selection directly into the field. This parameter operates in a hierarchical manner, meaning that a **Material** tag with a designated **Selection** field will project the material onto all child objects that have a corresponding **Selection** tag. This function is useful, for instance, when you want to add labels to objects.

Projection Display

The options in the **Projection Display** drop-down list allow you to define how the projection assistance display can be adjusted in the viewport. There are three options available:

- **Simple:** Only the projection shape is displayed (see Figure 5).
- **Grid:** Displays he yellow grid that was present in previous versions of Cinema 4D before R20 (see Figure 6).
- **Solid:** A solid grid is displayed that provides an easy way to determine the orientation. (see Figure 7).

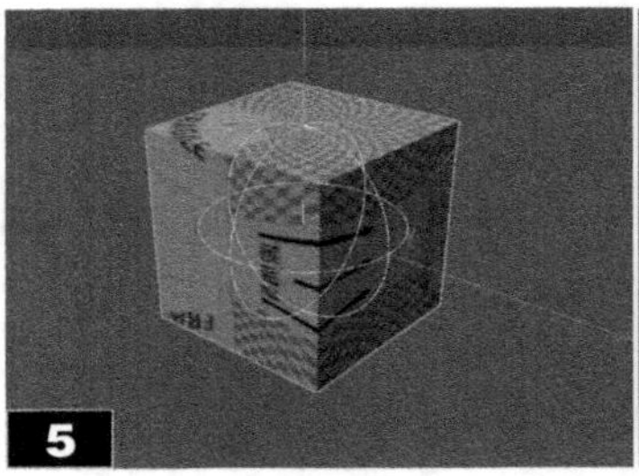

5

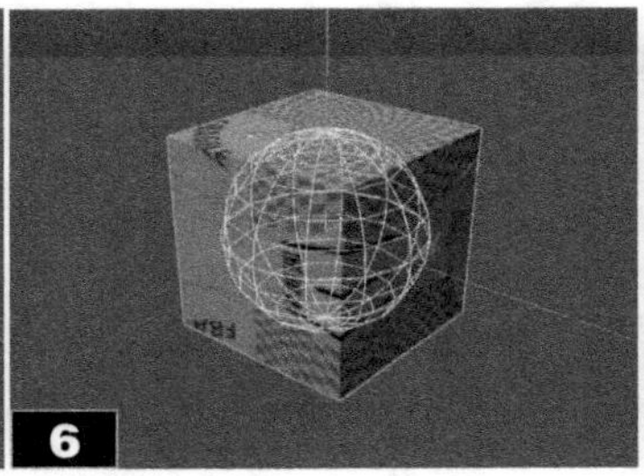

6

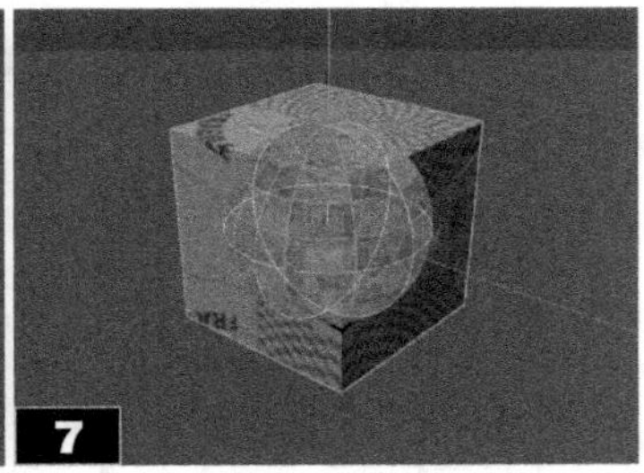

7

Projection

The options in the **Projection** drop-down list are used to define the type of UV projection. Given below is a quick rundown:

- **Spherical:** This option projects the texture onto the object in a spherical form.
- **Cylindrical:** It projects the texture onto the object in a cylindrical form.
- **Flat:** It projects the texture onto the object in a planar direction.
- **Cubic:** This option projects the texture onto all six sides of a texture cube.
- **Frontal:** This option allows you to project the texture from the camera position onto the object.
- **Spatial:** This mapping technique resembles flat projection. Nevertheless, with spatial mapping, the texture is shifted up and to the left as it moves through the object.
- **Flat:** In contrast to spatial mapping, this technique does not cause any distortion.

- **UVW Mapping:** If an object has UVW coordinates, you have this option to select them as the projection type.
- **Shrink Wrap:** When using this projection type, the texture's center is fixed to the north pole of a sphere while the rest of the texture is stretched over it. The benefit of this mapping method is that the texture only meets itself at the south pole, which eliminates the need for a seam running between the poles.
- **Camera Mapping:** This option is used to project the texture from the camera onto the object.

Add Material

By selecting this checkbox, the material becomes additive, allowing you to combine multiple textures. However, only certain channels can be additive, including **Color**, **Transparency**, **Reflectance**, **Bump**, **Displacement**, and **Luminance**. To use an additive material, it must be positioned to the right of the texture to which it should be added in the **Object Manager**. Nevertheless, using a **Layer** shader is a superior option for blending materials, as it provides numerous controls for defining the material.

Seamless

When you select the **Seamless** checkbox, the tiles are mirrored to prevent visible seams. This option is not useful for photographed textures but can produce interesting patterns, especially for materials like wood, marble, and others with a repetitive pattern.

Offset UV/Length UV

The **Offset** and **Length** options specify the texture's position and size on the texture envelope in the **U** and **V** axes. For example, if **Length U** and **Length V** are both set to **100%**, the texture entirely fills the envelope.

Tiles UV

The **Tiles** values determine how many times the texture fits onto the texture envelope in the **U** and **V** directions (**Length U** and **Length V**).

Repetitions UV

These values are used to determine how frequently the tiling should repeat in all directions.

6. Change **Projection** to **UVW Mapping** in the **Attribute Manager**.

WHAT JUST HAPPENED?

Cinema 4D's default projection type is ***UVW Mapping****. This projection type is only applicable to objects with UVW coordinates. By default, all primitive and generator objects have UVW coordinates. In the* ***Object Manager****, all polygon objects have a* ***UVW*** *tag, whereas primitive and generator objects have internal UVW coordinates. They do not have a* ***UVW*** *tag in the* ***Object Manager****. The tag appears when you convert them to editable polygon objects.*

WHAT ARE UVW COORDINATES?
*You might be wondering why we need a third dimension if a texture image is only two dimensions. Textures in the conventional sense have two dimensions: horizontal position **X** (**U**) and vertical position **Y** (**V**).These two coordinates are adequate for conventional shaders, but 3D shaders require a third dimension. In order to properly overlay textures on the objects, these shaders require a third dimension (**W**).*

WHAT IS THE STRUCTURE OF THE UVW COORDINATES?
*A UV grid is divided into two directions: **U** and **V** (see Figure 8). The range begins at **0** and ends at **1**.*

A texture is stretched between four coordinates. The grid represents a standard 2D texture. Perhaps you're wondering where the third coordinate W is. It is only created when needed and acts similarly to UV coordinates.

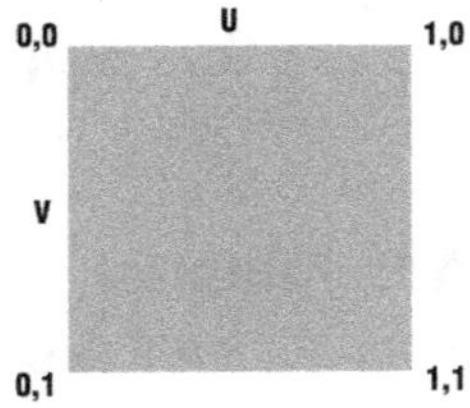

8

7. Switch to the **UVEdit** layout.

8. Choose **File > Open Texture** from **Texture UV Editor** menu (see Figure 9). Navigate to the **cardboard_texture.png** file and then click **Open**, the texture appears in the **Texture View** (see Figure 10).

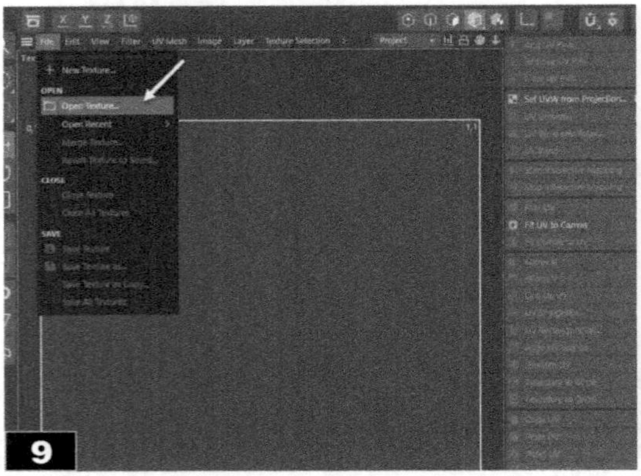
9

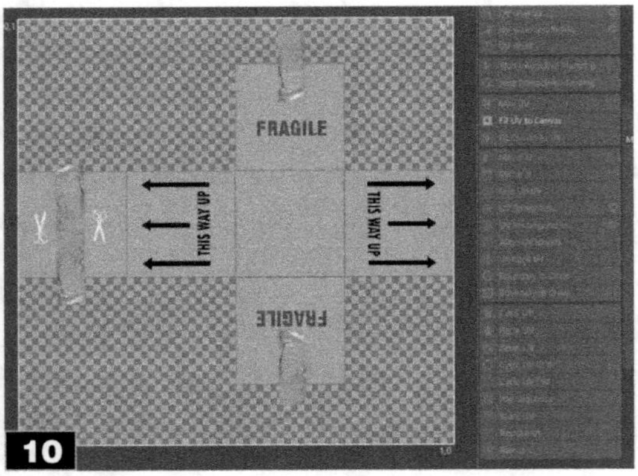

10

9. Activate the **Polygons** mode and then press **Ctrl A** to select all polygons. In the **UV Manager > Projection** tab, click **Cubic 2**, the selected polygons are unwrapped and displayed in the **Texture View** (see Figure 11). Notice in the viewport, the text **THIS WAY UP** is not oriented in the right direction (see Figure 12). Now, we will fix it.

WHAT JUST HAPPENED?
*When you activate a component mode, Cinema 4D allows you to select and modify UVs using a variety of tools. The **Cubic 2** mapping type applies textures onto the cube's six sides while also relaxing them.*

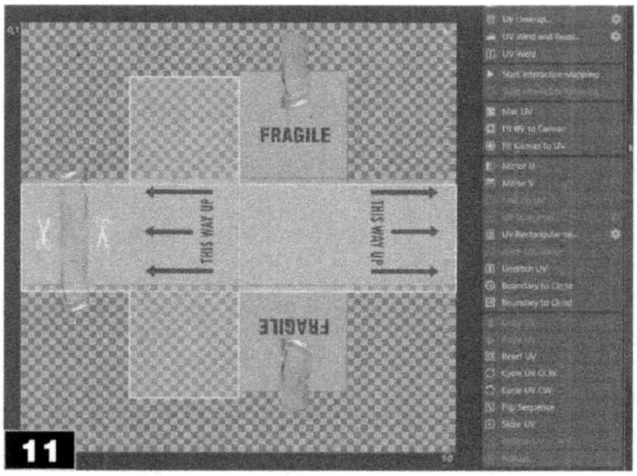

11

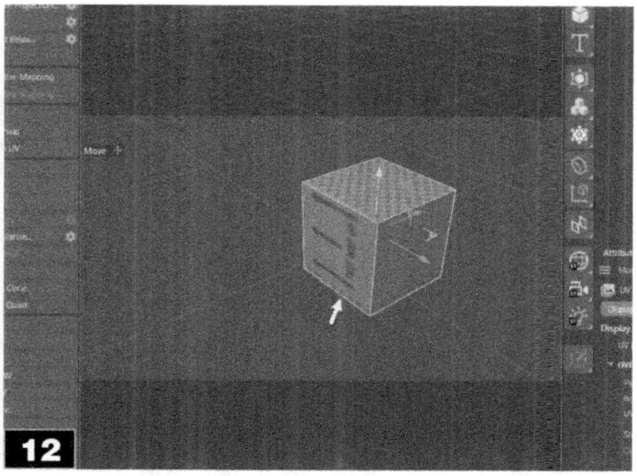

12

10. Activate the **Points** mode and select the bottom four points of the cube (see Figure 13). Choose **UV Mesh > PINS > Add UV Pins** from the **Texture UV Editor** menu (see Figure 14).

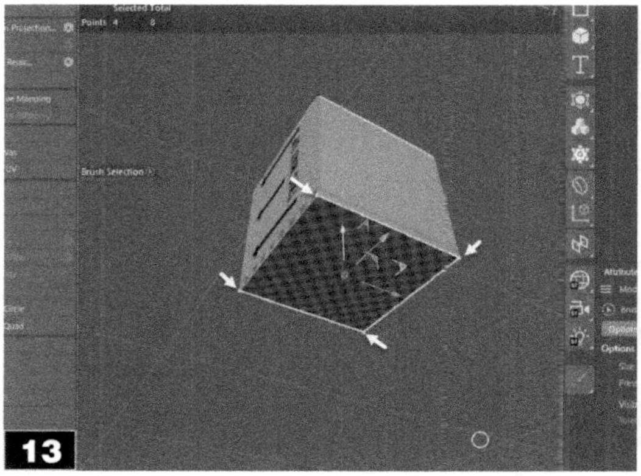

13

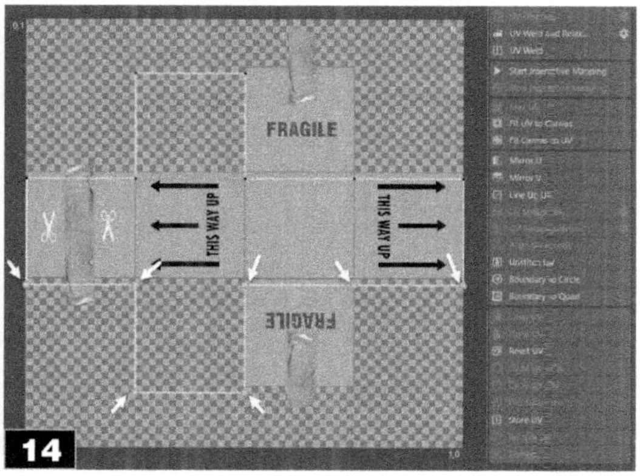

14

WHY THESE POINTS ARE SELECTED?
As you relax UVs in the following steps of the tutorial, these four points will be pinned (locked) to their present location and will not move. The goal here is to keep the bottom face in place while unfolding the other faces around it.

11. Activate the **Polygons** mode and then select all polygons by pressing **Ctrl A**. Switch to the **Top** viewport and then go to the **Projection** tab in the **UV Manager**. Then, click on the **Frontal** button.

12. Switch to the **Perspective** viewport and then select the edges, as shown in Figure 15.

WHY THESE EDGES ARE SELECTED?
Cuts (seams) are applied on these edges of the cube to avoid UV-coordinate distortion.

13. In the **UV Manager > Relax UV** tab, select the **Use UV Pins**, **Cut Selected Edges**, and **Auto Realign** checkboxes. Select **ABF** from the drop-down list located above

the **Apply** button. Then, click on the **Apply** button (see Figure 16); polygons are unwrapped in **Texture View**.

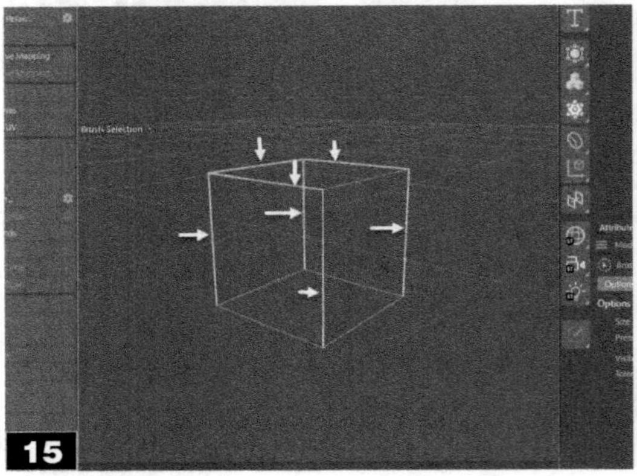

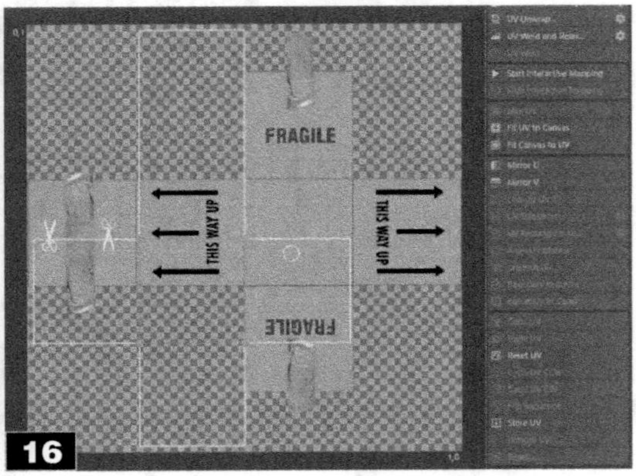

Relaxing

Relaxing UVs is a technique for improving the UV mesh. When you relax a mesh, Cinema 4D adds invisible springs to the UVs and then extends them to prevent overlap. To remove the overlaps, keep clicking **Apply**. This command is applied to the whole mesh if no UVs are selected. **ABF** and **LSCM** are the two modes accessible for UV relaxation. The **ABF** mode is superior to **LSCM**, however it is somewhat slower. It is advised that **ABF** be used with organic forms.

When you select the **Pin Border Points** checkbox, the UV points at the selection's edge are locked in place. When the **Pin to Neighbors** checkbox is selected, UV points that are related to unselected polygons are fixed in place. It allows you to disentangle complex parts of a UV mesh. If both checkboxes are deselected, the UV mesh will shrink with each click of the **Apply** button.

Select **Use UV Pins** checkbox if you have pinned some UVs to avoid some regions from shrinking together or being distorted while relaxing UVs. If you have created a selection tag that you want to use with relaxing UVs, enable the **Use Tag** checkbox and then drag the tag to the field underneath the **Use UV Pins** checkbox. Select the **Cut Selected Edges** checkbox if you wish to cut the selected edges. You may also use a selection tag with this parameter.

14. Activate the **Polygons** mode and then press **Ctrl A** to select all polygons. In the **UV Manager > Transform** tab, enter **-180** in the **Rotate** field and then click **Apply** to rotate the polygons. Then, use the **Move** and **Scale** tools to roughly fit polygons on the texture (see Figure 17).

15. Activate the **Points** mode and then adjust the points using the **Move** tool to perfectly align polygon edges with the texture (see Figure 18).

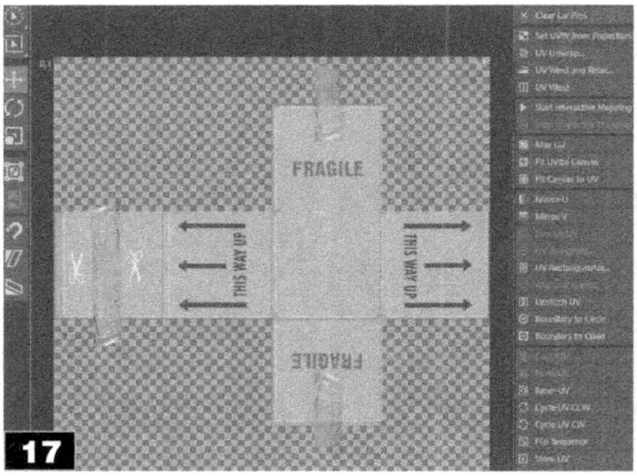

17

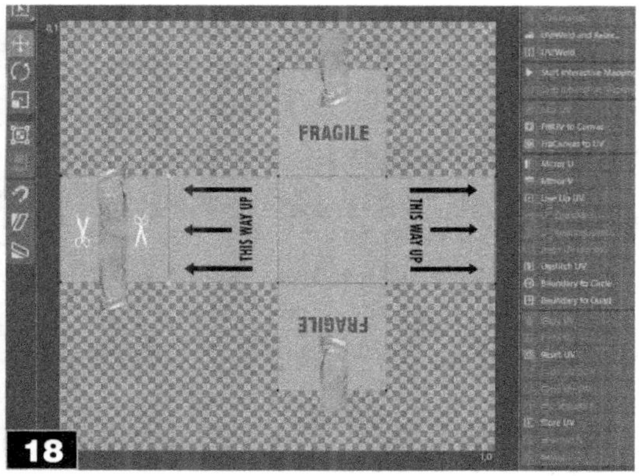

18

TEXTURING A DICE

In this tutorial, we will texture a dice (see Figure 1).

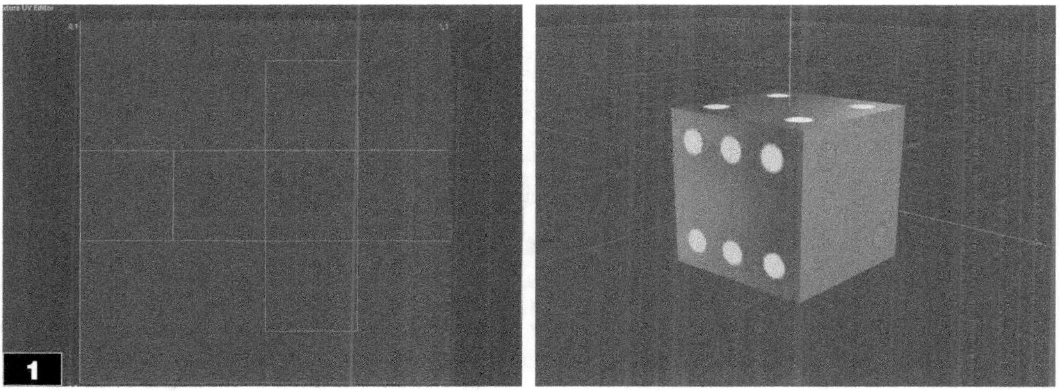

1

Summary	
Topics	Getting Started Texturing the Dice
Resources folder	**intro-uvmapping**
Start file	**dice-start.c4d**
Final file	**dice-finish.c4d**

Getting Started

Open open **dice-start.c4d** and then switch to the **UVEdit** layout.

Texturing the Dice

Follow these steps:

1. Choose **File > New Texture** from the **Texture UV Editor** menu to open the **New Texture** dialog box. In this dialog box, rename the texture as **diceText**. Change **Color**

to white and then click **OK**. Notice **diceText.tif** is selected in the **Texture View's Textures** menu (see Figure 2).

EMPTY CANVAS
*Choose **Empty Canvas** from the **Textures** menu to see the empty canvas. This command removes the currently active texture from the **UV Editor**. To display a standard UV texture, select **UV Map**. It can be used to assess distortion.*

2. Choose **Layer > ADD > New Layer** from the **Texture UV Editor** menu to create a new layer. Choose **Window > UV EDIT AND PAINT > Layer Manager** from the main menu to open the **Layers** window. Notice in the **Layers** window, a new layer with the name **Layer** appears in the **Layers** window. The **Background** layer is the layer created when you assigned the white color using the **New Texture** dialog box. Double-click on **Layer** label in the **Layers** window and rename it as **Outlines** (see Figure 3).

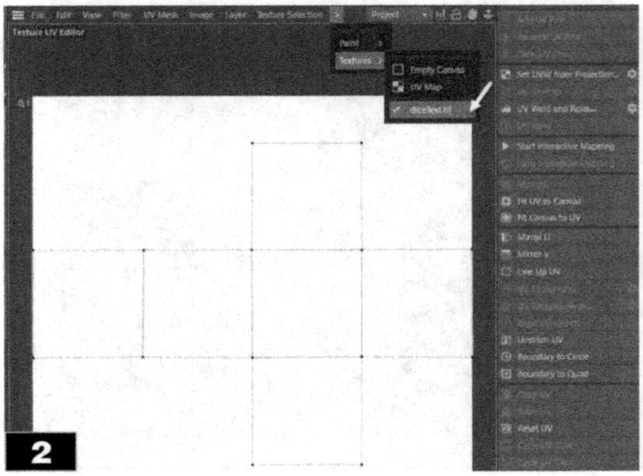

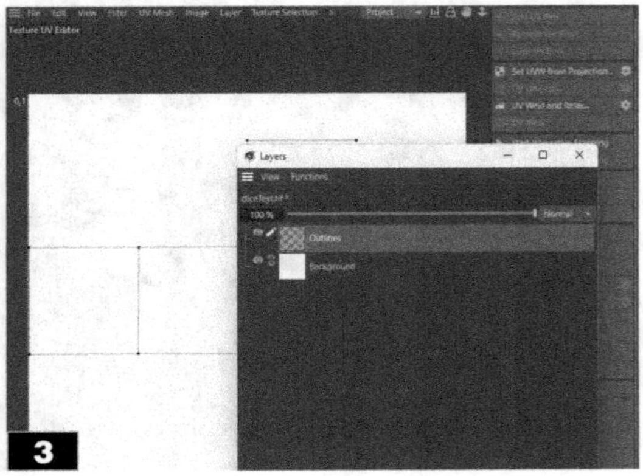

WHY NEW LAYER?
*Initially, a texture contains only one layer (canvas) called **Background**. You can use layers to accomplish non-destructive editing. You can paint on each layer separately. Each layer can be edited separately from the canvas and other layers. I wanted to make outlines for the polygons here so that when the **UV Template** is opened in Photoshop, the outlines display on a separate layer.*

3. Switch to the **Polygons** mode and ensure the **Outlines** layer is selected. Choose **Layer > Outline Polygons** from the **Texture UV Editor** menu. Now, if you switch to the **Model** mode and click the eye icon of the **Background** layer to turn it off, you will notice that the outlines are created in white color (see Figure 4).

4. Choose **Image > MODIFY > Texture Size** from the **Texture UV Editor** menu to open the **Scale Texture** dialog box. In this dialog box, set **Width** and **Height** to **1024** each (see Figure 5). Then, click **OK**.

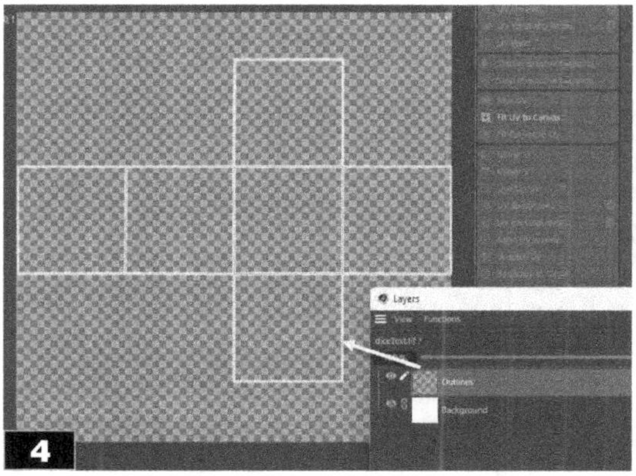
4

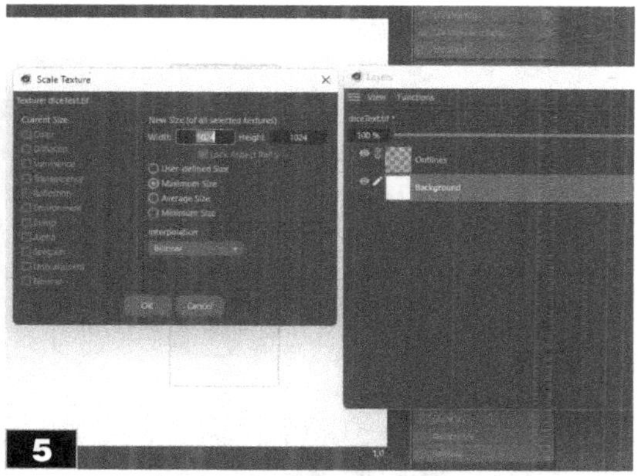
5

5. Turn on the visibility of the **Background** layer. Choose **File > SAVE > Save Texture As** from the **Texture UV Editor** menu to open the **Please choose the file format** dialog box. In this dialog box, select **PSD (*.psd)** option from the **Save File as** drop-down list and then click **OK**. In the **Save Channel as *.psd** dialog box that appears, save the texture with the name **diceTextPSD**.

6. Launch **Photoshop** and open **diceTextPSD.psd**. Notice in the **Layers** panel, two layers **Background** and **Outlines** appear. These are the layers we created in Cinema 4D. Fill the **Background** layer with **Black** color (see Figure 6).

7. Create dots on the dice layout using white color (see Figure 7).

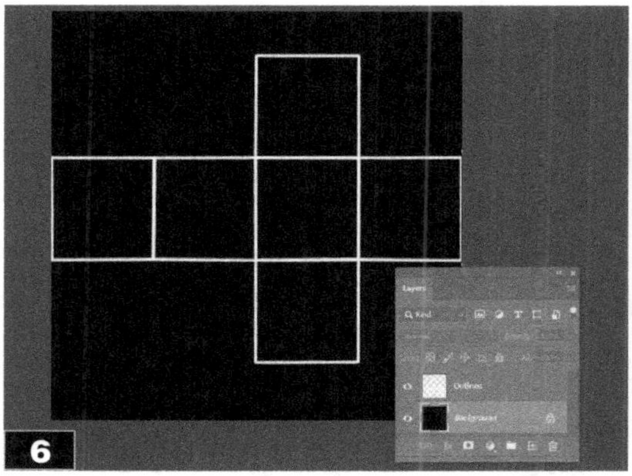
6

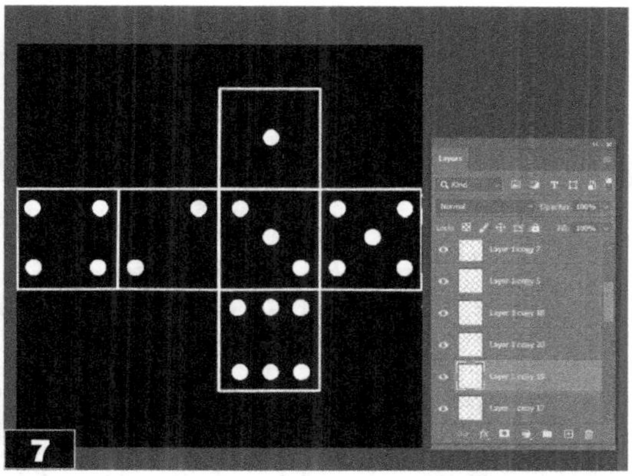
7

8. Delete the **Outlines** layer and then merge all dots layers. Also, create an alpha channel for the dots (refer to Figure 8). Now, rename dots layer as **DiceDots** and alpha channel as **diceAlpha**. Hide the **Background** layer and then save the Photoshop file.

9. Select the **Mat** node in the **Material Manager**. In the **Attribute Manager > Mat > Color** tab, change **HSV** to **233**, **90**, and **87**, respectively. In the **Reflectance** tab, click **Add** and then choose **Phong** from the popup to create a Phong reflectance layer with the name **Layer 1**. In the **Layer Color** section, change **Brightness** to **50**.

10. Create another material and then apply it to the **Cube**. In the **Attribute Manager > Color** tab, click the folder icon corresponding to the **Texture** parameter and then load the **diceTextPSD.psd**. In the **Basic** tab, select the **Alpha** checkbox to activate the **Alpha** channel. In the **Alpha** tab, click triangle next to the **Texture** label and then choose **Bitmaps > diceTextPSD.psd** from the popup menu. Make sure the order of the material should be same as shown in Figure 9. Render the scene.

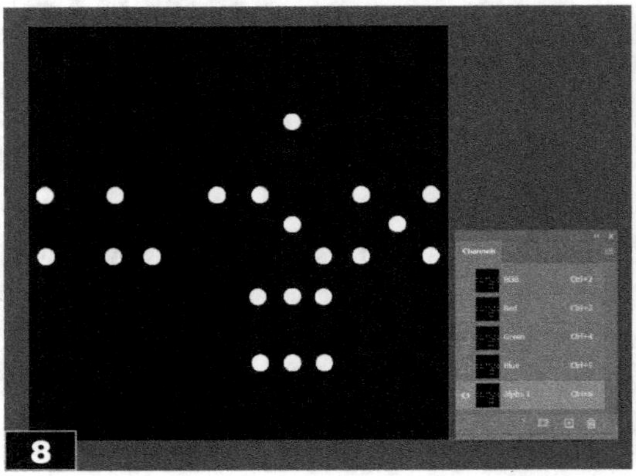

8

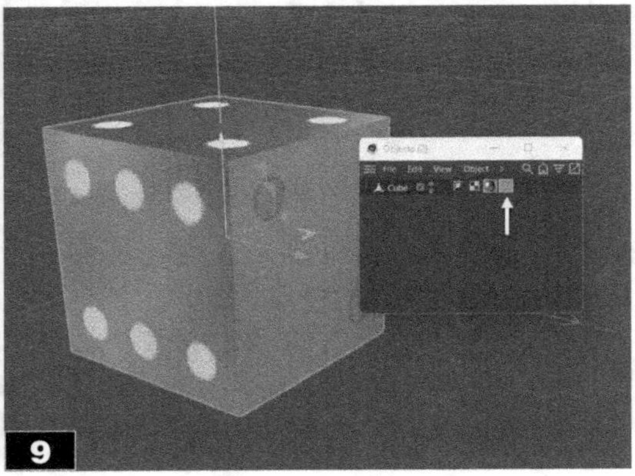

9

WHAT ALPHA IS REQUIRED?
You can use the alpha channel to mask off areas of the material. The objective is to define the region of the material that becomes non-existent and reveals the underlying material. In this case, I've created a blue material, and we also have an alpha channel in the PSD. When we applied the ***diceTextPSD.psd*** *to the material's alpha channel, the dots occluded the blue material while allowing the remainder of the blue to show through.*

RELAXING A HEAD MODEL

In this tutorial, we will unwrap a head model by relaxing UVs (see Figure 1).

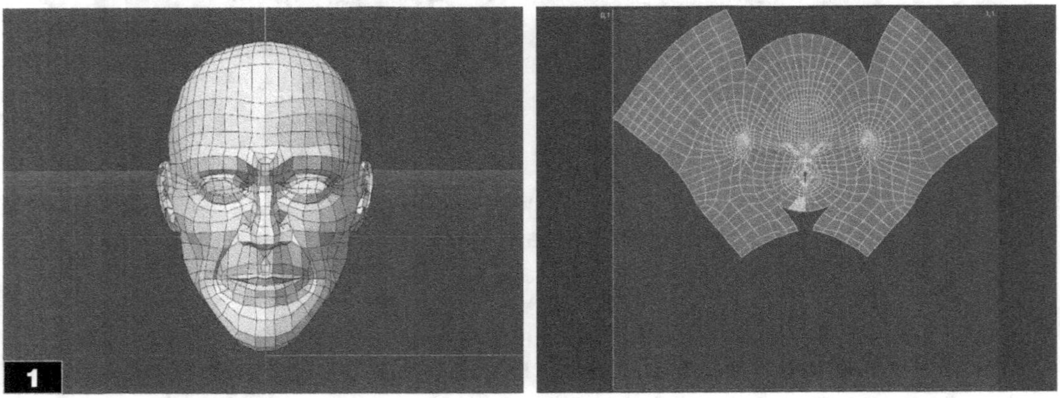

1

Summary	
Topics	Getting Started Unwrapping the Head Model
Resources folder	**intro-uvmapping**
Start file	**head-start.c4d**
Final file	**head-finish.c4d**

Getting Started

Open the **head-start.c4d** file and then switch to the **UVEdit** layout.

Unwrapping the Head Model

In order to relax the UVs, we will first define the lock points and cut edges. Follow these steps:

1. Activate the **Polygons** mode and then press **Ctrl A** to select all polygons. Switch to the **Front** view and then in the **UV Manager > Projection** tab, click **Frontal** (see Figure 2).

2. Activate the **Points** mode and then select the points shown in Figure 3. Choose **UV Mesh > PINS > Add UV Pins** from the **Texture UV Editor** menu.

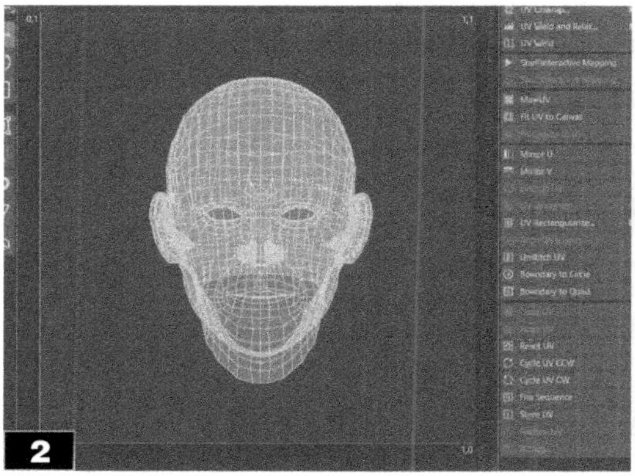

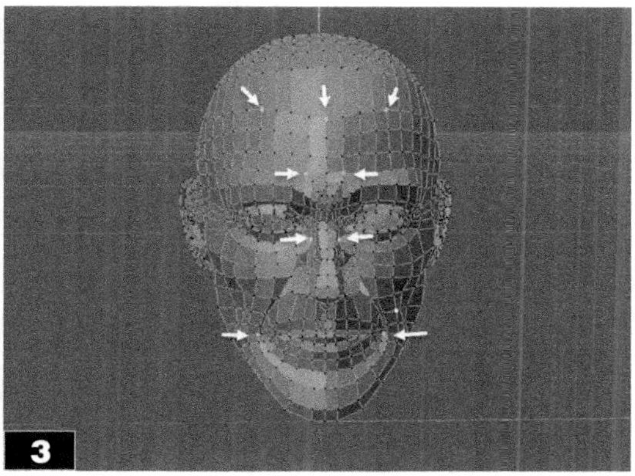

3. Now, activate the **Edges** mode and select the edges as shown in Figure 4.

4. In the **UV Manager > Relax UV** tab, select the **Use UV Pins**, **Cut Selected Edges**, and **Auto Realign** checkboxes. Select **ABF** from the drop-down list located above the **Apply** button. Then, click on the **Apply** button; polygons are unwrapped in **Texture View**.

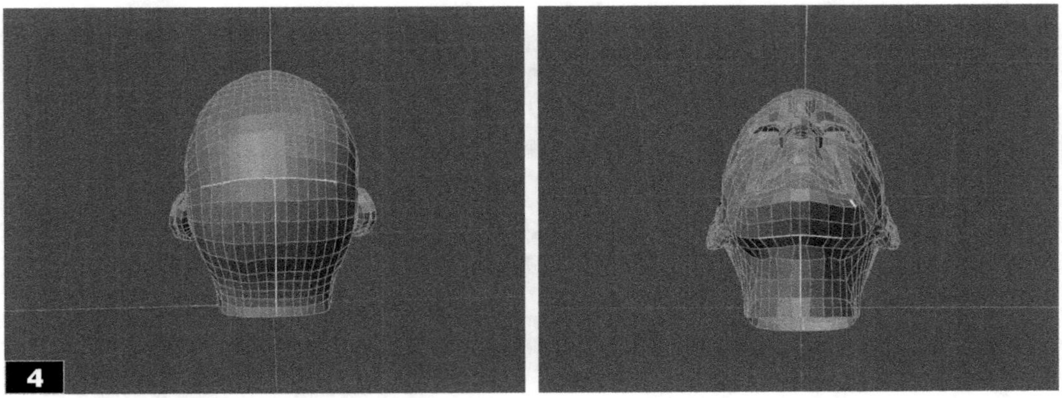

4

WHAT AUTO REALIGN DOES?
This checkbox makes sure that the relaxed mesh fits the texture.

UNWRAPPING MESHES

In this tutorial, we will unwrap several meshes.

Summary	
Topics	Getting Started Unwrapping Meshes
Resources folder	**intro-uvmapping**
Start file	**model-a.c4d**
Final file	**model-a-finish.c4d**

Getting Started

Switch to the **UVEdit** layout.

Unwrapping Meshes

Follow these steps:

1. Open **model-a.c4d**. Then, choose **Mode > UV Settings** from the **Attribute Manager** menu. In the **Display > OVERLAYS** section, set **Shading** to **Distortion**.

UV Settings

The **Display** section contains settings for defining how UV elements are presented in the viewport. It provides visual feedback on the position and quality of UVs. Because I have **Shading** set to **Distortion**, distortion will be color coded in the viewport. The blue color represents stretched UVs, the red color represents squashed UVs, and the light gray color represents undistorted UVs.

Other options in the Shading drop-down list include:

- **Lines:** The UV Islands will not be colored, and the backdrop or texture beneath the UV mesh will be entirely visible.
- **Overlapping Polygons:** It shows overlapping UVs in bright red.
- **Filled Polygons:** This option fills UV Islands with a single color so that available UV surfaces can be clearly identified.
- **Multi-Color Islands:** It assigns a random color to each UV island.

The **UV Display** checkbox controls whether UV-specific components are displayed in the **Texture UV Editor**. By default, **Seams** is selected in the **Boundaries** drop-down list. As a result, the UV Seams will be highlighted in the viewport, as will the UV Islands. If you select **Connectivity**, UV Seams that share an edge will be rendered in the same color. This lets you to see where the UV Islands dock. The **UV Mesh** checkbox toggles the visibility of the UV mesh's points, edges, or polygons in the **Texture UV Editor**. Selected items will continue to be displayed regardless of this setting.

2. Select **Cylinder** in the **Object Manager**. **RMB** click on **Cylinder** in the **Object Manager** and then choose **Material Tags > Set UVW from Projection** from the context menu to apply a blank projection tag to the object; UVs are displayed in the **Texture UV Editor** (see Figure 1). Also, notice the distortion in the UVs.
3. Activate the **Edges** mode and then select edge loops, as shown in Figure 2.

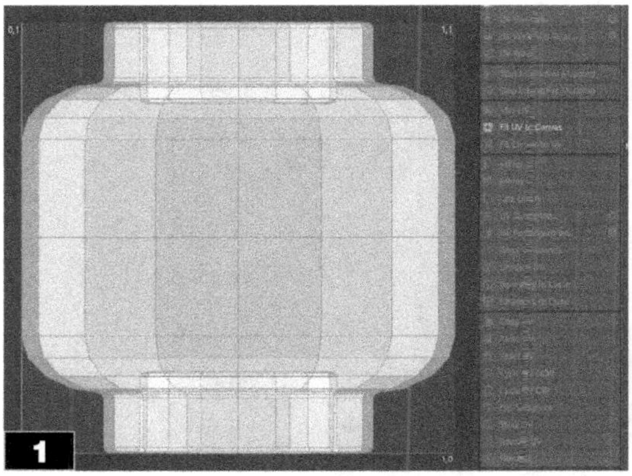
1

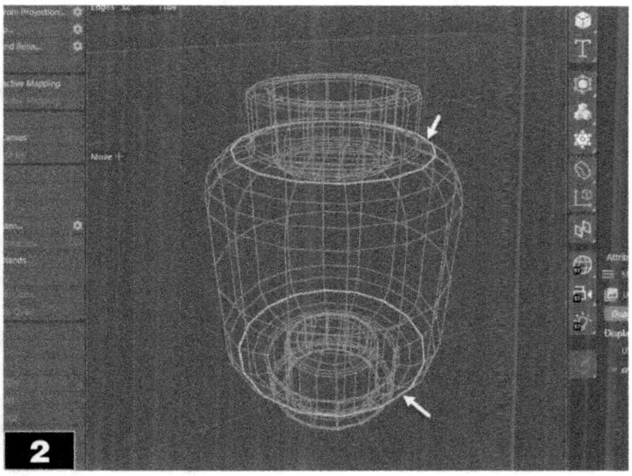
2

4. Choose **UV Mesh > UNWRAP > UV Unwrap - Gear Icon** from the **Texture UV Editor** menu or click the **UV Unwrap > Gear Icon** in the palette (let's call it the **UV Tools** palette) displayed to the right of the **Texture UV Editor** (see Figure 3); the **UV Unwrap** window is displayed. Make sure the **Auto Align** checkbox is selected in the window and then click **OK** (see Figure 4).

WHAT JUST HAPPENED?

Cinema 4D has generated seams from the edge loops I selected. Cinema 4D opens the UV Mesh, relaxes it, and then rearranges it. The ***ABF*** *algorithm is used to relax the UV mesh. Congruent selections will be recognized as islands (and an edge selection will be placed around the islands) and unwrapped separately if you first select polygons and then unwrap them. This command does not operate on meshes without a border.*

ORGANIC OBJECTS

If you are unwrapping an organic mesh, you can achieve good results, if the original projection is done using ***Frontal, Flat*** *or* ***Shrink*** *projection and then you define UV Seams using edge selections.*

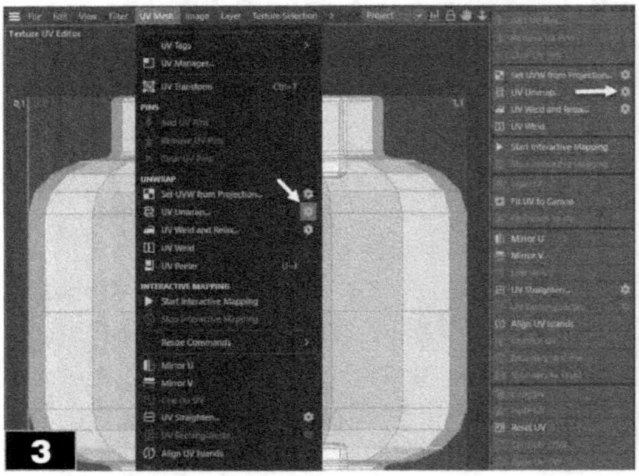
3

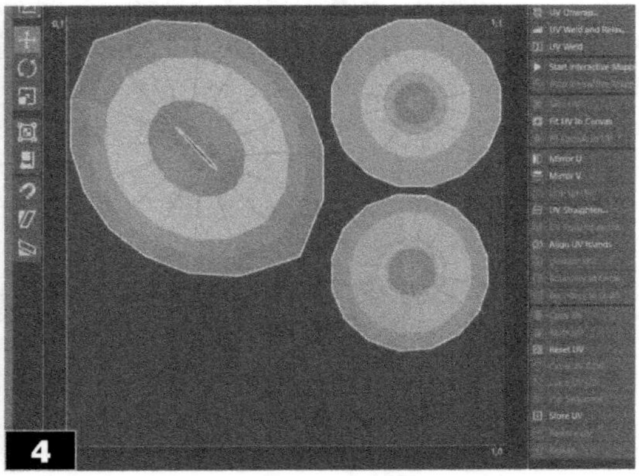
4

5. Select the edges, as shown in Figure 5 and then click on the **UV Unwrap** button in the **UV Tools** palette (see Figure 6).

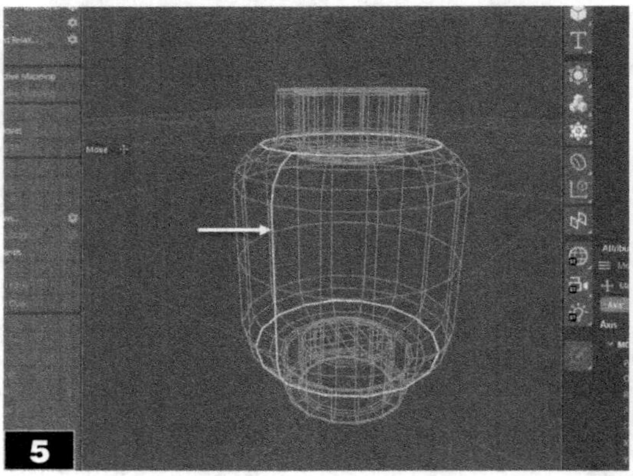
5

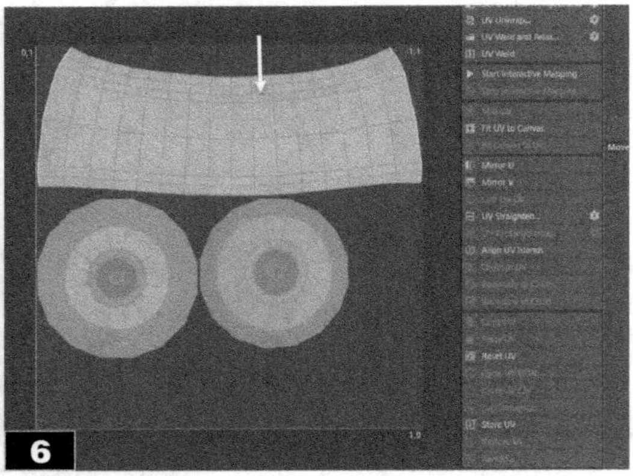
6

6. Save the Cinema 4D file; we'll return to it once we've finished testing with some tools.

There are some tools available in the **Tools** palette on the left side of the **Texture UV Editor**: **UV Transform**, **UV Peeler**, **Shear U**, and **Shear V**. These tools are also available via the **Texture UV Editor**'s **UV Mesh** menu.

The **UV Transform** tool allows you to modify UVs within the texture view and can be accessed using the **Ctrl T** keyboard shortcut. It provides support for snapping and quantizing and can perform various actions such as scaling, rotating, shearing, and non-uniform scaling (refer to Figure 7). Before using this tool, it is necessary to select the UV components that you wish to transform. Upon activating the tool, a rectangular frame will appear with transformation controls, including Move (**A**), Scale (**B**), Rotate (**C**), Non-Uniform Scale (**D**), and Anchor Point (**E**), for adjusting the selected UV components (refer to Figure 7).

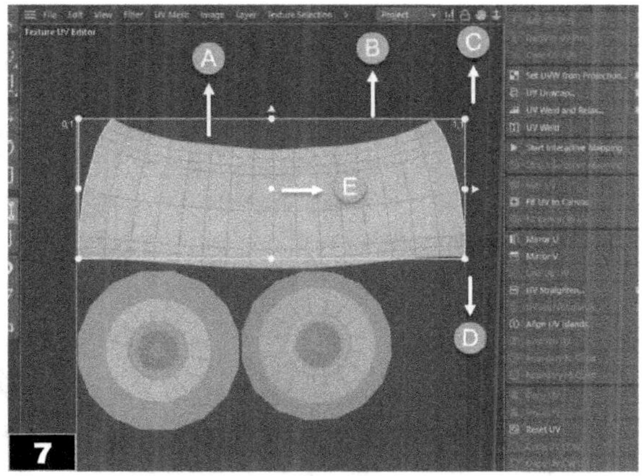

7

To shear UVs relative to the opposite edge, **Ctrl**-click and drag from the center point along the transform control edge. However, if you **Ctrl**-click a corner point of the frame, it will result in a non-uniform transform that distorts it horizontally or vertically.

The following keyboard shortcuts apply:

To constrain UV movement to either horizontal or vertical, simply hold down the **Shift** key while moving the UVs. When using the corner control, holding **Shift** enables you to scale UVs without restrictions. If you grab a control located at the center or edge of the UV, Cinema 4D will scale the UVs horizontally or vertically. By pressing **Alt** and grabbing the corner, center, or edge control, Cinema 4D scales the UVs around the anchor point proportionally. When you hit **Shift Alt** at the same time, Cinema 4D will combine the tasks described above.

When using the **UV Transform** tool, you can use the following shortcuts to perform specific actions:

- **Ctrl Shift:** Scale the selected UVs freely relative to the opposite edge.
- **Ctrl Alt:** Shear the selected UVs along the edge relative to the anchor point.
- **Ctrl Shift Alt:** Shear the selected UVs freely relative to the anchor point.

While using the **UV Transform** tool, the following shortcuts can be used to achieve specific transformations:

- **Ctrl Shift:** Scale the selected UVs freely.
- **Ctrl Alt:** Scale the selected UVs horizontally or vertically with a mirrored effect on the opposite edge.
- **Ctrl Shift Alt:** Distort the selected UVs into a trapezoid shape.

The **Shear U** and **Shear V** tools can tilt the selected UV elements around the closest UV coordinate to the cursor. Shearing can occur in either a horizontal (**Shear U**) or vertical (**Shear V**) direction. To shift the UV polygons, utilize the **Magnet** tool by dragging in the **UV Editor**. The UV polygons closest to the **Magnet** tool will be the most impacted. If specific UV components are selected, the **Magnet** tool will only manipulate those selected components. In order to apply a UV mesh to cylindrical objects, such as elongated objects, the **UV Peeler** tool is utilized. This tool has the capability to be applied to multiple objects simultaneously.

7. Revert back to the saved file. Activate the **Polygons** mode and then double-click on the polygon island to select it. Then, click on the **UV Rectangularize** button in the **UV Tools** palette (see Figure 8).

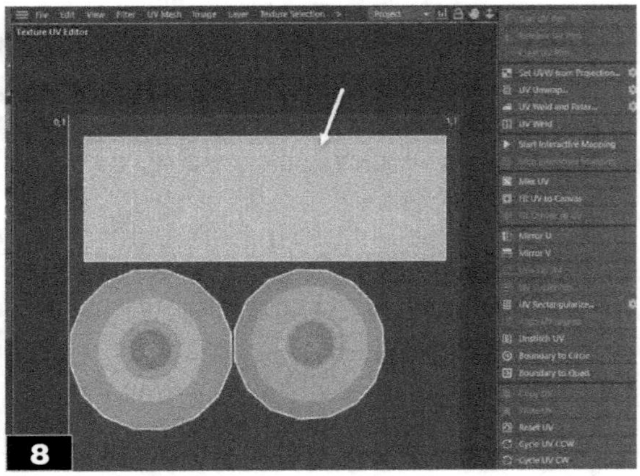

UV Rectangularize

I utilized the **Rectangularize** tool to transform the selected UV Polygons into a rectangular shape. However, there are certain requirements that must be met for this tool to work correctly:

- The selection must consist solely of coherent quads.
- The selection must create a rectangle as a whole or be convertible to a rectangle.
- The selection must include at least 2x2 polygons.

By clicking on the gear icon corresponding to this tool, you can access additional options. Enabling the **Equidistant Distribution** checkbox will result in Cinema 4D arranging the UV points at a constant distance from each other, resulting in a more homogeneous UV mesh. Additionally, selecting the **Auto Align** checkbox allows you to orient the rectangular section horizontally or vertically, depending on the axis to which the rectangle tends.

8. Select the edges, as shown in Figure 9. Then, choose **Select > COMPONENTS TOOLS > Symmetrize Selection** from the main menu or press **UV**. Click on the **UV Unwrap** button in the **UV Tools** palette (see Figure 10).

9. Select the edge, as shown in Figure 11 and then click on the **UV Unwrap** button in the **UV Tools** palette (see Figure 12). Make UVs rectangular using the **Rectangularize** tool (see Figure 13).

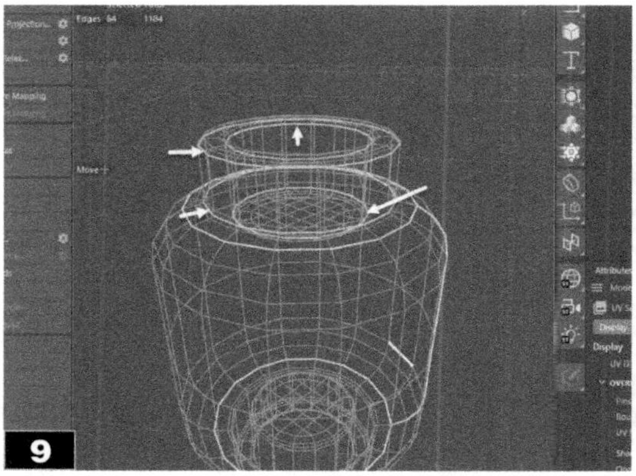

9

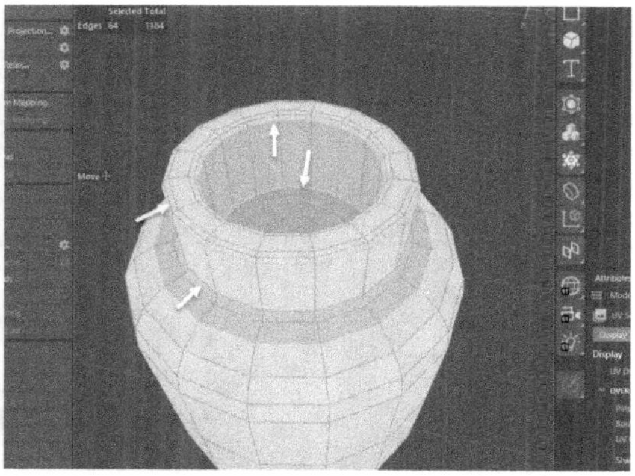

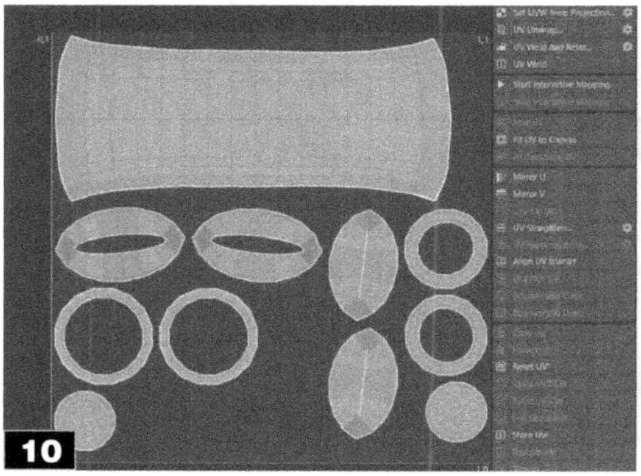

10

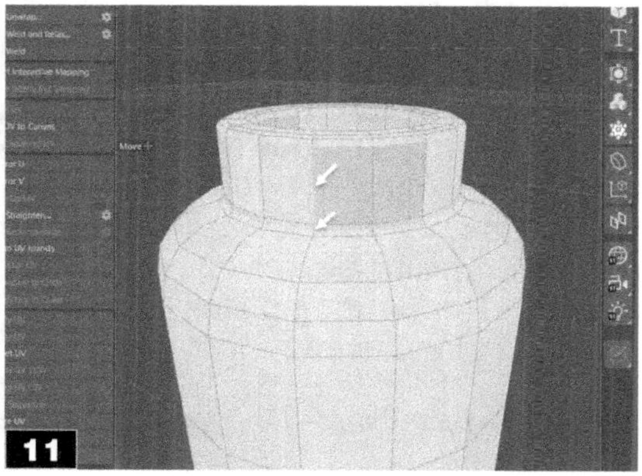

11

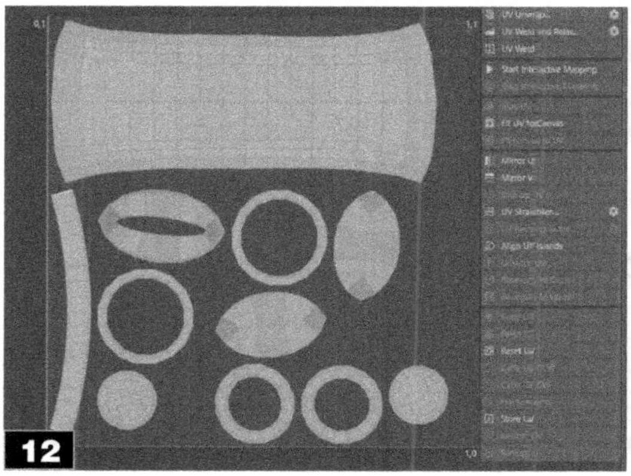

12

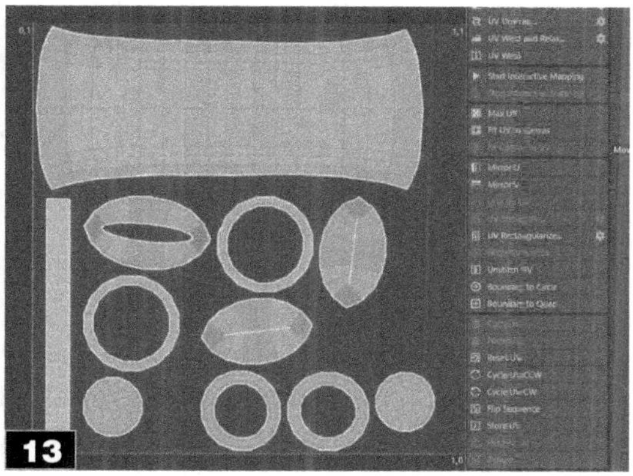

13

10. Likewise unwrap all cylindrical UVs (see Figure 14).

11. Select all polygons. In the **UV Manager > UV Packing** tab, select **Geometric** from the **UV Mapping** section. Select **Texture Space** from the drop-down list located to the right of the **Geometric** checkbox. Set **Target Resolution X** and **Target Resolution Y** to **2048** each. Set **Gap Size** to **10** and then select the **Preserve Orientation** and **Equalize Island Size** checkboxes. Then, click **Apply** (see Figure 15).

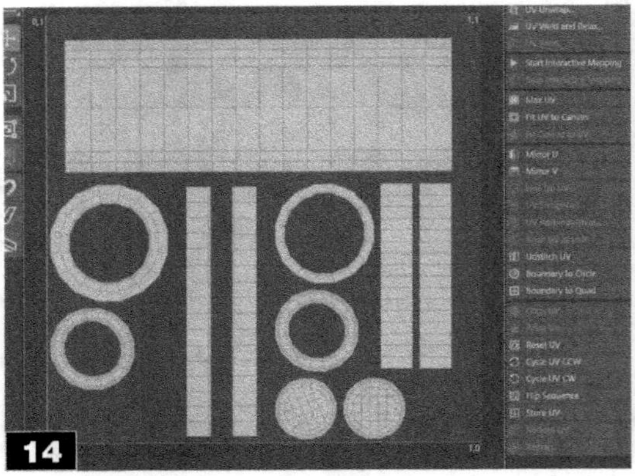

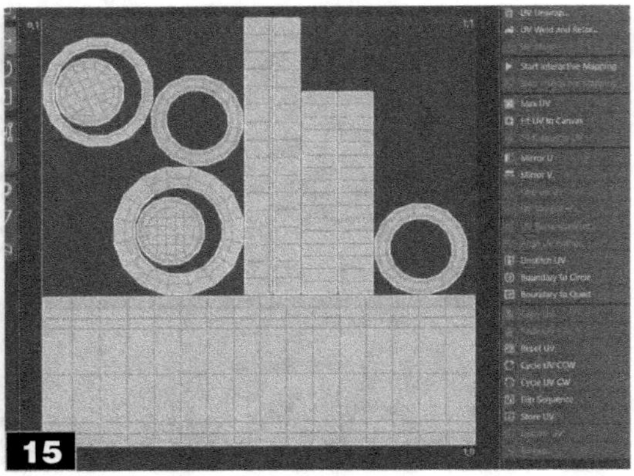

UV Packing

The **UV Packing** tab in the **UV Manager** provides options to efficiently organize UV Islands in the **Texture UV Editor**. There are three modes available for packing UVs: **Rasterized**, **Geometric**, and **Bounding Box**. When working with a large number of UV Islands, the **Rasterized** mode should be used. However, it should not be used together with overlapping UVs. The **Geometric** mode is the most effective mode in terms of generating optimal results. However, if there are many UV Islands, it may take longer to render than the other two modes. The **Bounding Box** mode is a legacy mode that results in more wasted UV surface than the other two modes.

The **Texture/UV Space** drop-down list offers two choices:

- **Texture Space:** Use this option if you have knowledge of the final texture size. You can define the desired resolution using the **Target Resolution X** and **Target Resolution Y** parameters. The UV coordinates will be distorted according to the aspect ratio of the resolution you specify. Moreover, you can set the **Gap Size** parameter to determine the gap size between Islands.
- **UV Space:** This mode allows you to input the minimum distance as a percentage of the UV tile size. Use the **Spacing** parameter to specify the distance.

It is important to note that using high values for **Gap Size/Spacing** in the **Texture/UV Space** drop-down list can result in a loss of valuable texture space, particularly for smaller UV Islands. To avoid color overlapping, a smaller distance between the islands is necessary.

12. Activate the **Polygons** mode. Choose **Mode > UV Settings** from the **Attribute Manager**'s menu to open the **UV Settings**. Then, change **Shading** to **Filled Polygons**. Figure 16 shows various islands that are colored blue. It shows that the islands' orientation is incorrect.

13. There is an alternate method to verify the orientation of the UVs. You can go to **Textures > UV Map** from the **Texture UV Editor** menu, which will display an image with numbered boxes in both the **UV Editor** and the viewport (refer to Figures 17 and 18). In Figure 18, you may observe that the box numbers are appearing flipped in the viewport.

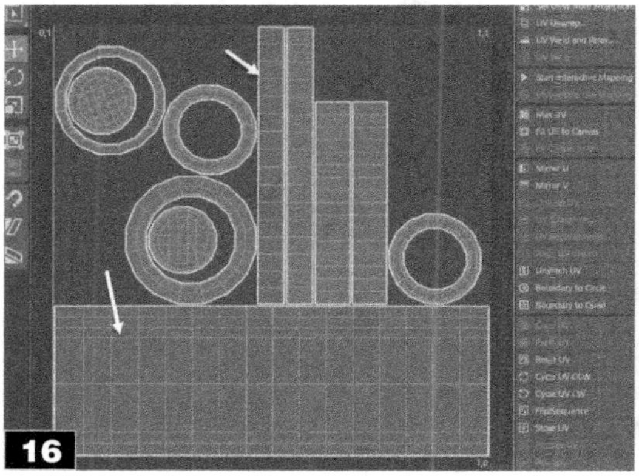
16

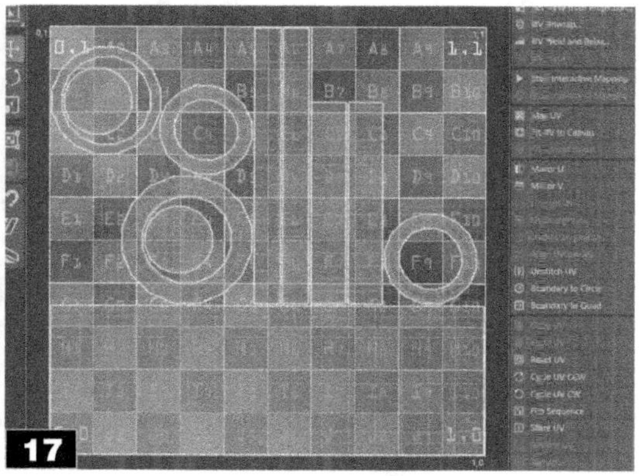
17

14. Double-click on one of the blue colored island to select all polygons and then click **Mirror U** in the **UV Tools** palette to flip them (see Figure 19). Repeat for other islands. Choose **Textures > Empty Canvas** from the **Texture UV Editor** menu.

18

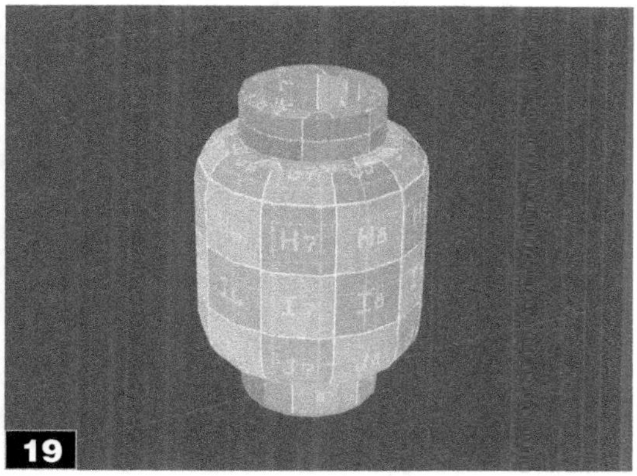
19

15. Switch to the **Model** mode and then create a new material and apply it to **Cylinder** in the viewport. Double-click on the **Mat** node to open the **Material Editor**. In the **Color** tab, click **Texture > Triangle** button > **Surfaces** > **Checkerboard** to apply checkerboard map to the **Texture** parameter (see Figure 20).

16. Select the **Material** tag in the **Object Manager** and then in the **Attribute Manager** > **Tag** tab, change **Tiles U** and **Tiles V** to **2** each. In the **Attribute Manager**, enable the **Subdivision Surface** object (see Figure 21).

20

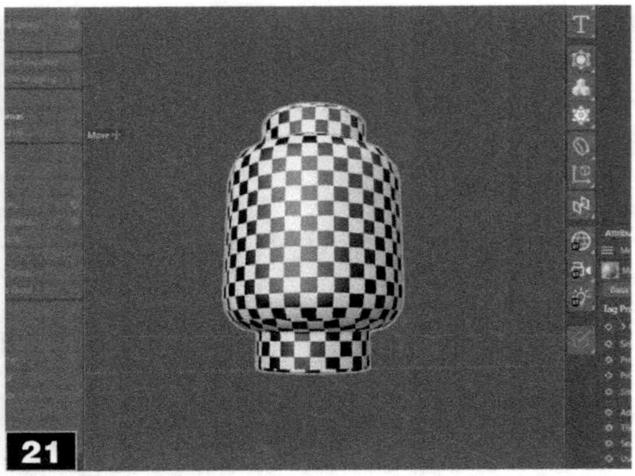

21

17. Open **model-b.c4d** and then switch to the **UVEdit** layout.

18. **RMB** click on **Cylinder** in the **Object Manager** and then choose **Material Tags > Set UVW from Projection** from the context menu to apply a blank projection tag to the object.

19. Choose **Mode > UV Settings** from the **Attribute Manager**'s menu to open the UV Settings. Then, change **Shading** to **Multi-Color Islands**. Lock the **Attribute Manager**.

20. Activate the **Edges** mode and then select the loops, as shown in Figure 22. Click on the **UV Unwrap** button in the **UV Tools** palette (see Figure 23).

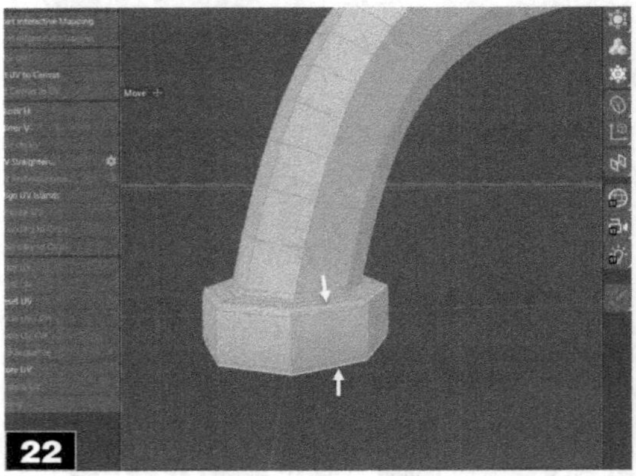

22

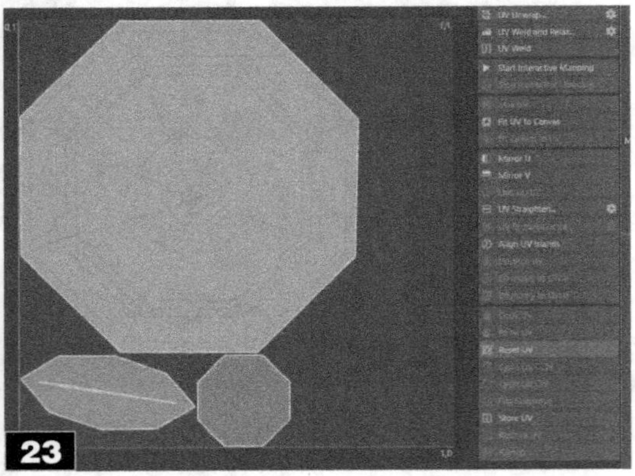

23

21. Select the edges, as shown in Figure 24. Then, click on the **UV Unwrap** button in the **UV Tools** palette (see Figure 25).

22. Repeat the process for the other end of the cylinder (see Figure 26).

23. Select the edges, as shown in Figure 27, and then click on the **UV Unwrap** button in the **UV Tools** palette (see Figure 28). Rectangularize UVs using the **Rectangularize** button (see Figure 29).

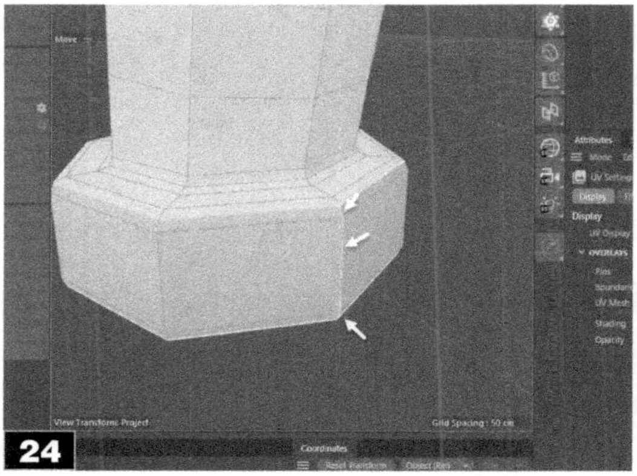

24

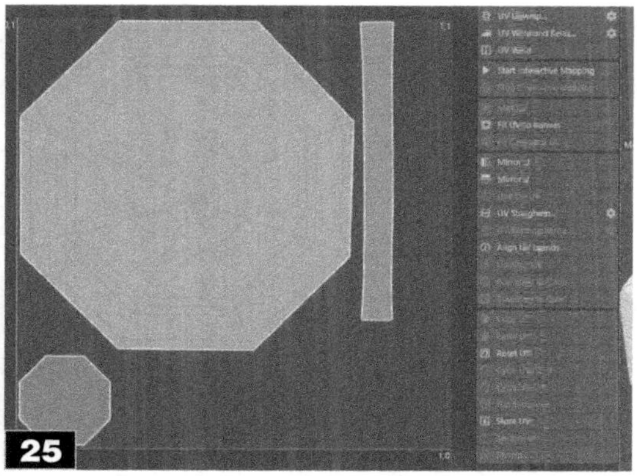

25

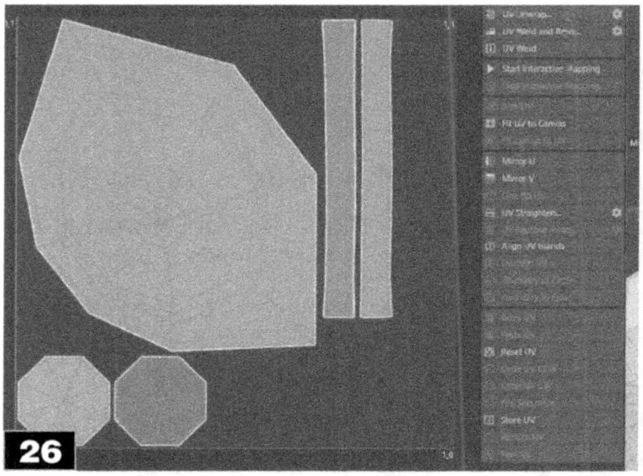

26

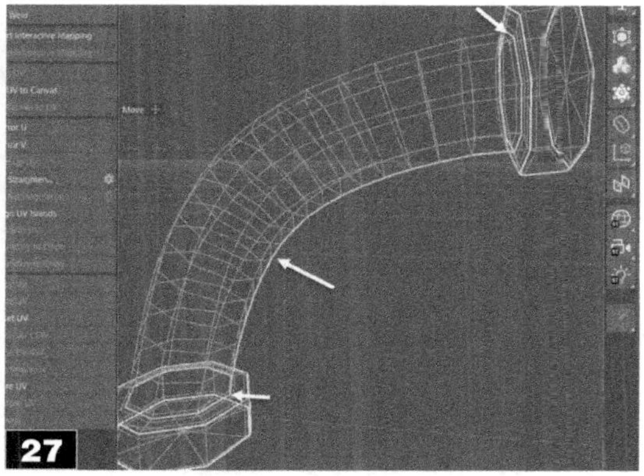

27

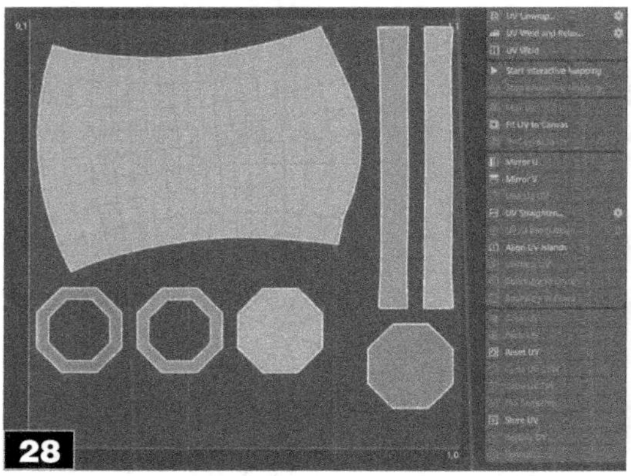

28

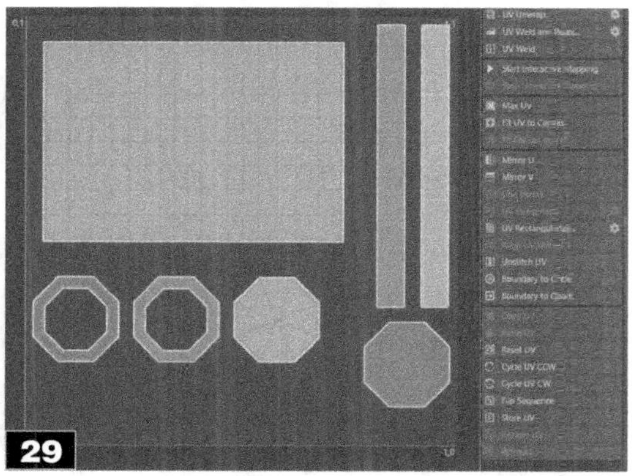

29

24. In the **Attribute Manager > UV Settings > OVERLAYS** section, set **Shading** to **Filled Polygons** (see Figure 30).

25. Mirror the Islands displayed in blue using the **Mirror** tools (see Figure 31).

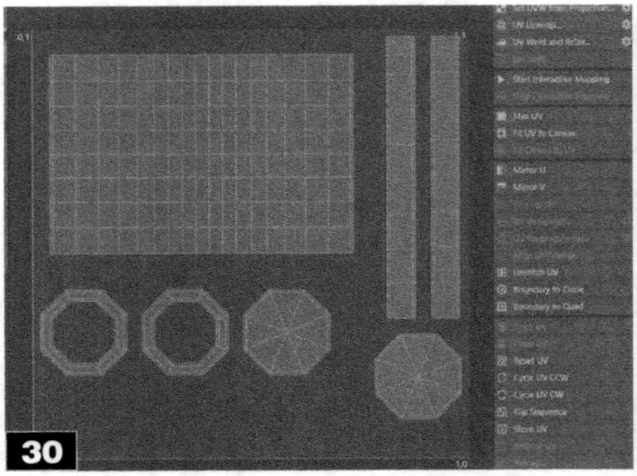
30

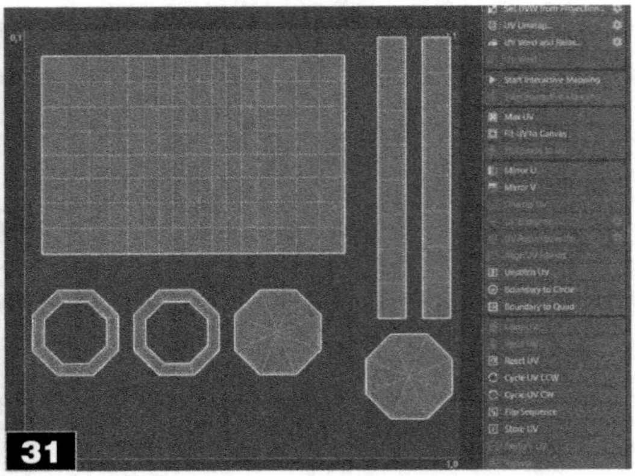
31

26. Select all polygons. In the **UV Manager > UV Packing** tab, select **Geometric** from the **UV Mapping** section. Select **Texture Space** from the drop-down list located to the right of the **Geometric** checkbox.

27. Set **Target Resolution X** and **Target Resolution Y** to **2048** each. Set **Gap Size** to **10** and then select the **Preserve Orientation** and **Equalize Island Size** checkboxes. Then, click **Apply** (see Figure 32).

28. Switch to the **Model** mode and then create a new material and apply it to **Cylinder** in the viewport. Double-click on the **Mat** node to open the **Material Editor**. In the **Color** tab, click **Texture > Triangle** button > **Load Image** to open the **Load File** dialog box. Then, select **check-2.png**, click **Open**. Unlock **Attribute Manager**.

29. Select the **Material** tag in the **Object Manager** and then in the **Attribute Manager > Tag** tab, change **Tiles U** and **Tiles V** to **3** each. Select the material in the **Material Manager** and then in the **Attribute Manager > Viewport** tab, change **Texture Preview Size** to **1024x1024**.

30. In the **Attribute Manager**, enable the **Subdivision Surface** object (see Figure 33).

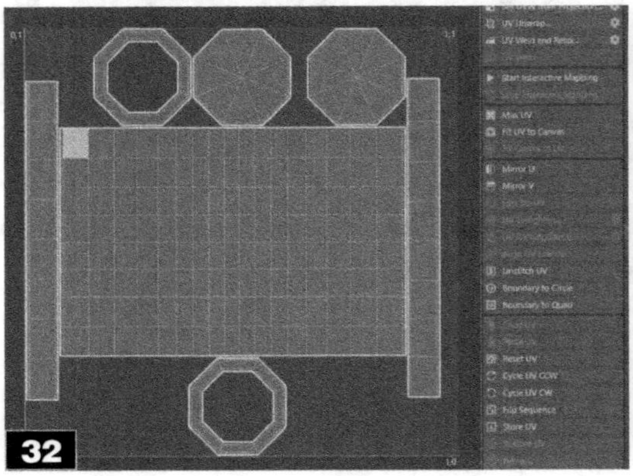
32

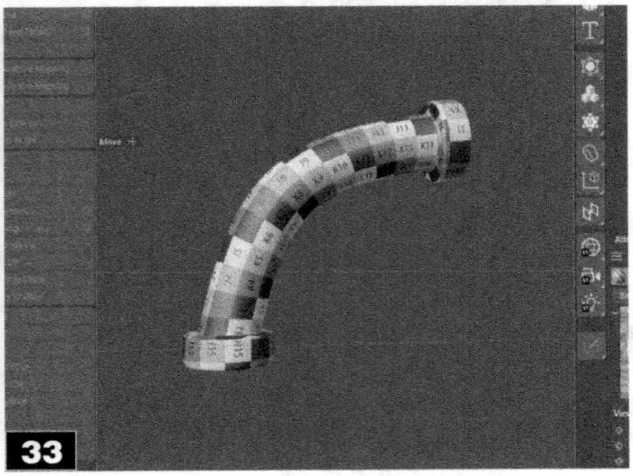
33

31. Open **model-c.c4d** and then switch to the **UVEdit** layout.

32. **RMB** click on **tankGeo** in the **Object Manager** and then choose **Material Tags > Set UVW from Projection** from the context menu to apply a blank projection tag to the object. Choose **Textures > UV Map** from the **Texture UV Editor** menu.

33. Activate the **Edges** mode and then select the edge loops, as shown in Figure 34. Click on the **UV Unwrap** button in the **UV Tools** palette (see Figure 35).

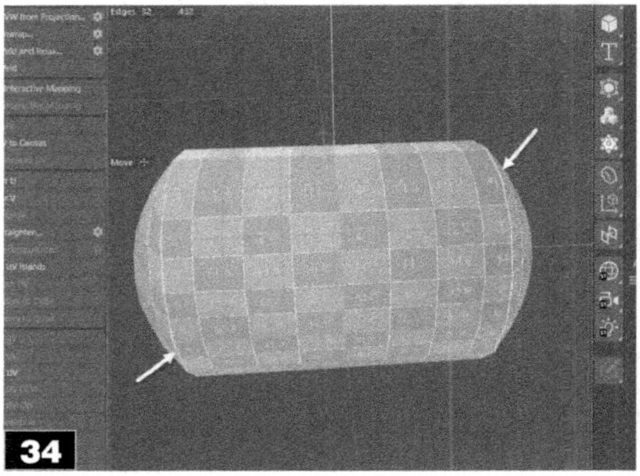

34

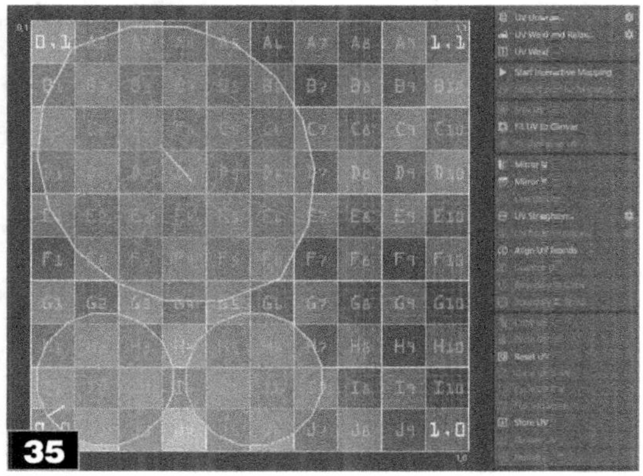

35

34. Press **UF** and then click on a middle polygon to select all polygons between the selected edges loops (refer to Figure 34).

35. Click on the **Start Interactive Mapping** button in the **UV Tools** palette. In the **Attribute Manager** > **Material** tag > **Tag Properties** section, set **Projection** to **Cylindrical** (see Figure 36).

36. Rotate and scale gizmo to adjust UVs (see Figure 37). Then, click on the **Stop Interactive Mapping** button in the **UV Tools** palette (see Figure 38).

37. Rotate Island to fix the orientation of UVs (see Figure 39).

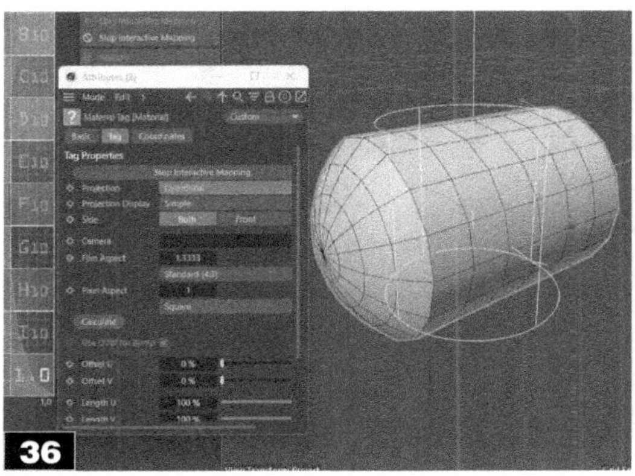

36

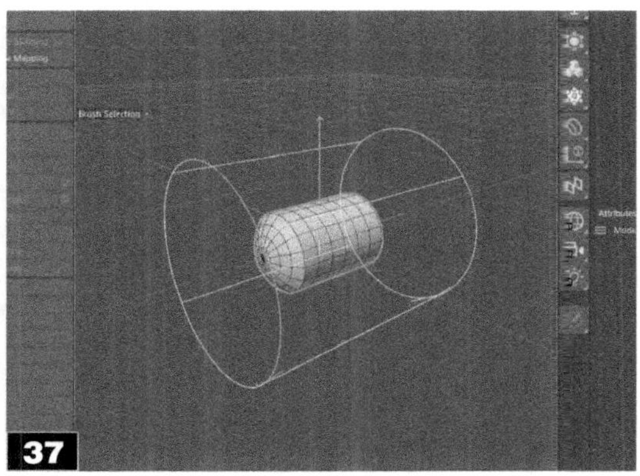

37

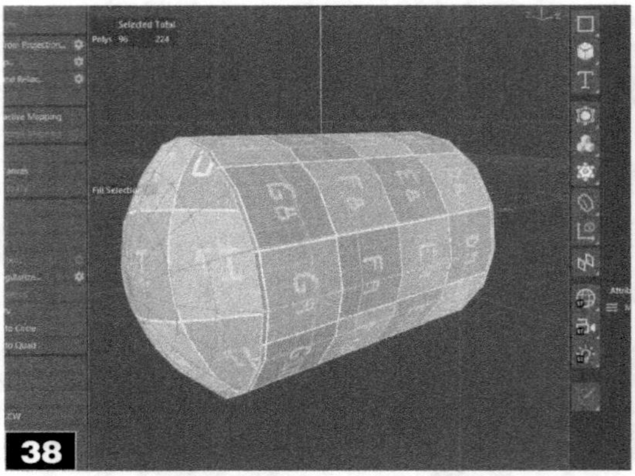
38

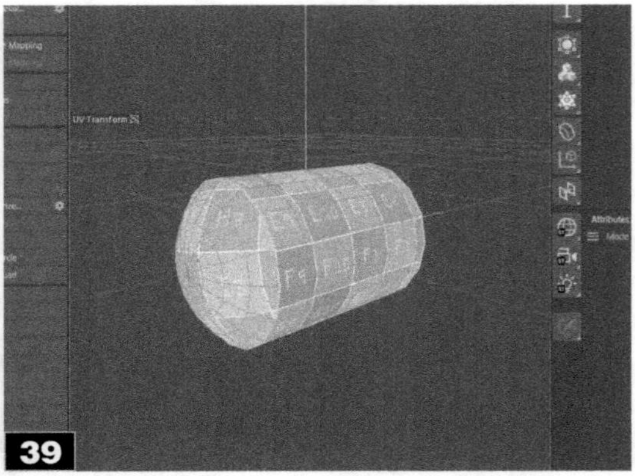
39

CHAPTER 2: STANDARD RENDERER

The default renderer in Cinema 4D is the **Standard** renderer, which is typically fast and stable for most use cases. However, if you need special effects like depth-of-field or motion blur, you may want to use the **Physical** renderer instead. The **Physical** renderer and other built-in renderers in Cinema 4D will be discussed in detail in upcoming chapters.

EXPLORING RENDER SETTINGS WINDOW

The **Render Settings** window contains the **Standard** renderer options (see Figure 1). To access this window, go to the main menu and select **Render > CONFIGURE > Edit Render Settings**, or press **Ctrl B**. Alternatively, under the **Standard** palette > **Render** command group, select the **Modify Render Settings** button. You can also access these settings through the **Attribute Manager** (see Figure 2) by choosing **Mode > Render Settings** from the **Attribute Manager**'s menu.

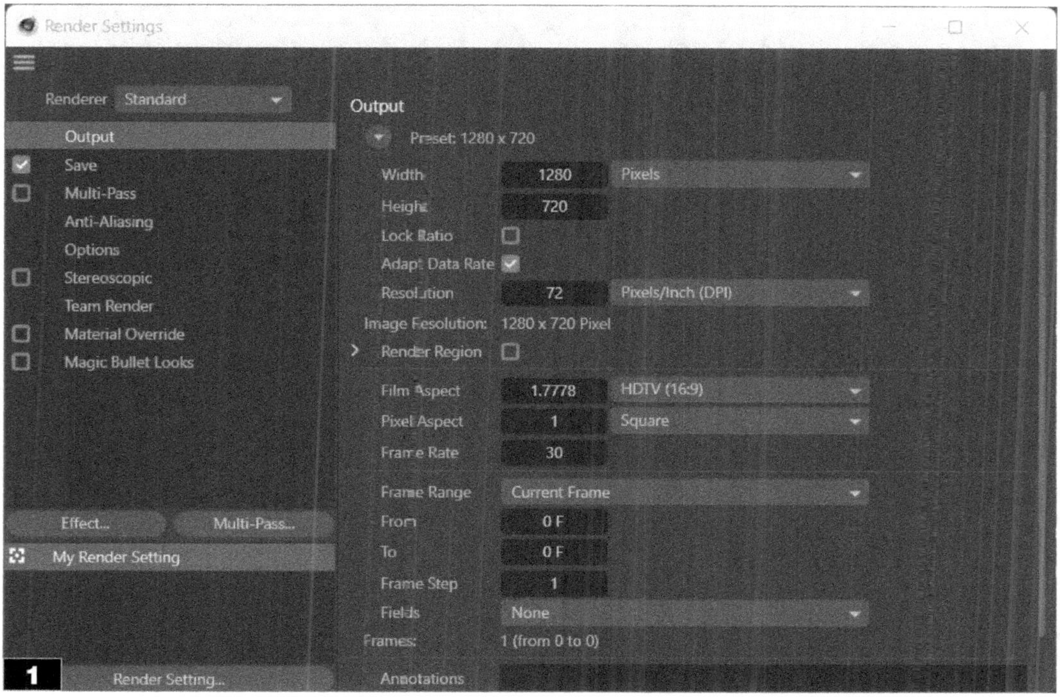

1

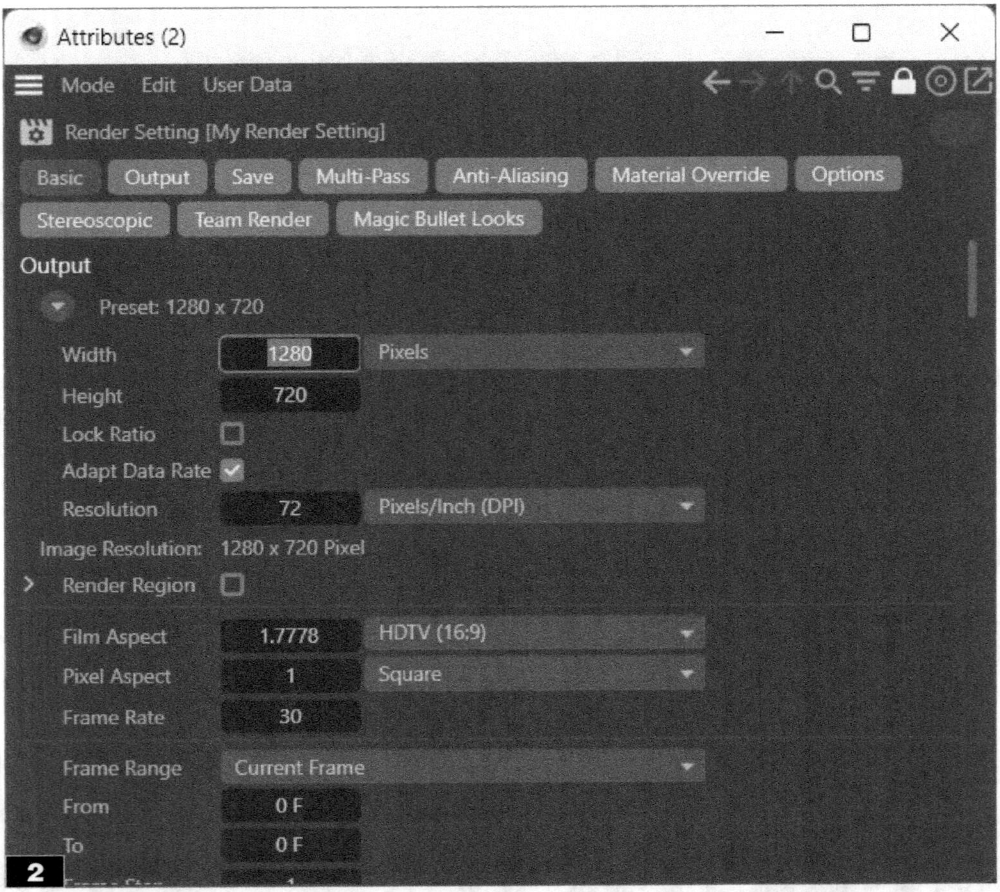

2

The **Render Settings** window is split into two sections. The render categories are listed in the left pane. When you select an option from the left pane, the settings for that option appear in the right pane. By clicking the **Effect** and **Multi-Pass** buttons, you can add post and multi-pass effects, respectively. Most of the options in the left pane have a checkbox to the left of them. This checkbox allows you to enable or disable the associated option. If the **Standard** renderer is not selected by default, you can select it from the **Renderer** drop-down list in the **Render Settings** window's top-left corner.

When you select an option from the window's left pane, the corresponding options for modification appear in the right pane. If you change an option in the right pane, the related label will appear in boldface since the values differ from the default values. Let's explore the commonly used rendering options available in the left pane of the **Render Settings** window.

OUTPUT

The **Output** settings in solely influence the rendering displayed in the separate render window, and have no effect on the rendering shown within the viewport. At the top-left corner, an **Arrow** button is available. Clicking on this button reveals the commonly used resolution settings for print, video, mobile devices, and films. For example, if you want to use the **HDV 1440x1080** resolution, click on the **Arrow** button and then choose **Film/ Video** > **HDV 1080 25** or **HDV 1080 29.97** option.

The **Width** and **Height** parameters specify the image's width and height, respectively. The unit of measurement is selected using the drop-down list to the right of the **Width** parameter. In this drop-down list, the **Pixels** option is selected by default. When you use a preset, the other options, including as resolution, aspect ratio, frame rate, and so on, are automatically configured. Enabling the **Lock Ratio** checkbox enables the image to dynamically adjust its width or height whenever either dimension is modified.

BIT RATE
*If you're rendering a video and wish to specify a bit rate, select the **Adapt Data Rate** checkbox then select the **Save** render option from the left pane. Choose a video format, such as **MP4**, from the **Format** drop-down list in the right pane. Next, expand the **Format** group by clicking the triangle to the left of the **Format** label and provide a bit rate using the **Data Rate (kBit)** field (see Figure 3).*

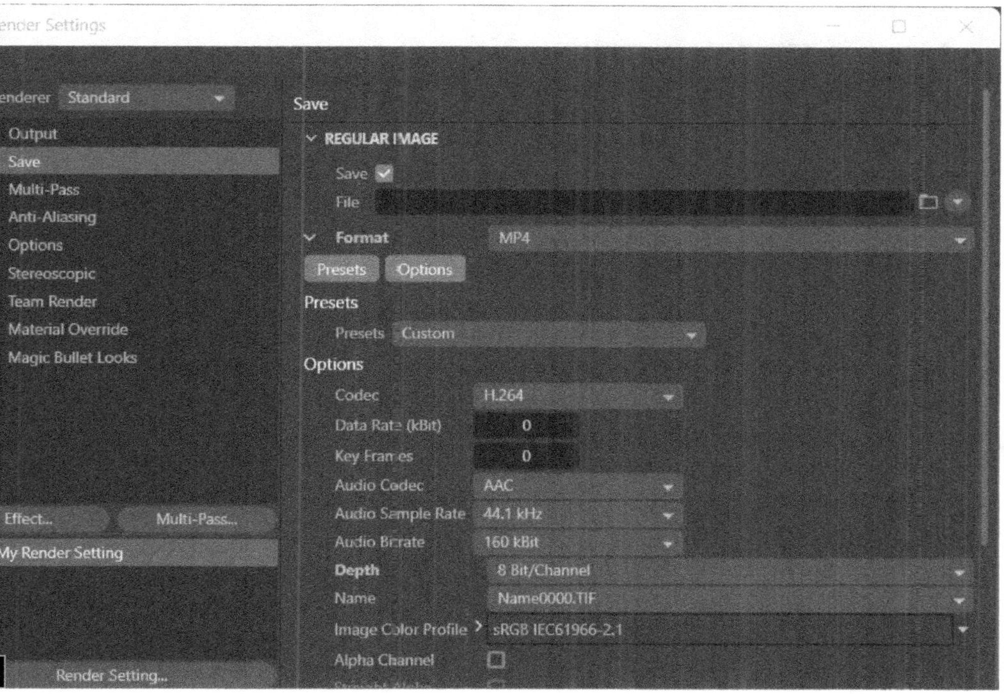

3

The **Resolution** parameter does not apply to a video, but if you are rendering an image for printing, you can use it to provide a DPI value. If you made a minor change to the scene that only impacts a smaller area, you can render a small zone rather than the entire image. You can render a specific part of the scene using the **Render Region** function. To define an area, expand the **Render Region** group and then use the **Left Border**, **Top Border**, **Right Border**, and **Bottom Border** parameters to define the region (see Figures 4 and 5).

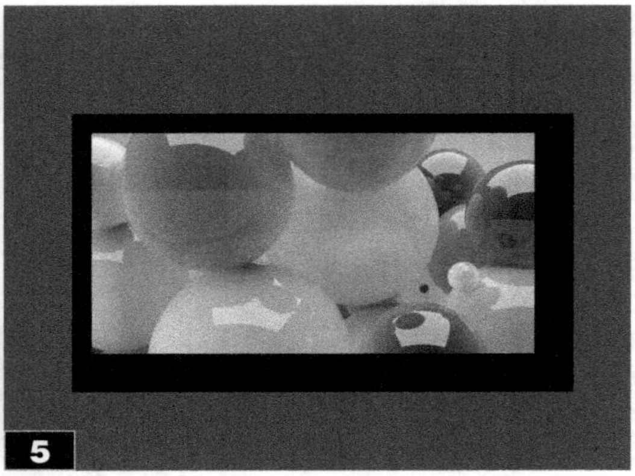

In Figure 5, I set the **Left Border**, **Top Border, Right Border**, and **Bottom Border** parameters to **50**, **50**, **100**, and **100**, respectively. You must render the scene to the **Picture Viewer** to get the outcome shown in Figure 5. It will not appear in the editor view. Choose **Render > OFFLINE RENDERING > Render to Picture Viewer** from the main menu or press **Shift R** to render to the **Picture Viewer**. Alternatively, in the **Standard** palette > **Render** command group, click **Render to Picture Viewer**. [**render-region.c4d**]

COPYING SETTINGS FROM IRR
*If you have defined an interactive render region in the viewport, you can quickly set the values for the **Left Border, Top Border, Right Border,** and **Bottom Border** parameters by clicking the **Copy from IRR** button; Cinema 4D will populate values for these parameters using the IRR dimensions. You can enable IPR from the main menu by choosing **Render > ONLINE RENDERING > Interactive Render Region** or by pressing **Alt R**. Then, create an interactive render region by dragging in the viewport.*

The **Film Aspect** parameter represents the file's **X:Y** ratio, whereas the **Pixel Aspect** parameter determines a pixel's **on-screen-width:on-screen-height** ratio. Most displays have a pixel aspect ratio of **1:1**. The **Frame Rate** parameter determines the render's frame rate. The **Frame Range** drop-down list lets you select frame or set of frames to render. If you select an option from this drop-down list, the **From** and **To** parameters are updated to reflect the associated frame numbers. The **Frame Step** parameter can be used to skip frames during rendering. For example, if you set this value to **5**, just the **fifth** frame will be rendered, providing a rough estimate of the final product.

SAVE

You can save a picture, a video, or a sequence of images to the **Picture Viewer** window using the **Save** settings. The right pane has two groups: **REGULAR IMAGE** and **COMPOSITING PROJECT FILE**. These groups are discussed next:

Regular Image

The **File** parameter specifies the location where the files should be saved. If you enter a file name without a path, the image or image sequence will be saved in the folder of the active scene. If you wish to utilize relative paths, start the path name with a **Period**. Let's see how it works:

1. Create a folder with the name **path** and then create a sub-folder with the name **x**. Create another sub-folder with the name **y** inside the **x** folder. Now, start a new project .

2. Create a **Cube** just for testing purposes. Save the scene with the name **test.c4d** inside the **x** folder.

3. In the **Render Settings** window, specify path as **./y/diffuse** and then press **Shift R** to render the scene; the rendered image with the name **diffuse** will be saved in the **path > y** folder.

The absolute path is indicated by a single dot (.) in the path name. You can give a relative path from the location where the scene file is saved by using two dots (..). When you specify **../diffuse** as the path, the control moves one level up in the directory from where the scene file is saved (the file was saved in the **x** folder). As a result, the **diffuse** file will be stored in the parent folder directory.

FILE NAME

*The maximum length of the filename is **22** characters. Out of **22, 4** characters are reserved for the file extension (for example **.png**) and **5** characters are reserved for numbering frame sequences (for example **_0025**). Keep in mind that you can use only the following characters in the file name: **A - Z, a- z, 0-9, _**.*

Tokens

You can use variable path and file names known as **Tokens** in the **File** input field. Tokens are simple text variables, when they are rendered or displayed in the **Picture Viewer** window, they will be replaced by parameters such as name of the project, the current camera, take, and so on. The following tokens are available:

- **$prj:** Project file name
- **$camera:** Current camera name
- **$take:** Current take name
- **$pass:** Multi-Pass or object channel name (the defined multi-pass names). Primarily to be used as directory name. (the **Channel Name as Suffix** option will be disabled internally)
- **$userpass:** Multi-Pass or object channel name (the multi-passes renamed via double-click in the **Render Settings** (opened Multi-Pass tree view). Primarily to be used as a directory name.
- **$frame:** Current animation frame
- **$rs:** Current **Render Setting** name

- **$res:** Image resolution
- **$range:** Animation range
- **$fps:** Frame rate
- **$username:** Operating system user name
- **$height:** Render output as defined in the **Render Settings** menu, e.g., 720
- **$computer:** Operating system machine name
- **$YY:** The current year (only last 2 digits)
- **$YYYY:** The complete current year date with all 4 digits
- **$mm:** The current time (only minutes)
- **$MM:** The current month
- **$ss:** The current time (seconds only)
- **$hh:** the current time (hours only)
- **$DD:** The current day
- **$author:** The author defined in the **Info** tab
- **$renderer:** The render engine defined in the **Render Settings** menu, e.g., **Redshift**

You can input these tokens or click the arrow button next to the **File** button parameter to open a flyout and then select desired option from the flyout. Follow these steps:

1. Create a folder with the name **tktest** in your system.
2. Open the **tokens-start.c4d** file. Then, in the **Render Settings** window, specify path for the folder ./**tktest**.
3. Append / at the end of the path and then choose **Current Camera** from the **Tokens** flyout; Cinema 4D shows the new path; **/tktest/$camera**.
4. Append / at the end of the path and then choose **Render Settings** from the **Tokens** flyout; the new path will be displayed as follows; **tktest/$camera/$rs**.
5. Add / at the end then type **tk-seq** as the file name. The complete path should now read like follows; **tktest/$camera/$rs/tk-seq**.

Notice in the **Object Manager**, **RN_CAM** is the name of the camera. Also, notice in the bottom-left corner of the **Render Settings** window, the name of the active render settings is **Low Res**. Now, press **SHIFT R** to render the sequence. Then, navigate to the **tktest** folder and then check the directory structure (see Figure 6). [**tokens-finish.c4d**]

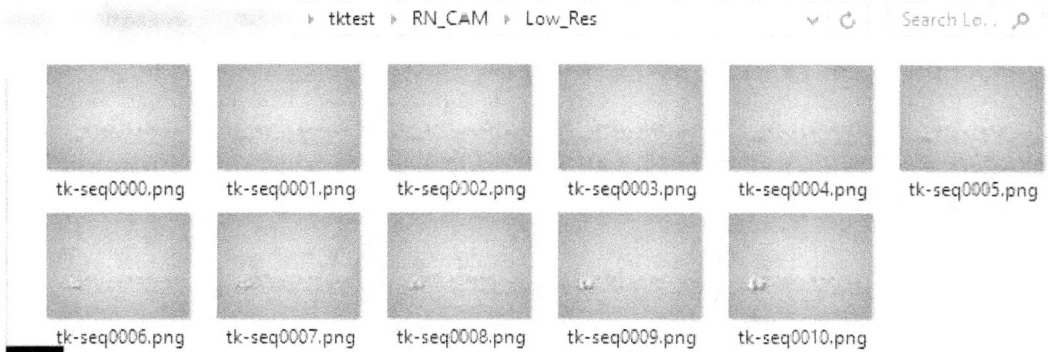

6

The **Format** drop-down list contains options for selecting the file format for the image or image sequence. When you expand the **Format** group, the **Presets** drop-down list appears. It includes options (if any) for the format you select from the **Format** drop-down list.

For example, if you select **WMV** from the **Format** drop-down list, you will notice that there are some presets available for the selected format. The **Options** section is located below the **Presets** area and allows you to configure numerous settings for the selected parameters.

The **Depth** parameter specifies the image's bit depth per channel. The **Depth** drop-down list allows you to choose between **8 Bit/Channel**, **16 Bit/Channel**, and **32 Bit/Channel**. These settings are used for 24-bit color, 48-bit color, and 98-bit color, respectively.

The options in the **Name** drop-down list are used to number the image files sequentially. The letters **TIF** signify the file format extension, such as **JPG**. For example, if you select **JPG** as file format and **beauty** as filename:

- **Name0000.TIF** will result in **beauty1234.JPG**
- **Name0000** will result in **beauty1234**
- **Name.0000** will result in **beauty.1234**
- **Name000.TIF** will result in **beauty123.JPG**
- **Name000** will result in **beauty123**
- **Name.000** will result in **beauty.123**

You can use the **Image Color Profile** setting to define which color profile should be embedded in the rendered image.

COLOR PROFILE
*Some of the programs are incapable of reading color profiles. Windows 7, for example, only reads profiles in part. In most cases, the default **sRGB** profile is the proper profile.*

COLOR PROFILE

*If you use the **Linear** color profile (for example, with the HDR format) with the multi-pass feature, it is advised that you render images with the **16-bit** color depth since multi-passes are saved with the **Linear** color profile. When color profile management is disabled, no color profiles are included in the rendered images. Expand the **Image Color Profile** group; a vertical arrow button will appear on the right. Click this button to see the color profile selection possibilities.*

To compute a pre-multiplied alpha channel, select the **Alpha Channel** checkbox. The alpha channel contains the same resolution grayscale image as the color image.

PRE-MULTIPLIED ALPHA

When you render an image with pre-multiplied alpha, the alpha channel picture is antialiased to ensure a soft transition in the composited picture. The white pixels in the alpha channel indicate the presence of the object whereas the black pixels indicate there is no object. The alpha channel can be used to composite multiple images. Using the alpha channel, the image on top may be blended with the one on the bottom. If the alpha value is white (opaque), the top color overwrites the destination color, if black (transparent), the color at the top is not visible. As a result, allowing the background to show through.

If you multiply the color and alpha channels, the alpha channel will result in a dark seam because both channels are antialiased, and black gets multiplied twice. To prevent the dark seam, you can check the **Straight Alpha** checkbox.

STRAIGHT ALPHA

The use of straight alpha is typically limited to compositing images and may not be useful for conventional images.

Alpha channels are typically included in image formats that support them, meaning they are saved together with the color image. However, if you need to save the alpha channel as a separate image, you can do so by enabling the **Separate Alpha** checkbox. The resulting alpha channel files will be saved in the same format as the color files.

Enabling the **8 Bit Dithering** checkbox adds random patterns to colors in order to prevent color banding. While this can improve image quality, it also increases the file size. Therefore, it is generally not recommended to use this option for rendering web graphics, where smaller file sizes are often desirable.

If you select one of the video formats from the **Format** drop-down list, select the **Include Sound** checkbox to integrate a sound file into the video.

BITRATE FOR VIDEOS

*Bitrate refers to the amount of bits that can be processed per unit of time, with **1** byte being equal to **8** bits. Video data rates are typically measured in bits per second, and the data rate for a video file is its bitrate. In Cinema 4D, you have the ability to define* *the bitrate for both the video and audio components of a file. To do this, you can expand the **Format** group and navigate to the **Options** section, where you can specify the video bitrate using the **Data Rate (kBit)** option and the audio bitrate using the **Audio Bitrate** option.*

Multi-Pass Image

Enabling the **Multi-Pass** render option in the left pane of the **Render Settings** window provides access to the **Multi-Pass Image** section (as shown in Figure 7). By default, the **Multi-Layer File** checkbox is enabled, which saves all layers in a multi-layer file format like Photoshop (**PSD**), BodyPaint (**B3D**), or **TIFF**. Additionally, Cinema 4D creates a separate file for each pass, and adds a suffix to each file name to differentiate them.

If you have selected a format from the **Format** drop-down list that does not support multi-layer files, each layer will be saved as a separate file. Enabling the **Layer Name as Suffix** checkbox will append the name of the layer (such as "**_diffuse**", "**_reflection**", etc.) to the end of the file name.

By default, each multi-pass in Cinema 4D is given a specific name such as "**Ambient**" or "**Diffuse**". However, if you prefer to use your own custom names for these passes, you can do so by double-clicking on the pass name in the left pane of the **Render Settings** window and typing in a new name. Once you have done this, you can enable the **User Defined Layer Name** checkbox to ensure that your custom names are used for the passes instead of the default ones.

Compositing Project File

The options located in this section, as shown in Figure 8, allow you to generate a compositing file comprised of multiple layers, each of which can be edited individually. You can choose the desired target application for the project from the **Target Application** drop-down list, with available options including **After Effects**, **Nuke**, **Motion**, and **Fusion**.

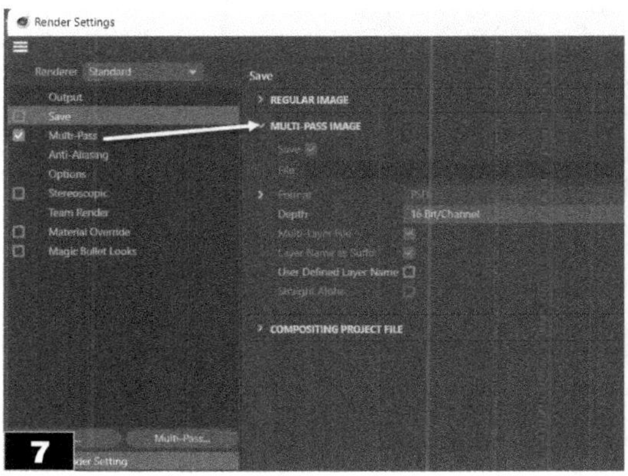

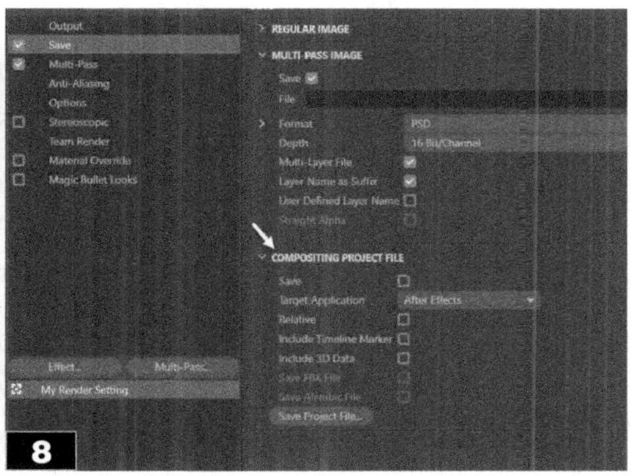

ANTI-ALIASING

The settings corresponding to the **Anti-Aliasing** option allow you to remove jagged edges from your images. The process works by first breaking down each pixel into sub-pixels and then calculating and averaging several color values to produce the final color for the pixel. The commonly used options are discussed next.

The default method is **Geometry** which smooths all object edges using a **16x16** sub-pixels. Figures 9 and 10 show the render with **Anti-Aliasing** set to **None** and **Geometry**.

9

10

The **Best** method uses more sub-pixels as well as Cinema 4D's adaptive antialiasing. Adaptive antialiasing is activated for pixels whose values differ significantly from those of their neighbors. It also has an impact on the color edges and the items hidden behind transparency.

The **Min Level** option determines the minimum number of sub-pixels that will always be rendered. In most circumstances, the default setting of **1x1** is sufficient. Nevertheless, if you see any artifacts, such as shadow swelling, a greater number should be used.

The **Max Level** parameter specifies the sub-pixel dispersion that will be applied to the crucial region, such as color edges and object edges behind transparency. In most circumstances, the default setting of **2x2** is sufficient. The higher the value you specify, the longer the render time.

The **Threshold** value specifies the degree of color divergence at which the **Max Level** value is applied to a specific pixel. Figures 11 and 12 show the rendered output when **Anti-Aliasing** is set to **Best** and the **Max Level** is set to **2x2** and **8x8**. [**anti-aliasing.c4d**]

OPTIONS

The **Options** settings are used to define various parameters that affect the rendering. These settings are discussed next:

11

12

Transparency

Use the **Transparency** checkbox to def ne whether or not **Transparency** or **Alpha** channel should be included in the render calculations. By default, this checkbox is enabled. Figure 13 show the rendered output when the **Transparency**, **Refraction**, **Reflection**, and **Shadow** options are enabled. Figure 14 shows the output when **Transparency** is disabled. [**rays.c4d**]

13

14

Refraction

The **Refraction** checkbox controls whether the refraction index is included in the render calculations for transparent materials. This checkbox is enabled by default. Compare Figures 13 and 15; Figure 15 shows the output when **Refraction** is disabled.

REFRACTION INDEX

When materials like glass and water are rendered with refraction index, they seem more realistic, but they also take longer to render. However, if the scene has no materials that reflect light, the ***Refraction*** *option will not add any additional render time.*

RENDERING TRANSPARENCY

Increase the value of the ***Ray Depth*** *parameter if transparent objects that are behind other transparent objects are displayed dark. The* ***Ray Depth*** *parameter is set to* ***15*** *by default.*

Reflection

Use the **Reflection** checkbox to define whether or not reflection should be included in the render calculations. By default, this checkbox is enabled. Compare Figures 13 and 16. Figure 16 shows the output when **Reflection** is disabled.

15

16

Shadow

Use the **Shadow** checkbox to define whether or not shadows should be included in the render calculations. If you select the **Limit Shadows to Soft** checkbox, Cinema 4D will render soft shadows that render fast. Note that the rendering area or hard shadows is much more computationally intensive than the soft shadows. The soft shadows appear more realistic than the hard shadows. Compare Figures 13 and 17; Figure 17 shows the output when **Shadow** is disabled.

17

Limit Reflections to Floor/Sky

Use this checkbox to instruct the raytracer to compute the reflection of the floor and sky onto the scene's reflecting surfaces rather than other objects. This option when selected takes less time to render. Therefore, you can utilize it for test rendering or when you have to meet a deadline.

Blurriness

The **Blurriness** checkbox determines whether the blur effect for the **Roughness** and **Transparency** material channels (blurriness caused by Roughness value) should be included in render calculations.

Cache Shadow Maps

Each light in the scene that creates a soft shadow is assigned a shadow map in Cinema 4D. A shadow map specifies where shadows will be displayed. If shadow maps are rendered in a complex scene, the render time increases significantly. When you enable the **Cache Shadow Maps** checkbox, the shadow map is saved when you render the scene for the first time. The shadow map will be stored as ****.c4d.smap** in the scene's **Illum** folder. If there is no such folder, one will be created automatically.

Active Object Only

When this checkbox is enabled, only the selected objects will be included in the render calculations.

Default Light

If you do not have a defined light source in the scene, a default light is used to render the scene. As soon as a light source is added, Cinema 4D automatically disables the default light.

> ***DEFAULT LIGHT***
> *When you use a **Sky** object with the **HDR** texture, the auto light is not disabled If you add GI to scene, the auto light will be disabled when you render the scene.*

Textures

Textures can be enabled or disabled while rendering using the **Textures** checkbox. This checkbox can be disabled for a test render or while using the **Cel** renderer. If this checkbox is not selected, bitmaps will be substituted with the color black. When a texture is missing while rendering, a dialog box appears. If the **Show Texture Errors** checkbox is enabled and you confirm the alert, the rendering will continue without the missing texture. If you enable this checkbox, rendering will be cancelled after you confirm the alert.

Volumetric Lighting

Shadows will be cast in visible light if this checkbox is enabled. Because this feature is render intensive, you can disable it for test renders.

Use Display Tag LOD

If this checkbox is enabled, the renderer will use the level of detail specified in **Display** tags.

Render HUD

Select this checkbox, if you want to include HUD in the rendered image or image sequence (see Figure 18).

Render Doodle

Use this checkbox to define whether or not the **Doodle** function should be included in the rendered output.

18

Sub Polygon Displacement

You can use this option to deactivate sub-polygon displacement globally rather than individually for each sub-polygon displacement material. This checkbox can be disabled for test renders.

Post Effects

Use this checkbox to enable or disable post effects globally.

Identical Noise Distribution

When utilizing low render settings with various Cinema 4D effects, the outcome may appear grainy and is commonly referred to as "Noise". Some of these effects are:

- Area shadows
- Subsurface Scattering (in the **Direct** mode)
- Depth-of-field
- Motion blur
- General sampling in the **Physical** renderer
- Post effects like **Global Illumination**, **Ambient Occlusion**, etc

Enabling the **Identical Noise Distribution** checkbox ensures that the distribution of noise will be random for every frame rendered, even if there are no parameter changes in the animation. This means that the noise distribution will differ for each consecutive frame.

> ***NOISE DISTRIBUTION***
> *It is recommended to disable this option when working with animations, as it can lead to unexpected outcomes. However, if you are aiming to create static images that are as similar as possible to each other, you can enable this checkbox.*

> ***NOISE DISTRIBUTION***
> *Even with options such as multi-threading enabled, some degree of randomness can still be present. This is noticeable in GI rendering, where slight variations may occur even if the* ***Identical Noise Distribution*** *checkbox is selected.*

Subsurface Scattering

Use this checkbox to define whether or not to enable or disable **Subsurface Scattering** for the entire project.

Bucket Sequence

Buckets are the square render regions (shown in Figure 19), each of which is generated utilizing a single processor or processor core. This leads to efficient rendering, especially when rendering render instances. To describe how buckets should process, select an option from the **Bucket Sequence** drop-down list. You can select any option from the drop-down list; no sequence is superior than the others.

The **Automatic Size** checkbox is enabled by default. As a result, a bucket size between **8x8** and **64x64** is determined automatically based on the number of Processors and image size. Smaller buckets use less memory than bigger buckets, however this has no impact on render performance.

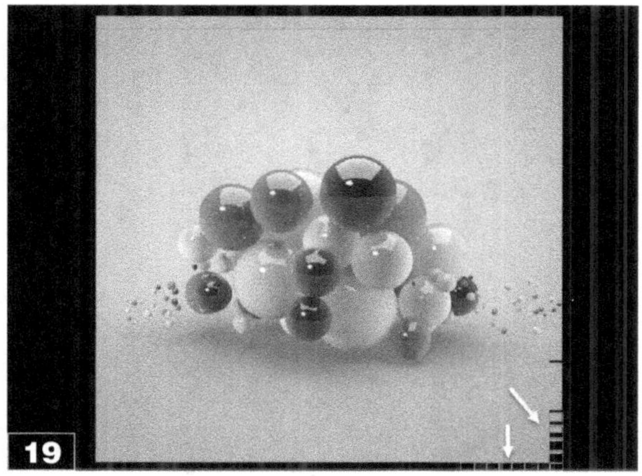

If you expand the **Automatic Size** group, the **Bucket Width** and **Bucket Height** parameters will be revealed. They are only available if you disable the **Automatic Size** checkbox. You can use these parameters to define a custom bucket region.

Ray Threshold

The **Ray Threshold** parameter controls the movement of rays in the scene. Rays cease moving from the camera to the scene when their brightness falls below the value you set for the **Ray Threshold** parameter. This value can be used to optimize render time because **90%** of processed rays contribute less than **10%** to the overall brightness and color of the image in a scene with many reflecting and transparent surfaces. The bigger the value you specify for the **Ray Threshold** parameter, the more tiny reflections and transparencies will be taken into account, resulting in longer render times.

Ray Depth

The **Ray Depth** parameter determines how many transparent objects the renderer will penetrate. The lower the value you specify for this parameter, the fewer the number of objects can be seen through. A value of **1** indicates that a pixel's computations are complete as soon as the ray collides with something in the scene. Areas that the renderer cannot penetrate are shown in black.

A value of **2** indicates that once a ray strikes a surface, a second ray is fired to determine transparency. Figure 20 shows the rendered result with the **Ray Depth** parameter set to **1** on the left and **2** on the right. Figure 21 shows the rendered result when the **Ray Depth** parameter is set to **3** on the left or **8** on the right. [**rays.c4d**]

Reflection Depth

When a ray is shot into the scene, it is reflected by the reflective surfaces. You can use the **Reflection Depth** parameter to limit the number of reflective rays (maximum number of rays) sent into the scene. Figure 22 shows the rendered output with **Reflection Depth** parameter set to **2** on the left, **4** on the center, and **8** on the right. [**reflection-depth.c4d**].

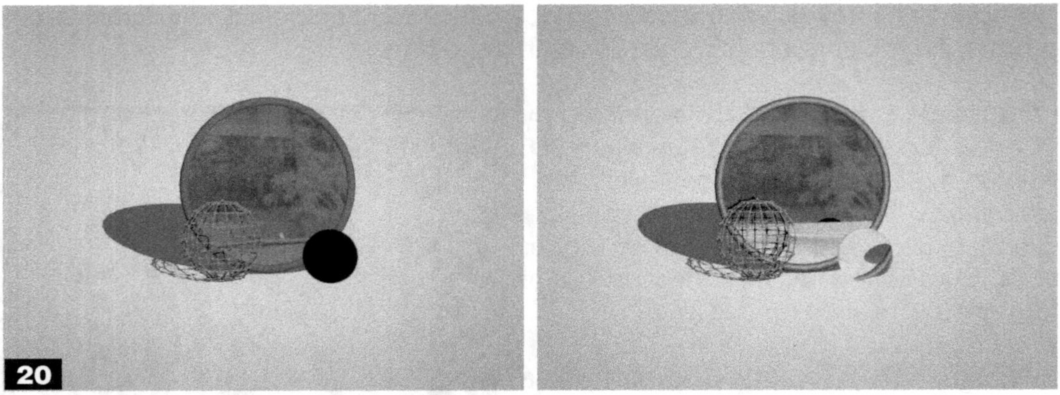

20

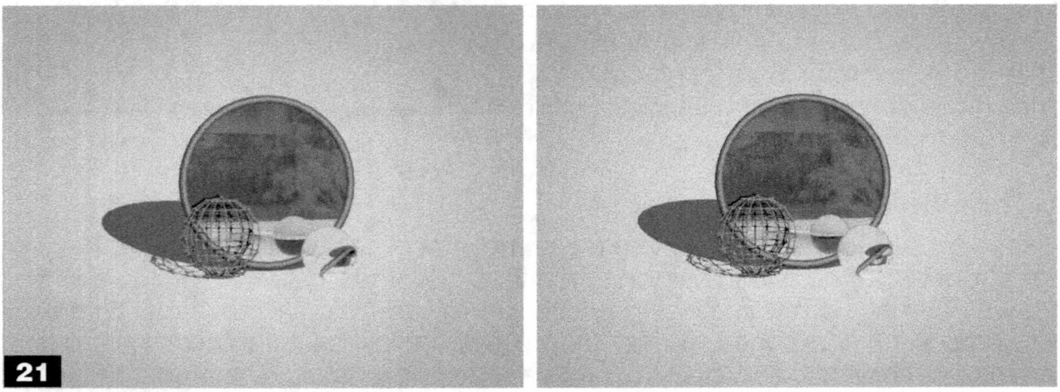

21

22

REFLECTION DEPTH
In most cases, only the initial set of reflections are crucial. Additional rays tend to have a minor impact on the image quality, while significantly increasing the render time.

Shadow Depth

The behavior of the **Shadow Depth** parameter is similar to that of the **Reflection Depth** parameter. When a surface is obscured by another object's shadow, this parameter can be utilized to send extra shadow rays in order to determine which shadow should be directed towards the light source. Figure 23 illustrates the rendered output when the **Shadow Depth** parameter is set to **1** (left), **3** (center), and **5** (right). [**shadow-depth.c4d**]

23

MATERIAL OVERRIDE

Occasionally, it can be beneficial to render an object in a neural gray color to assess elements such as shadows and light balance. This technique is known as "**clay rendering**". By enabling the **Material Override** checkbox, all materials in the scene will be substituted with the defined material. If you wish to exclude specific materials from being replaced, you can select the desired mode and drag the materials that you want to include or exclude from the **Material Manager** into the **Materials** list. If you want to preserve specific channels, you can do so by enabling the corresponding checkboxes in the **Preserve** section. The available channels are: **Diffuse Color**, **Luminance**, **Transparency**, **Reflectance**, **Bump**, **Normal**, **Alpha**, and **Displacement**.

NODE MATERIALS
*Node materials are not supported by the **Material Override** option.*

MAGIC BULLET LOOKS

The **Magic Bullet Looks** option is used to enable the **Magic Bullet Looks** suite (see Figure 24) that is used to color-grade/color correct rendered images.

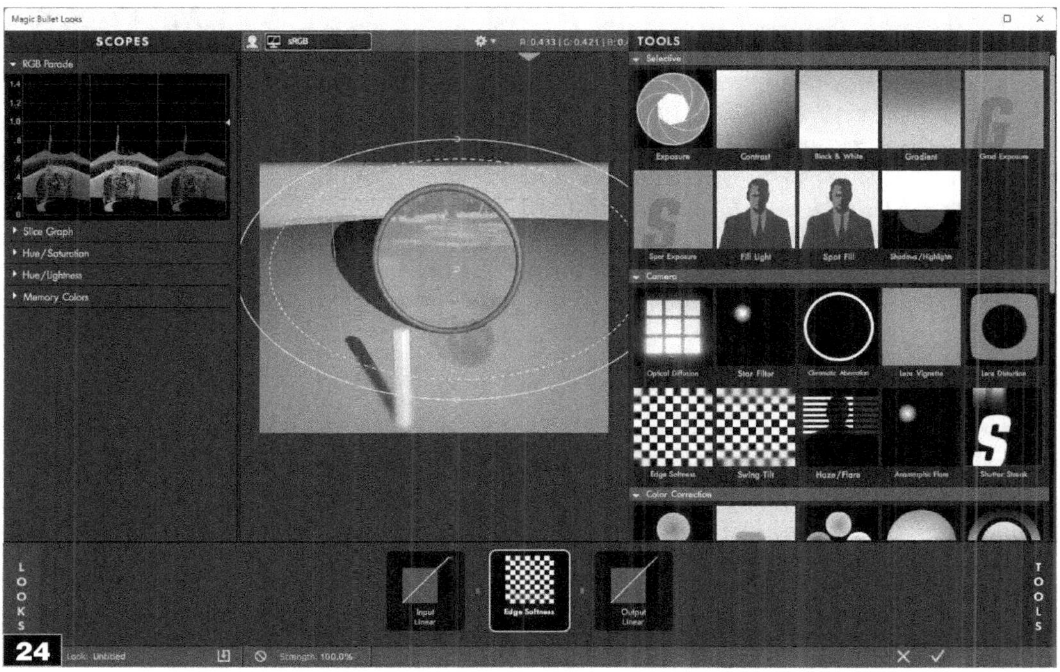

24

RENDER SETTINGS CONTEXTUAL MENU

If you click on the **Render Settings** button located at the bottom-left corner (see Figure 25) of the **Render Settings** window, a menu will be displayed. The options in this menu allow you to save presets for the render settings. You can also open this flyout by **RMB** clicking in this area located below the **Effect** and **Multi-Pass** buttons. For example, you can make a preset for low-res settings and one for high-res settings. By default, the **My Render Setting** preset is used for saving the current settings. You can double-click on it to rename it.

To add a new preset, click on the **Render Settings** button and then choose **New**. You can also copy and paste the presets using the **Ctrl C** and **Ctrl V** key combinations. Alternatively, you can also duplicate a preset by **Ctrl** dragging. You can create a child preset by choosing **New Child** from the menu. To make a preset active, either choose **Set Active** from the flyout or click on the icon to the left of the preset. If you want to create a preset that contains only the modified (bold) parameters, choose **Apply/Save Difference Preset** from the menu.

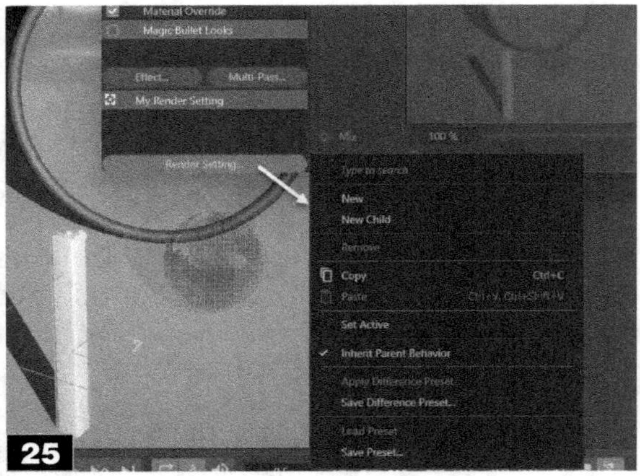

25

NOTE: ATTRIBUTE MANAGER COMPATIBILITY

*When you select an option from the left pane of the **Render Settings** window, the corresponding options that you can modify will be displayed in the right pane. These settings are compatible with the **Attribute Manager** which gives you access to all relevant **Attribute Manager** commands as well as two additional commands, namely **Inherit Parent Setting** and **Override Parent Setting** (see Figure 26). Choose **Mode > Render Settings** from the **Attribute Manager**'s menu to see the render settings in the **Attribute Manager**.*

26

If you select the **Inherit Parent Setting** option, parameters that have no values to be inherited (bold text) will reset. Selecting the **Override Parent Setting** option will prevent any parent values from being assumed. Also, the parameter name will be made black and in bold face.

Let's see this in action, follow these steps:

1. Open the **Render Settings** window and then rename the default **My Render Setting** preset to **High-Res**.

2. Select **Options** from the left pane and then in the right pane, change **Ray Depth** and **Shadow Depth** parameters to **20** each. Notice that parameters names are shown in bold face (see Figure 27).

3. **RMB** click on **High-Res** and then choose **New Child** from the context menu. Rename it as **Low-Res**. Notice that the **Ray Depth** and **Shadow Depth** parameters inherited values from the parent settings **High-Res** (see Figure 28) and their labels are not in bold face.

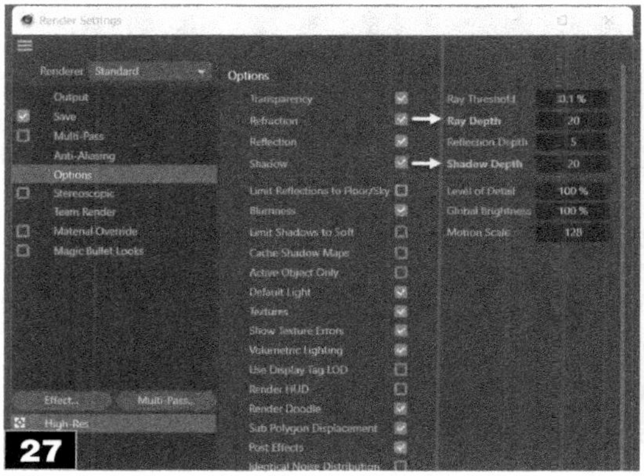
27

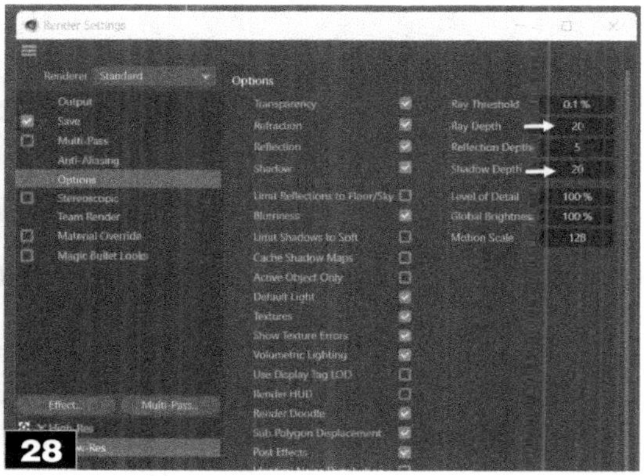
28

4. Change the **Ray Depth** and **Shadow Depth** parameters to **10** each. These parameters labels are now shown in boldface (see Figure 29). Now, switch to **Low-Res** and change **Ray Threshold** to **0.2**; its label is shown in boldface.

5. Switch to **High-Res**; its label is still in the default state. Change **Reflection Depth** to **6** and switch to **Low-Res**; notice the value has changed but label is still in the normal state.

6. **RMB** click on **Ray Depth** and choose **Inherit Parent Setting** from the menu. Notice that value has been changed to **20** and also the color of the label is now changed to normal state (see Figure 30).

7. **RMB** click on **Ray Depth** and choose **Override Parent Setting** to change the state of the label (see Figure 31).

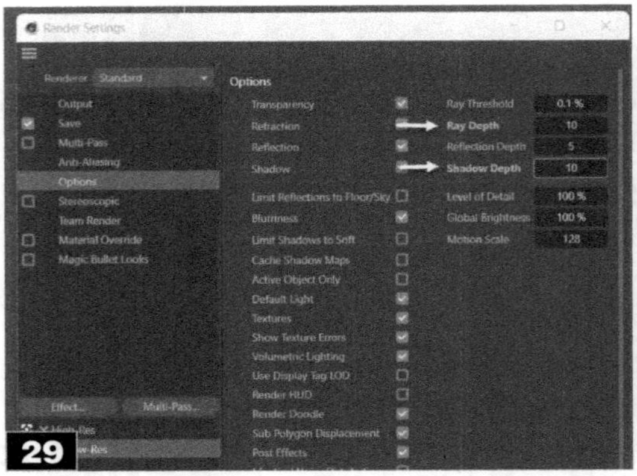

29

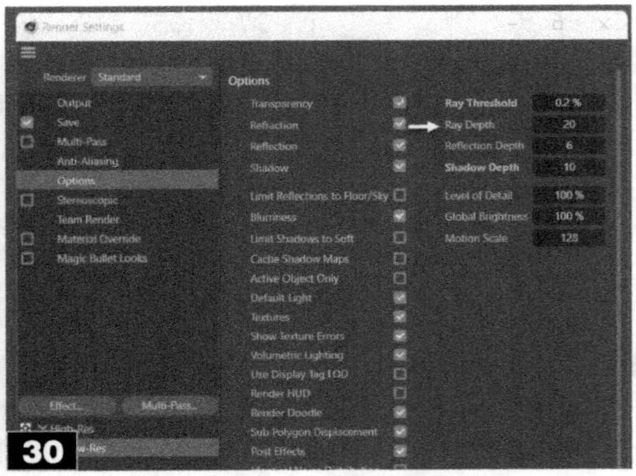

30

8. Delete **Low-Res**, select **High-Res**, and then change **Ray Depth**, **Reflection Depth**, and **Shadow Depth** to **6** each. Now, **RMB** click on **High-Res** and choose **Save Difference Preset** from the contextual menu to open the **Save High-Res** window. In this window, type **Name** as **Difference** and then click **OK**.

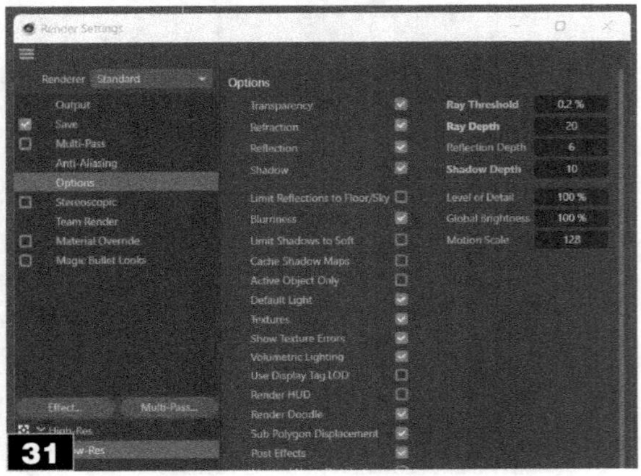

31

9. Create a new preset, **RMB** click on it, and then choose **Apply Difference Preset > Difference** to change the render settings that contain only the bold values.

You can use these presets in variety of scenarios such as:

- Rendering images without antialiasing, shadows, and so on for test renderings.
- Rendering a specific range of animation.
- Creating presets for the final rendering.
- Creating presets for multi-pass rendering and so on.

WORKING WITH EFFECTS

A popup will appear when you click the **Effect** button in the **Render Settings** window's left pane. You can add any effect from this popup to the scene. The selected effect displays in the list of render effects on the **Render Settings** window's left pane. To change the corresponding options, select the effect; the options will be displayed in the window's right pane.

The post effects are generated after the image has been rendered. Therefore, you will not see the effects until the image is fully rendered. To remove an effect, **RMB** click on it and then select **Remove** from the contextual menu. You can enable or disable an effect without removing it from the list. To do so, select or clear the checkbox to the left of a given effect.

ORDER OF THE EFFECTS
The order of the effects is important. To move an effect up or down in the list, click-drag the desired effect at the new location.

You can also copy and paste the effects including their parameters using the **Copy** and **Paste** options. These options are available in the **Effect** popup. You can also save and load effect presets using the **Load Preset** and **Save Preset** options from the popup. Many of the post effects' parameters can be animated just like you animate any parameter using the **Attribute Manager**. Let's explore some of the most commonly used effects available in the **Effect** popup.

GLOBAL ILLUMINATION

When light strikes an object's surface in real life, part of it is absorbed, and some is reflected back. GI governs how light interacts with the objects. It allows you to render realistic evenly lit scenes. Follow these steps to understand global illumination:

1. Open the **gi-start.c4d** file. This file contains several objects. A self-illuminating material is applied to **Sphere** in the scene. This scene has no lights.
2. Press **Ctrl B** to open the **Render Settings** window. Click on the **Effect** button and then choose **Global Illumination** from the popup menu to enable GI in the scene. Similarly, add the **Ambient Occlusion** effect. Render the scene (see Figure 32).

WHAT JUST HAPPENED?
*The **Global Illumination** (GI) and **Ambient Occlusion** (AO) effects have been added. **AO** lets you decide how much of each surface point is visible and then darkens it proportionately. When **AO** is enabled, regions such as corners, holes, or objects that are near to one other appear darker.*

EFFECTS
***GI** and **AO** are post effects, which means they are generated after the image has been rendered. They won't be visible until the entire image is rendered. Remember that the sequence of the effects in the **Render Settings** window is important. You can rearrange the effects by dragging and dropping them.*

WHAT NEXT?
Figure 32 shows a render with very little illumination. Let us enhance that.

3. Press **Shift F2** to open the **Material Manager**. Double-click on the self-illumination material **Mat** to open the **Material Editor** and then select **Illumination** from the left pane. In the right pane, change the **Generate GI** option's **Strength** to **1000**. Render the scene (see Figure 33).

32

33

WHAT JUST HAPPENED?
*The **Generate GI** checkbox is enabled by default in the **Material Editor**. As a result, the specified material has an impact on the other objects in the scene. The **Strength** option determines how much light this material emits. **Strength** has been set to **1000**, which is ten times the default value of **100**. The highest value that can be specified is **10000**. Figure 33 shows that the brightness has increased significantly, but the shadows are still incorrect.*

4. In the **Material Editor**, select the **Polygon Light** checkbox and then render the scene (see Figure 34). Notice that we have much better render now.

34

POLYGON LIGHT
*When the **Polygon Light** checkbox is enabled, the object serves as an area light. Such objects contain a material with an active **Luminance** channel.*

UBER AND NODE MATERIALS
*Using this option on an **Uber** or **Node** material with an active **Emission** channel will result in focused sampling during GI calculation. As a result, GI artefacting may be avoided. When displaying this material in rough reflections, it's also a good idea to check the Polygon Light checkbox. The material reflection will take a little longer to render, but the quality will be better.*

5. Open the **Render Settings** window by pressing **Ctrl+B**. Select **Global Illumination** from the left pane.

The **Preset** drop-down list is located at the top of the **General** tab in the right pane. This drop-down list has options for selecting a GI setting. These settings serve as a starting point and can be then be fine-tuned to maximize render speed and quality. Presets are divided into two categories: interior and exterior. Here's a basic rundown of the settings available:

- **Interior:** The GI of interior areas is more difficult to calculate. As a result, use interior settings in scenes with fewer or smaller light sources.
- **Exterior:** In open scenes that are set up beneath the open sky or space, use exterior options.
- **Custom:** The **Custom** preset is enabled as soon as you change the GI parameters.
- **Default:** The **Default** preset uses the **Irradiance Cache** method with **Diffuse Depth** set to **1**. This is the quickest GI method.
- **Object Visualization:** These presets are utilized in situations when the items are brightly lit and in the center of the scene. As a result, less light reflections are required.
- **Progressive:** These presets are used in conjunction with the **Physical** renderer's **Progressive Sampler** option.

The following table summarizes the methods used with the presets:

Primary and Secondary Methods		
Preset	**Primary Method**	**Secondary Method**
Interior - Preview	Irradiance Cache	Radiosity Maps
Interior - Preview (High Diffuse Depth)	Irradiance Cache	Light Mapping
Interior - Preview (Small Illuminants)	Irradiance Cache	Light Mapping
Interior - High	Irradiance Cache	Irradiance Cache
Interior - High (High Diffuse Depth)	Irradiance Cache	Light Mapping
Interior - High (Small Illuminants)	Irradiance Cache	Light Mapping
Exterior - Preview	Irradiance Cache	Radiosity Maps
Exterior - Physical Sky	Irradiance Cache	QMC
Exterior - HDR Image	Irradiance Cache	QMC

Primary and Secondary Methods		
Preset	**Primary Method**	**Secondary Method**
Object Visualization Preview	Irradiance Cache	Light Mapping
Object Visualization High	Irradiance Cache	Irradiance Cache
Progressive No Prepass	QMC	QMC
Progressive Fast Complete Diffuse	QMC	Light Mapping

The table shows that **Irradiance Cache** is the main primary method, whereas **Light Mapping** is the major secondary method. The **Radiosity Maps** method is used with the preview settings since it is ideally suited for quick rendering previews. Less reflected light is used in this method. The term **High Diffuse Depth** refers to the effects of several rays (light) reflections that provide a considerably more realistic image. The term **Little Illuminants** refers to scene lighting provided mostly by tiny lights. GI portals or polygon lights are used to define these lights.

The **Exterior - Physical Sky** preset differs from the **Exterior - HDR Image** preset in that the **Force Per-Pixel** checkbox is enabled while using the **Exterior - HDR Image** preset. This checkbox appears when you expand the **Discrete Sky Sampling** section in the **General** tab. When you choose the **Force Per-Pixel** checkbox, the computation of the light emitted by the sky is divided from the cache and performed independently for each pixel. This checkbox is relevant when you use **Irradiance Cache** as the primary method.

For exterior scenes, **Irradiance Cache+QMC** is the best combination. As a secondary method, **Irradiance Cache** works well in interior spaces with small lights specified as polygon or GI gateway lights.

Observe that the **Primary Method** is set to **Irradiance Cache** in the **Render Settings** window. Many pre-passes are computed in this method in which the scene is evaluated to identify the indirect lighting regions, also known as shading points. The brightness and color values of these spots will be kept as entries in the irradiance cache. The **Cache Files** tab contains options that allow you to preserve and reuse cache data.

CACHE FILES
*The cache files are only utilized while rendering the scene in the **Picture Viewer** window, not in the viewport.*

In comparison to the **Irradiance Cache** option, the other mode, **Quasi-Monte Carlo (QMC)**, provides the best GI quality. **QMC** is the most precise method, but it is also the slowest. It works really well when **Light Mapping** is used as a secondary method.

FLICKERING
*When used with animations, the **Irradiance Cache** mode tends to flicker. When you utilize bright and small polygon lights in the scene, it flickers more.*

FLICKERING
*The **QMC+QMC** combo delivers flicker-free results with animations. **Irradiance Cache+QMC** is prone to flickering as well. **QMC** works effectively as a secondary method with **Light Mapping**.*

If you expand the **Primary Method** area, you would see two settings: **Intensity** and **Saturation**. These settings are used to adjust the GI brightness and color saturation.

6. In the **Render Settings** window, change **Secondary Method** to **Light Mapping**. Render the scene (see Figure 35).

The **Secondary Method** options allow you to specify the mode for calculating secondary bounces. The **Light Mapping** as secondary method works well when there are lots of lights in the scene. **Light Mapping** offers very fast GI calculations.

LIGHT LEAKS
*Light leaks can occur when **Light Mapping** is used. To correct it, reduce the value of the **Sample Size** parameter in the **Light Mapping** tab. Additionally, instead of using single polygon surfaces, use thicker objects.*

Light Mapping emits samples from the camera's field of view. When geometry is struck, these samples are reflected back and colors are determined. If you want brighter results, simply lower the **Intensity** setting.

7. In the **General** tab, change **Maximum Depth** to **32** and then render the scene (see Figure 36).

35

36

WHAT JUST HAPPENED?
You are already aware that when ***Light Mapping*** *is utilized as a GI technique, samples are emitted from the camera's point of view. Depending on the* ***Maximum Depth*** *setting, these samples are frequently reflected in the scene. As the light mapping rays strike the geometry, the colors are determined. The colors are then recorded in a cell pattern (which can be saved to a file and reused later) and made available to the primary method algorithm, in this instance* ***Irrandiance Cache****. The* ***Maximum Depth*** *setting increases light dispersion without increasing render time.*

GAMMA
The ***Gamma*** *setting in the* ***General*** *tab affects just the indirect GI illumination. It can be used to lighten up the darker renders. Be cautious of the gamma value; excessive levels tend to eliminate contrast and flatten the image.*

LIGHT REFLECTION
If you use ***Irradiance Cache*** *or* ***QMC*** *as a secondary method, you will have access to the* ***Diffuse Depth*** *parameter, which lets you specify how frequently light should be reflected off a surface. High values will lengthen the rendering time.*

The **Path Count (x1000)** setting in the **Light Mapping** tab is one of the important settings to control the quality of the light map. The value you specify is internally multiplied by **1000**. This setting defines the number of samples that should be calculated for the entire scene. The higher the value you specify, the more homogeneous the light dispersion will be, and the longer will be the corresponding render time.

You are already aware that in light mapping, colors are saved in a cell pattern. You can use the **Sample Size** setting in the **Light Mapping** tab to control the size of the cells. If you want to see the progress of cell sampling during the render process, select the **Show Preview Paths** checkbox (see Figure 37).

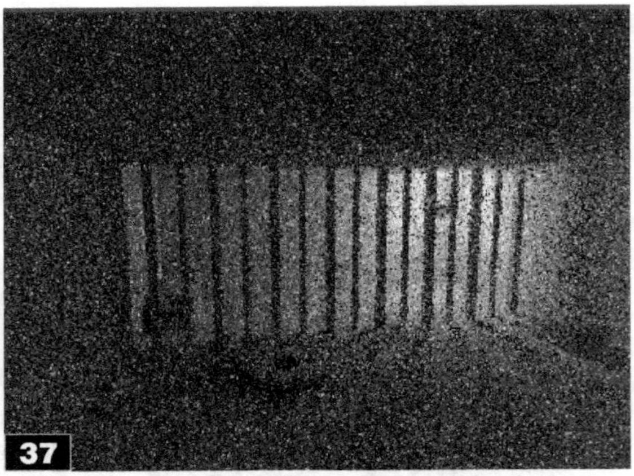
37

8. Switch to the **General** tab. Change **Maximum Depth** back to **16**, the default value.

In the **General** tab, notice that the **Medium** option is selected from the **Samples** drop-down list. The options in this drop-down list control the **Accuracy** and **Sample Count** settings. You can view these settings by expanding the **Samples** section. The **Low**, **Medium**, and **High** options in the **Samples** drop-down list let you set the **Accuracy** setting to **50%**, **75%**, and **90%**, respectively. The **Accuracy** setting automatically defines the optimized sample count. If you want to specify your own accuracy or custom sample settings, select the **Custom Sample Count** or **Custom Accuracy** option from the **Samples** drop-down list.

The number of samples you specify here will also be used by the **Discrete Area Sampling** and **Discrete Sky Sampling** settings if you haven't defined a specific number of samples for them.

HIGHER SAMPLE VALUE
*A larger **Custom Sample Count** number results in a greater render quality. If you use the **QMC** method, it will eliminate graininess from the render, and if you use the **Irrandiance Cache** method, it will remove spots from the render.*

WHAT IS A SAMPLE?
A sampler takes a sample of the scene's cache (colors+brightness) from the camera's point of view. In other terms, a sample is a color and brightness combination of a shading point. The greater the number of computed samples, the more exact the GI estimate.

9. In the **General** tab, change **Samples** to **Custom Sample Count** and **Sample Count** to **8**. Render the scene (see Figure 38). Notice there are lots of spots in the render. Change **Sample Count** to **64** and notice the change in the render quality (see Figure 39).

38

39

10. Switch to the **Irrandiance Cache** tab.

In this tab, we have the **Record Density** drop-down list at the top. Expand the **Record Density** area to see the corresponding options. The options available in the **Record Density** drop-down list are: **Preview**, **Low**, **Medium**, and **High**. If you change any of the default options in the **Record Density** area, the **Custom** option will be active.

These settings are used to fine tune the results. The **Preview** mode offers a quick preview of the final result. The **Record Density > Density** parameter adjusts the general dispersion of the shading points. The higher the value you set for this parameter, the higher the shading point density will be.

Shaded points and their positions are calculated point by point via GI techniques. When rendering, the point-by-point brightness dispersion must be transformed to a planar dispersion. **Smoothing** takes care of it for you. To draw a particular pixel, it interpolates the brightness of nearby points. The greater the **Smoothing** parameter value, the more samples will be used for rendering at a particular position. Smaller values yield a spotty outcome.

SMOOTHING VALUE
Smoothing *is a setting whose value you will rarely have to modify.*

11. In the **General** tab, change **Secondary Method** to **Off**. Render the scene (see Figure 40). In the **Irradiance Cache** tab, change **Color Refinement** to **100**. Render the scene (see Figure 41).

40

41

WHAT JUST HAPPENED?
Compare Figures 40 and 41. Figure 40 has more defined shadows. The ***Color Refinement*** *setting enhances render quality in locations where GI illumination changes abruptly, such as GI shadows and bright polygon lights. When you utilize the* ***Color Refinement*** *setting, more shading points are generated, which increases the render time.*

CAUTION: SPOTTY REGIONS
It is important that you increase the value of ***Record Density*** *sufficiently to ensure that the light dispersion is homogeneous; otherwise, the render would have spotty regions.*

GI CAUSTICS
GI caustics also benefits from the higher values.

12. In the **General** tab, change **Primary Method > Intensity** to **200**, **Secondary Method** to **Light Mapping**, **Secondary Method > Maximum Depth** to **32**, and **Samples > Sample Count** to **256**. Render the scene. Notice in Figure 42, we have a better looking result now. [**gi-finish.c4d**] You can also increase the **Radius** of the **Sphere** to get more illumination in the scene.

AMBIENT OCCLUSION

42

Ambient Occlusion lets you determine how much of each surface point is exposed before darkening it. When **Ambient Occlusion** is enabled, places such as corners, holes, or close-together objects seem darker. Ambient Occlusion in Cinema 4D may be defined in two places: Using the **Effect** button in the **Render Settings** window. You can also output ambient occlusion as a multi-pass channel.

As a channel shader for a material, you can access it by choosing **Texture > Arrow** button **> Effects > Ambient Occlusion** (see Figure 43) in the **Material Editor**. You should use this effect in the **Diffusion** channel. You can also use channels for special effects such as applying dirt textures in the corners.

When you select **Ambient Occlusion** in the **Render Settings** window's left pane, the relevant options appear in the right pane (see Figure 44). **[ambient-occlusion.c4d]**

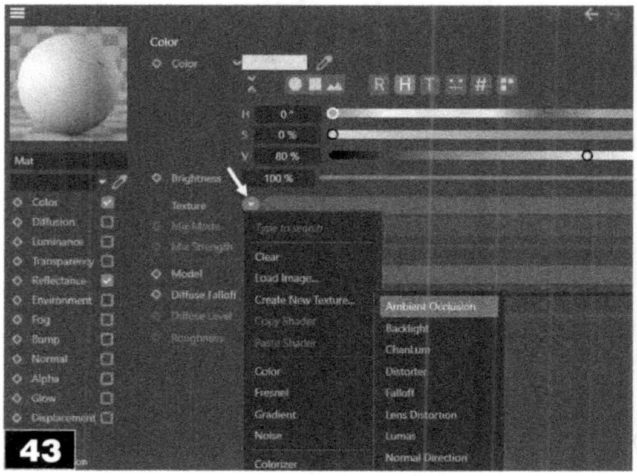

43

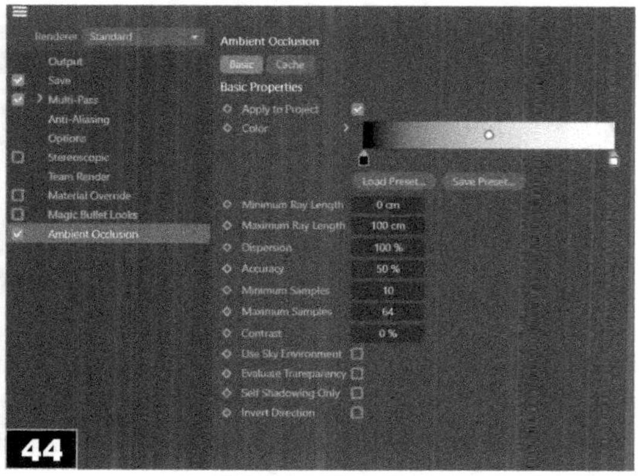

44

The first option at the top is the **Apply to Project** checkbox, which is by default selected. As a result, you can enable **Ambient Occlusion** without having to create or edit materials. Figure 45 shows the render with and without the **Ambient Occlusion** effect.

COMPOSITING TAG
*You can remove ambient occlusion from individual objects using the **Compositing** tag.*

AMPLIFIED EFFECT
*If you define **Ambient Occlusion** in the **Render Settings** window, it will be applied to all objects globally. The objects that have the **Ambient Occlusion** shader applied, ambient occlusion calculations will be done twice. As a result, the **Ambient Occlusion** effect will be amplified for these objects.*

45

The **Color** option allows you to define a color gradient for the effect. Generally, a simple black to white gradient is used. However, you can define any color for special effects. Figure 46 shows the render when a gradient is used as **Color**.

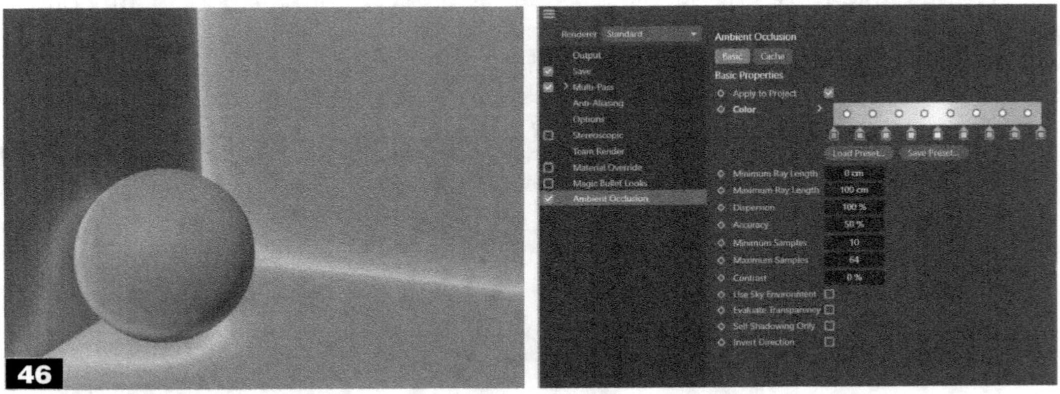

46

The **Minimum Ray Length** parameter determines how the defined gradient between exposed and non-exposed regions is rendered. It is recommended that you leave this option alone and leave it at its default value of **0**. The **Maximum Ray Length** parameter specifies the distance between surfaces. Figure 47 shows the rendered output with the **Maximum Ray Length** set to **10**, **30**, **60**, and **200**. In general, smaller values for the **Maximum Ray Length** parameter should be used.

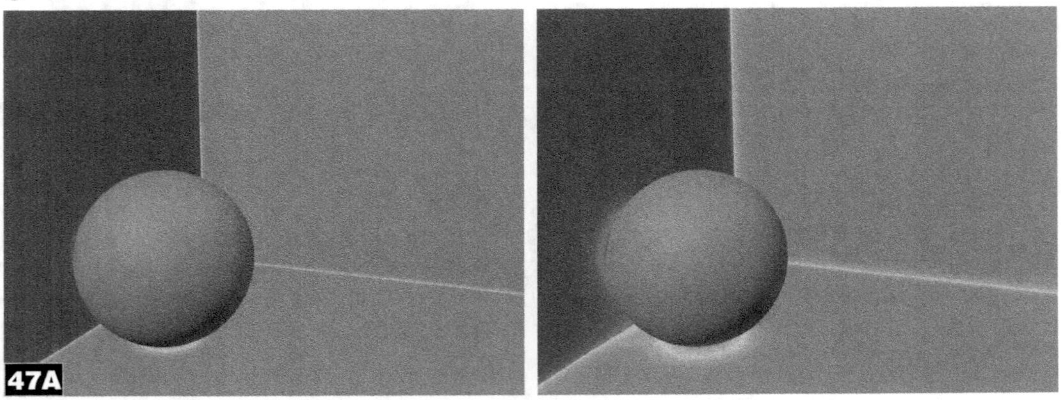

47A

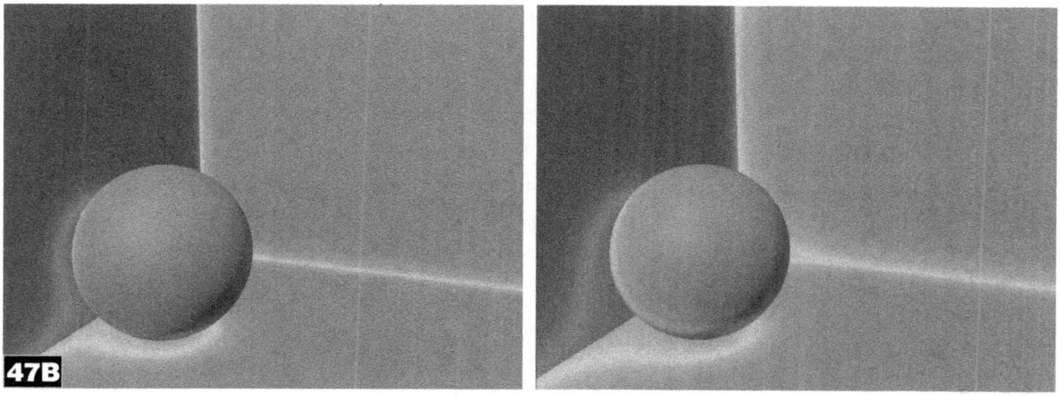

47B

The **Dispersion** parameter determines which samples are utilized for **Ambient Occlusion** calculations. Many samples or rays are released during the computations for each point inside a virtual hemisphere. These rays determine whether or not geometries fall inside the **Maximum Ray Length** parameter value. A **Dispersion** number of **100** considers the whole hemisphere, whereas a value of **0** considers only the zenith (the areas perpendicular to each point) of the hemisphere. Figure 48 depicts the rendered result with the **Dispersion** value set to **0**, **50**, and **100**.

48

The quality of the **Ambient Occlusion** effect is controlled by the **Accuracy**, **Minimum Samples**, and **Maximum Samples** parameters. The more samples you use, the more uniform the result, and the longer the render time necessary for computations. The **Minimum Samples** and **Maximum Samples** settings are used to manage the scene's critical and less important parts. The **Accuracy** option specifies how the samples should be spread in order to achieve the best possible results. The **Contrast** setting controls the contrast of the **Ambient Occlusion** effect. Figure 49 shows the rendered result with the **Contrast** value set to **0**, **50**, and **100**.

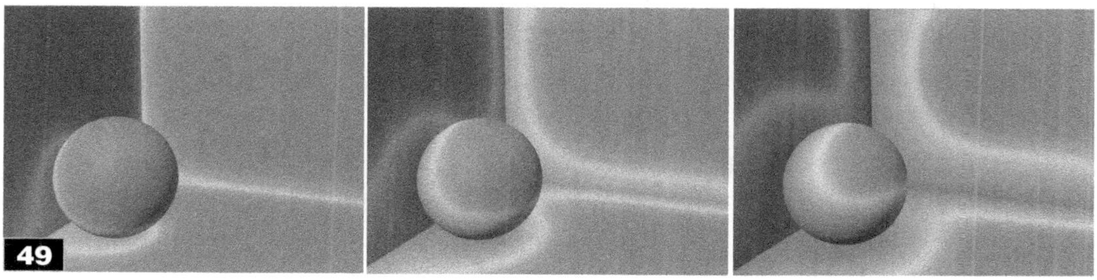

49

When the **Self Shadowing Only** checkbox is enabled, separate objects will not see each other, they will only see themselves (see Figure 50). The **Invert Direction** switch allows you to invert the **Ambient Occlusion** effect. As a result, outward pointing edges and corners/peaks will be ascertained for the **Ambient Occlusion** effect (see Figure 51). [**ambient-occlusion-2.c4d**]

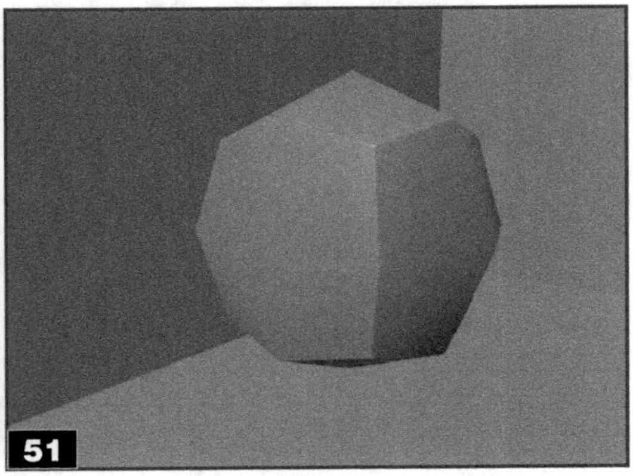

ALPHA CHANNEL
You can place the ***Ambient Occlusion*** *shader into the alpha channel of a material; the respective material will only have an effect on the outward pointing edges and corners/peaks.*

POINTS TO REMEMBER

Render Settings

- **Tokens** are simple text variables that can be used in the **File** input field as a path string.
- To compute a pre-multiplied alpha channel, select the **Alpha Channel** checkbox. The alpha channel contains the same resolution grayscale picture as the color image. The presence of an object is shown by white pixels in the alpha channel, whereas the absence of an object is indicated by black pixels. Select the **Straight Alpha** checkbox to prevent the black seam in the composition. Straight alphas are only used for compositing images; they are not useful for conventional images.
- **Geometry** is the default anti-aliasing method, which smooths all object edges with **16x16** sub-pixels. The **Best** method uses more sub-pixels as well as Cinema 4D's adaptive antialiasing. In most circumstances, the default setting of **2x2** for the **Max Level** option is sufficient. If the **Refraction** option is enabled but no materials in the scene reflect light, no additional render time is added.
- Increase the value of the **Ray Depth** parameter if transparent objects that are behind other transparent objects are displayed dark.
- The area or hard shadows are substantially more computationally costly to render than the soft shadows. Hard shadows seem more realistic than soft shadows.

- When you select the **Active Object Only** option, only the objects you've selected will be included in the render calculations.
- The **Textures** checkbox controls whether or not textures are enabled or disabled during rendering. This checkbox can be disabled for a test render or while using the **Cel** renderer. When this option is not checked, bitmaps are replaced with black.
- When you enable the **Volumetric Lighting** checkbox, the shadows will be projected in visible light. Because this option is render heavy, you can deactivate it for test renderings.
- The **Ray Threshold** parameter governs the movement of rays in the scene. Rays stop moving from the camera to the scene when their brightness falls below the value you set for the **Ray Threshold** parameter. Because **90%** of the processed rays contribute less than **10%** to the overall brightness and color of the image in a scene with numerous reflecting and transparent surfaces, you may use this value to improve the render time.
- The **Ray Depth** parameter determines how many transparent objects the renderer will penetrate.
- The **Reflection Depth** parameter can be used to restrict the number of reflective rays (maximum number of rays) that are sent into the scene. Adding additional rays tends to improve image quality while increasing render time.
- When you select the **Material Override** checkbox, the defined material replaces all other materials in the scene. You may use this option to enable or disable features such as shadows and light balancing (commonly known as "clay rendering").

Global Illumination

- When the image is rendered, post effects are generated. They won't be visible until the entire image is displayed. Remember that the sequence of the effects in the **Render Settings** window is important.
- When you use a **Sky** object with the **HDR** texture, the auto light is not disabled. If you add GI to the scene, the auto light will be disabled.
- When the **Generate GI** checkbox for the material is enabled, the specified material has an effect on other objects in the scene. The **Strength** option determines how much light this material emits.
- The **Primary Method** only brightens surfaces that are directly lit, whereas the **Secondary Method** accounts for additional reflected light. The primary method computes the impact of diffuse depth, which is the light emitted by polygon lights and surfaces illuminated by actual lights or **Physical Sky**. In most cases, a blue sphere lit by white light reflects blue light. The **Secondary Method** computes the brightness of surfaces that do not have to lie in the camera's field of view. Figure 52 shows the surfaces illuminated by the primary method on the left and the primary + secondary methods on the right. [**summary-1.c4d**]

52

- The **Diffuse Depth** parameter is only accessible if the **Irradiance Cache** or **QMC** method is used as a secondary method. It determines how frequently light should be reflected from a surface. The rendered result is shown in Figure 53, with **Diffuse Depth** set to **2** on the left, and **3** on the right. It should be noted that it brightens the image but increases the render time. A value greater than **3** gets less and less noticeable in a regular scene; the render scene simply becomes brighter.

53

- The **Maximum Depth** parameter is available when **Light Mapping** is used as **Secondary Method**. Higher values create homogeneous dispersion of light with no increase in render time. The increase in brightness is less noticeable in interior scenes. No other GI method calculates high **Diffuse Depth** values as fast as **Light Mapping**.
- The **Samples** settings lets you set the number of samples and **Accuracy** setting. You can use the **Sample Count** setting to optimize the scene.
- The **Discrete Area Sampling** settings only work if **Polygon Light** is active for the polygon lights (or for GI Portals). These settings send additional samples to polygon lights.
- The **Discrete Sky Sampling** settings are only advantageous when **Irradiance Cache** is used as primary method. For bright region such as Sun, the **Irradiance Cache** method has some limitations which results in the spotty rendering. To fix this, you can use the **Discrete Sky Sampling** setting.

- The **Radiosity Maps** method is used with the preview settings since it is ideally suited for quick rendering previews.
- A sampler samples the cache (colors+brightness) of the scene from the camera's point of view.
- For exterior scenes, **Irradiance Cache+QMC** is the best combination. As a secondary method, **Irradiance Cache** works well in interior environments with small lights specified as polygon lights or GI portals lights.
- A higher **Custom Sample Count** value results in a greater render quality. This option will eliminate graininess from the render if you use the **QMC** method, and it will remove spots if you use the **Irrandiance Cache** method.
- The cache files are only used while rendering the scene in the **Picture Viewer** window, not in the viewport.
- In comparison to the **Irradiance Cache** method, the **QMC** method provides the best GI quality. **QMC** is the most precise method, but it is also the slowest. It works really well when **Light Mapping** is used as a secondary method.
- When used with animations, the **Irradiance Cache** mode tends to flicker. When you utilize bright and small polygon lights in the scene, it flickers more.
- Using animations, the **QMC+QMC** combination offers flicker-free output. **Irradiance Cache+QMC** is prone to flickering as well. **QMC** works effectively as a secondary method with **Light Mapping**.
- When **Light Mapping** is used, light leakage might occur. To correct it, reduce the values of the **Sample Size** parameter in the **Light Mapping** tab. Additionally, instead of using single polygon surfaces, use thicker objects.
- The **Maximum Depth** setting increases light dispersion without increasing render time.
- The **Gamma** setting in the **General** tab affects just the indirect GI illumination. It may be used to lighten up the darker renderings. Be cautious of the gamma value; high values tend to eliminate contrast and flatten the image.
- If you use **Irradiance Cache** or **QMC** as a secondary method, you will have access to the **Diffuse Depth** parameter, which lets you specify how frequently light should be reflected off a surface.
- It is important that you increase the value of **Record Density** sufficiently to ensure that the light dispersion is homogeneous; otherwise, the render would have patchy sections. The higher levels are also beneficial to GI caustics.
- The **QMC** approach requires a lot of CPU resources to render the animation.

Ambient Occlusion

- **Ambient Occlusion** allows you to decide how much of each surface point is exposed before darkening it. When **Ambient Occlusion** is enabled, areas such as corners, holes, or areas where objects are near to each other appear darker.

- The **Ambient Occlusion** effect can be applied using a material.
- The **Compositing** tag can be used to eliminate ambient occlusion from particular objects. If you apply the **Ambient Occlusion** shader to an object while also enabling the global **Ambient Occlusion** effect in the **Render Settings** window, the ambient occlusion computations will be repeated. As a result, the ambient occlusion effect for the object will be amplified.
- The quality of the **Ambient Occlusion** effect is controlled by the **Accuracy**, **Minimum Samples**, and **Maximum Samples** parameters.
- When the **Self Shadowing Only** checkbox is enabled, separate objects will only see themselves and will not see each other.
- You can place the **Ambient Occlusion** shader in a material's alpha channel; the material will only affect the outward pointing edges and corners/peaks.

CEL RENDERER

The **Cel Renderer** post-effect allows you to create cartoon-style images and animations. The render time increases linearly with the amount of polygons in the scene when this effect is used. Open the **cell-renderer.c4d** file and then press **Ctrl B** to open the **Render Settings** window. In this window, click the **Effect** button to open the **Effect** popup and then choose **Cel Renderer** from the popup to add the effect to the left pane of the **Render Settings** window. Select it in the left pane; the corresponding parameters will be displayed in the right pane (see Figure 54). By default, the **Outline** checkbox is enabled. As a result, an outline will be drawn around the silhouette of objects (see Figure 55).

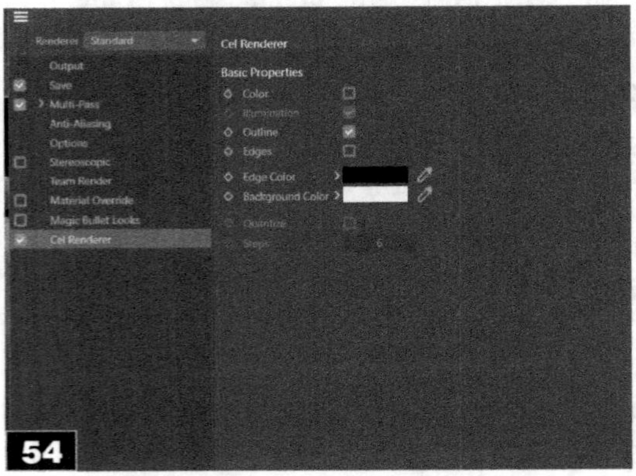

54

55

If you clear both the **Color** and **Outline** checkboxes, only background color will be displayed. The background color is controlled by the **Background Color** swatch. Figure 56 shows the render with both the **Color** and **Outline** checkboxes selected. The **Quantize** checkbox and the **Steps** parameter can be used to render the cartoon effect with color steps. Figure 57 shows the render with **Steps** set to **6**. If you select the **Edges** checkbox, all polygon edges will be outlined in black creating shaded wireframe feel (see Figure 58). The color of the edges can be changed using the **Edge Color** swatch.

56

57

If the **Illumination** checkbox is enabled, the shading of the objects will be affected by illumination in the scene. If the **Illumination** checkbox is cleared, each color will be displayed in a monotone color (see Figure 59). [**cell-renderer-finish.c4d**] The color will be defined using the right-most texture tag in the **Object Manager**. Also, shadows will not be rendered.

58

59

COLOR CORRECTION

The **Color Correction** post-effect allows you to make common color corrections in Cinema 4D without having to switch to a post-application such as **Photoshop** or **After Effects**. I recommend that instead of using color correction as post effect, you can use it as a filter in the **Picture Viewer** window for greater control (see Figure 60). When you use it as post effect, it affects the internal rendering process in 32-bit full color width. You can also use the **Magic Bullet Looks** feature to color correct your image using advanced parameters.

COLOR MAPPING

When you use GI with a low ray depth to render a scene, the rendered output appears very bright in some regions and very dark in others. **Color Mapping** helps you to achieve consistent illumination by establishing an excellent balanced allocation of color and brightness. Figure 61 shows the options corresponding to the **Color Mapping** effect.

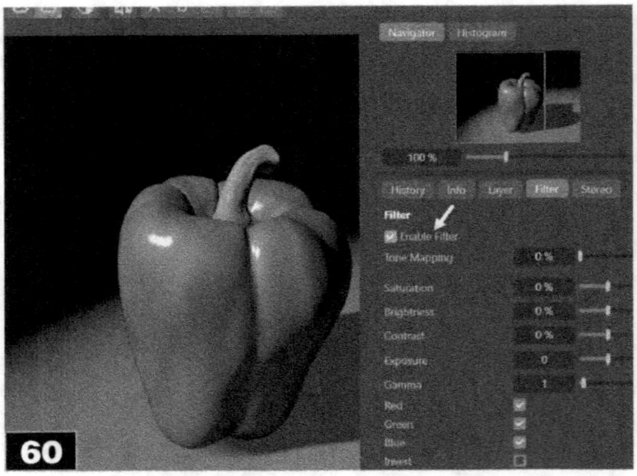

60

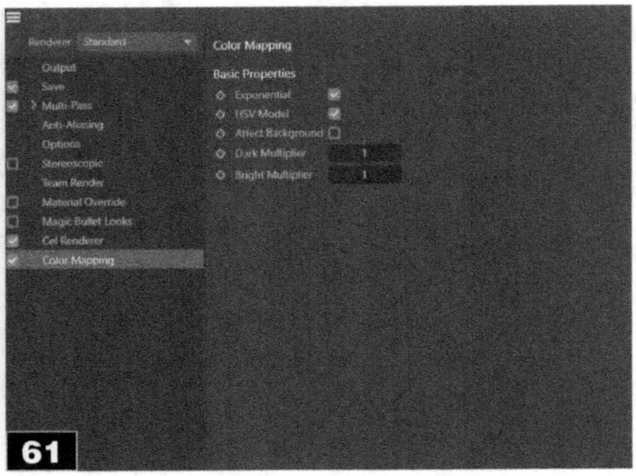

61

You can achieve this in one of two ways:

- Export the rendered image in 32-bit depth before using an external compositor/editor.
- You can use the **Color Mapping** effect to have it compute internal interpolation for you. This post-effect is applied before Cinema 4D's sub-pixel anti-aliasing and gives better results than the external application method.

By default, the color dispersion is controlled linearly. The **Exponential** checkbox allows you to control dispersion exponentially. The exponential dispersion results in an even and harmonious color progression.

Open the **color-mapping.c4d** file. In this file, we have a blue backdrop and a **Disc** object is serving as a light source in the scene. A bright white material is applied on the disc with very high brightness in the **Luminance** channel. Also, the **Polygon Light** checkbox is enabled for the material. Render the scene (see Figure 62). Notice in Figure 62 that the blue backdrop is lit strongly (also referred to as burnout) in the vicinity of the disc.

Press **Ctrl B** to open the **Render Settings** window. In this window, click the **Effect** button to open the **Effect** popup and then choose **Color Mapping** from the popup to add the effect to the left pane of the **Render Settings** window. Select it in the left pane; the corresponding parameters will be displayed in the right pane. In the right pane, clear the **HSV Model** checkbox and then select the **Affect Background** checkbox. Render the scene (see Figure 63).

Notice in Figure 63 the color progression on the blue backdrop is harmonious. The **HSV Model** checkbox allows you to convert colors to HSV model and only the **V** component (**brightness**) component will be affected; the colors will remain identical. If there is any background present in the scene such as a **Sky** or a **Background** object, you can use the **Affect Background** checkbox to define whether or not **Color Mapping** should affect the background.

The **Dark Multiplier** and **Bright Multiplier** settings allow you to strengthen or weaken the dark and light colors. The left image in Figure 64 shows the render with no **Color Mapping** applied. In the right image, the **Exponential** and **Affect Background** checkboxes are selected. The **HSV Model** checkbox is cleared, the **Dark Multiplier** and **Bright Multiplier** parameters are set to **3** and **1**, respectively. [**color-mapping-2.c4d**]

WHAT IS THE HSV MODEL?
*The **HSV** model specifies color by combining three elements: hue, saturation, and value (Brightness). To define an HSV color, no prior knowledge of primary colors (red, green, and blue) is necessary. As a result, this model allows you to intuitively create the color palettes and this is the reason Cinema 4D employs HSV model for the color wheels. This model gets close to capturing the human eye's sense of color. The hue is defined by the **H** value, which is represented as an angle on the color wheel. The saturation of hue is defined by the **S** value. The color's brightness is defined by the **V** value. A value of **0** creates the color black.*

CYLINDRICAL LENS

The **Cylindrical Lens** post effect allows you to generate 360-degree rendering. If you're a matte painter, this effect is quite beneficial. Get a rough scene from the modeling department and render it using the **Cylindrical Lens** effect. You can now paint your scenery using the rendered output.

Open the **cylindrical-lens.c4d** file. It contains a **Sphere** object that is cloned using the **Cloner** object. Create a **Camera** in the scene and then make it the current camera. Press **Shift C** to open the **Commander** window and then execute the command **Reset Transform**. This command zero outs all position and rotation coordinates.

ANGLE OF VIEW
*Ensure that the angle of view should be parallel to the floor which essentially means that the **R.P** and **R.B** values for the camera should be zero.*

Press **Ctrl B** to open the **Render Settings** window. In this window, select **Output** from the left pane and then in the right pane, set **Width** and **Height** to **1500** and **200**, respectively. Note that the **Width** value should be larger in relation to the **Height** value.

Click the **Effect** button to open the **Effect** popup and then choose **Cylindrical Lens** from the popup to add the effect to the left pane of the **Render Settings** window. Select it in the left pane; the corresponding parameters will be displayed in the right pane. Now, change **Horizontal Field of View** to **360** and **Vertical Size** to **300**. You have to tweak the value of **Vertical Size** to get rid of any distortion. Render the scene, refer to Figure 65. [**cylindrical-lens-finsh.c4d**]

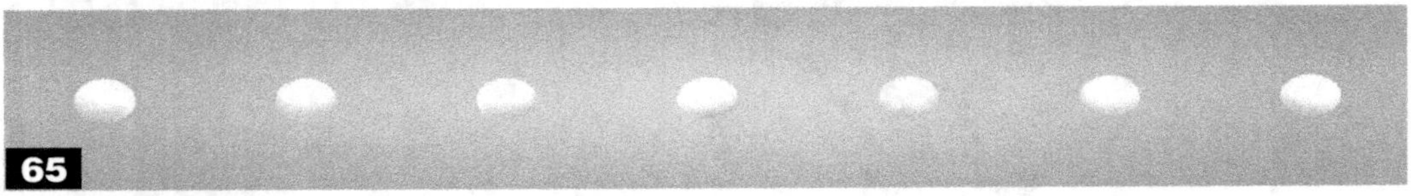

65

DEPTH OF FIELD

The **Depth of Field** effect is a post-effect that calculates quickly but has several limitations. Artifacts may appear, for example, when blurred objects are viewed in reflections or behind clear surfaces. With the **Physical** renderer, you can generate a higher quality depth of field effect. The technique of producing depth-of-field effects with the **Physical** renderer is covered in the next chapter.

GLOW

The **Glow** post effect allows you to simulate glow of LEDs, neon lights, incandescent lights, and so on. This effect also allows you to:

- Control the transparency of glow.
- Restrict glow to edges or specific colors.
- Apply fractal noise to glow.
- Use additive or non-additive glow to surfaces.
- Prevent unwanted overexposures.
- Change glow according to the surface normals.

GLOW EFFECT

*This effect can b calculated to a maximum width and height of **4096** pixels.*

GLOWING M RIALS

*The **Glow** c el of a material differs from the **Glow** effect. Glow is always generated by glowin rials, whereas the **Glow** effect creates glow based on the brightness of the di d pixels. It is important to note that if there are no lights in the scene, the glo rials will always emit glow, however the **Glow** effect will not.*

RENDER

The o e **Render** menu are used to render an image or an image sequence. Let's se options.

R W

ider > ONLINE RENDERING > Render View (Ctrl R)

der the active viewport using the **Render View** option. In Cinema 4D, an active s a thick gray border. If you're working in a four-panel view, you can render each cession. Make a view active, then choose **Render > ONLINE RENDERING > iew** from the main menu. You can also click on the **Render View** icon in the d palette > **Render command** group. Now, you can use the **Tab** key to cycle the views and render them one by one. You can stop the rendering anytime by g **Esc** or by clicking in the view.

RENDERING SUPPORT

While rendering the active viewport, all methods of rendering (for example, multi-passes) are not supported. Moreover, certain post-processing effects, such as motion blur, will not be displayed. The rendering process is shown as a blue bar in the lower left corner of the Cinema 4D interface.

RENDER REGION

Main Menu: Render > ONLINE RENDERING > Render Region

You can render a specified region of the view using the **Render Region** tool. This tool is handy for fine-tuning a specific area of the view. You can also invoke this tool by holding the **LMB** on the **Render View** icon in the **Standard** palette > **Render** command group and then choose **Render Region** from the popup menu. You can stop the rendering anytime by pressing **Esc** or by clicking in the view.

INTERACTIVE RENDER REGION

Main Menu: Render > ONLINE RENDERING > Interactive render region (Alt R)

The **Interactive Render Region** tool or IRR tool is used for test renderings. The IRR can be freely positioned and resized in a scene (see Figure 66).

GLOW EFFECT
*This effect can be calculated to a maximum width and height of **4096** pixels.*

GLOWING MATERIALS
*The **Glow** channel of a material differs from the **Glow** effect. Glow is always generated by glowing materials, whereas the **Glow** effect creates glow based on the brightness of the displayed pixels. It is important to note that if there are no lights in the scene, the glow materials will always emit glow, however the **Glow** effect will not.*

RENDER MENU

The options in the **Render** menu are used to render an image or an image sequence. Let's explore these options.

RENDER VIEW

Main Menu: Render > ONLINE RENDERING > Render View (Ctrl R)

You can render the active viewport using the **Render View** option. In Cinema 4D, an active viewport has a thick gray border. If you're working in a four-panel view, you can render each view in succession. Make a view active, then choose **Render > ONLINE RENDERING > Render View** from the main menu. You can also click on the **Render View** icon in the **Standard** palette > **Render command** group. Now, you can use the **Tab** key to cycle through the views and render them one by one. You can stop the rendering anytime by pressing **Esc** or by clicking in the view.

RENDERING SUPPORT
While rendering the active viewport, all methods of rendering (for example, multi-passes) are not supported. Moreover, certain post-processing effects, such as motion blur, will not be displayed. The rendering process is shown as a blue bar in the lower left corner of the Cinema 4D interface.

RENDER REGION

Main Menu: Render > ONLINE RENDERING > Render Region

You can render a specified region of the view using the **Render Region** tool. This tool is handy for fine-tuning a specific area of the view. You can also invoke this tool by holding the **LMB** on the **Render View** icon in the **Standard** palette > **Render** command group and then choose **Render Region** from the popup menu. You can stop the rendering anytime by pressing **Esc** or by clicking in the view.

INTERACTIVE RENDER REGION

Main Menu: Render > ONLINE RENDERING > Interactive render region (Alt R)

The **Interactive Render Region** tool or IRR tool is used for test renderings. The IRR can be freely positioned and resized in a scene (see Figure 66).

Click-drag the handles of the region to scale the box. Hover the mouse pointer over one of the region boundaries and drag when the mouse pointer icon turns to a hand to move. A triangular slider (see Figure 67) at the right edge of the IRR allows you to alter the render resolution. Move the triangle all the way to the top for the highest render quality. But, as is often the case, the higher the render quality, the longer it will take to render the preview. **RMB** click on one of the edges to open a context menu (see Figure 67). Using the options available in this menu, you can define the behavior of IRR.

66

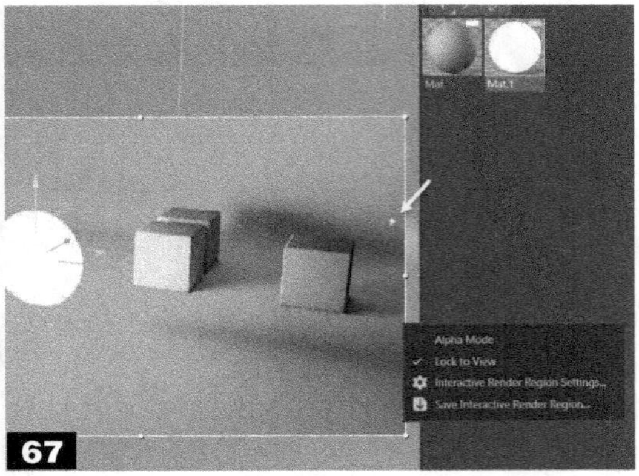

67

RENDER TO PICTURE VIEWER

Main Menu: Render > OFFLINE RENDERING > Render to Picture Viewer (Shift R)

The **Render to Picture Viewer** command renders the scene in the **Picture Viewer** window. This command can also be accessed by clicking the **Render to Picture Viewer** button in the **Standard** palette > **Render** command group. A progress indicator shows in the status bar once rendering begins. This bar displays the amount of time that has passed since the rendering began. While rendering an animation, the bar displays the current frame number as well as the overall number of frames. Use **Esc** to cancel the rendering. Figure 68 shows the **Picture Viewer** window.

The **Picture Viewer** is one of Cinema 4D's output windows. This window displays the rendered image and animations. Render images from a session are saved in the **History** tab, and images rendered for a specific session can be accessed from this tab at any time. The **Image Viewer** includes a ram player which you can use to play the animation without first saving it as a video. The sound can also be loaded into the **Image Viewer**. Let's have a look at the **Picture Viewer**.

At the top-right corner of the viewer are navigation icons. The first icon is used to maximize the display area. It toggles the visibility of the **Navigator** and **Histogram** tabs. The next icon is used to open a new **Picture Viewer**. The next icon is used to move the **Picture Viewer's** clipping region. The right-most icon is used to scale the **Picture Viewer's** clipping region.

68

Following options are available for the display view:

- Click-drag in a clipping region to move it.
- Press and hold the **2** key on the main keyboard and then click drag to scale the image. The mouse wheel scroll will perform the same function.
- Double-click on the display to scale it to **100%**; double-click again to fit to full screen.
- If you **RMB** click in the clipping region, a context menu will open. You can use the options in this menu to select an alternate background color.

Ram Player

The ram player (see Figure 69) is used to load and play the image sequence. It loads the sequence temporarily into the dynamic memory of the system so that it can be played back in real-time - even HD quality.

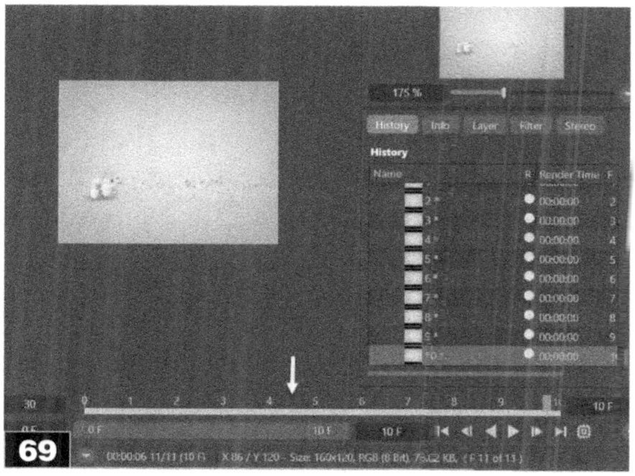

69

MEMORY
Images in the RAM player are not compressed. As a result, a large amount of RAM is utilized.

TIMELINE
*You can scale the timeline by holding the **2** key on the main keyboard and then dragging the mouse pointer in the timeline. Similarly, you can use the **1** key to move.*

Navigator

The **Navigator** tab displays the rendered image at preview size. The viewable region will be represented with a moveable square depending on the zoom level. You can set zoom level to **100%** by double-clicking on the navigator. To move the square freely, click and drag. The **Shift** drag action allows you to move the square horizontally or vertically. **Ctrl** dragging can be used to define a separate square zone.

Histogram

The **Histogram** tab shows a static distribution of an image's brightness, color, and luminance information. Peaks in the **Histogram** show values that occur more frequently. The color channel will be determined by the drop-down list below the histogram (see Figure 70). The **Display Filer** checkbox is only accessible, if you have turned on **Enable Filter** in the **Filter** tab (see Figure 71). On selecting this checkbox, histogram will take the effect of the filter into account.

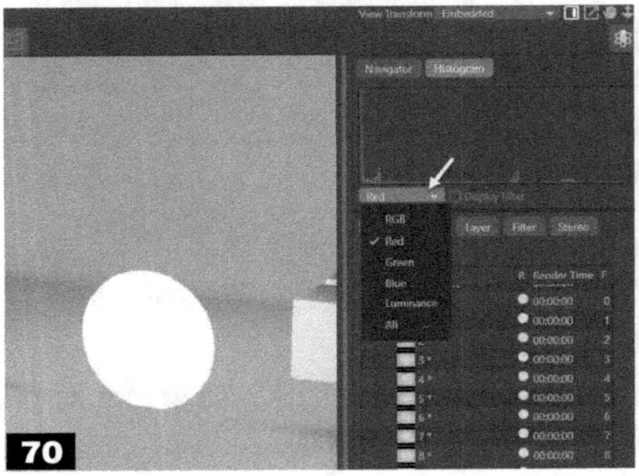

70

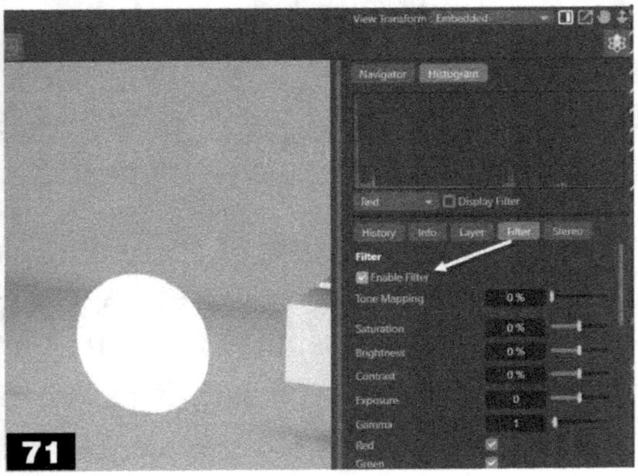

71

> ***HUMAN EYE***
> *The green value is more important than the red and blue values. Green appears brighter to the human eye than red/blue.*

History

The **History** tab displays a list that shows the all the rendered or loaded images for the current session. The list remains empty until a rendering or render session takes place. Click on one of the entries to display it in the **Picture Viewer**. Image names with a * next to them represent images that have not been saved.

The **History** tab contains the following columns:

- **Name:** The name of the image or directory.
- **R:** Displays image state. **Green:** Cached, **Gray:** Not Cached, **Orange:** Currently being rendered, **A/B:** Images currently being compared.
- **Render Time:** Displays the time system took to render the image.

- **F:** Frame number
- **Resolution:** The image resolution in pixels.

The **Shift** and **Ctrl** keys can be used to select images in the list. Individual images or entire directories can be dragged and dropped to a different location in the hierarchy. You can also create a copy of an image by **Ctrl** dragging. The arrow keys may be used to navigate up and down the hierarchy, as well as to open (right arrow) and close (left arrow) directories.

You can also compare images in the **Picture Viewer** window. You can only compare images with same resolution. To compare images, select the first image and then choose **Compare > Set As A** from the viewer's menu or press **A**. Now, select the second image and then choose **Compare > Set As B** from the viewer's menu bar or press **B**; a dividing line appears in the display (see Figure 72).

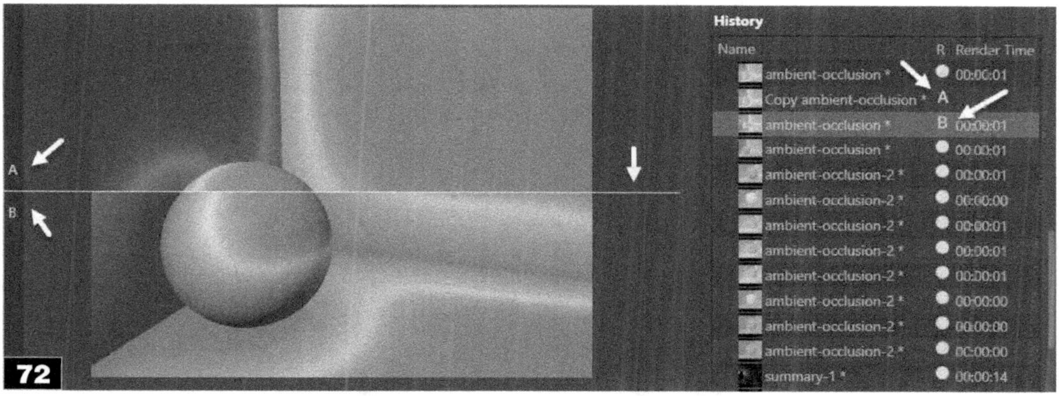

72

Now, you can drag the line to compare the two images. You can toggle the display of the line by choosing **Compare > AB Compare** from the viewer's menu bar. To swap the AB images choose **Compare > Swap AB** from the viewer's menu bar or press **S**. To toggle the orientation of the line choose **Compare > Swap Vert./Horiz.** from the viewer's menu.

These options are also available via the context menu that appears when you **RMB** click an image in the **History** list. When you select **Show File in Explorer/Finder** from the context menu, Cinema 4D launches the corresponding application on your system and displays the file, if it was loaded using the **Picture Viewer**. If you've done several test renders with different render settings and want to pick the best one, you can use the **Create Render Setting from Render** command to establish a new, distinct render preset for rendered images or image sequences for the current Cinema 4D session.

Info

The **Info** panel provides an array of self-explanatory details about the selected image. This tab indicates the render time per image and the overall render time for newly rendered scenes. The size of the title safe and action safe frames is controlled by the **Title Safe** and **Action Safe** parameters, respectively. The **Pixel Aspect** parameter is used to distort the aspect ratio. The viewer's **View** menu allows you to enable the **Title Safe** and **Action Safe** settings.

Layer

The **Layer** tab displays the images selected in the **History** tab, including all passes and alpha channel. There are three radio buttons in the **Layer** area: **Image**, **Single-Pass**, and **Multi-Pass** (see Figure 73). On selecting the **Image** radio button, only the layer defined as "**background**" will be shown.

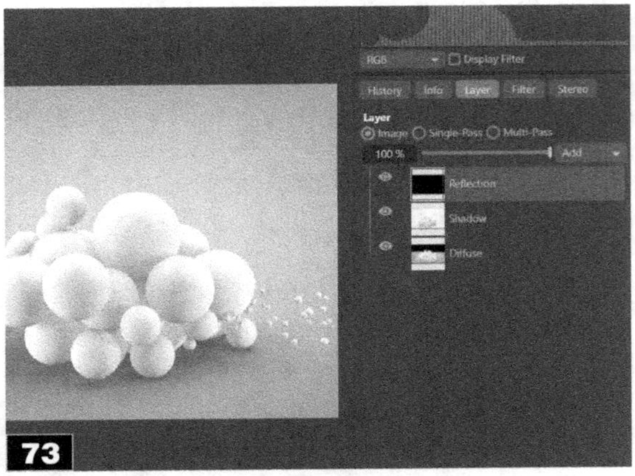

73

If you select the **Single-Pass** radio button, you can display an individual pass by selecting it. Figure 74 shows the **Shadow** pass. When you select the **Multi-Pass** radio button, the image mode is switched to **Multi-Pass** mode, you can now select blending mode from the drop-down list in this tab.

Also, you can adjust the mix strength using the float slider available on the left of the drop-down list. Figure 75 shows the mix strength and blending mode set to **34** and **Multiply**, respectively, for the **Shadow** pass. [**layer.c4d**]

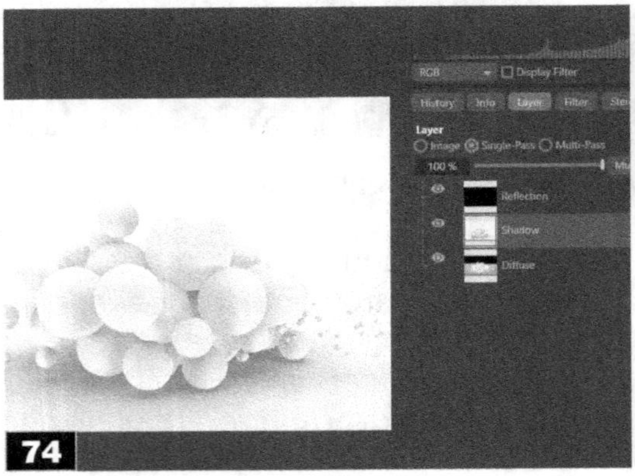

74

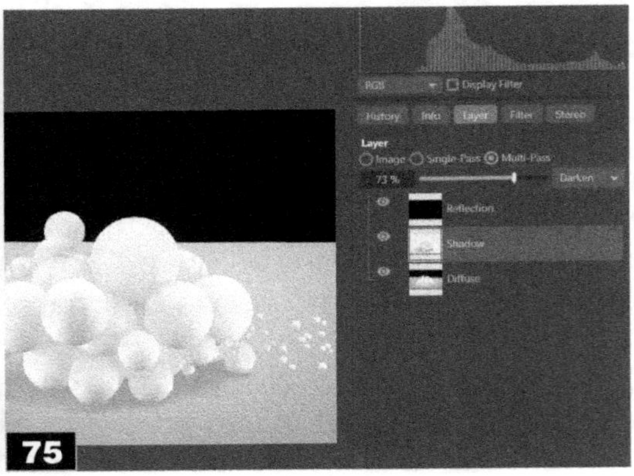

75

Filter

The options in the **Filter** tab are used to color correct images. The effect are temporarily applied to the loaded or rendered sequence. Only when the images are saved with the **Enable Filter** option enabled, the **Filter** actually be applied to the images.

RENDER TO PICTURE VIEWER (TEAM RENDER)

Main Menu: Render > OFFLINE RENDERING > Render to Picture Viewer (Ctrl Shift R)

The functionality of this command is same to that of the **Render to Picture Viewer** command, only that rendering will be done using **Team Render**.

TAKES

Main Menu: Render > OFFLINE RENDERING > Takes

The **Render All Takes to PV** and **Render Marked Takes to PV** options are used to render all or marked **Takes** in succession to the **Picture Viewer (PV)**. The **Team Render All Takes to PV** and **Team Render Marked Takes to PV** options are used to render all or marked takes in succession to the **Picture Viewer (PV)** using **Team Render**. These options are also available in the **Render to Picture Viewer** popup.

ADD TO RENDER QUEUE

Main Menu: Render > RENDER QUEUE > Add to Render Queue

You can use the **Add to Render Queue** command to add currently opened scene to the list of **Render Queue** window.

RENDER QUEUE

Main Menu: Render > RENDER QUEUE > Render Queue

The options in the **Render Queue** window (see Figure 76) allow you to batch render any number of files without supervision.

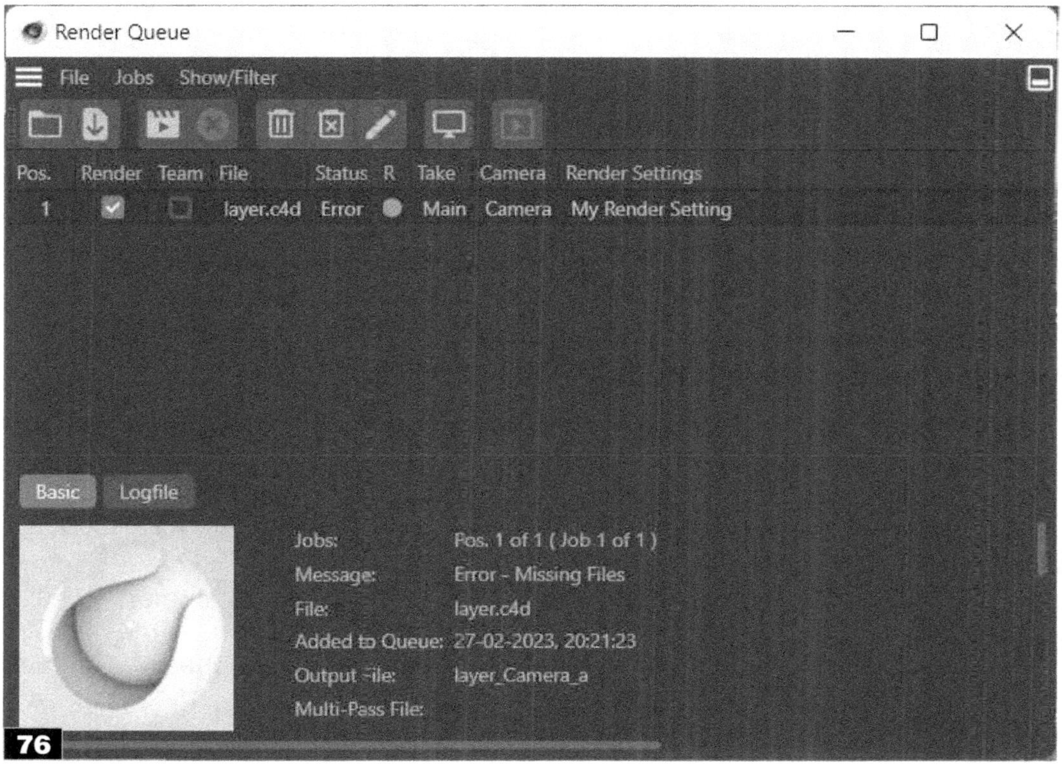

76

The following functions are available in this window:

- Render any number of files consecutively without any supervision.
- Redirect save paths, select cameras, select takes, and render settings without opening the files itself.
- Extensive **Render Queue** configurations can be saved as presets.
- Log files can be saved and viewed.
- Rendered images are displayed in a preview window during rendering.
- Animation rendering can be interrupted and then resumed automatically at the same location. It is important to note that you cannot interrupt and resume a video; only individual frames can be continued.
- Simultaneous rendering in the **Picture Viewer** and the **Render Queue**.
- Scenes can be rendered without opening them in the view, which saves memory.

The job list in the **Render Queue** contains the following information:

- **Pos:** The task sequence number. Drag-and-drop operations can be used to reposition the tasks.
- **Render:** You can enable or disable a job using the checkbox available in this column.
- **Team:** Select the checkbox in this column to define which jobs should be rendered using **Team Render**.
- **Status/R:** Displays the current status of the job. **In Queue/R -** ready to render, **In Progress** - is being rendered, **Take** - the Take selected for rendering, **Finished** - render completed successfully, **Stopped** - render was halted before being completed, and **Error** - error occurred during rendering
- **Camera:** The camera from which the scene is rendered.
- **Render Settings: Render Settings** with which the file is rendered.
- **Message:** Relevant notifications are displayed here, such as if a file is missing, information for saving, and so on.

When you select a job from the job list, the **Render Queue** window displays pertinent information such as render progress, estimated render time, take name, render parameters, camera, output file name path, and so on. You can alter these parameters to suit your needs. An existing job list will be maintained even if you close Cinema 4D. When Cinema 4D is reopened and the **Queue Manager** is opened, the list will reappear.

EDIT RENDER SETTINGS

Main Menu: Render > CONFIGURE > Edit Render Settings (Ctrl B)

This command opens the **Render Settings** window. The options in this window have already been discussed. Below the **Edit Render Settings** option in the **Render** menu, the render preset are listed. You can activate the preset by selecting it. You can create these presets in the **Render Settings** window, as discussed previously in the chapter.

NODE SPACE

Main Menu: Render > CONFIGURE > Node Spaces

The options in the **Node Spaces** sub-menu are used with the nodes. Cinema 4D supports many 3rd party renderers (**Arnold**, **Redshift**, etc) as well as the native **Standard** and **Physical** renderers. If you wish to create a **Node** material for the **Standard** renderer, you won't need any nodes in the **Asset** list that only operate with the installed third-party renderers. The following options can be selected from the menu:

- **Current (Standard/Physical):** The renderer specified in the **Render Settings** will always use the **Node Space**. The **Node Space** is determined by the defined renderer.
- **Standard/Physical:** You can configure the **Node Space** for all open documents using this and the following menu items such as **Arnold**, **Redshift**, etc.

TEAM RENDER MACHINES

Main Menu: Render > TEAM RENDER > Team Render Machines

With **Team Render**, you can quickly and simply render on many computers (all of which must be running the same version of Cinema 4D) across a local network with the click of a mouse. When you select the **Team Render Machines** option, the **Team Render Machines** window will appear. This window allows you to control network rendering.

SHARE MACHINE OVER NETWORK

Main Menu: Render > TEAM RENDER > Share Machine Over Network

The **Share Machine Over Network** command is used to delete or add the current computer to Team Render. This command can be used to temporarily free up memory on the machine on which you are currently working. If you delete the current computer while rendering, the operation will resume when you add the computer again using this command.

FLUSH ILLUMINATION CACHES

Main Menu: Render > Flush Illumination Caches

If you enable cache on the **Render Settings** window > **Global Illumination** or **Caustics** tabs, files will be saved in the **Illum** folder of the scene so that subsequent renders can reuse the data. Choose the **Flush Illumination Caches** option to delete these files. If you have selected the **Cache Shadow Maps** checkbox in the **Render Settings** window > **Options** > **Options** area, this command will also flush cached shadow maps.

MISSING TEXTURES
If Cinema 4D is unable to find textures when you render, it will display an alert. If you choose to continue rendering, materials will be used without the missing texture.

PATHS
When you render, Cinema 4D searches for texture in the following locations:

- The same folder as the scene file.
- In the **Tex** sub-folder of the scene's folder.
- In the **Text** sub-folder of the Cinema 4D installation folder.
- If you have specified an absolute path, Cinema 4D will search only in that path.
- If you are using assets from the Cinema 4D libraries, the corresponding path can be specified in texture's file name parameter.
- And finally, Cinema 4D also searches in the paths specified in the **Preferences** window. To define the path, open the **Preferences** window and then select **Files > Paths** in the left pane of the window. Now, in the right pane, add paths in the **FILE ASSETS** area.

COMPOSITING TAG

The **Compositing** tag contains several options that affect rendering. You can add compositing tag by choosing **Tags > Render Tags > Compositing** from the **Object Manager** menu or **RMB** clicking on an object and then choosing **Render Tags > Compositing** from the context menu. Select the tag's icon in the **Object Manager**, the corresponding parameters will be displayed in the **Attribute Manager** (see Figure 77).

You can use the **Cast Shadows** and **Receive Shadows** checkboxes to enable/prevent objects from casting or receiving shadows. If you want an object to cast shadows onto other objects but not on itself, clear the **Self Shadowing** checkbox.

SOFT SHADOWS
If you are using soft shadows in the scene, you cannot disable self shadowing.

If the **Seen by Camera** checkbox is enabled, all first generation rays; visual rays from the camera through which the scene is being seen will see a specified object. If you clear the **Seen by Camera** checkbox, Cinema 4D will not completely conceal the associated object from view because it will still be visible in transparent or reflecting surfaces depending on the settings used.

If the **Seen by Rays** checkbox is enabled, subsequent (higher) generations of rays (those of a reflection or refraction) will be computed as well. These rays can in turn be applied separately in conjunction with the checkboxes (**Seen by Transparency**, **Seen by**

Refraction, and **Seen by Reflection**). If you want the object to generate global illumination, select the **Seen by GI** checkbox. If you clear this checkbox, the object will not generate global illumination. You can use the **Global Illumination** effect in the **Render Settings** window to globally enable or disable GI.

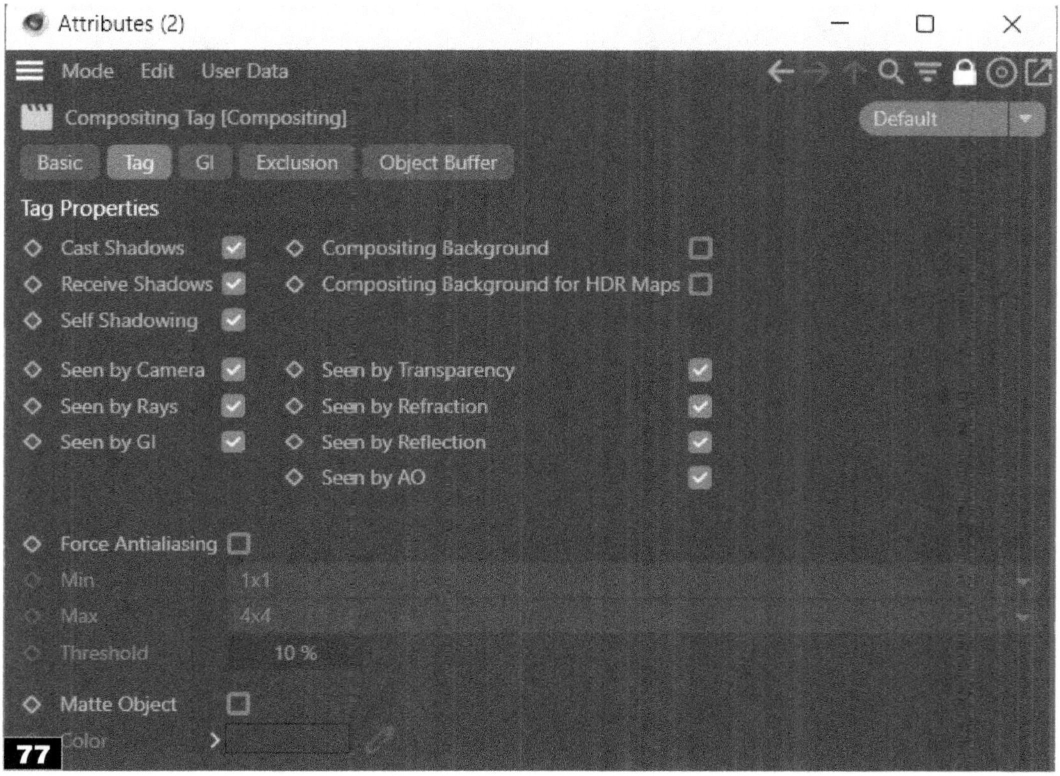

When you select the **Compositing Background** checkbox, the object will be self-illuminated and will receive shadows. The object in question must have its own material. Select the **Compositing Background for HDR Maps** checkbox to integrate rendered objects in a scene that was illuminated using the GI and HDRI textures. The HDRI textures must be assigned to the **Sky** object. You can then apply the **Compositing** tag to the **Floor** object; light and shadows from GI will then be combined with the background image.

> ***SHADOW CATCHER SHADER***
> *The **Shadow Catcher** shader can do pretty much the same. However, the shader works more flexibly with the **Alpha** channel.*

The **Seen by GI** checkbox can be used to exclude individual objects from the GI calculations. This can be useful, for example, when you are using multiple **Sky** objects: one for direct visibility, one for reflected/refracted rays, and one for generating GI.

When the **Seen by Transparency** checkbox is clear, an object with this **Compositing** tag setting will not be visible when behind transparent objects. The **Seen by Refraction** setting only applies when **Refraction** in the material's **Transparency** channel menu is not equal to **1**. Otherwise, the **Seen by Transparency** setting will apply. When this checkbox is clear, the object with this **Compositing** tag setting will no longer be visible behind transparent objects that have a refraction index.

If **Seen by Reflection** checkbox is clear, the object with this **Compositing** tag setting will no longer be visible in reflective objects. You can use the **Seen by AO** checkbox to define whether or not an object should be included in **Ambient Occlusion**.

The global antialiasing settings are defined in the **Render Settings** window. To override the global settings, select the **Force Antialiasing** checkbox and then you can use the **Min**, **Max**, and **Threshold** parameters to define new antialiasing settings.

When you select the **Matte Object** checkbox, the **Color** parameter will be activated. The object to which the **Compositing** tag is assigned will be colored with only the color defined using the **Color** parameter. No shading or lighting will be applied. Compare Figures 78 and 79; the **Compositing** tag is assigned to red spheres and pink color is assigned to the **Color** parameter. The object in question will not appear in the **Alpha** channel. [**matte.c4d**]

78

79

TUTORIALS

RENDERING A FLICKER FREE ANIMATION

One of the most common issues when rendering an image sequence from a GI enabled scene is removing flicker from the generated output. In this tutorial, we will look at various scenarios. The following table summarizes the tutorial:

Summary	
Difficulty level	Intermediate
Topics	Getting Started Rendering the Animation

Summary	
Resources folder	**standard-renderer**
Start file	**flicker-free-start.c4d**
Final file	**flicker-free-finish.c4d**

Getting Started

Open the **flicker-free-start.c4d** file. This file has an animated MoGraph setup. To see the animation, scroll through the timeline. Before you begin rendering a scene, you must ensure that the lighting and shadows are proper. You don't require global illumination in the scene if you adequately illuminate it. Check the quality of the shadows in the scene as well.

To test the quality of area shadows in the scene, add a neutral-gray material to all objects in the scene. Isolate each light, then examine the shadows it casts in the scene.

Select the light and then go to the **Shadow** tab in the **Attribute Manager**. The **Density**, **Color**, **Accuracy**, **Minimum Samples**, and **Maximum Samples** parameters in this tab control the quality of the area shadows.

Follow the steps given next to use optimal settings for shadows:

1. Find out the grainy areas in the scene.
2. Set the **Minimum Samples** and **Maximum Samples** parameters to the same value and then render the grainy areas using the **Render Region** feature.
3. Raise the values of the **Minimum Samples** and **Maximum Samples** parameters to same value until you get good results.
4. Lower the value of the **Minimum Samples** parameter to **25%** of the **Maximum Samples** parameter's value and set **Accuracy** to **50%**. Now, raise the **Accuracy** value until you see the good result.

After you're happy with the results, you can apply the materials to the objects and start rendering. The **flicker-free-start.c4d** file has already been optimized for shadows. Let's see how the render appears without the **Global Illumination** effect and with the default render settings.

Rendering the Animation

Follow these steps:

1. Press **Ctrl B** to open the **Render Settings** window. Make sure **Standard** selected from the **Renderer** drop-down list.

2. Select **Output** from the left pane of the window, if not already selected. In the right pane, select the **Lock Ratio** checkbox and then change **Width** to **320**; the **Height** automatically changes to **180**. You can set a higher resolution as per the configuration of your computer.

3. Select **All Frames** from the **Frame Range** drop-down list. The **From** and **To** parameters reflect the frame range.

4. Select **Save** from the left pane. In the **Regular Image** area of the right pane, click the folder icon corresponding to the **File** parameter to open the **Save File** dialog box. In this dialog box, navigate to the location where you want to save the file and then create a new folder with the name **flicker-free**. Now, create a sub-folder with the name **no-gi** and then open this folder. Now, type **render-no-gi** in the **File name** field and then click **Save**. Change **Format** to **PNG** and then change **Name** to **Name.0000.TIF**.

WHAT JUST HAPPENED?
*I have set the **Name** parameter to **Name.0000.TIF**. As a result, the rendered **PNG** files will be named as **render-no-gi.0000.png**, **render-no-gi.0001.png**, **render-no-gi.0002.png**, and so on.*

5. Save the file as **render-no-gi.c4d**. Then, press **Shift R** to render animation in the **Picture Viewer** window. Figure 1 shows the render at frames **10** and **42**, respectively.

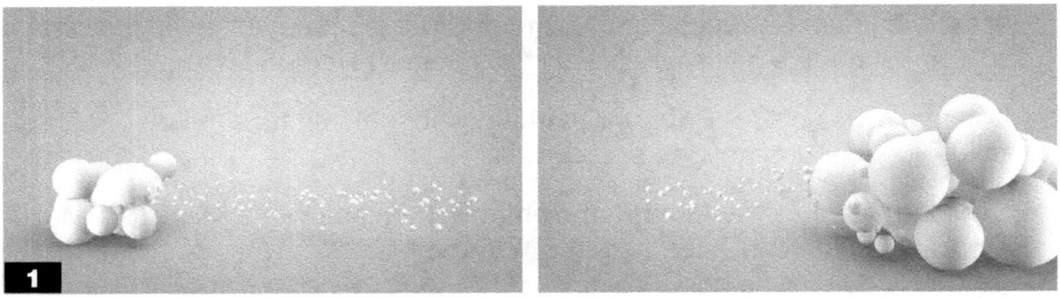
1

Once the render is complete, click the **Play Forwards** button in the **Picture Viewer** window. This render without GI took **0.44** seconds on my system.

If you want to skip rendering, you can open the render sequence available with the resources of this book. To do so, choose **File > Open Image** from the **Picture Viewer** window's menu to open the **Load File** dialog box and then navigate to the location where you have downloaded the sequence. Select the file and then click **Open**. In the **Open** dialog box that is displayed (see Figure 2), click **OK** to load the sequence in the window.

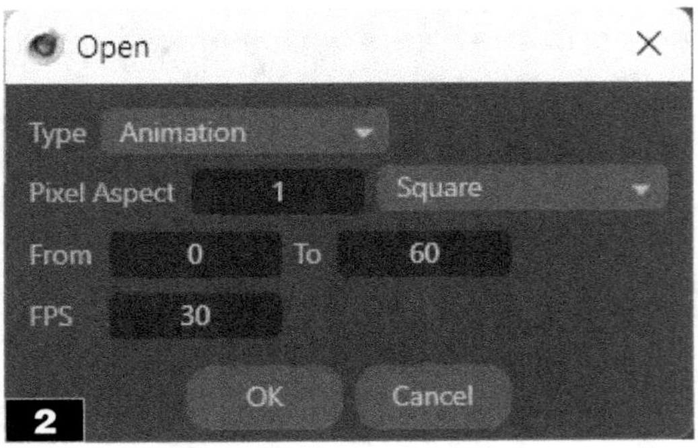

2

During playback, you can see that we have nearly no flicker or noise. Avoid using GI with animation wherever feasible and instead attempt to illuminate the scene with the various lights available in Cinema 4D.

WHAT NEXT?
*Now, we already have the scene with optimized shadows. Before we apply the **Global Illumination** settings, we must ensure that our materials are in good shape. If there is a problem, we must resolve it before proceeding. In the next steps, you will apply materials as well as provide the optimum render parameters.*

6. Save the file with the name **render-materials-no-gi.c4d**. Apply the **Green**, **Violet**, **Red**, and **Yellow** materials to **Sphere**, **Sphere.1**, **Sphere.2**, and **Sphere.3**, respectively.
7. Press **Ctrl B** to open the **Render Settings** window. Select **Save** from the left pane. In the **Regular Image** area of the right pane, click the folder icon corresponding to the **File** parameter to open the **Save File** dialog box. In this dialog box, navigate to **flicker-free** folder and then create a new sub-folder with the name **materials-no-gi**. Open this folder and then type **render-materials-no-gi** in the **File** name field and then click **Save**.
8. Select **Anti-Aliasing** from the left pane. In the **Anti-Aliasing** area, change **Anti-Aliasing** to **Best**, **Max Level** to **2x2**, and **Threshold** to **20**.
9. Select **Options** from the left pane. In the **Options** area, change **Ray Depth** to **6**, **Reflection Depth** to **3**, and **Shadow Depth** to **3**. Clear the **Automatic Size** checkbox and then expand the **Automatic Size** area. Now, change **Bucket Width** and **Bucket Height** to **32** each.
10. Choose the **Effect** button from left pane and then choose **Ambient Occlusion** to add the **Ambient Occlusion** effect. Ensure it is selected in the left pane and then in the **Basic** tab, change **Maximum Ray Length** to **30**.
11. Press **Ctrl S** to save the file. Press **Shift R** to render the animation in the **Picture Viewer** window.

If you now play the rendered sequence, you will notice that we have now acceptable render quality and there is no flicker in the scene. This render took **1.21** minutes on my system.

WHAT NEXT?
*We saw the rendered output with no GI in the scene. Let's turn on the GI and check what the rendered output looks like. We already know that **Irradiance Cache** gives flickering results, so let's have a look at how flicker appears in this case.*

12. Save the scene as **render-ic-low.c4d**. Press **Ctrl B** to open the **Render Settings** window.

13. Select **Save** from the left pane. In the **Regular Image** area of the right pane, click the folder icon corresponding to the **File** parameter to open the **Save File** dialog box. In this dialog box, navigate to **flicker-free** folder and then create a new sub-folder with the name **ic-low**. Open this folder and then type **render-ic-low** in the **File** name field and then click **Save**.

14. Choose the **Effect** button from left pane and then choose **Global Illumination** to add the **Global Illumination** effect. Ensure it is selected in the left pane and then in the **General** tab, change **Preset** to **Interior - Preview**. Notice that **Irradiance Cache** and **Radiosity Maps** are selected as **Primary Method** and **Secondary Method**, respectively.

15. Press **Ctrl S** to save the file. Now, press **Shift R** to render the animation in the **Picture Viewer** window. This render took **2.32** minutes on my system. Notice that the render time increased as we introduced GI in the scene.

WHAT NEXT?
Observe the image sequence; you will notice that the rendered sequence contains numerous artifacts. The preview settings are ideal for testing renderings. Let's have a look at what happens when we use high GI levels.

16. Save as the file with the name **render-ic-high.c4d**. Press **Ctrl B** to open the **Render Settings** window.

17. Select **Save** from the left pane. In the **Regular Image** area of the right pane, click the folder icon corresponding to the **File** parameter to open the **Save File** dialog box. In this dialog box, navigate to **flicker-free** folder and then create a new sub-folder with the name **ic-high**. Open this folder and then type **render-ic-high** in the **File** name field and then click **Save**.

18. Select **Global Illumination** from the left pane. In the **General** tab, change the **Primary Method** and the **Secondary Method** to **Irradiance Cache** and **Light Mapping**, respectively. Change **Samples** to **Custom Sample Count** and **Sample Count** to **1000**.

19. Expand the **Discrete Sky Sampling** area and then select the **Custom Count** checkbox. Also, change **Sample Count** to **3000**.

20. In the **Irradiance Cache** tab, change **Record Density** to **Medium**. In the **Light Mapping** tab, change **Path Count (x1000)** to **6000**.

21. Press **Ctrl S** to save the file. Now, press **Shift R** to render animation in the **Picture Viewer** window. This render took **12.13** minutes on my system.

WHAT NEXT?
*Even with a high **Sample Count** value, there is still flickering in the rendered sequence. Let's now use high settings.*

22. Save the file with the name **render-ic-rm-high.c4d**.

23. In the **Render Settings** window, select **Save** from the left pane. In the **Regular Image** area of the right pane, click the folder icon corresponding to the **File** parameter to open the **Save File** dialog box. In this dialog box, navigate to **flicker-free** folder and then create a new sub-folder with the name **ic-rm-high**. Open this folder and then type **render-ic-rm-high** in the **File** name field and then click **Save**.

24. Select **Global Illumination** from the left pane and then in the **General** tab of the right pane, change **Secondary Method** to **Radiosity Maps**. In the **Radiosity Maps** tab, change **Sampling Subdivisions** to **2** and then save the file.

25. Press **Shift R** to render animation in the **Picture Viewer** window. Play the animation, and you'll find that the rendered output still has flickering. On my machine, this render took **10.34** minutes.

WHAT NEXT?
*We already know that the **QMC+QMC** algorithm generates flicker-free output, but if you use **QMC** for both the primary and secondary GI methods, the rendering process would be extremely slow. Let's see if we can use a different strategy for secondary bounces.*

26. Save the file with the name **render-qmc.c4d**.

27. Press **Ctrl B** to open the **Render Settings** window. Select **Save** from the left pane. In the **Regular Image** area of the right pane, click the folder icon corresponding to the **File** parameter to open the **Save File** dialog box. In this dialog box, navigate to **flicker-free** folder and then create a new sub-folder with the name **qmc**. Open this folder and then type **render-qmc** in the **File** name field and then click **Save**.

28. In the **Global Illumination > General** tab, change the **Primary Method** and the **Secondary Method** to **QMC** and **Light Mapping**, respectively. Change **Samples** to **Medium**. In the **Light Mapping** tab, change **Path Count (x1000)** to **1000**.

29. Save the file. Now, press **Shift R** to render animation in the **Picture Viewer** window.

Play the animation when the render is finished. You'll notice that the rendered result is now flicker- and noise-free. After experimenting with various render settings, it is clear that **QMC + Light Mapping** is the ideal combo for rendering GI scenes. Rendering **60** frames at **320x180** resolution took **29.20** minutes on my system.

RENDERING A SPECIFIC REGION OF THE SCENE

If you find an issue in a specific region of the render, you can use the **Interactive Render Region** tool to render only that portion of the scene and then fix the incorrect image in post. You will save a lot of time since you will not have to render the entire image again. We will use the **Interactive Render Region** tool in this tutorial to render a selected region of the scene.

Summary	
Difficulty level	Beginner
Topics	Getting Started Using the Interactive Render Region Tool
Resources folder	**standard-renderer**
Start file	**render-region-start.c4d**
Final file	**render-region-finish.c4d**

Getting Started

Open **render-region-start.c4d**.

Using The Interactive Render Region Tool

Follow these steps:

1. Make sure the **Camera** view is active and then render the scene in the **Picture Viewer** window (see Figure 1). Notice in Figure 1 that the front landscape is not rendered as low poly. Save the image using the image format of your choice.

1

WHAT NEXT?
Now, instead of rendering the whole image, we will just render the problematic region.

2. Choose **Render > ONLINE RENDERING > Interactive Render Region** from the menu. Now, place the render region, as shown in Figure 2.

3. Place the quality triangle all the way to the top (see Figure 3) and then in the **Object Manager**, delete the **Phong Tag** corresponding to the **L5** object.

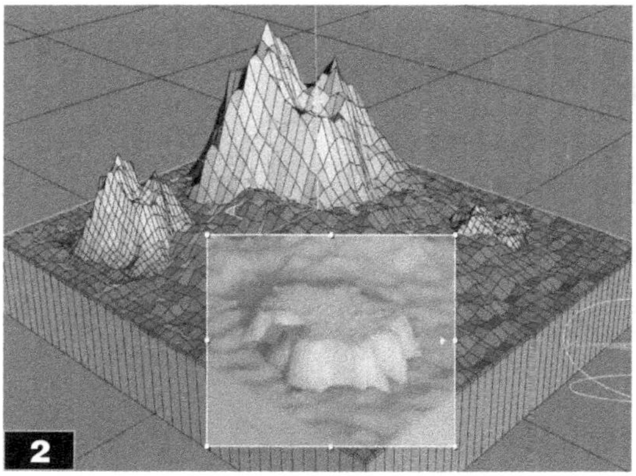

2

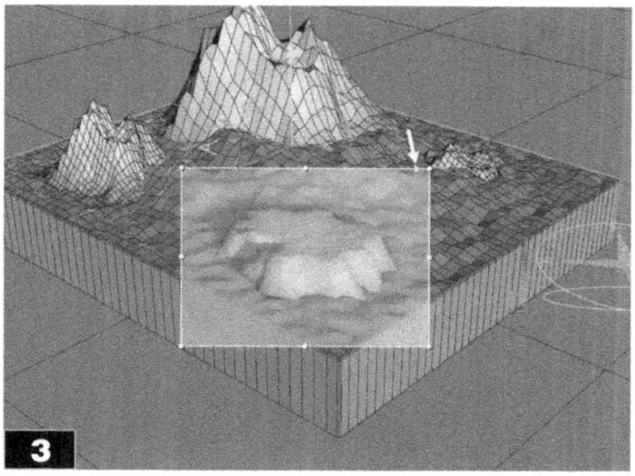

3

WHAT JUST HAPPENED?
*I removed the **Phong** Tag so that the corresponding item appears low poly in the render. I've assured that the IRR tool will use the render settings defined in the **Render Settings** window by anchoring the quality triangle at the top.*

4. Open the **Render Settings** window and then select **Output** from the left pane of the window. In the right pane, select the **Render Region** checkbox and then expand the **Render Region** area. Now, click on the **Copy from IRR** button.

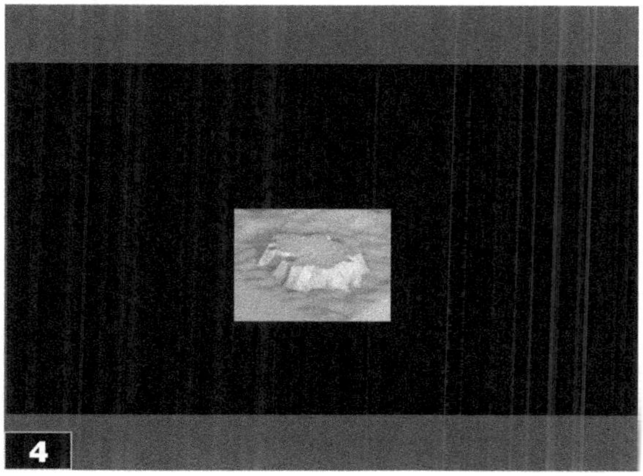

4

5. Select **Save** from the left pane and then in the right pane, select the **Alpha Channel** checkbox. Render the scene in the **Picture Viewer** (see Figure 4).Save the image using the image format of your choice. Now, you can composite the two saved images in a post-production application such as Nuke, Photoshop, or After Effects.

DYNAMICALLY CONTROLLING THE DEPTH-OF-FIELD EFFECT

In this tutorial, we will create the dynamic depth-of-field effect using the **Standard** renderer and the **Depth** pass (see Figure 1). We will use the **Lens Blur** filter in **Photoshop** to create and control the blur effect.

Summary	
Difficulty level	Intermediate
Topics	Getting Started Create the Effect

Summary	
Resources folder	**standard-renderer**
Start file	**dof-depth-start.c4d**
Final file	**dof-depth-finish.c4d**

Getting Started

Open **dof-depth-start.c4d**.

Creating the Effect

Follow these steps:

1. Open the **Render Settings** window and then make sure that **Renderer** is set to **Standard**.
2. Select the checkbox corresponding to the **Multi-Pass** option and then click on the **Multi-Pass** button to open a popup. Choose **Depth** from the popup to add the **Depth** pass.
3. Select the checkbox corresponding to the **Save** option and then click on the **Save** option. In the **REGULAR IMAGE** area, make sure the **Save** checkbox is enabled and then type **beauty-pass** in the **File** field. Also, change **Format** to **PNG**.
4. In the **Multi-Pass Image** area, make sure the **Save** checkbox is enabled and then type **depth-pass** in the **File** field. Also, change **Format** to **PNG** and clear the **Layer Name as Suffix** checkbox.
5. Select the **Ant-Aliasing** option from the left pane and then in the right pane, select **Best** from the **Ant-Aliasing** drop-down list. Close the **Render Settings** window.
6. Select **Camera** in the **Object Manager** and then in the **Attribute Manager > Object** tab, change **Focus Distance** to **856.566**. In the **Attribute Manager > Details** tab, select the **DOF Map Front Blur** and **DOF Map Rear Blur** checkboxes.

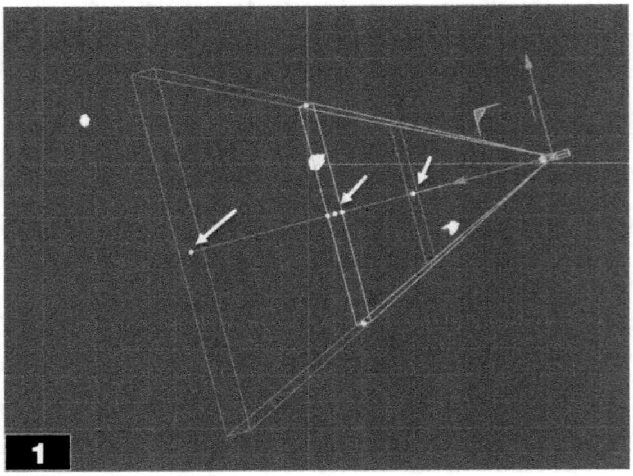

7. Change **DOF Map Front Blur > End** to **306.428** and **DOF Map Rear Blur > End** to **564.673** (see Figure 1). Leave the **Start** values at **0**. Now, make sure **Camera** view is active and then render the scene. Figures 2 and 3 show the beauty and depth render passes, respectively.

2

3

WHAT JUST HAPPENED?
*The **DOF Map Front Blur** and **DOF Map Rear Blur** parameters allow you to define which part of an images should be in focus and which out of focus.*

8. Start **Photoshop** and then open the **diffuse-pass.png** and then place the **depth-pass.png** file in another layer (see Figure 4).

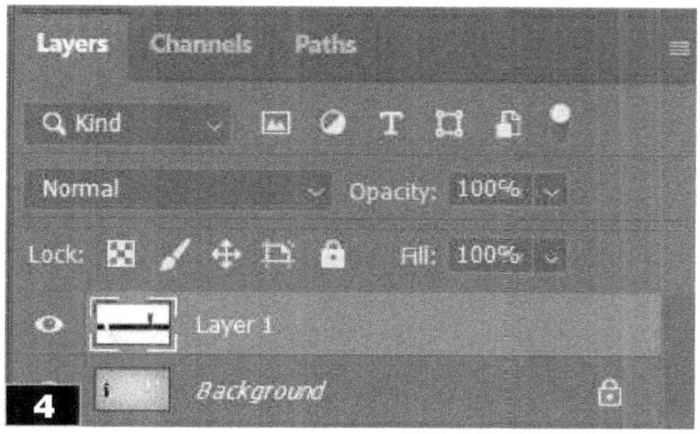

4

9. Press **Ctrl A** to select all pixels, press **Ctrl C**, and then switch to the **Channels** panel. In this panel, click the **Create new channel** icon and then press **Ctrl V**. Switch to the **RGB** channel.
10. Switch to the **Layers** panel and then press **Ctr D** to clear the selection. Hide the top layer. Select the **Background** layer and then choose **Filter > Blur > Lens Blur** from the menubar to open the **Lens Blur** window. In the **Depth Map** area of this window, change **Source** to **Alpha1** and **Blur Focal Distance** to **0**.
11. In the **Iris** area, change **Shape** to **Octagon (6)**, **Radius** to **8**, and **Blade Curvature** to **87**. Click **OK**. Save the file as **dynamic-dof.psd**.

CHANGING FOCUS
*In the **Lens Blur** window, use the **Blur Focal Distance** parameter to dynamically change the focus. The strength of the effect can controlled using the **Radius** parameter.*

This page is intentionally left blank

CHAPTER 3: PHYSICAL RENDERER

The **Physical** renderer can be utilized for generating special visual effects like depth-of-field, motion blur, vignetting, and chromatic aberration. While the robust and speedy **Standard** renderer can be used for most applications, the **Physical** renderer should be used to achieve these visual effects.

VIGNETTING
Vignetting refers to the gradual decrease in brightness or saturation towards the edges of an image, in contrast to the center of the image.

CHROMATIC ABERRATION
Chromatic aberration is an optical effect that occurs when a lens is unable to converge all colors to the same focal point, resulting in color fringes or seams appearing at edges within the image.

RENDERING SPEED
*If you are rendering multiple effects such as motion blur with depth-of-field, area shadows, and others, the **Physical** renderer is generally faster than the **Standard** renderer.*

There some drawbacks with the **Physical** renderer:

- It requires more calculations and time to render special effects like depth-of-field and motion blur. However, there are optimization settings available to help with this issue
- It cannot be used in combination with some effects, including the **Sketch and Toon** effect, the **Cel Renderer** post effect, specular lights, the **Cylindrical Lens** effect, and others available in the **Effects** menu.
- Motion blur is not compatible with certain elements like **PyroCluster**, visible lights, and object glow.
- Hair rendering is much slower, and hair multi-passes cannot be rendered.
- It only supports area shadows and cannot render hard shadows.

EXPLORING PHYSICAL RENDERER

To make the **Physical** renderer active renderer, press **Ctrl B** to open the **Render Settings** window. Select **Physical** from the **Renderer** drop-down list located at the upper-left corner of the window. An entry with the name **Physical** will be added in the left pane. Select it; the corresponding options will be displayed on the right pane under the **Basic** and **Advanced** tabs (see Figure 1). These options are discussed next.

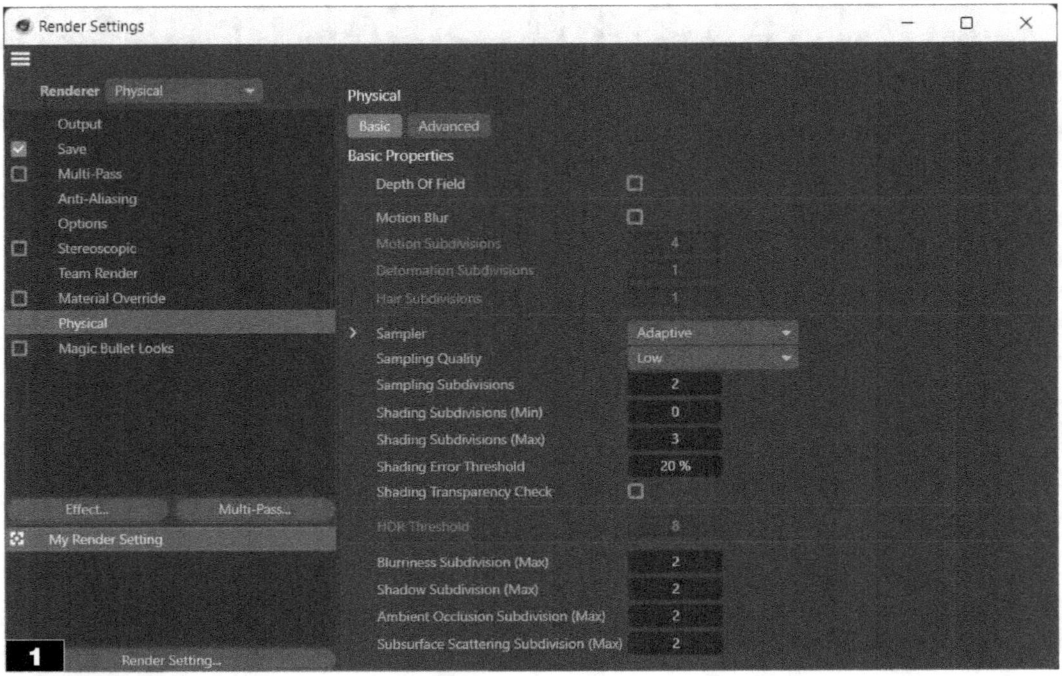

SAMPLER

A sampler extracts the cache (colors) of the scene from the camera's point of view. It controls which portions of the scene must be sampled repeatedly in order to achieve the render quality, such as anti-aliasing and blur effects like depth-of-field and motion blur. The number of samples (colors/cache) gathered by the sampler exceeds the number of actual pixels. These samples in the end are turned into pixels color using an anti-aliasing filter.

There are three methods available in Cinema 4D for sampling: **Adaptive**, **Fixed**, and **Progressive**. You can select these modes from the **Basic** tab > **Sampler** drop-down list. These modes are discussed next:

Fixed

The **Fixed** method uses an unchangeable, fix per-pixel sample number. This is comparable to the default renderer's **Best** and **Min/Max** anti-aliasing settings. When you select this method, the **Sampling Subdivisions** parameter is made available. It defines the number of shading samples required per pixel.

Progressive

The sampler in the **Progressive** technique can run forever and will continually pick (calculate) the samples. During this time, the result will continuously improve. The longer you run the render with the **Progressive** method, the better the quality of the anti-aliasing and blur effects will be. The improved quality will be seen in areas of blur effects such as depth-of-field, motion blur, and area shadows rather than on the homogeneously colored surfaces.

UNBIASED RENDERING
*The **Physical** renderer does not offer unbiased rendering. GI is biased in this type of rendering, which essentially implies that GI is pure in terms of physical accuracy and precision. As a result, the GI effect is continuously improved with time. The **Progressive** method does not offer this functionality.*

When the **Progressive** method is selected, all sampling parameters are disabled. This method is primarily suitable for fast preview renderings because it allows you to assess the overall quality of the render. No other method offers such a fast rendition of the quality of the entire image.

Click on the black triangle at left to **Sampler** to make numerous settings visible related to the **Progressive** method (see Figure 2). The default **Progressive Mode** is **Infinite**. As a result, the render will never end. If you want to end the render after a specified number of passes, change **Progressive Mode** to **Pass Count** and then specify the count using the **Progressive Pass Count** parameter. You can also run render for a specified time by first changing **Progressive Mode** to **Time Limit** and then specifying time in minutes using the **Progressive Time Limit (minutes)** parameter.

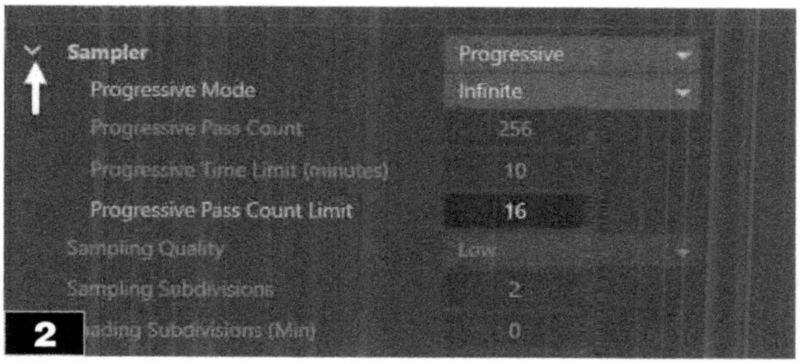

Adaptive

The **Adaptive** sampling method is often recommended because it strikes a good balance between rendering speed and image quality. This method is generally faster than the **Fixed** sampling method, and it employs more samples in critical or important areas of the scene. This is similar to the Best anti-aliasing setting used by the default renderer in Cinema 4D.

DETAILED TEXTURES AND SHARP EDGES
*It is worth noting that the **Adaptive** sampling method may produce slightly less sharp edges than the **Fixed** sampling method. Therefore, if you want to render a highly detailed texture with sharp edges, it may be preferable to use the **Fixed** sampler instead.*

The **Adaptive** sampler gives good results but it's hard to control as it uses four settings to sample pixels: **Sampling Subdivisions**, **Shading Subdivisions (Min)**, **Shading Subdivisions (Max)**, and **Shading Error Threshold**. However, the options in the **Sampling Quality** drop-down list make your life easier by automatically defining the parameter combination. There are five combinations available: **Preview**, **Low**, **Medium**, **High**, and **Automatic**. When you change any parameter manually, **Sample Quality** changes to **Custom**. The higher the settings you specify, the less the grain will be in the image, and the longer it will take to render.

ALPHA CHANNEL AND TRANSPARENCY
If you are rendering an animated object with the alpha channel and motion blur, select the ***Shading Transparency Check*** *checkbox to fix artifacts in the transparent motion blurred regions. When you select this checkbox, render time might increase drastically, if you are rendering a complex project.*

FIXING ANTI-ALIASING/BLUR
Use the ***HDR Threshold*** *field if you're having trouble rendering antialiasing and/or blur effects owing to excessively strong lighting from HDR sources or bright light sources. But, if this field is used, the render output will lose part of its dynamic. To regulate the brightness, a number between* ***2*** *and* ***8*** *is ideal.*

SUBDIVISIONS

The four subdivision settings: **Blurriness Subdivision (Max)**, **Shadow Subdivision (Max)**, **Ambient Occlusion Subdivision (Max)**, and **Subsurface Scattering Subdivision (Max)** are the quality settings for the respective effects such as blurriness, area shadows, and ambient occlusion. These settings have scene wide effect, they are not set at the material level or the object level.

PROGRESSIVE MODE
While previewing the render in ***Progressive*** *mode, it is advised that subdivision settings be set to* ***0*** *for quicker calculations.*

The **Blurriness Subdivision (Max)** parameter allows you to define the quality (graininess) for the blurriness effects. These blur values are defined in the **Transparency** and **Reflectance** channels of the material. Larger values produce less grain but take longer to render.

RENDER TIME
Whenever you increase the value by a factor of ***1****, the render time will double.*

The **Shadow Subdivision (Max)** parameter controls the quality of the shadows. Note that the **Physical** renderer simulates the shadows maps because it cannot calculate them. Use the **Ambient Occlusion Subdivision (Max)** parameter to control the quality of the ambient occlusion effect.

If the **Mode** is set to **Direct** for the **SSS** material, you can define the quality of SSS using the **Subsurface Scattering Subdivision (Max)** parameter. The larger the value you specify here, the better (high-quality) the result will be, and the longer it will take to render. If you want to specify SSS subdivisions for materials or object, in the **Multiple** tab of the **Subsurface Scattering** shader, select the **Custom Sampling** checkbox and then specify a value for the **Sampling Subdivision** parameter (see Figure 3).

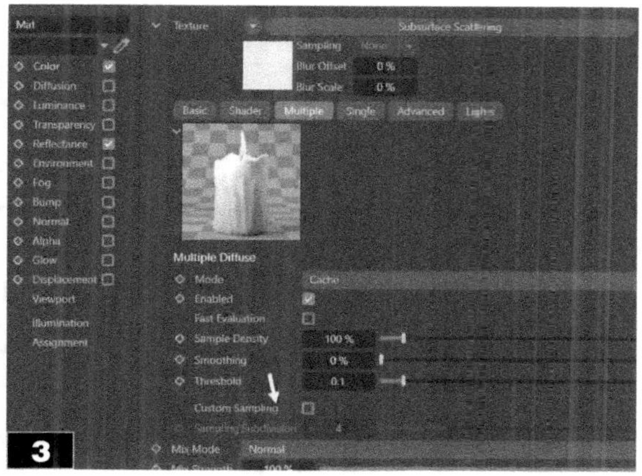

ADVANCED SETTINGS

The advanced settings for the **Physical** renderer are available under the **Advanced** tab. The **Raytracing Engine** drop-down list allows you to select **Embree** technology. This technology was developed by Intel and is only compatible with the most recent generation of CPUs that support **SSE3**. This technology is especially useful if the scene contains a large number of polygons/objects, glass objects with high refraction, areas shadows, ambient occlusion, blur effects, and complex textures. This method renders substantially quicker but with apparent quality loss.

The **Physical** render engine requires least memory to render. The **Embree (Faster)** engine is the fastest embree engine and requires most amount of memory. The **Embree (Smaller)** engine is slightly slower than the **Embree (Faster)** engine but it requires less memory.

The options in the **Quick Preview** drop-down list allow you to generate quick preview of the image. A rough preview is generated as soon as possible which is then immediately replaced by the bucket-by-bucket rendering. The **Preview Only** option renders a quick preview not the final render quality. Use the **Progressive Mode** option, if you are using the **Progressive** sampler mode. The **All Modes** option always enables the **Quick Preview** (for all modes). Select **Never** to disable **Quick Preview**.

The **Debug Information Level** drop-down list options display internal render data in the console. This information is irrelevant to you as a Cinema 4D user, but it can be utilized by support staff to troubleshoot.

VIEWPORT RENDERER

You can use the **Viewport Renderer** to render images and animations at a lower quality for preview purposes. This renderer use the same technology as the viewport display (GPU framework and graphics card). Select **Viewport Renderer** from the **Renderer** drop-down list to activate it. Select **Viewport Renderer** from the left pane; the corresponding options will be displayed in the right pane. Figure 4 shows the **Options** MEV menu and corresponding **Viewport Renderer** options.

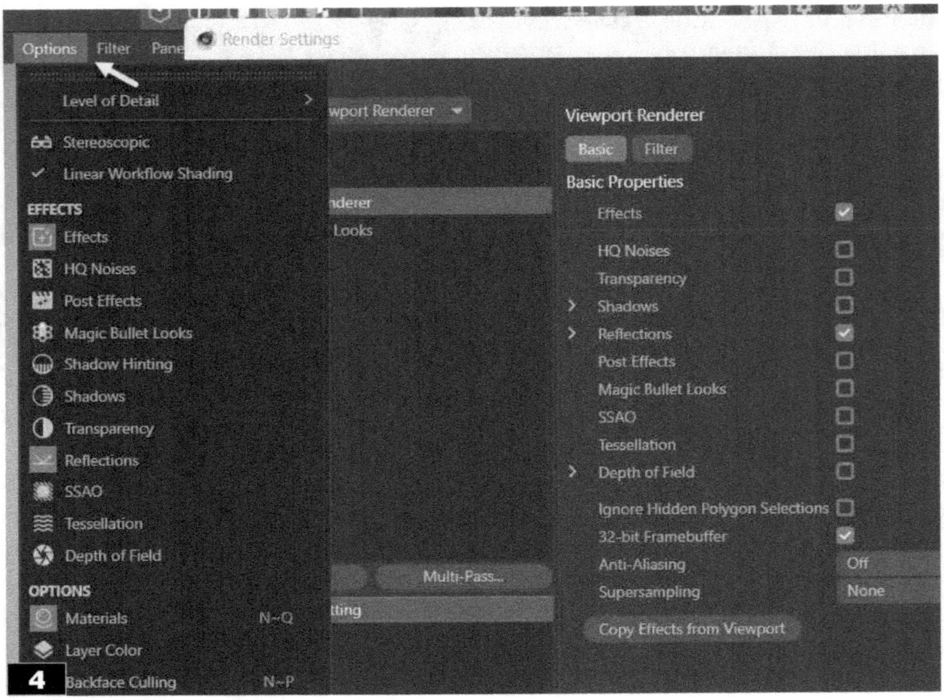

4

TUTORIALS

CREATING A STUDIO LIGHT SETUP

In this tutorial, we will create a simple studio light setup (see Figure 1). We will use **Area** lights to create the setup.

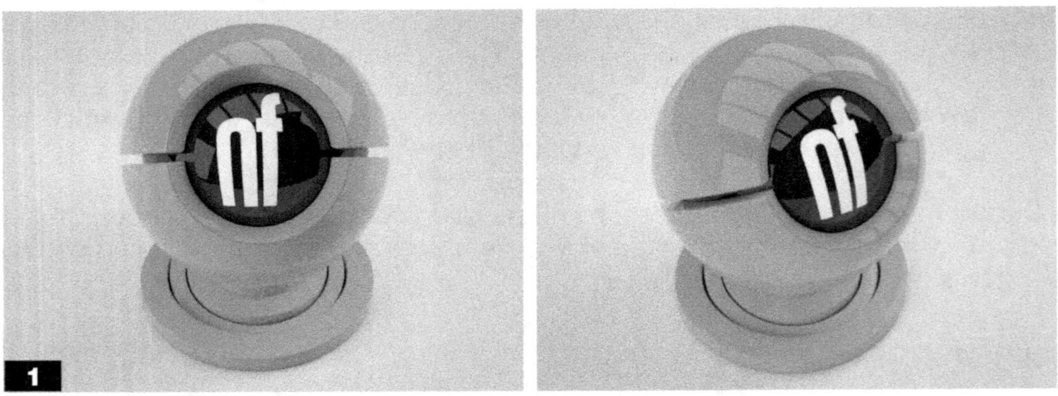
1

Summary	
Topics	Getting Started Creating the Setup
Resources folder	**physical-renderer**

Summary	
Start file	**shader-ball-start.c4d**
Final file	**shader-ball-finish.c4d**

Getting Started

Open the **shader-ball-start.c4d** file in Cinema 4D.

Creating the Setup

We will first define the render settings for the scene. We will be using the **Physical** renderer in this tutorial. Follow these steps:

1. Click **Edit Render Settings** on the **Standard** palette to open the **Render Settings** window. Click the **Render Settings** button on the bottom-left corner of the window and then choose **New** from the popup. Double-click on the **My Render Setting.1** label and then rename it as **PhysicalTest**.

WHAT JUST HAPPENED?
I've made a preset for test renderings here. We'll make one more preset for the final renders. Presets allow you to quickly swap between different render settings.

2. Make sure the **PhysicalTest** preset is selected and then **RMB** click on it. Choose **Set Active** from the popup. Change **Renderer** to **Physical** at the top-left corner of the window. Ensure **Output** is selected in the left pane of the window and then select the **Lock Ratio** checkbox in the right pane. Now, change **Width** to **500**.
3. Click the **Effect** button and then choose **Global Illumination** from the popup. Repeat the process to choose **Ambient Occlusion**.
4. Open the **Render Settings** window and select **Physical** (available below **Material Override**) from the left pane. In the **Basic** tab of the right pane, set **Sampler** to **Progressive**. Expand the **Sampler** area by clicking on the small triangle and then set **Progressive Mode** to **Pass Count**, and **Progressive Pass Count** to **10**. Close the window.
5. Render the scene.

WHAT JUST HAPPENED?
Because there is no light in the scene and no environment to reflect on the surfaces we have in the scene, the shader ball is rendered entirely dark (see Figure 2). Let's start by adding some light sources and then revisit the render parameters.

6. Click **Area Light** in the **Objects** palette > **Light** command group to create an area light in the editor view.

AREA LIGHTS

In Cinema 4D, area lights are two or three dimensional lights that are used to create realistic lighting. If you enable ***Area*** *shadows, you can create realistic shadows as well. However,* ***Area*** *shadows take longer to render. The following options are available in Cinema 4D for creating area light shapes:* ***Disc, Rectangle, Line, Sphere, Cylinder, Cylinder (Perpendicular), Cube, Hemisphere,*** *and* ***Object/Spline****. When you use 3D area light types such as cube or sphere, the objects within the volume of the light source require high sampling rates, especially when* ***Area*** *shadows are used. You can use the parameters given next to adjust the sampling quality:*

For diffuse lighting: *The* ***Samples*** *parameter in the* ***Details*** *tab.*
For Area shadows: *The* ***Accuracy, Minimum Samples,*** *and* ***Maximum Samples*** *parameters in the* ***Shadow*** *tab.*

But, these options will not be available if you are using the ***Physical*** *renderer. The scene-wide quality settings are controlled from the* ***Render Settings*** *window.*

7. In the **Attribute Manager** > **Light** > **Details** tab, change **Size X** and **Size Y** to **500** and **400**, respectively. In the **General** tab, change **Intensity** to **95**. Now, in the **Coordinates** tab, change **P.X**, **P.Y**, and **P.Z** to **-371**, **395**, and **651**, respectively. Also, change **R.H**, **R.P**, and **R.B** to **-153**, **-18**, and **-5**, respectively (see Figure 3).

2

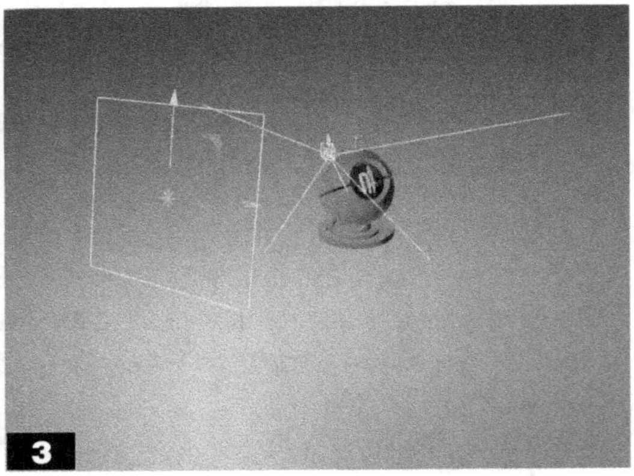

3

WHAT JUST HAPPENED?

For the area light, we're going to use the standard ***Rectangle*** *shape. I've made the rectangle* ***500x400*** *in size. If you wish to illuminate a bigger region in the scene, raise the size of the light. The larger the size of the light, the more the diffuse light it will emit.*

8. Ensure light is selected in the **Object Manager** and then in the **Attribute Manager > General** tab, change **Shadow** to **Area**. Render the scene; notice that now we have soft shadows in the scene (see Figure 4) but the falloff of the light is not correct.

PROGRESSIVE PASSES
*Note at the bottom of the **Picture Viewer** window, status of the progressive passes is displayed in the status line as Cinema 4D calculates them. Do not worry about the grain in the render, we will fix it later.*

9. In the **Details** tab, select **Inverse Square (Physically Accurate)** from the **Falloff** drop-down list. Also, select the **Z Direction Only** checkbox. Render the scene (see Figure 5).

4

5

LIGHT DECAY
*In real-world, the brightness of the light is strongest at its origin and it decreases or decays (luminosity absorbed) further away from the light source. To achieve this, Cinema 4D provides several options that you can access from the **Falloff** drop-down list. When you use the **Inverse Square (Physically Accurate)** or **Inverse Square Clamped** option, the light will reach to the distance defined by the **Radius/Decay** parameter and then will fade away proportionally opposite to the square of the original distance.*

10. In the **Details** tab, select the **Show in Reflection** checkbox.

WHAT JUST HAPPENED?
*By selecting this checkbox, the light's shape (**500x400** rectangle in this case) will appear in the reflections on the objects. If you select the **Show in Render** checkbox, the area light shape will be visible in the render except for the **Line** shape type and splines. You can control brightness of the visible area light or its reflection using the **Visibility Multiplier** parameter.*

11. Change **Radius/Decay** to **950** and then in the **General** tab, change **Intensity** to **100**. Render the scene (see Figure 6).

12. Click **Null** in the **Objects** palette to create a null in the editor view. Rename **Null** as **LeftLight** and then make **Light** its child.

WHY LIGHT IS GROUPED?
*Placing light under a **Null** will help us placing the axis at the origin and then we can easily create and align copy of the light by **Ctrl** dragging. The new light will rotate around the origin (0, 0, 0).*

13. Activate the **Rotate** tool, hold **Ctrl**, and then rotate **LeftLight** around the **Y** axis to create a copy of the **LeftLight** (see Figure 7). Rename the copied null as **RightLight**. Render the scene (see Figure 8).

6

7

WHAT NEXT?
*Now, we will create a **Cloner** setup that we will use to create reflections on the shader ball.*

14. Click **Plane** in the **Standard** palette > **Mesh** command group to create a plane in the editor view. In the **Attribute Manager > Object** tab, change **Width**, **Height**, **Width Segments**, **Height Segments** to **619**, **174**, **1**, and **1**, respectively (see Figure 9).

8

9

15. Select **Plane** in the **Object Manager** and then choose **Cloner** from the **MoGraph** menu with **Alt** held down to create a **Cloner** object and to make **Plane** its child. Select **Cloner** and then in the **Attribute Manager > Object** tab, change **Mode** to **Linear**, **Count** to **4**, **P.X** to **0**, **P.Y** to **0**, and **P.Z** to **202**. Now, align **Cloner**, as shown in Figure 10.

16. **RMB** click on **Cloner** and then choose **Render Tags > Compositing** from the context menu. Select tag from the **Object Manager** and in the **Attribute Manager > Tag** tab, clear the **Cast Shadows**, **Receive Shadows**, and **Seen by Camera** checkboxes.

17. Create a new material, rename it as **RefMat** and then open it in the **Material Editor.** Enable the **Luminance** channel and then disable the **Color** channel. Apply this material to **Cloner**. Render the scene (see Figure 11).

WHAT NEXT?
*Now, let's adjust the **Global Illumination** and **Ambient Occlusion** effects.*

18. Open the **Render Settings** window and select **Global Illumination** from the left pane, the settings are displayed in the right pane. Notice in the **General** tab, there is a **Preset** drop-down list. You can use one of these presets as quick starting point. Leave the **Primary Method** to **Irradiance Cache** and then change **Secondary Method** to **Light Mapping**.

19. In the **General** tab, change **Samples** to **Custom Sample Count**. Expand the **Samples** area and then set **Sample Count** to **100**.

20. In the **Light Mapping** tab, change **Path Count (x1000)** parameter to **1500**. Render the scene (see Figure 12).

21. Select **PhysicalTest** and press **Ctrl C** and then press **Ctrl V** to create a copy of the preset. Rename the pasted preset as **PhyscialFinal**. Ensure the **PhyscialFinal** preset is selected. **RMB** click on it and then choose **Set Active** from the popup, if not already active.

WHAT NEXT?
Now, let's specify the final settings for GI.

22. In the **General** tab, set **Primary Method > Intensity** to **110** and **Samples** to **Custom Sample Count**. Now, change **Sample Count** to **600**. In the **Irradiance Cache** tab, change **Record Density** to **Medium** and **Smoothing** to **60%**. In the **Light Mapping** tab, set **Path Count (x1000)** to **3000**. Render the scene (see Figure 13).

12

13

WHAT JUST HAPPENED?
*These settings in the **Record Density** area are used to fine tune the results. The **Preview** mode offers a quick preview of the final result. The **Density** parameter adjusts the general dispersion of the shading points. The higher the value you set for this parameter, the higher the shading point density will be.*

WHAT NEXT?
*Let's now specify the settings for the **Physical** renderer for final rendering.*

23. Select **Physical** from the left pane of the **Render Settings** window. In the **Basic** tab, change **Sampler** to **Adaptive** and **Sampling Quality** to **Automatic**. Set **Shading Error Threshold** to **8**.

24. Change **Shadow Subdivision (Max)**, **Blurriness Subdivision (Max)**, and **Ambient Occlusion Subdivision (Max)** to **3** each.

WHAT ARE THESE SETTINGS?
*The **Shadow Subdivision (Max)** setting controls the quality of the shadows. Larger values produce better results but at the cost of the render time. The **Ambient Occlusion Subdivision (Max)** setting controls the quality of the ambient occlusion effect.*

25. Select **Ambient Occlusion** from the left pane of the **Render Settings** window. In the right pane, change **Maximum Ray Length** to **20**. Render the scene (see Figure 14).

26. Click on the **Effect** button in the **Render Settings** window and then choose **Color Mapping** to add the **Color Mapping** post-effect. Select it and then in the right pane, select the **Exponential** checkbox, clear the **HSV Model** checkbox, and then select the **Affect Background** checkbox. Now, change **Dark Multiplier** to **2**. Render the scene (see Figure 15).

14

15

RENDERING SCENES WITH GI, THINGS TO REMEMBER

*When you are using the **Global Illumination** effect, consider the following points:*

i. *First render the scene at very low resolution such as **320x240**. It will allow you to quickly check the brightness of the scene.*

ii. *Use the **Progressive** sampler for fast previews.*

iii. *Use the **Interactive Render Region** tool at low resolutions to check the brightness and light dispersion.*

iv. *Check if you need additional light sources.*

v. *Once you are satisfied, you can use high quality settings for GI.*

vi. *If you see spotty rendering, most of the time you can fix it by increasing **Samples** value in the **General** tab.*

WHY RENDERING IS SLOW?

Well, there might be numerous reasons for slow rendering but here's is list that you can use to diagnose the problem:

- *Have you specified high values for **Samples** and **Record Density**?*
- *Are you using **OMC+QMC** as primary and secondary methods? The **QMC+QMC** model produces best quality but this combination is the slowest.*
- *Have you turned on the **Force Per-Pixel** checkbox for the polygon and portal lights?*
- *Are you using very high settings for the **Physical** renderer?*

USING POLYGON LIGHTS

In this tutorial, we will use polygon lights to illuminate a scene (see Figure 1).

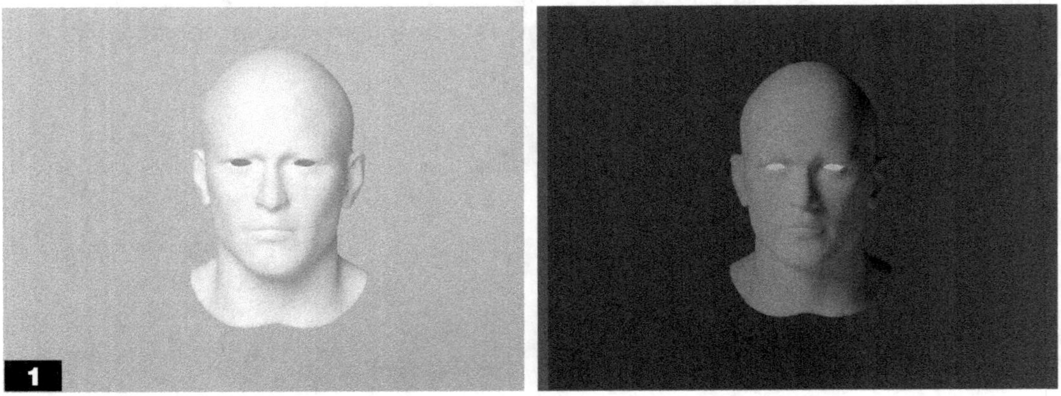

Summary	
Topics	Getting Started Using Lights
Resources folder	**physical-renderer**
Start file	**polygon-lights-start.c4d**
Final file	**polygon-lights-finish-1.c4d** **polygon-lights-finish-2.c4d**

Getting Started

Open **polygon-lights-start.c4d**.

Lighting the Scene

Follow these steps:

1. Double-click in the **Material Manager** to create a new material and then rename the material as **diffuseMat**. Apply the material to **Head** and **Back Drop**.

2. Select **diffuseMat** in the **Material Manager** and then in the **Attribute Manager > Basic** tab, clear the **Color** checkbox. Make sure the **Reflectance** checkbox is enabled.

3. In the **Reflectance** tab > **Default Specular** section, change **Type** to **Lambertian (Diffuse)** and **Attenuation** to **Average**. Change **Reflection Strength** to **100** and **Specular Strength** to **0**. In the **LAYER COLOR** section, change **Color** to **HSV** (**0**, **0**, **83**).

4. Open the **Render Settings** window and then select **Physical** from the **Renderer** drop-down list. Close the window.

WHAT NEXT?
Now, we will create a spherical polygon light to illuminate the head geometry in the scene.

5. Create a **Sphere** in the scene and then in the **Attribute Manager** > **Object** tab, change **Radius** to **20**. Then, align the sphere, as shown in Figure 2.
6. Double-click in the **Material Manager** to create a new material and then rename the material as **matLight**. Assign this material to the sphere in the scene. In the **Attribute Manager** > **matLight** > **Basic** tab, clear the **Color** and **Reflectance** checkboxes and then select the **Luminance** checkbox.
7. Render the scene (see Figure 3).

2

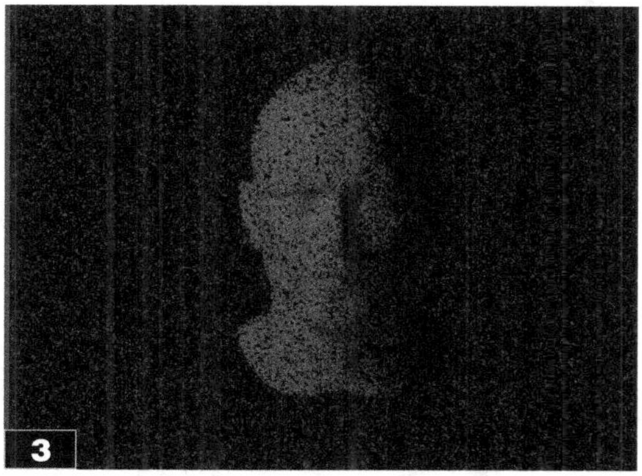
3

8. In the **Attribute Manager** > **matLight** > **Illumination** tab, select the **Polygon Light** checkbox. Render the scene (see Figure 4).

4

WHAT JUST HAPPENED?
*Figures 3 and 4 show that by making the sphere a polygon light, we were able to eliminate a significant amount of noise. When you select the **Polygon Light** checkbox, the manner an (luminous) item is included in the GI calculation is optimized. In Figure 4, you'll notice that we have a dark render. The **Luminance** channel settings will be our next area of emphasis, but first, let's switch the **Sampler** to **Progressive**.*

9. Open the **Render Settings** window and then change **Sampler** to **Progressive**. Also, change the **Blurriness Subdivisions (Max)** to **4**.

WHAT JUST HAPPENED?
I have increased the value of the ***Blurriness Subdivisions (Max)*** *parameter. This parameter can be used to minimize noise (graininess) in the picture. Higher values result in higher quality, but they also increase render times. Render time for a particular effect will double for every factor of one increase in this parameter. We will utilize adaptive sampling for the final render.*

10. In the **Attribute Manager > matLight > Luminance** tab, change **Brightness** to **500**. In the **Object Manager**, move the **Eyes** texture tag to the right and then render the scene (see Figure 5).

11. Change **Radius** of the **Sphere** to **80** and then render the scene (see Figure 6). In the **Attribute Manager > matLight > Luminance** tab, change **Brightness** to **200**. Render the scene (see Figure 7).

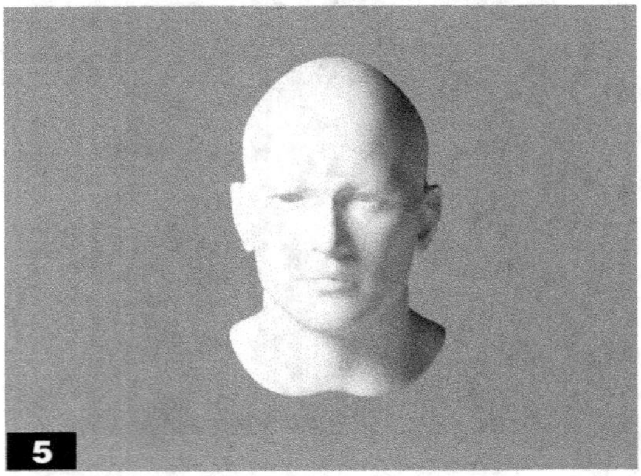

5

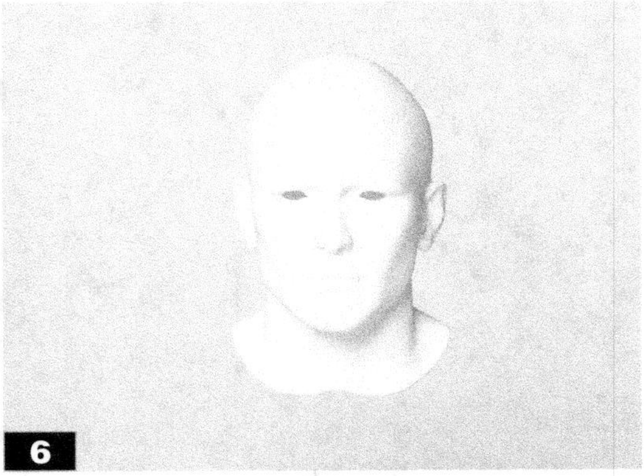

6

WHAT JUST HAPPENED?
Figure 6 shows an overly bright render. We changed the brightness of the material to achieve the desired lighting in the scene (see Figure 7). To get the ideal illumination, we can use the size of the light and the luminance strength of the material.

12. Open the **Render Settings** window and then select **Physical** from the left pane. In the right pane, change **Sampler** to **Adaptive**. Change **Sampling Subdivisions** to **0**, **Sampling Subdivisions (Min)** to **1**, **Sampling Subdivisions (Max)** to **3**, and **Shading Error Threshold** to **10**. Render the scene (see Figure 8). [**polygon-lights-finish-1.c4d**]

NOTE: THINGS TO REMEMBER-I
Keep the following in mind:

- **i.** *A small light, in relation to its distance from an object, will cast harsh shadows. See Figures 9 and 10. [**polygon-lights-hard-shadows.c4d**]*
- **ii.** *A big light with the same intensity as the small light will produce soft shadows. In the real world, photographers use umbrellas and soft boxes to achieve the similar*

*effect. To create soft shadows, they adjust the location of the umbrella or soft box. Simply put, they create a bigger light from a small one by placing an umbrella or soft box in front of it. The closer the diffuser is to the light, the harsher the shadows produced (see Figures 11 and 12). [**polygon-lights-soft-shadows.c4d**]*

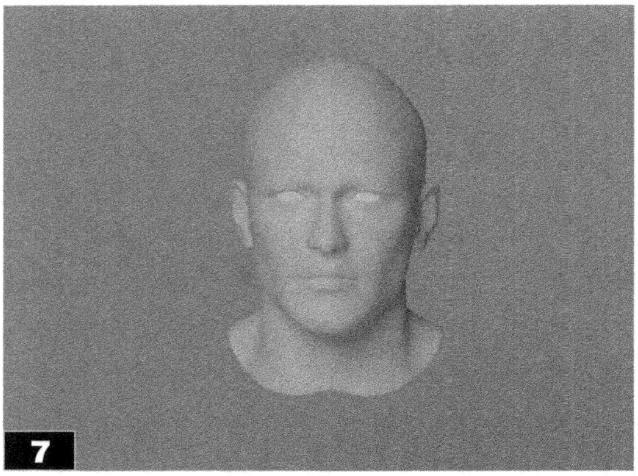
7

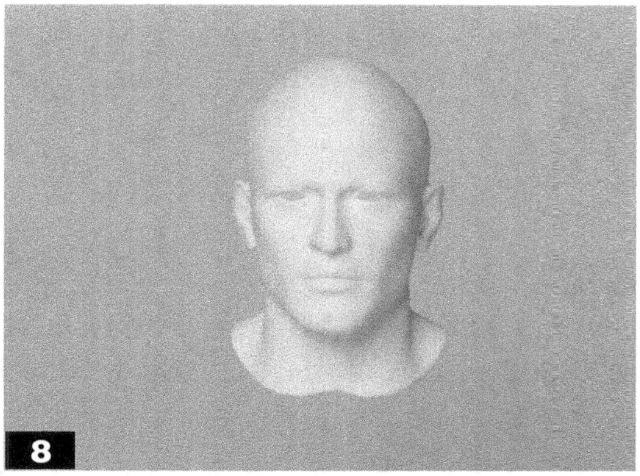
8

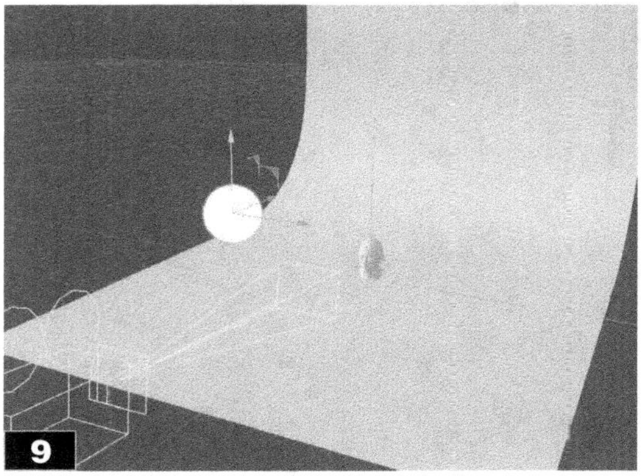
9

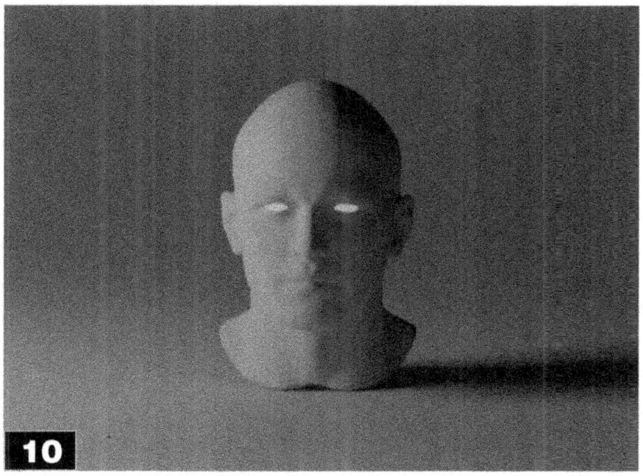
10

iii. *To eliminate the noise you can use higher values for the **Shading Subdivisions (Max)** and **Blurriness Subdivision (Max)** parameters. Keep in mind the higher values take longer to render*

iv. *If you are using the depth-of-field effect, you need to increase the value of the **Sampling Subdivisions** parameter. You can set it to **0** if you are not using the depth-of-field effect.*

WHAT NEXT?
In step 11, we lowered the intensity of the light by lowering the brightness strength of the polygon light. Let's now work on the exposure controls on the camera to lower the exposure without adjusting the intensity of the light. Additionally, see point 2 in the preceding note.

11

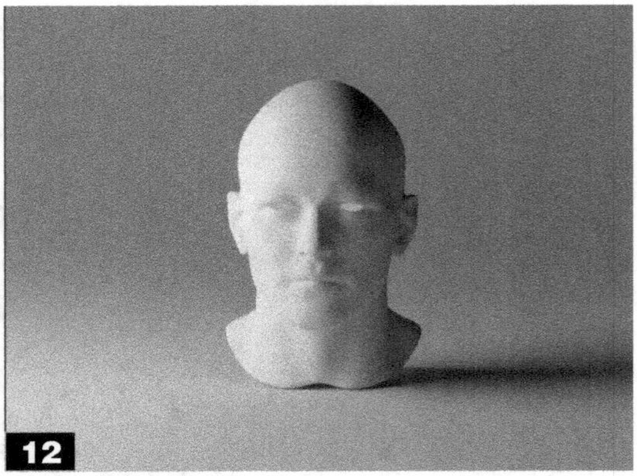

12

13. In the **Attribute Manager > matLight > Luminance** tab, change **Brightness** back to **500**. If you render the scene (see Figure 13), you will notice that scene is over exposed.

14. Select **Camera** and then in the **Attribute Manager > Physical** tab, select the **Exposure** checkbox. Now, change **F-Stop** to **5.6**, **ISO** to **200** and **Shutter Speed** to **1/125**. Render the scene (see Figure 14).

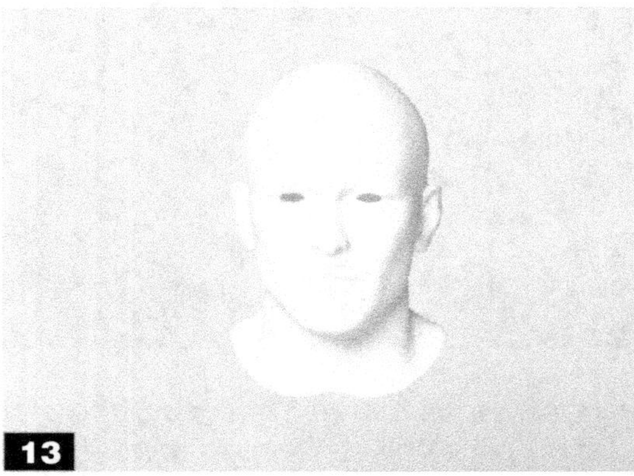

13

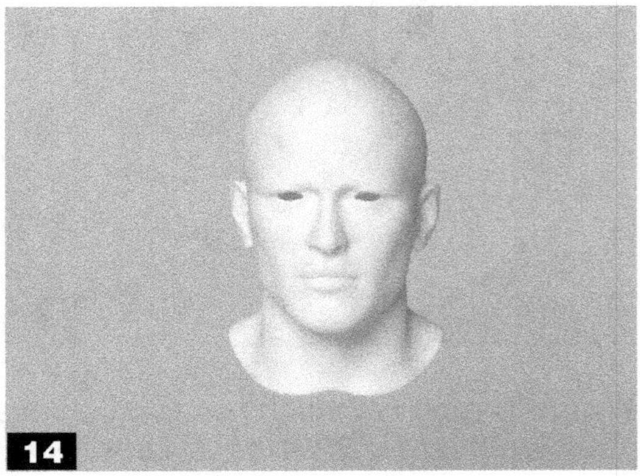

14

15. In the **Render Settings** window, select **Physical** in the left pane and then set **Sample Quality** to **Automatic**, and **Shading Error Threshold** to **8**. Render the scene.

THINGS TO REMEMBER-II
*Because we're using a polygon light, we can't utilize the Cinema 4D light's Include/Exclude technique. If you don't want the light from the polygon light to spill over into the background, you can use a plane with black material (black card) to block the light. Refer to Figures 15 and 16. [**polygon-lights-blackcard.c4d**]*

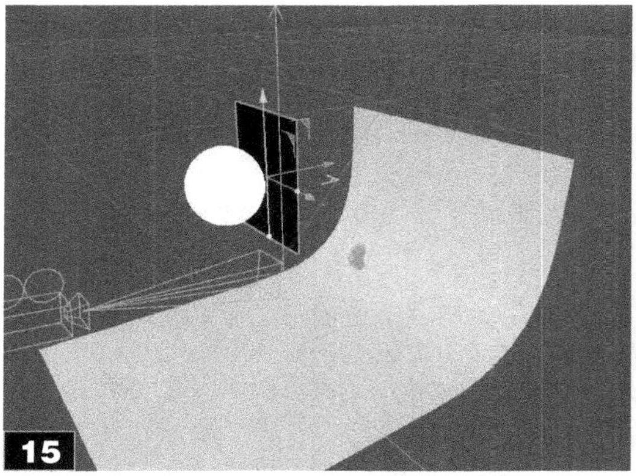

15

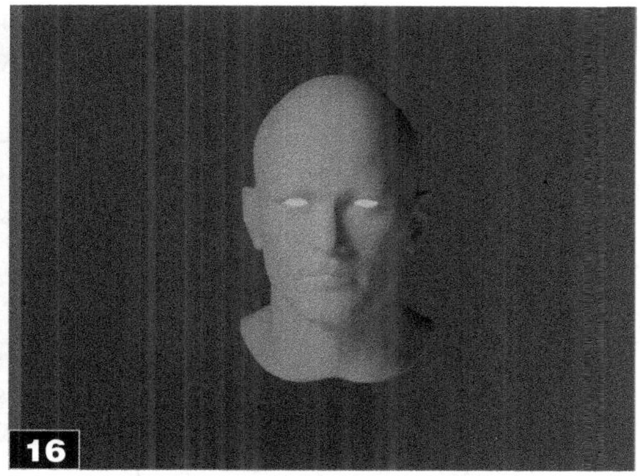

16

WORKING WITH THE DEPTH-OF-FIELD EFFECT

In this tutorial, we will create the depth-of-field effect using the **Physical** renderer (see Figure 1).

1

Summary	
Topics	Getting Started Creating the Effect
Resources folder	**physical-renderer**
Start file	**dof-start.c4d**
Final file	**dof-finish.c4d**

Getting Started

Open **dof-start.c4d**.

Creating the Effect

Follow these steps:

1. Open the **Render Settings** window. In this window, select **Physical** from the **Renderer**

drop-down list. Select **Physical** from the left pane of the window and then in the right pane, select the **Depth Of Field** checkbox. Close the window.

2. Select **Camera** in the **Object Manager** and then in the **Attribute Manager > Physical** tab, change **F-Stop (f/#)** to **0.2**.

WHAT JUST HAPPENED?
*I have used the **F-Stop** value to adjust the focal aperture. The larger the focal aperture (i.e. the smaller the **F-Stop** value), the smaller the depth-of-field will be and vice-versa. The smaller the **F-Stop** value, the more pronounced the depth-of-field effect will be.*

3. In the **Attribute Manager > Object** tab, click the eyedropper icon corresponding to the **Focus Distance** parameter and then click on the middle character in the view. Make sure the camera view is active and then render the scene (see Figure 2).

WHAT JUST HAPPENED?
I have defined the focus distance which is the distance measured from the camera's origin out (=film or sensor plane). It defines the distance to a plane that lies perpendicular to the angle of view, on which all objects are displayed perfectly in focus. In front of and behind this plane, all objects are rendered progressively blurred. You can also interactively change the focus distance using camera's center front handle (see Figure 3).

2

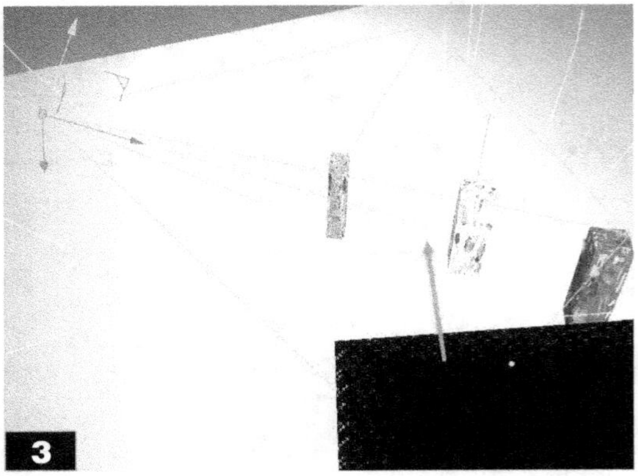
3

WHAT NEXT?
Notice in Figure 2 that the quality of the blur is not good. Next, we will adjust the quality settings to get a better looking results.

4. In the **Render Settings** window, change **Sampler** to **Adaptive** and **Sampling Quality** to **High**. Also, change **Blurriness Subdivision (Max)** to **4**. Render the scene.

WORKING WITH THE MOTION BLUR EFFECT

In this tutorial, we will create the motion blur effect using the **Physical** renderer (see Figure 1).

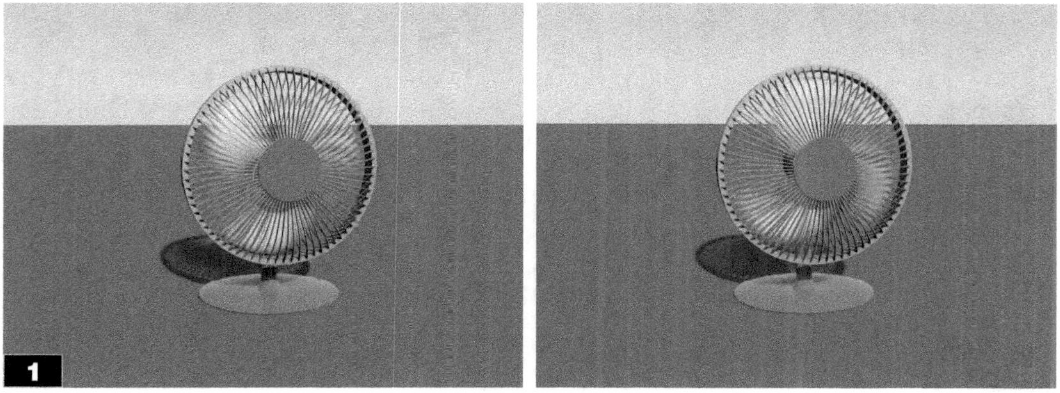

Summary	
Difficulty level	Intermediate
Topics	Getting Started Creating the Effect
Resources folder	**physical-renderer**
Start file	**mb-start.c4d**
Final file	**mb-finish.c4d**

Getting Started

Open **mb-start.c4d**.

Creating the Effect

Follow these steps:

1. Open the **Render Settings** window. In this window, select **Physical** from the **Renderer** drop-down list. Select **Physical** from the left pane of the window and then in the right pane, select the **Motion Blur** checkbox. Close the window.
2. Select **Camera** in the **Object Manager** and then in the **Attribute Manager** > **Physical** tab, change **Shutter Speed (s)** to **0.125**. Render the scene (see Figure 2).

Shutter Speed

The **Shutter Speed** parameter is generally used with the **Exposure** settings. It controls the amount of light that reaches the film. In other words, it defines how long the shutter will remain open when a picture is taken. If **Motion Blur** is enabled, it controls the amount of motion blur. The slower the shutter speed is, the greater the motion blur will be.

3. Open the **Render Settings** window. Select **Physical** from the left pane of the window and then in the right pane, change **Motion Subdivisions** to **6**. Render the scene (see Figure 3).

2

3

WHAT JUST HAPPENED?
It is important to compute the position between animation frames while computing motion blur for rapid circular motion. The degree of subdivision between two successive frames of animation is defined by the ***Motion Subdivisions*** *parameter. Higher values take up more memory. It is noticeable if motion blur is added to multiple objects, in regular settings it will not make much difference. For still images, you should apply a value greater than* ***4*** *to ensure the maximum quality.*

4. In the **Render Settings** window, change **Sampler** to **Adaptive** and **Sampling Quality** to **High**. Also, change **Blurriness Subdivision (Max)** to **4**. Render the scene.

CHAPTER 4: MATERIAL PRESETS

A material defines how objects in a scene reflect and transmit light. Surface attributes like color, reflectivity, roughness, and bumpiness are all simulated using materials. They aid in the creation of realistic-looking renderings.

You can use the **Material Editor** (see Figure 1) to create and edit materials as well as to assign them to the objects in the scene. You can open the **Material Editor** by double-clicking on the material node in the **Material Manager**. The parameters of the material can be modified from the **Material Editor** as well as using the **Attribute Manager** (see Figure 2). In the **Material Editor**, the channels are displayed at the left whereas in the **Attribute Manager** they are in the **Basic** tab.

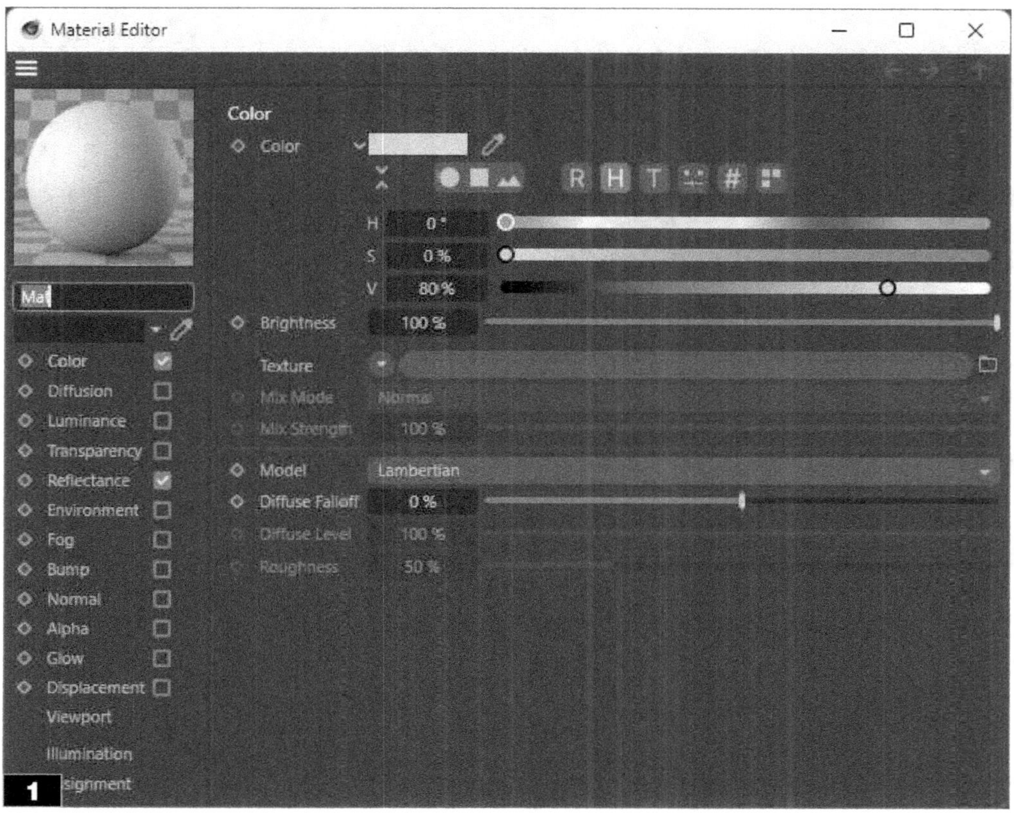

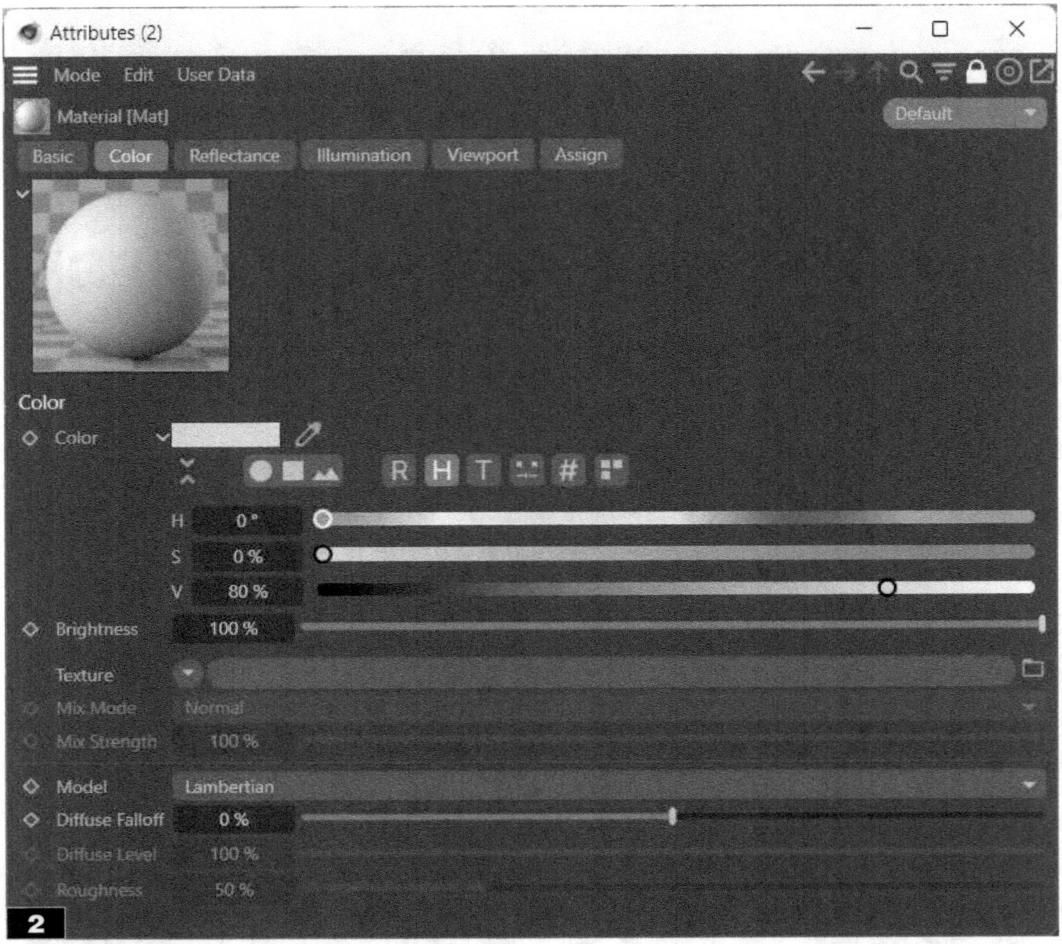

2

The **Material Editor** is divided into two panes. At the top-left corner of the left window, a preview of the content is displayed. You can adjust the shape of the preview by **RMB** clicking on it and then selecting an option from the context menu. For instance, if you wish to see a preview using a torus knot, select **Knot** from the popup menu. When you select the **Open Window** option, a floating window containing the preview emerges. You may enlarge the preview by resizing the window.

A list of channels is provided below the preview. Activate the channels by selecting the checkboxes next to each one. Most of the time, you don't need all channels. The selection of channels depends on the type of material you are creating. The following table summarizes the channels name and what they control:

Channels in the Material Editor	
Channel	**Description**
Color	Controls the color of the surface.

Channels in the Material Editor	
Diffusion	Controls the irregularities in the color of the surface by darkening or brightening the color channel.
Luminance	Controls the luminescent color which is light independent color.
Transparency	Controls the transparency and refraction index.
Reflectance	Controls the reflection on the surface.
Environment	Controls the reflection from the environment.
Fog	Controls the fog effect.
Bump	Creates bumps on the surface.
Normal	Creates bumps on the surface like the **Bump** channel but the bumps are lit realistically when you use the **Normal** channel.
Alpha	Controls the localized texture invisibility.
Glow	Creates a halo around the object.
Displacement	Creates realistic bumps on the surface.
Editor	Controls material display in the viewport.
Illumination	Controls the global illumination, caustics, and illuminations functions.
Assignment	It lists all object that use the material.

When you select a material in the **Material Manager**, its preview is displayed in the **Attribute Manager** (see Figure 3).

You can collapse or expand the preview area by clicking on the arrowhead next to the preview. To rotate the preview, **RMB Drag** or **Shift Drag** the preview.

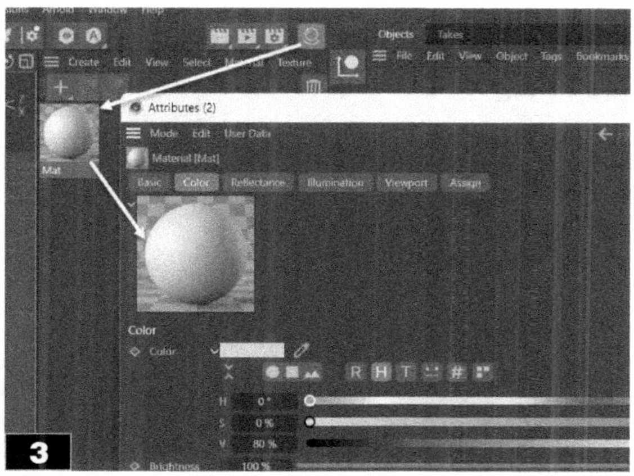

PREVIEW
Not all parameter adjustments will have an effect on the material preview, but they will have an influence on the rendering.

COLOR PICKER
*This tip only applies to the **Material Editor**, not the **Attribute Manager. Ctrl** clicking in the preview will transform the pointer into a color picker for the current channel color.*

ANIMATION FOR THE PREVIEW
*If you want to switch on the animation for the preview, **RMB** click on the preview and then choose **Animate** from the context menu; the animation will be played automatically, without moving the **Timeslider**, according to the **Frame Rate (FPS)** settings in the **Preferences** window > **Material** category > **MATERIAL PREVIEW** area.*

COPYING TEXTURES
The bitmaps and shaders can be easily copied between materials and/or channels by dragging the preview image on the targets. For example, if you have a bitmap attached to the ***Texture*** *parameter in the* ***Color*** *tab and wish to duplicate it to the* ***Texture*** *parameter in the* ***Bump*** *tab, drag the* ***Texture****'s preview image from the* ***Color*** *tab and then hover the mouse over the* ***Bump*** *tab. When the* ***Bump*** *tab's content appears, drag the preview onto the* ***Texture*** *parameter's arrow or button. This method is also applicable in the* ***Material Editor****.*

MATERIAL PRESETS
Cinema 4D includes a variety of material presets that can be used to quickly apply materials to objects. These presets are available in the ***Asset Browser****'s* ***Materials*** *category. In this chapter, we will analyze several of these material presets.*

TUTORIALS

CREATING PLASTIC MATERIALS

In this tutorial, we will create various plastic materials.

Summary	
Topics	Getting Started Creating Plastic Materials
Resources folder	**materials**
Start file	**shadeGeo.c4d**
Final file	**plastic-finish.c4d**

Getting Started

Open the **shadeGeo.c4d** file.

Creating Plastic Materials

Follow these steps:

1. Double-click in the **Material Manager** to create a new material. Rename the material as **matShinyPlastic**. Apply the material to the **Geo-1** and **Geo-2** objects in the **Object Manager**.

WHAT JUST HAPPENED?
I added material to the objects. When you apply a material to an object, it automatically receives a texture tag (see Figure 1). This tag specifies how the texture should be mapped or put on the object. The tag's settings are displayed in the ***Attribute Manager****.*

2. Select **matShinyPlastic** in the **Material Manager** and then in the **Attribute Manager > matShinyPlastic > Basic** tab, select the **Normal** checkbox.

WHAT JUST HAPPENED?
*I've selected the **Normal** checkbox. This operation enabled the **Normal** channel, as well as the **Normal** tab in the **Attribute Manager**. Normal mapping is achieved using the options available in the **Normal** tab.*

WHAT IS NORMAL MAPPING?
The phrase "normal mapping" is derived from computer game development. In this technique, a detailed texture is applied to a low-poly object thus reducing the render time. Normal mapping is distinct from bump mapping. A grayscale image is used to create height data in bump mapping, whereas an RGB texture including the orientation of the normals is used in normal mapping. The normals' orientation is used for generating height data.

3. In the **Color** tab > **Color** area, change **H**, **S**, **V** to **0**, **0**, **9**, respectively. Render the scene (see Figure 2).

WHAT JUST HAPPENED?
*Using the **HSV** model, I assigned the surfaces a dark gray hue. The hue, saturation, and value (or brightness) of a color are defined by the **HSV** model. The hue is defined by **H** and is represented as an angle on the color wheel. The saturation of the hue is defined by **S**, while the brightness of the color is defined by **V**. We have created a black surface, but it does not appear to be glossy. Next, we will adjust the reflectivity of the surface..*

4. In the **Reflectance** tab, click **Remove** to remove the **Default Specular** layer. Click **Add** and then choose **GGX** from the popup, a new reflectance layer with the name **Layer 1** appears in the **Attribute Manager**. Rename it as **Reflection** by double-clicking on the label and typing the new name (see Figure 3). Render the scene (see Figure 4).

Reflectance Channel

The **Color**, **Specular**, and **Reflection** channels are the most important aspect of creating a material. The other channels are essentially used for creating special or enhanced effects. The **Color**, **Specular**, and **Reflection** channels have been combined into a single improved channel called **Reflectance** in Cinema 4D. Layers are used in this model to construct complicated materials. Each layer's alpha, bump, and normal channels are distinct. You can now make a material using only the **Reflectance** channel. You can disregard the **Color** channel, however this should not be done consistently.

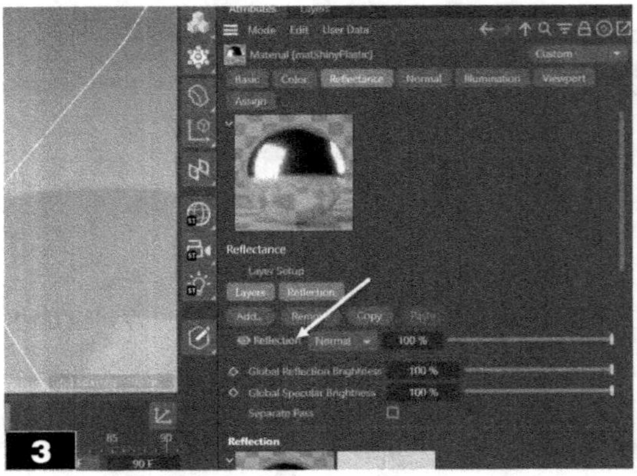

COLOR CHANNEL

*The **Global Illumination** function gets data from the **Color** channel not from the **Reflectance** channel. Keep in mind that ignoring the **Color** channel will prevent you from creating a **Global Illumination** solution.*

Type

The **Beckman**, **GGX**, **Phong**, and **Ward** are four most important reflection types available in **Type** drop-down list. They evenly weaken the reflections from the ideal reflection angle or angle of incidence. **Backmann** should be used in most cases since it gives physically correct results and is faster to calculate than other types. Because of its higher dispersion, the **GGX** type is ideal for generating metallic surfaces. It creates bright specular highlights that fade in brightness. **Ward** should be used on soft surfaces like rubber or skin.

5. Change **Attenuation** to **Average**, **Roughness** and **Reflection Strength** to **100** each, and then change **Specular Strength** to **0**. Render the scene (see Figure 5).

Attenuation

The options in the **Attenuation** drop-down list control how the **Color** channel should be mixed with the value of the **LAYER COLOR > Color** parameter with various **Reflection Strength** settings. If you have disabled the **Color** channel, the **Attenuation** parameter will have no effect.

The following options are available for this parameter:

- **Average:** This mode produces most realistic looking results. In this mode, both colors are averaged. This does not differ from the **Maximum** mode, if no color is defined for the **LAYER COLOR > Color** parameter.
- **Maximum:** This mode is used to generate colored reflections. The **Color** channel's effect will be reduced and the color defined using the **LAYER COLOR > Color** parameter will dominate.
- **Additive/Metal:** These two modes are available for reasons of compatibility if an older project is loaded.

Roughness

A finely polished surface is made up of numerous microscopic reflective facets. Each facet is oriented differently. The rougher surfaces have a random distribution of those facets, resulting in highlights that are scattered out. The **Roughness** parameter causes the objects' highlights to be spread out. Later in this tutorial, we'll use the **Layer** shader to build a texture for the **Roughness** parameter. You can apply a texture to the **Roughness** parameter, by first clicking on the arrow next adjacent to it and then assigning a shader or bitmap to the **Texture** parameter.

Reflection Strength

The **Reflection Strength** parameter specifies how strongly the material should reflect. According to energy conservation rules, the strength of the **Color** channel decreases as the reflection strength increases. If you set this parameter to **0**, the material will not reflect at all. A number of **100** produces the most reflection. To reveal the **Texture** and **Colored** parameters, click the arrow adjacent to the **Reflection** parameter. When the **Colored** checkbox is selected, the color defined in the material's **Color** channel is utilized as the reflection color.

CREATING REALISTIC MATERIALS
Every material in nature reflects to some extent, even if it is little. Remember this if you want to build realistic materials in Cinema 4D.

Specular Strength

The **Specular Strength** parameter defines the strength of the specular highlights. You can use the specular highlight as a trick to add reflection to the material without significantly increasing the render speeds. In nature, specular highlights are simply light sources reflected on the surfaces of objects. Set this value to **0** and use the **Reflection Strength** parameter instead to create a realistic environment.

COMBINED REFLECTIVE STRENGTH
*The combined reflective and specular strength of multiple layers can be adjusted together using the **Global Reflection Brightness** and **Global Specular Brightness** parameters.*

6. In the **Reflectance** tab > **Reflection** > **LAYER FRESNEL** section, change **Fresnel** to **Dielectric** and **Preset** to **PET**. Render the scene (see Figure 6).

Fresnel

The fresnel reflections are defined by the **Fresnel** setting. They are affected by the angle of view and the index of refraction. Figure 7 shows the distinction between normal and fresnel reflections.

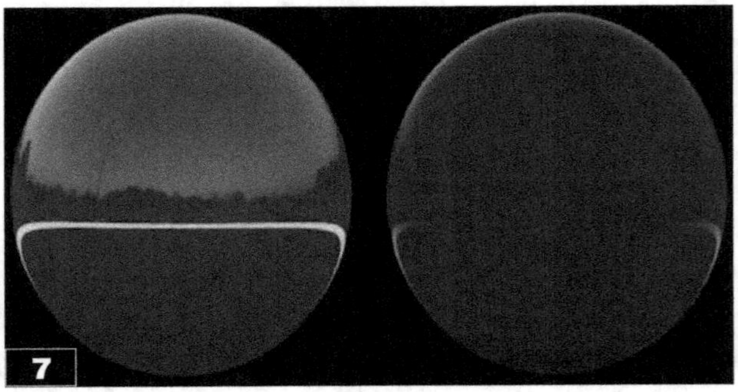

The fresnel model in Cinema 4D has two options. The **Dielectric** option is used for transparent and reflecting materials like glass and water, whereas the **Conductor** option is used for opaque and reflective materials like metals. The **IOR** of the **PET** preset is **1.575**.

The **Fresnel** setting defines the fresnel reflections. They depend on the angle of view and index of refraction. Figure 7 shows the difference between the normal reflection and fresnel reflection. Cinema 4D provides two options for the fresnel model. The **Dielectric** option is used for materials such as glass and water whereas the **Conductor** option is used for opaque and reflective materials such as metals. The **PET** preset has an **IOR** of **1.575**.

RENDER TIME
The render time increases if you use a high value for the ***Roughness*** *setting. Also, this value should be greater than* ***0*** *for the calculation of specular highlights and anisotropy.*

7. Click **Roughness** > **Texture** > **Triangle** button (you need to first expand the **Roughness** settings by clicking on the triangle) and then choose **Layer** from the popup (see Figure 8). Now, click the **Layer** button to open the **Layer Shader** settings (see Figure 9).

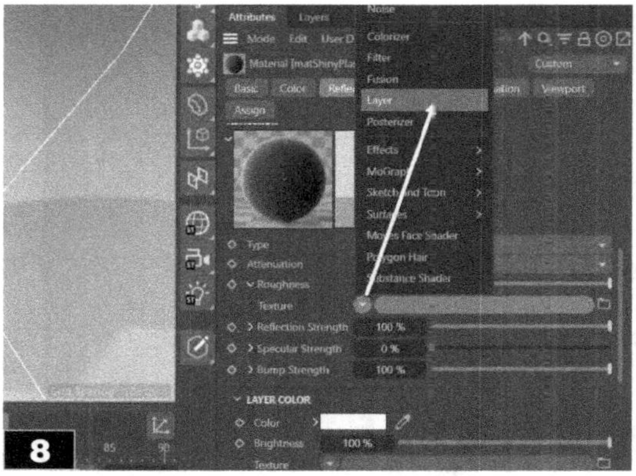

8

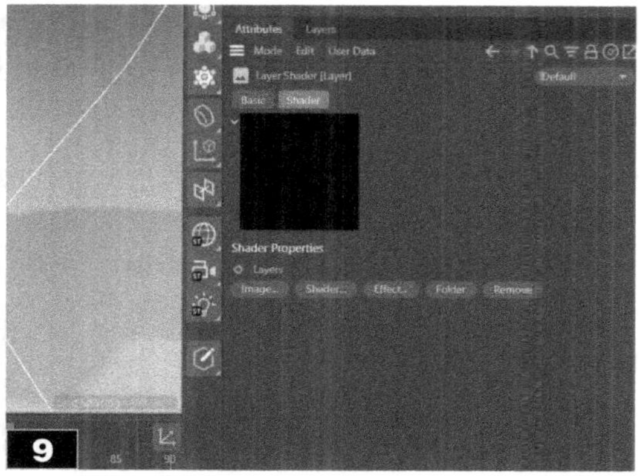

9

LAYER SHADER

*The **Layer Shader** is a powerful shader that is used to combine other shaders and bitmaps. You can stack shaders and bitmaps in layers and folders. To change the order of the layers, you can drag and drop them to their new positions.*

8. Click **Folder** to create a new folder and then rename it as **Roughness** by double-clicking on its label. Now, click **Image** and load **dc.jpg**. Click **Effect** and then choose **Colorize** from the popup. Click below the gradient bar to create two knobs and position them, as shown in Figure 10. Double-click on first knob to open the **Gradient Knot Settings** dialog box. Change **V** to **9%** and then click **OK**. Similarly, change **V** to **10%** for the other knob. Render the scene (see Figure 11).

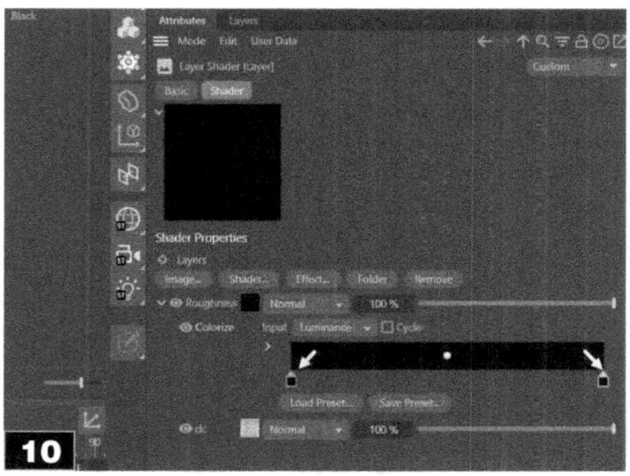

10

11

WHAT JUST HAPPENED?

*A layer can have various effects applied to it. The effect affects all layers below it in the list. The **Colorize** effect in this example takes a value from a channel (**Luminance** in this case) and remaps it using a gradient. The **Layer Shader** preview appears at the top of the **Layer Shader** area, but it is dark since we picked fairly dark gray values for the gradient. **RMB** click on the preview and then select **Open Window** from the context menu if you want to see it clearly. You need to enlarge the window.*

9. Click **Shader** and then choose **Gradient** from the popup. Rename it as **EdgeFalloff**. Make sure the gradient layer is at the top of the stack (see Figure 12). You can drag and drop layers to change their order.

10. Click on the gradient swatch to open the **Gradient Shader** settings. Change **Type** to **2D-V** and then change gradient as shown in Figure 13. Double-click on the second knob to open the **Gradient Knot Settings** dialog box. Then, set **Knot Position** to **20**.

11. Click the **Up Arrow** button in the **Attribute Manager** menu to go back to the **Layer Shader** settings.

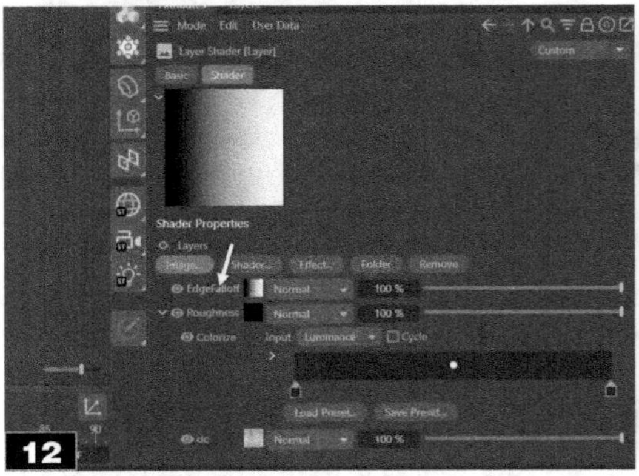
12

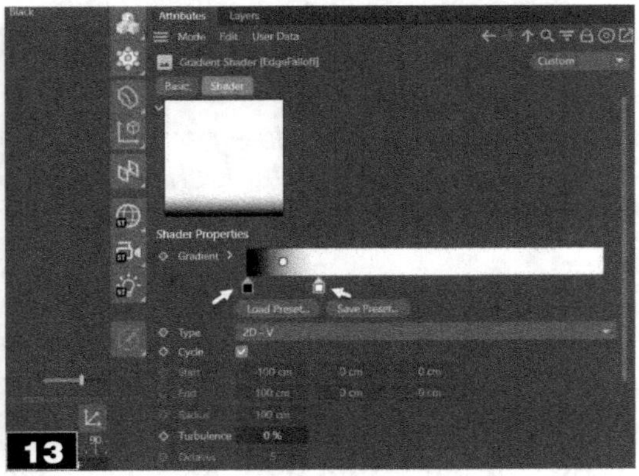
13

12. Change **Edge Falloff** drop-down list to **Multiply** (see Figure 14). Click the **Up Arrow** button in the **Attribute Manager** menu to go back to the **matShinyPlastic** settings. Render the scene (see Figure 15).

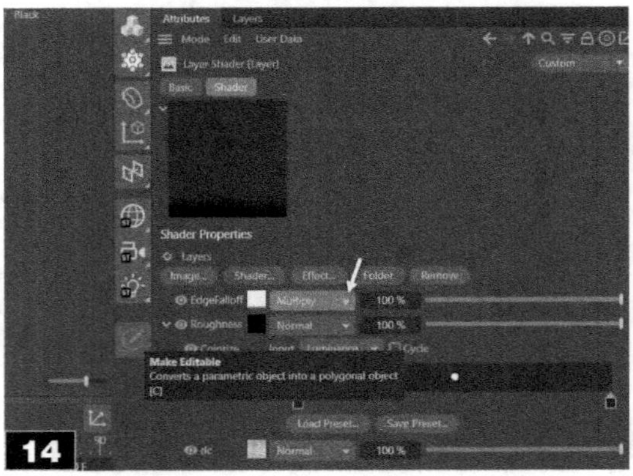
14

15

WHAT JUST HAPPENED?
At the top of the stack, I've added a gradient layer. It will create roughness on the edges by distributing highlights. Changing the mix mode to ***Multiply*** *ensures that the gradient's white color has no effect on the edge roughness.*

ROUGH PLASTIC
*If you want to create rough plastic material, change **Colorize's** gradient knobs to **25** and **30**, respectively and then render the scene, refer to Figure 16.*

WHAT NEXT?
Let's create a matte plastic material.

13. Create a new material and rename it as **matMattePlastic**. To replace the materials for **Geo-1** and **Geo-2**, simply grab the material from the **Material Manager** and drag it over the corresponding material tags in the **Object Manager**. This action will replace the original material tags with the new ones.

14. Select the material in the **Material Manager** and then in the **Basic** tab, select the **Diffusion** checkbox.

WHAT JUST HAPPENED?
*I have selected the **Diffusion** checkbox to enable the **Diffusion** channel. The **Diffusion** channel is used to make the material look dirty. It darkens or lightens a material using a diffusion map. The darker the area in the diffusion map, the darker the corresponding region of the material will be.*

15. In the **Attribute Manager > matMattePlastic > Color** tab, change **V** to **100** to make the color white and then change **Brightness** to **90**. Render the scene (see Figure 17).

16

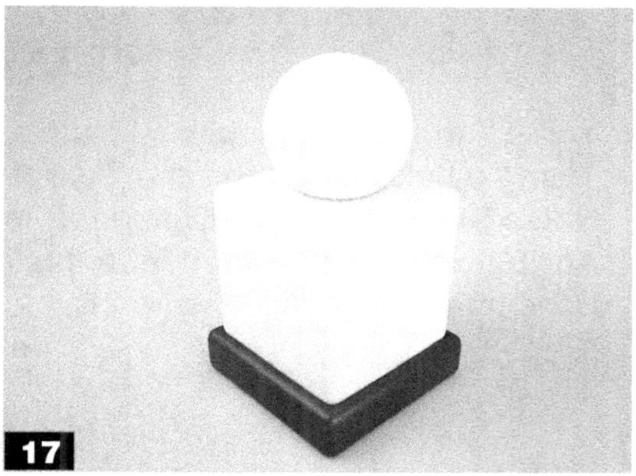
17

Brightness

This parameter governs the color brightness of the **Color** channel. It is a multiplier which can be adjusted to a value greater than **100%**.

16. Click **Texture > Triangle** button and then choose **Fresnel** from the popup. Click the **Fresnel** button to open the **Fresnel Shader** settings. Render the scene (see Figure 18). Specify the value **76** for the **V** parameter for the second knob. Render the scene (see Figure 19).

18

19

17. In the **Attribute Manager > matMattePlastic > Color** tab, change **Mix Mode** to **Multiply**, **Model** to **Oren-Nayar**, **Diffuse Falloff** to **-20**, and **Roughness** to **30**. Render the scene (see Figure 20).

WHAT JUST HAPPENED?
*I changed the model to **Oren-Nayar**. This type is appropriate for producing matte materials. The **Diffuse Falloff** option governs the brightness falloff between the specular highlights. The higher the value, the more consistent the brightness, up to the point of generating uniform hues (comic-like look). When negative values are used, the regions from which light is reflected are proportionally smaller. **Roughness** is only available for the **Oren-Nayer** model and provides more diffuse light dispersion. As a result, the material will become darker and less glossy.*

18. In the **Attribute Manager > matMattePlastic > Diffusion** tab, click **Texture > Triangle** button and then choose **Noise** from it. Click the **Noise** button to open the **Noise Shader** settings. Change **Noise** to **Voronoi 1** and **Global Scale** to **5**. In the **Attribute Manager > matMattePlastic > Diffusion** tab, change **Mix Strength** to **8**. Render the scene (see Figure 21).

20

21

WHAT JUST HAPPENED?
*I've used the **Noise** shader as diffusion map. The **Noise** shader is a special type of shader that can produce **32** types of noise. The **Global Scale** setting scales the noise in the **UVW** directions. The **Relative Scale** setting allows you to individually scale the noise in the **UVW** directions. The **Mix Strength** setting controls the mixing between the **Color** channel and texture. The **Octave** parameter controls octaves of details in the noise.*

19. In the **Reflectance** tab, click **Remove** to remove the **Default Specular** layer. Click **Add** and then choose **Ward** from the flyout, a new reflectance layer with the name **Layer 1** appears in the **Attribute Manager**. Rename it as **Reflection** by double-clicking on the label and typing the new name.

20. Change **Attenuation** to **Average**, **Roughness** to **7**, **Reflection Strength** to **12**, **Specular Strength** to **0**. In the **LAYER FRESNEL** area, change **Fresnel** to **Dielectric** and **IOR** to **1.44**. Render the scene (see Figure 22).

WHAT NEXT?
Now, let's create a red plastic material.

21. Double-click on the **Material Manager** to create a new material. Rename the material as **matRedPlastic**. To replace the materials for **Geo-1** and **Geo-2**, simply grab the material from the **Material Manager** and drag it over the corresponding material tags in the **Object Manager**. This action will replace the original material tags with the new ones.

22. In the **Attribute Manager > matRedPlastic > Basic** tab, select the **Normal** checkbox. In the **Color** tab, change **HSV** to **0**, **80**, **94**, respectively. In the **Reflectance** tab, delete the **Default Specular** layer. Click **Add** and then choose **Beckman** from the popup. Change **Specular Strength** to **0**. In the **LAYER FRESNEL** area, change **Fresnel** to **Dielectric** and **IOR** to **1.5**. Render the scene (see Figure 23).

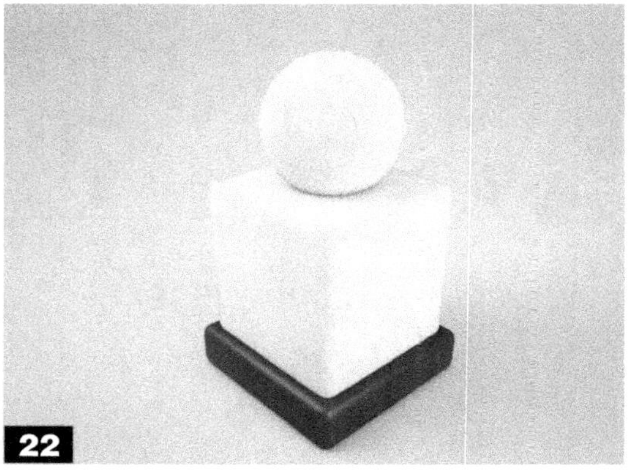
22

23

23. In the **Attribute Manager > matRedPlastic > Normal** tab, click **Texture > Triangle** button and then choose **Effects > Normalizer** from the popup menu. Click on the **Normalizer** button. In the **Normalizer Shader** properties section, click **Texture > Triangle** button, and then choose **Load Image** from the popup to open the **Open File** dialog box. Select **noise.jpg** and click **Open**. Render the scene (see Figure 24). Now, change **Strength** to **3** and **Filter** to **Sobel 4x**. Render the scene (see Figure 25).

24

25

WHAT JUST HAPPENED?

*To produce grain on the surface, I used an image with the **Normalizer** shader. The shader's overall strength is controlled by the **Strength** setting. The **Filter** setting lets you choose a method for calculating the normal texture. The **Condensed** method is appropriate for very fine surfaces, whereas the **Sobel** method is appropriate for rougher surfaces. The **Condensed** method is faster than the **Sobel** method. Figure 26 shows the normal texture with **Strength** set to **50** on the left and **100** on the right.*

26

WHAT NEXT?

*Now, let's create a plastic material with **Subsurface Scattering (SSS)**.*

WHAT IS SSS?
***SSS** stands for **Subsurface Scattering**. This technique is used to simulate light's penetration in slightly transparent surfaces. In a SSS material, light travels through partially or fully and some of it is absorbed.*

24. Double-click in the **Material Manager** to create a new material. Rename the material as **matSSSPlastic**. To replace the materials for **Geo-1** and **Geo-2**, simply grab the material from the **Material Manager** and drag it over the corresponding material tags in the **Object Manager**. This action will replace the original material tags with the new ones.

25. In the **Attribute Manager > matSSSPlastic > Basic** tab, select the **Normal** and **Luminance** checkboxes and clear the **Color** checkbox.

26. In the **Luminance** tab, change **HSV** to **222**, **25**, and **100**, respectively. Click **Texture > Triangle** button and then choose **Effects > Subsurface Scattering** from the popup. Click on the **Subsurface Scattering** button.

27. In the **Subsurface Scattering Shader > Shader** tab, change **HSV** to **224**, **83**, and **80**, respectively. Render the scene (see Figure 27). Change **Path Length** to **1**. Expand the **Path Length** area and then change **Blue** to **200**. Render the scene (see Figure 28).

27

28

WHAT JUST HAPPENED?
*I've assigned a color using the **Color** parameter that will represent the general color of the **SSS** effect. The **Path Length** parameter controls how far light travels beneath the surface. The lower the value you specify for this parameter, the longer will be the render time. The **Red**, **Blue**, and **Green** parameters in the **Path Length** section are multipliers for the **Path Length** parameter. You can use these parameters to define which color penetrates deeper beneath the surface.*

PATH LENGTH PARAMETERS
*You can use values less than **100%** for these parameters but on doing so render time will increase.*

28. In the **Subsurface Scattering Shader > Advanced** tab, change **Index of Refraction** to **1.5**. In the **Multiple** tab, change **Mode** to **Direct** and **Minimum Threshold** to **0.01**. Render the scene (see Figure 29).

29

Index of Refraction

The **Index of Refraction** parameter controls the refraction index associated with the SSS effect. The greater the value, the darker the SSS effect.

Single Mode

The **Single** checkbox enables the **Single** mode. SSS is available in two modes: **Single** and **Multiple**. Light is diffused once in the **Single** mode and then continues to travel in a straight path. The angle at which light enters has a significant impact on the SSS effect. This is why, while using the **Single** mode, you must have genuine light sources in the scene. The effect cannot be produced only through **Global Illumination**.

Multiple Mode

In the **Multiple** mode, the light is dispersed multiple times until it reaches to the surface at some other point on the surface. The direction of the light is irrelevant in this case. The **Direct** mode does not use a cache and does not compute lighting for each pixel. This method works best for small **Path Length** values. The process will be delayed if you use this option with large **Path Length** settings. This setting is also incompatible with **Global Illumination**. In the **Cache** mode, points are spread out across the object's surface as evenly as possible before being cached. Then, light dispersion is calculated on each point and then spread across the whole surface.

ARTIFACTS
*Render artifacts may appear on the sharp edges as well as on the surfaces that drastically changes directions within short distances. To fix such issues, you should increase the **Minimum Threshold** value in the **Multiple** tab.*

29. In the **Attribute Manager > matSSSPlastic > Luminance** tab, change **Mix Mode** to **Multiply**. Render the scene (see Figure 30).

30. In the **Reflectance** tab, change **Type** to **GGX**, **Attenuation** to **Average**, and **Roughness** to **100**. Now, create a **Layer** shader for the **Roughness** parameter as done earlier when you created shiny plastic material. Change **Specular Strength** to **0** and **Reflection Strength** to **100**. In the **LAYER FRESNEL** area, change **Fresnel** to **Dielectric** and **IOR** to **1.5**. Render the scene (see Figure 31).

30

31

31. In the **Normal** tab, click **Texture > Triangle** button and then choose **Effects > Normalizer** from the popup menu. Click on the **Normalizer** button. In the **Normalizer Shader** properties section, click **Texture > Triangle** button and then choose **Load Image** from the popup to open the **Open File** dialog box. Select **noise.jpeg** and then click **Open**. Now, change **Strength** to **3** and **Filter** to **Sobel 4x**. Render the scene (see Figure 32). You need to increase the value of the **Subsurface Scattering Subdivision (Max)** parameter in the **Render Settings** window to get noise free SSS.

32

WHAT NEXT?
Now, let's create a plastic grid material.

32. Double-click in the **Material Manager** to create a new material. Rename the material as **matPlasticGrid**. To replace the materials for **Geo-1** and **Geo-2**, simply grab the material from the **Material Manager** and drag it over the corresponding material tags in the **Object Manager**. This action will replace the original material tags with the new ones.

33. Select the material in the **Material Manager** and then in the **Attribute Manager > matPlasticGrid > Basic** tab, select the **Bump** and **Alpha** checkboxes.

WHAT JUST HAPPENED?
*I enabled the **Bump** and **Alpha** channels. We need to create holes in the geometry to make a grid. We will use the **Alpha** channel to do this. Using the **Tiles** shader, we will generate alpha data, which we will then utilize to mask off parts of the material to create holes.*

34. In the **Attribute Manager > matPlasticGrid > Color** tab, change **Color** to white and **Brightness** to **20**. In the **Reflectance** tab, change **Type** to **Phong**, **Attenuation** to **Average**, **Roughness** to **28**, **Reflection Strength** to **35**, and **Specular Strength** to **0**. In the **LAYER FRESNEL** section, change **Fresnel** to **Dielectric** and **Preset** to **PET**. Render the scene (see Figure 33).

33

35. In the **Attribute Manager > matPlasticGrid > Bump** tab, click **Texture > Triangle** button and then choose **Surfaces > Tiles** from the popup.

36. Click on the **Tiles** button to open the **Tile Shader** settings. Change **Grout Color** to **white**. Change **Tiles Color 1**, **Tiles Color 2**, and **Tiles Color 3** to black. Change **Pattern** to **Circle 1**. Change **Grout Width** to **20**.

WHAT JUST HAPPENED?
*I've added the **Tiles** shader to create the patterns for the holes. You can use this shader to create different patterns. The **Grout Color** is the color between the tiles. The **Tiles Color 1**, **Tiles Color 2**, and **Tiles Color 3** parameters are the colors of the tiles. **Grout Width** defines the width of the grout as a percentage of tile.*

37. Select the texture tag corresponding to **Geo-2** and then in the **Attribute Manager > Tag** tab, change **Length U** and **Length V** to **40** and **50**, respectively. Render the scene (see Figure 34).

38. In the **Attribute Manager > matPlasticGrid > Bump** tab, **RMB** click on **Texture** label and choose **Copy** from the popup.

39. In the **Attribute Manager > matPlasticGrid > Alpha** tab, **RMB** click on **Texture** label and choose **Paste** from the popup menu. Render the scene (see Figure 35).

CREATING ABSTRACT MATERIALS

Let's now create different types of abstract materials.

Summary	
Topics	Getting Started Creating Abstract Materials
Resources folder	**materials**
Start file	**shadeGeo.c4d**
Final file	**abstract-finish.c4d**

Getting Started

Open the **shadeGeo.c4d** file.

Creating Abstract Materials

Let's start by creating a two sided color material. Follow these steps:

1. Double-click in the **Material Manager** to create a new material. Rename the material as **matAbs1**. Apply the material to the **Geo-1** and **Geo-2** objects in the **Object Manager**. Select material in the **Material Manager** and then in the **Attribute Manager** > **matAbs1** > **Basic** tab, clear all checkboxes except the **Transparency** checkbox. In the **Transparency** tab, change **Refraction** to **1.6**.

WHAT JUST HAPPENED?
*I have used the **Transparency** channel to define the transparency. If the material has color and we enable this channel, the color of the material is reduced to incorporate transparency. If a material has **100%** transparency, there will be no color.*

Refraction

The index of refraction of the material can be managed by adjusting the **Refraction** parameter. In a subsequent section of this tutorial, we will diminish the color by **40%**, and allocate the remaining **60%** to the **Transparency** channel to generate the desired outcome.

2. Click **Texture > Triangle** button and then choose **Effects > Normal Direction** from the popup. Click on the **Normal Direction** button. In the **Normal Direction Shader** settings, change **Color 1** to **HSV (228, 76, 97)** and **Color 2** to **HSV (128, 78, 66).** In the **Attribute Manager > matAbs1 > Transparency** tab, change **Mix Mode** to **Multiply**. Render the scene (see Figure 1).

WHAT THE NORMAL DIRECTION SHADER DOES?
The object is shaded according to the orientation of its surface normals. Those areas on the surface where the normals are facing towards the rendering ray are assigned ***Color 1****, while the remaining areas of the surface are assigned* ***Color 2****.*

3. In the **Attribute Manager > matAbs1> Basic** tab, select the **Reflectance** checkbox. In the **Reflectance** tab > **Default Specular** section, change **Type** to **Beckmann**, **Roughness** to **35**, **Reflection Strength** to **7**, and **Specular Strength** to **45**. In the **Layer Color** area change **Color** to **HSV (128, 78, 66)**. Render the scene (see Figure 2).

WHAT JUST HAPPENED?
I have modified the filter color of the layer from its default white to green. As a result, the reflection colors will be influenced by this green color.

4. In the **Attribute Manager > matAbs1> Basic** tab, select the **Color** checkbox. Copy the **Normal Direction** shader from the **Transparency** tab and then paste on the **Texture** parameter in the **Color** tab. Change **Mix Mode** to **Multiply**. Render the scene (see Figure 3).

WHAT JUST HAPPENED?
*As shown in Figure 3, two colors are visible, but they are not very noticeable. This is because the **Transparency** channel's effect is mostly obscured by the **Color** channel. In the following step, we will address this issue.*

5. In the **Color** tab, change **Brightness** to **40%** and render the scene (see Figure 4).

3

4

WHAT NEXT?
We will now generate a material that has stripes.

6. Double-click on the **Material Manager** to create a new material. Rename the material as **matStripe**. To replace the materials for **Geo-1** and **Geo-2**, simply grab the material from the **Material Manager** and drag it over the corresponding material tags in the **Object Manager**. This action will replace the original material tags with the new ones.

7. Select material in the **Material Manager** and then in the **Attribute Manager > matStripe > Color** tab, change **Color** to **HSV (44, 73, 100)**. Click **Texture > Triangle** button and then choose **Layer** from the popup. Click on the **Layer** button.

8. In the **Layer Shader** settings, click **Shader** and then choose **Gradient** from the popup. Click on the **Gradient** swatch to open the **Gradient Shader** settings. Change **Type** to **2D-U**. Click on the **Load Preset** button and then select the **Scheme 2** preset. Change the **Gradient**, as shown in Figure 5.

9. Select the texture tag corresponding to **Geo-2** and then in the **Attribute Manager > Tag** tab, change **Length U** to **40**. Render the scene (see Figure 6).

WHAT JUST HAPPENED?
*As you can observe, the **Gradient** setting has replaced the **Color** settings. In the following step, we will rectify this issue.*

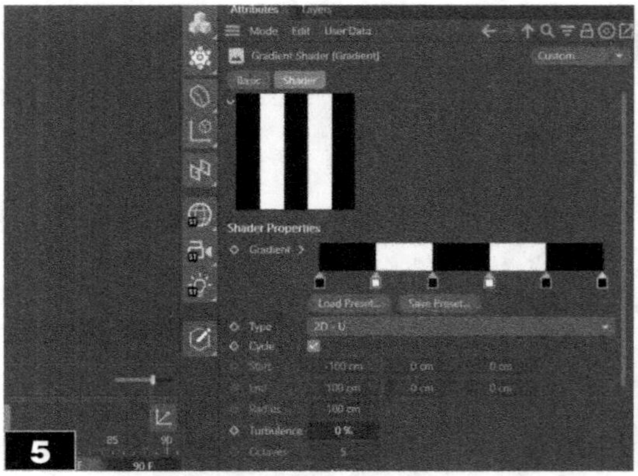

5

6

10. In the **Attribute Manager > matStripe > Color** tab, change **Mix Mode** to **Multiply**. Render the scene (see Figure 7).

7

WHAT JUST HAPPENED?
*When you switch the **Mix Mode** to **Multiply**, the color will be visible in areas where the gradient is white. As a general guideline, keep in mind that **Multiply** eliminates white, while **Screen** eliminates black.*

11. Switch to the **Layer Shader** setting area in the **Attribute Manager**. Click **Shader** and then choose **Effects > Lumas** from the popup. Click on the **Lumas** swatch to open the **Lumas Shader** settings.

WHAT JUST HAPPENED?
*I have generated a **Lumas** shader layer, which is an illumination shader that includes options for emulating three specular highlights and the capability to simulate anisotropic highlights.*

12. In the **Shader** tab, change **Color** to **black**. In the **Specular 1** tab, change **Glare** to **100**. In the **Specular 2** tab, change **Color** to **HSV (103, 5, 77)**, **Size** to **10%**, and **Glare** to **100%**.

8

13. In the **Specular 3** tab, change **Color** to **HSV (233, 13, 53)**. In the **Anisotropy** tab, select the **Active** checkbox and then change **Projection** to **Planar** and **Y Roughness** to **200%**. Render the scene (see Figure 8).

WHAT JUST HAPPENED?
*Within the **Shader** tab, the **Color** parameter has been set to black, which determines the basic diffuse color of the surface. The three Specular tabs have identical settings. The **Glare** parameter influences the Intensity by utilizing an edge falloff. The **Projection** parameter is utilized to establish uneven scaling of the specular highlights.*

14. Switch to the **Layer Shader** properties in the **Attribute Manager** and then change blending mode to **Soft Light** for the **Lumas** layer. Render the scene (see Figure 9). Notice that we need to reduce the effect of the **Lumas** layer so that more color is visible. To do so, change mix strength of the **Lumas** layer to **30%** and render the scene (see Figure 10).

9

10

15. In the **Attribute Manager** > **matStripe** > **Reflectance** tab, change **Type** to **GGX**, **Roughness** to **5**, **Reflection Strength** to **10**, and **Specular Strength** to **0**. In the **LAYER FRESNEL** area, change **Fresnel** to **Conductor** and **Preset** to **Chromium**. Render the scene (see Figure 11).

16. In the **Attribute Manager** > **matStripe** > **Basic** tab, select the **Bump** checkbox and then in the **Attribute Manager** > **matStripe** > **Bump** tab, click **Texture** > **Triangle** button and then choose **Noise** from the popup.

17. Click the **Noise** button to open the **Noise Shader** properties. Change **Color 1** to **HSV (0, 0, 50)**, **Noise** to **Turbulence**, **Global Scale** to **2**, and **Delta** to **50**.

18. In the **Attribute Manager** > **matStripe** > **Bump** tab, change **Strength** to **5**. In the **Attribute Manager** > **matStripe** > **Color** tab, change **Brightness** to **80**. Render the scene (see Figure 12).

11

12

Delta

The **Delta** parameter is a scaling factor used to sample the noise. It is used to determine the slope that will be utilized in the **Bump** channel. This feature enables the creation of precise bumps with fine details.

WHAT NEXT?
Let's now generate a slightly more intricate material with stripes.

19. Double-click on the **Material Manager** to create a new material. Rename the material as **matStripe1**. To replace the materials for **Geo-1** and **Geo-2**, simply grab the material from the **Material Manager** and drag it over the corresponding material tags in the **Object Manager**. This action will replace the original material tags with the new ones.

20. Select material in the **Material Manager** and then in the **Attribute Manager > matStripe1 > Color** tab, change **Color** to **HSV (44, 0, 100)** and **Brightness** to **80**. Click **Texture > Triangle** button and then choose **Layer** from the popup.

21. Click on the **Layer** button. In the **Layer Shader** settings, click **Shader** and then choose **Layer** from the popup. Click on **Layer** color swatch to switch to the **Layer Shader** properties.

22. Click **Shader** and then choose **Gradient** from the popup. Create a gradient, as shown in Figure 13. In the **Gradient** settings, change **Type** to **3D - Linear**, **Start** to **(-100, -40, 0)**, and **End** to (**100**, **75**, **0**).

WHAT JUST HAPPENED?
*The **Start** and **End** parameters interact with 3D gradients and determine the beginning and ending points of the gradient. These parameters can be utilized to rotate the gradient.*

__SAVING GRADIENTS__
*You have the option to save Gradient patterns using the **Save Preset** button and subsequently use that pattern with another shader. To load the preset, simply click on the **Load Preset** button.*

__PLACING KNOTS UNIFORMLY__
*You have the option to uniformly distribute knots along the gradient by utilizing the **Knot Position** parameter within the **Gradient** section. The leftmost position is **0%**, and the rightmost is **100%**. For instance, if you want to create ten bars, you can place the knots at 0%, 10%, 20%, 30%, 40%, 50%, 60%, 70%, 80%, 90%, and 100%, respectively.*

23. In the **Layer Shader** settings, **RMB** click on the **Gradient** layer as you created earlier and then choose **Copy Shader** from the popup. Now, **RMB** click and then choose **Paste Shader** from the popup menu to create another gradient layer.

24. Click **Folder** to create folder and then move the upper **Gradient** layer inside it (see Figure 14). Select the **Gradient** layer which is inside the **Folder** and then click **Effect** and then choose **Transform** from the popup. In the **Transform** layer, change **Scale** to **0.1**, **0.1**, and **0.1**.

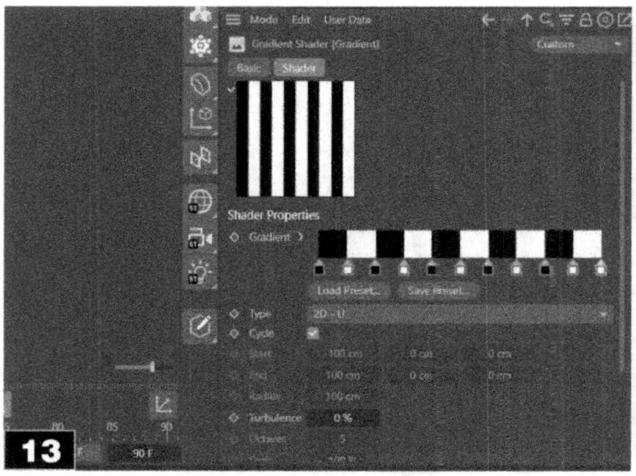

13

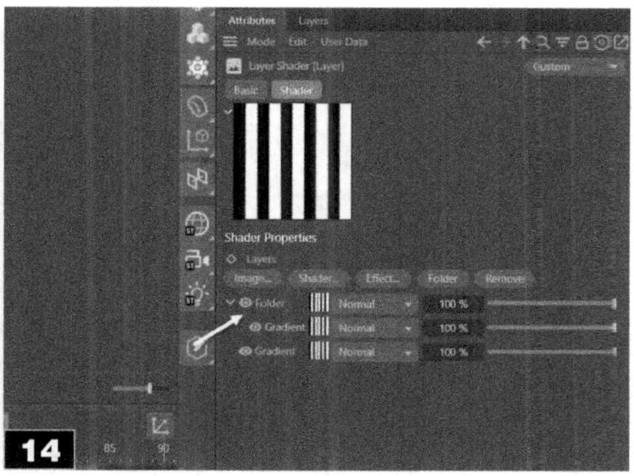

14

__WHAT TRANSFORM EFFECT DOES?__
*The **Transform** effect is employed to manipulate (move, scale, and rotate) the output of the underlying layers. In this case, I have scaled the **Gradient** layer to generate several vertical strips. Next, we will blend it with the other **Gradient** layer using the **Soft Light** mode to produce variations in the final gradient.*

25. Change **Folder's** blending mode to **Soft Light** and strength to **25** (see Figure 15).

26. In the **Attribute Manager > matStripe1 > Color** tab, change **Mix Mode** to **Multiply** and render the scene (see Figure 16).

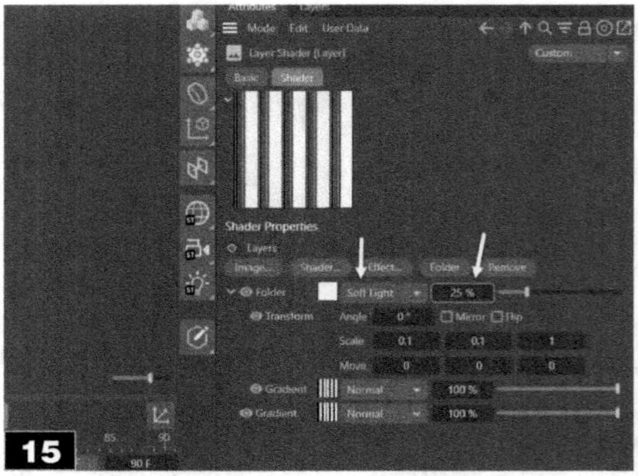

15

16

27. Click the **Layer** button to open the **Layer Shader** settings. Click **Shader** and then choose **Effects > Lumas** from the popup menu. Drag the **Lumas** layer at the bottom of the stack. Now, specify the settings for the **Lumas** layer as done earlier. Disable **Anisotropy** from the **Lumas** layer. Change blending mode to **Add** for the **Layer** layer that you created initially (see Figure 17).

28. In the **Attribute Manager > matStripe > Reflectance** tab, change **Type** to **GGX**, **Roughness** to **5**, **Reflection Strength** to **10**, and **Specular Strength** to **0**. In the **LAYER FRESNEL** area, change **Fresnel** to **Conductor** and **Preset** to **Chromium**. Render the scene (see Figure 18).

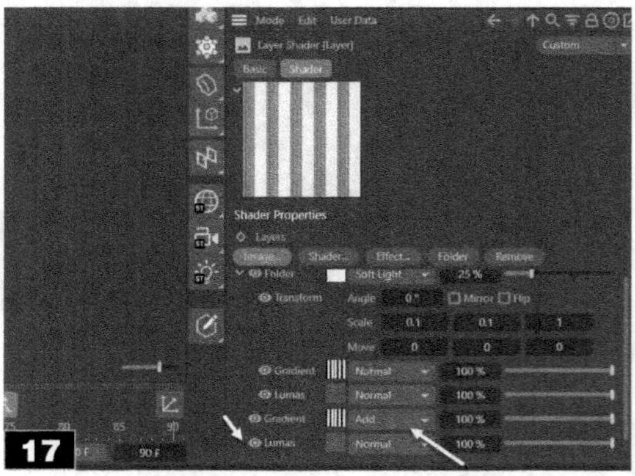

17

18

CREATING EFFECTS USING MATERIALS

We will now utilize materials to create special effects.

Summary	
Topics	Getting Started Creating Effects Using Materials
Resources folder	**materials**

Summary	
Start file	**shadeGeo.c4d**
Final file	**effects-finish.c4d**

Getting Started

Load the **shadeGeo.c4d** file.

Creating Effects Using Materials

Follow these steps:

1. Choose **Create > Extensions > Cheen** from the **Material Manager** menu to create a new material. Rename the material as **matEffect1**. Apply the material to the **Geo-1** and **Geo-2** objects in the **Object Manager**.

> ***WHEN TO USE THE CHEEN SHADER?***
> *The **Cheen** shader is intended for creating a microscopic appearance. It includes an extra **Gradients** channel for producing a range of effects.*

2. Select material in the **Material Manager** and then in the **Attribute Manager > matEffect1> Basic** tab, clear the **Diffuse** and **Roughness** checkboxes and select the **Transparency** checkbox. In the **Attribute Manager > Transparency** tab, change **Refraction Index** to **1**.

3. In the **Gradients** tab, create an additional knob for the **Opacity** gradient at **65%** and change its color to black. Change **Interpolation** to **Cubic** (see Figure 1). Render the scene (see Figure 2).

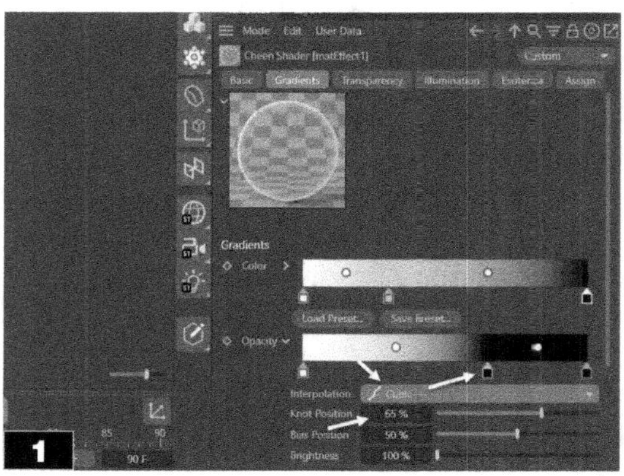

Color and Opacity

The **Color** gradient establishes the fundamental color of the object relative to the angle between the camera and the surface normals. The left segment of the gradient influences the object's edge, while the right segment influences its center. The **Opacity** gradient regulates the object's opacity based on the angle between the camera and the surface normal. The transparent knots are black, while the opaque knots are white. The left segment of the gradient influences the object's edge, while the right segment influences its center.

WHAT NEXT?
Let's create an X-Ray look now.

4. Double-click on the **Material Manager** to create a new material. Rename the material as **matEffect2**. To replace the materials for **Geo-1** and **Geo-2**, simply grab the material from the **Material Manager** and drag it over the corresponding material tags in the **Object Manager**. This action will replace the original material tags with the new ones.

5. Select material in the **Material Manager** and then in the **Attribute Manager > matEffect2 > Basic** tab, clear the **Color** checkbox and select the **Luminance** and **Alpha** checkboxes.

6. In the **Attribute Manager > matEffect2 > Luminance** tab, change **Color** to **HSV** (**229**, **15**, **100**) and **Brightness** to **50**. Click **Texture > Triangle** button and then choose **Fresnel** from the popup menu. Click the **Fresnel** button to open the **Fresnel Shader** settings.

7. Change first knob of the gradient to **HSV** (**175**, **28**, **91**). Render the scene (see Figure 3).

3

Fresnel Shader

The **Fresnel** shader is responsive to the camera's viewing angle of individual polygons on a 3D object. The **Gradient** parameter calculates the attenuation of the output by determining the angle or drop-off between the surface normals and the viewing angle. The gradient's left side influences the object's edges, while the right side influences the center. The **Render** parameter determines how the shader effect is displayed, with different options available for front, back, or both sides of the object. Here is a brief summary:

- **Front Only:** Calculates the falloff for the front of the object and then change back of the object to black, if it can be seen.
- **Front Trans:** Calculates the falloff for the front of the object and then change back of the object to white, if it can be seen.
- **Back Only:** Calculates the falloff for the back of the object and then change front of the object to black, if it can be seen.

- **Back Trans:** Calculates the falloff for the back of the object and then change front of the object to white, if it can be seen.
- **Front and Back:** Calculates falloff for the intercepted surface.

8. Select the **Transparency** checkbox in the **Attribute Manager > Basic** tab. In the **Transparency** tab, change **Brightness** to **65** and clear the **Total Internal Reflection** checkbox. Select the **Additive** checkbox. Click **Texture > Triangle** button and then choose **Fresnel** from the popup menu.

9. Click the **Fresnel** button to open the **Fresnel Shader** settings and then set the gradient, as shown in Figure 4.

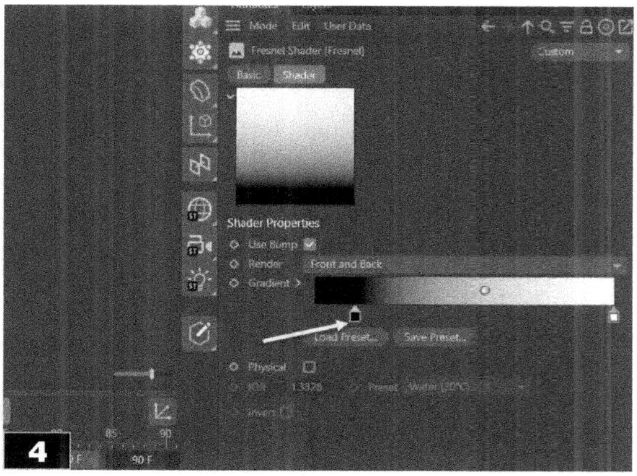

4

10. In the **Transparency** tab, change **Mix Mode** to **Multiply** and **Blurriness** to **10**. Render the scene (see Figure 5). In the **Alpha** tab, click **Texture > Triangle** button **> Effects** and then choose **Normal Direction** from the popup menu. Render the scene (see Figure 6).

5

6

WHAT NEXT?
Now, let's create the involution effect.

11. Double-click on the **Material Manager** to create a new material. Rename the material as **matEffect3**. To replace the materials for **Geo-1** and **Geo-2**, simply grab the material from the **Material Manager** and drag it over the corresponding material tags in the **Object Manager**. This action will replace the original material tags with the new ones.

12. Select material in the **Material Manager** and then in the **Color** tab, change **Color** to **HSV** (**120**, **4**, **100**) and **Brightness** to **80**. Click **Texture > Triangle** button and

then choose **Fresnel** from the popup menu. Click the **Fresnel** button to open the **Fresnel Shader** settings.

13. Create a gradient, as shown in Figure 7. In the **Color** tab, change **Mix Mode** to **Multiply**. Render the scene (see Figure 8).

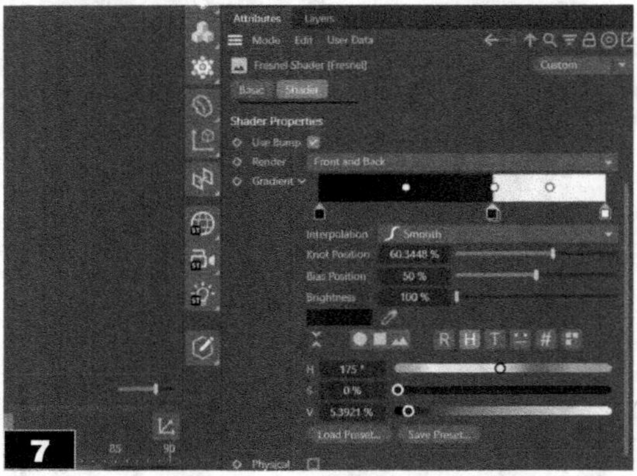

7

8

14. Select the **Luminance** checkbox in the **Attribute Manager > Basic** tab. In the **Luminance** tab, click **Texture > Triangle** button and then choose **Fresnel** from the popup menu. Click the **Fresnel** button to open the **Fresnel Shader** settings. Change color of the second knob to **HSV** (**0**, **0**, **22**). In the **Luminance** tab, change **Mix Mode** to **Multiply** and **Brightness** to **70**. Render the scene (see Figure 9).

15. Select the **Transparency** checkbox in the **Attribute Manager > Basic** tab. In the **Transparency** tab, change **Brightness** to **30**, **Refraction** to **2**, and the clear the **Total Internal Reflection** checkbox. Render the scene (see Figure 10).

9

10

CREATING VARIOUS MATERIALS

Let's now create different kinds of materials.

Summary	
Topics	Getting Started Creating Materials
Resources folder	**materials**
Start file	**shadeGeo.c4d**
Final file	**varmat-finish.c4d**

Getting Started

Load the **shadeGeo.c4d** file.

Creating Materials

Let's start by creating the roman aqua glass material. Follow these steps:

1. Double-click on the **Material Manager** to create a new material. Rename the material as **matRomanAqua**. Apply the material to the **Geo-1 and Geo-2** objects in the **Object Manager**. Select material in the **Material Manager** and then in the **Attribute Manager > Basic** tab, disbale all checkboxes except **Color**.

2. In the **Color** tab, change **Color** to **HSV** (**120**, **17**, **47**) and **Diffuse Falloff** to **80**. Click **Texture > Triangle** button and then choose **Fresnel** from the popup menu. Click the **Fresnel** button to open the **Fresnel Shader** settings. Change color of the second knob to **HSV** (**0**, **0**, **65**). In the **Color** tab, change **Mix Mode** to **Multiply**. Render the scene (see Figure 1).

3. In the **Attribute Manager > Basic** tab, select the **Diffusion** checkbox. In the **Diffusion** tab, click **Texture > Triangle** button and then choose **Noise** from the popup menu. In the **Noise Shader** settings, change **Noise** to **Cell Voronoi**, and **Global Scale** to **5**. In the **Diffusion** tab, change **Mix Strength** to **50%**. Render the scene (see Figure 2).

1

2

4. In the **Basic** tab, enable the **Transparency** channel and then in the **Transparency** tab, change **Color** to **HSV** (**201**, **27**, **100**) and **Refraction** to **1.5**. Clear the **Exit Reflections** checkbox and then change **Fresnel Reflectivity** to **70**. Render the scene (see Figure 3).

3

HOW TRANSPARENCY WORKS?
*If you raise the transparency of a material, the color will decrease automatically to adjust for the transparency. The formula for this is **Color % + Transparency % = 100%**. For example, if a white material has **0%** transparency, its color will be white. But if you increase transparency to **50%**, the color of the material will be gray. If you increase transparency all the way up to **100%**, the material will become colorless. This is the normal process. But if you want to stop this process, you can choose the **Additive** option.*

Exit Reflections

When a reflection ray penetrates a surface after being refracted, two kinds of reflections can be computed: one when the rays enter the medium, and the other when they exit the medium. Having a single reflection is visually more attractive than having a double reflection. To accomplish a single reflection, the **Exit Reflections** checkbox should be unchecked.

Fresnel Reflectivity

The **Fresnel Reflectivity** parameter controls the strength of the fresnel reflections.

Absorption Color and Absorption Distance

Transparent glass often has a subtle color due to the way light interacts with it. To create this effect in 3D, you can use the **Absorption Color** and **Absorption Distance** parameters. The **Absorption Color** defines a color that is multiplied by the original color of the glass as light passes through it over a certain distance specified by the **Absorption Distance** parameter. Additionally, you can adjust the transparency of the glass using the **Blurriness**, **Min Samples**, **Max Samples**, and **Accuracy** parameters to achieve a more realistic effect.

ABSORPTION
The absorption algorithm is optimized for closed volumes, meaning that if there are holes in the geometry, it may not produce expected results in Cinema 4D.

GLASS FILLED WITH FLUID
When creating a material for a glass filled with liquid, it is recommended to model the glass and fluid separately. This is because the liquid and glass have different refractive indices, which can cause visual artifacts if modeled as a single object. To

get predictable results, the fluid object should slightly extend into the glass object, ensuring that the two objects are in contact. This way, the refraction of light through the liquid and glass can be calculated accurately.

5. Click **Texture > Triangle** button and then choose **Noise** from the popup menu. In the **Noise Shader** settings, change **Noise** to **Luka**, **Octaves** to **8**, **Global Scale** to **500**, **Color 1** to **HSV** (**0**, **0**, **53**). In the **Transparency** tab, change **Mix Mode** to **Multiply**, **Absorption Color** to **HSV** (**195**, **20**, **81**). Render the scene (see Figure 4).

6. Select the **Reflectance** checkbox in the **Basic** tab. In the **Reflectance** tab, select **Type** to **GGX**, **Roughness** to **0**, **Reflection Strength** to **45**, and **Specular Strength** to **0**. In the **LAYER FRESNEL** area, select **Dielectric** from the **Fresnel** drop-down list and **Glass** from the **Preset** drop-down list.

7. In the **Basic** tab, select the **Bump** checkbox. In the **Bump** tab, Click **Texture > Triangle** button and then choose **Noise** from the popup menu. In the **Noise Shader** settings, change **Texture** to **Stupl**, **Global Scale** to **500**, and **Color 1** to **HSV** (**0**, **0**, **53**). Render the scene (see Figure 5).

4

5

WHAT NEXT?
Let's proceed to make the material for stained glass.

8. Double-click on the **Material Manager** to create a new material. Rename the material as **matStainedGlass**. Apply the material to the **Geo-1 and Geo-2** objects in the **Object Manager**. Select material in the **Material Manager** and then in the **Attribute Manager > Basic** tab, clear the **Color** checkbox and select the **Transparency** checkbox. In the **Transparency** tab, change **Color** to **HSV** (**94**, **57**, **65**) and **Refraction** to **1.5**. Render the scene (see Figure 6).

9. Clear the **Exit Reflections** checkbox and change **Fresnel Reflectivity** to **50**. Change **Absorption Color** to **HSV** (**147**, **17**, **100**) and change **Absorption Distance** to **50**.

10. In the **Reflectance** tab, select **Type** to **GGX**, **Roughness** to **11**, **Reflection Strength** to **100**, and **Specular Strength** to **20**. In the **LAYER FRESNEL** area, select **Dielectric** from the **Fresnel** drop-down list and **Glass** from the **Preset** drop-down list.

11. In the **Basic** tab, select the **Bump** checkbox. In the **Bump** tab, click **Texture > Triangle** button and then choose **Noise** from the popup menu. In the **Noise Shader** settings, change **Noise** to **Turbulence**, **Global Scale** to **5**, **Delta** to **50**, and **Color 1** to **HSV** (**0**, **0**, **50**). Render the scene (see Figure 7).

6

7

WHAT NEXT?
Let's proceed to make the tinted glass material.

12. Double-click on the **Material Manager** to create a new material. Rename the material as **matTintedGlass**. To replace the materials for **Geo-1** and **Geo-2**, simply grab the material from the **Material Manager** and drag it over the corresponding material tags in the **Object Manager**. This action will replace the original material tags with the new ones.

13. Select material in the **Material Manager** and then in the **Attribute Manager > Basic** tab, clear the **Color** checkbox and select the **Transparency** checkbox. In the **Transparency** tab, change **Brightness** to **80** and **Refraction** to **1.55**.

14. Clear the **Exit Reflections** checkbox and change **Fresnel Reflectivity** to **60**. In the **Reflectance** tab, select **Type** to **GGX**, **Attenuation** to **Average**, **Roughness** to **0**, **Reflection Strength** to **90**, and **Specular Strength** to **3**. In the **LAYER FRESNEL** area, select **Dielectric** from the **Fresnel** drop-down list and **Glass** from the **Preset** drop-down list.

15. Enable the **Color** channel in the **Basic** tab. Click **Texture > Triangle** button and then choose **Layer** from the popup menu. In the **Layer Shader** settings, click **Shader** and then choose **Shader > Effects > Falloff**. In the **Falloff** shader settings, change the gradient (use the **Heat 1** preset), as shown in Figure 8.

16. In the **Layer Shader** settings, click **Shader** and then choose **Fresnel** from the popup menu. Change the blending mode to **Multiply**. In the **Color** tab, change **Model** to **Oren-Nayar**, **Diffuse Falloff** to **-21**. Render the scene (see Figure 9).

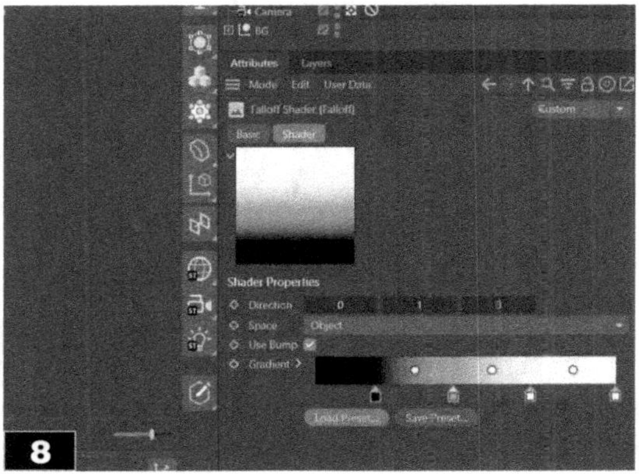

8

9

WHAT NEXT?
We will now proceed to create a material for the ground.

17. Double-click on the **Material Manager** to create a new material. Rename the material as **matGround**. To replace the materials for **Geo-1** and **Geo-2**, simply grab the material from the **Material Manager** and drag it over the corresponding material tags in the **Object Manager**. This action will replace the original material tags with the new ones.

18. In the **Attribute Manager** > **Color** tab, change **Color** to **HSV** (**200**, **0**, **100**). Click **Texture** > **Triangle** button and then choose **Layer** from the popup.

19. Click on the **Layer** button. In the **Layer Shader** settings, click **Shader** and then choose **Layer** from the popup. In the **Layer Shader** settings, click **Shader** and then choose **Noise** from the popup menu. In the **Noise Shader** settings, change **Color 1** to **HSV** (**18**, **68**, **38**), **Color 2** to **HSV** (**22**, **56**, **46**), **Noise** to **Wavy Turbulence**, **Octave** to **6**, and **Global Scale** to **85**.

20. In the **Layer Shader** settings, click **Shader** and then choose **Noise** from the popup menu. Change blending mode to **Multiply**. In the new **Noise Shader** settings, change **Noise** to **Blistered Turbulence**, and **Global Scale** to **10**. In the **Layer Shader** settings, change strength to **64** for the top noise layer. In the **Color** tab, change **Mix Mode** to **Multiply**. Render the scene (see Figure 10).

21. Add another **Noise** layer on the **Layer Shader** settings and then in the **Noise Shader** settings, change **Noise** to **Naki**, **Octave** to **7**, and **Global Scale** to **600**. In the **Layer Shader** settings, change blending mode to **Multiply** and strength to **33**. Render the scene (see Figure 11).

10

11

22. In the **Layer Shader** settings, click **Shader** and then choose **Fresnel** from the popup menu. In the **Fresnel Shader** settings, change second gradient knob color to **HSV** (**0**, **0**, **46**). In the **Layer Shader** settings, change blending mode to **Dodge** and strength to **22** for the **Fresnel** layer. Render the scene (see Figure 12).

23. In the **Layer Shader** settings, click **Shader** and then choose **Noise** from the popup menu. In the **Noise Shader** settings, change **Noise** to **Nutous**, **Global Scale** to **2000**, and **Octave** to **8**. In the **Layer Shader** settings, change blending mode to **Soft Light** and strength to **28**. Render the scene (see Figure 13).

12

13

24. In the **Color** tab, change **Model** to **Oren-Nayar**, **Diffuse Falloff** to **28**, and **Roughness** to **40**.

25. In the **Basic** tab, clear the **Reflectance** channel and then select the **Diffusion** channel. In the **Diffusion** tab, click **Texture** > **Triangle** button and then choose **Noise** from the popup. In the **Noise Shader** settings, change **Global Scale** to **2**. In the **Diffusion** tab, change **Mix Strength** and to **19**. Render the scene (see Figure 14).

26. Enable the **Bump** channel and then on the **Bump** tab, click **Texture > Triangle** button and then choose **Noise** from the popup. In the **Noise Shader** settings, change **Noise** to **Turbulence** and **Global Scale** to **125**. In the **Bump** tab, change **Strength** to **73**. Render the scene (see Figure 15).

14

15

This page is intentionally left blank

CHAPTER 5: CREATING MATERIALS

In the previous chapter, we examined certain pre-existing material presets within Cinema 4D. However, in this chapter, we will generate materials from the ground up.

TUTORIALS

CREATING DENIM FABRIC MATERIAL

In this tutorial, we will create the denim fabric material using Photoshop.

Summary	
Topics	Getting Started Creating the Material
Resources folder	**creating-materials**
Start file	**shadeGeo.c4d**
Final file	**denim-finish.c4d**

Getting Started

Open **shadeGeo.c4d** in Cinema 4D.

Creating the Material

Follow these steps:

1. Start **Photoshop**. Create a **1000 x 1000 px** document and fill it with **RGB** (**41**, **67**, **102**). Create a new layer and fill it with **50%** gray. Press **D** to switch to the default background and foreground colors.
2. Choose **Filter** > **Filter Gallery** > **Sketch** > **Halftone Pattern** from the menubar and then change the parameters as shown in Figure 1 and then click **OK**.
3. Choose **Filter** > **Pixelate** > **Mezzotint** from the menubar and then change the parameters, as shown in Figure 2. Then, Click **OK**.

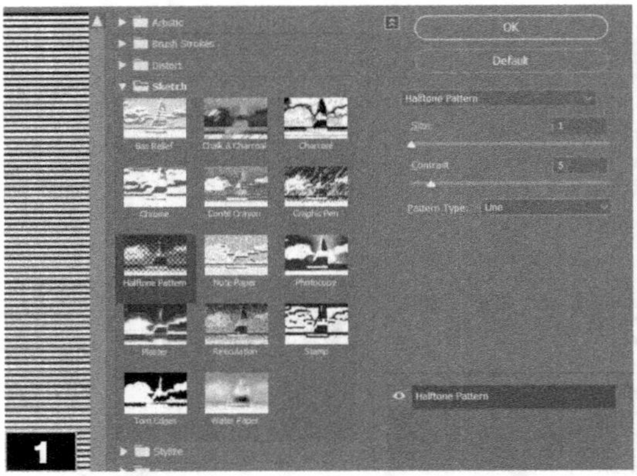

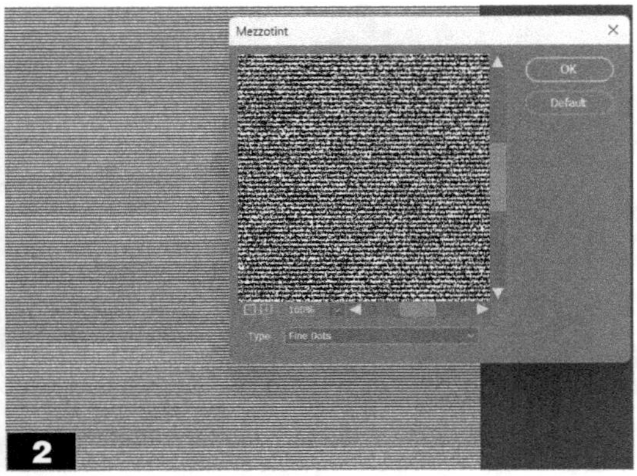

4. Duplicate the layer and rotate/scale the duplicate layer (see Figure 3). Choose **Filter > Blur > Gaussian Blur** from the menubar and then apply a blur of radius **1**. Change blending mode to **Multiply**. Also, change the blending mode of the middle layer (**Layer 1**) to **Softlight** (see Figure 4). Save the file as **denimFebric.jpg**.

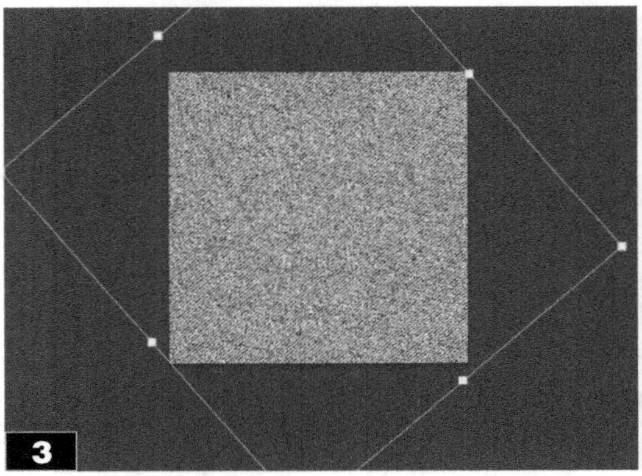

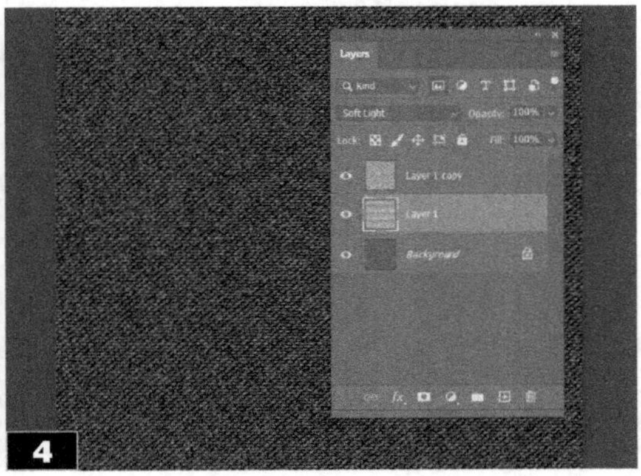

5. Choose **Layer > Flatten Image** from the menubar to flatten the image. Then, press **Ctrl Shift U** to desaturate the image. Apply **Levels** to bring back some contrast and then save it as **denimFebricBump.jpg**.

6. In Cinema 4D, double-click in the **Material Manager** to create a new material. Rename the material as **matDenim**. Apply the material to the **Geo-1** and **Geo-2** objects in the **Object Manager**. Select material in the **Material Manager** and then in the **Attribute Manager > matDenim > Basic** tab, clear the **Reflectance** checkbox. In the **Color** tab, change **Color** to **HSV** (**213**, **42**, **89**).

7. Click the **Texture > Triangle** button and then choose **Load Image** from the popup menu to open the **Open File** dialog box. In this dialog box, navigate to **denimFebric.jpg** and then click the **Open** button. Change **Mix Mode** to **Multiply**, **Model** to **Oren-Nayar** and **Diffuse Falloff** to **21**. Render the scene (see Figure 5).

8. In the **Attribute Manager > matDenim > Basic** tab, select the **Bump** checkbox. In the **Bump** tab, click the **Texture > Triangle** button and then choose **Load Image** from the popup menu to open the **Open File** dialog box. In this dialog box, navigate to **denimFebricBump.jpg** and then click the **Open** button. Change **Strength** to **57** in the **Bump** tab.

9. In the **Attribute Manager > matDenim > Basic** tab, select the **Diffusion** checkbox. In the **Diffusion** tab, click the **Texture > Triangle** button and then choose **Noise** from the popup menu. Click the **Noise** button to open the **Noise** shader settings. Click the **Noise** button to open the **Noise Shader** settings. Change **Noise** to **Voronoi 1** and **Global Scale** to **5**.

NOISE CLIPPING
*The **Low Clip** and **High Clip** parameters control the clipping value of the noise. Noise values less than the value specified for the **Low Clip** parameter will clipped to **0**. Similarly, noise values greater than the value specified for the **High Clip** parameter will clipped to **100**.*

10. In the **Diffusion** tab, change **Mix Mode** to **Add** and then render the scene (see Figure 6).

5

6

CREATING DENIM FABRIC MATERIAL USING REFLECTANCE MODEL

In this tutorial, we will create the denim fabric material using Cinema 4D's reflectance model.

Summary	
Topics	Getting Started Creating the Material
Resources folder	**creating-materials**
Start file	**shadeGeo.c4d**
Final file	**fabric-finish.c4d**

Getting Started

Start Cinema 4D and open the **shadeGeo.c4d** file.

Creating the Material

Follow these steps:

1. Double-click in the **Material Manager** to create a new material. Rename the material as **matDenim2**. Apply the material to the **Geo-1** and **Geo-2** objects in the **Object Manager**.

2. Select material in the **Material Manager** and then in the **Attribute Manager > matDenim2 > Basic** tab, clear all checkboxes except the **Reflectance** checkbox. In the **Reflectance** tab, change **Type** to **Irawan (Woven Cloth)**. Render the scene; notice that pattern that appears in the render (see Figure 1).

Irawan (Woven Cloth)

Irawan (Woven Cloth) is a cloth mode in Cinema 4D that allows you to simulate characteristic anisotropic specular highlights/reflections that are found on the real-world cloth objects. You can select a predefined cloth preset from the Preset drop-down list or you can apply your own customized settings.

3. In the **Layer Cloth** area, make sure **Preset** is set to **Blue Gabardine (Suits)** and then change **Pattern** to **Cotton Denim**. Change **Scale U** and **Scale V** to **30** each.

4. Change **Diffuse Warp**, **Diffuse Weft**, **Specular Warp**, and **Specular Weft** to **HSV** (**221**, **46**, **48**), **HSV** (**242**, **23**, **42**), **HSV** (**208**, **21**, **20**), and **HSV** (**207**, **13**, **61**), respectively. Render the scene (see Figure 2).

1

2

5. Change **Scattering - Uniform** and **Scattering - Forward** to **0.02** and **7**, respectively. Render the scene (see Figure 3).

6. In the **Attribute Manager** > **matDenim2** > **Basic** tab, select the **Color** checkbox. In the **Color** tab, change **Color** to **HSV** (**217**, **54**, **95**), **Brightness** to **20**, **Model** to **Oren-Nayer**, and **Diffuse Falloff** to **21**. Render the scene (see Figure 4).

3

4

Diffuse and Warp Settings

You can use these settings to specify separate diffuse and specular colors for the warp and weft threads.

Specular and Diffuse Colors

In order to achieve favorable outcomes from the fabric reflectance model, it is crucial to ensure that the specular color is consistently brighter than the diffuse color so that they blend well. You may also apply a texture to determine the color, which will be combined with the existing color. If you intend to employ a texture to define the color, set the color to white. The **Scattering - Uniform** parameter controls the overall specular and reflection intensity. Increasing this value will result in a brighter and more reflective cloth. The **Scattering - Forward** parameter affects the luminous regions of the fabric's specular highlight.

CREATING AN ABSTRACT MATERIAL - 1

In this tutorial, we will create an abstract material.

Summary	
Topics	Getting Started Creating the Material
Resources folder	**creating-materials**
Start file	**shadeGeo.c4d**
Final file	**abs1-finish.c4d**

Getting Started

Start Cinema 4D and open the **shadeGeo.c4d** file.

Creating the Material

Follow these steps:

1. Double-click in the **Material Manager** to create a new material. Rename the material as **matAbs1**. Apply the material to the **Geo-1** and **Geo-2** objects in the **Object Manager**.
2. Select **matAbs1** in the **Material Manager** and then in the **Attribute Manager > matAbs1 > Basic** tab, clear the **Reflectance** checkbox. In the **Color** tab, click **Texture > Triangle** button and then choose **Layer** from the popup menu. Click the **Layer** button to open the **Layer** shader settings.
3. Click **Shader** and then choose **Filter** from the popup menu. Then, in the **Filter** shader settings, click **Texture > Triangle** button and then load **granite-texture.jpg**. Change **Hue** to **305** and **Contrast** to **39**. Render the scene (see Figure 1).

Filter Shader

The **Filter** shader can modify the hue, brightness, contrast, saturation, gamma, and gradient curves of a bitmap or other shaders. The **Gamma** parameter influences the middle tones, with higher values resulting in brighter middle tones and lower values causing darker middle tones. If the **Colorize** checkbox is selected, the texture is transformed into grayscale, and the **Hue** and **Saturation** parameters can be used to colorize the image.

4. In the **Layer** shader settings, click **Shader** and then choose **Color** from the popup menu. In the **Color** shader settings and then change **Color** to **HSV (229, 91, 100)**. In the **Layer** shader settings, change blending mode **Luminance** and **Strength** to **88**. Render the scene (see Figure 2).

5. Select the **Reflectance** checkbox in the **Attribute Manager > Basic** tab. In the **Reflectance** tab, change **Type** to **Beckmann**, **Attenuation** to **Average**, **Roughness** to **10**, **Reflection Strength** to **15**, and **Specular Strength** to **0**.

6. Copy the texture from the **Color** tab and then paste it on the **Reflectance** tab > **Layer Color** area > **Texture** parameter (see Figure 3). Change **Brightness** to **7** and then render the scene (see Figure 4).

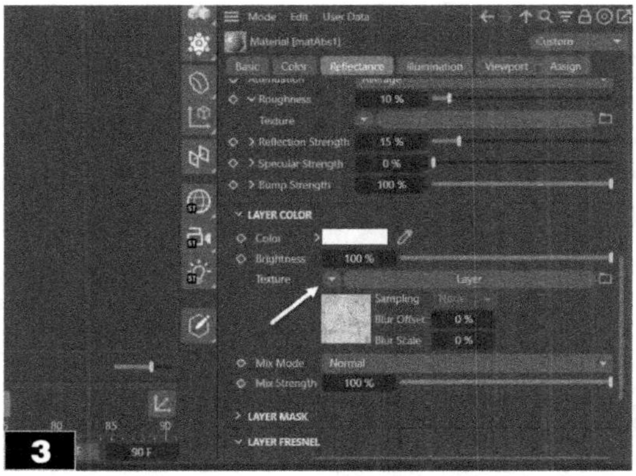

3

4

7. Select the **Bump** checkbox in the **Attribute Manager** > **Basic** tab. Copy the texture from the **Color** tab and then paste it on the **Bump** tab > **Texture** parameter. In the **Layer** shader settings, delete the **Color** layer and then switch to the **Filter** shader settings.

8. Change **Hue** to **0**, Saturation to **-100**, and **Contrast** to **26**. In the **Bump** tab, change **Strength** to **100** and then render the scene (see Figure 5).

5

CREATING AN ABSTRACT MATERIAL - 2

In this tutorial, we will create an abstract material.

Summary	
Topics	Getting Started Creating the Material
Resources folder	**creating-materials**
Start file	**shadeGeo-1.c4d**
Final file	**abs2-finish.c4d**

Getting Started

Start Cinema 4D and open the **shadeGeo-1.c4d** file.

Creating the Material

Follow these steps:

1. Double-click in the **Material Manager** to create a new material. Rename the material as **matAbs2**. Apply the material to the **Geo-1** and **Geo-2** objects in the **Object Manager**.

2. In the **Color** tab, click the **Texture > Triangle** button and then choose **Gradient** from the popup menu. In the **Gradient** shader settings, change **Type** to **2D-V** and then change the **Gradient** using the red and white colors, as shown in Figure 1.

3. Select the **Displacement** checkbox in the **Attribute Manager > Basic** tab. In the **Displacement** tab, click the **Texture > Triangle** button and then choose **Filter** from the popup menu.

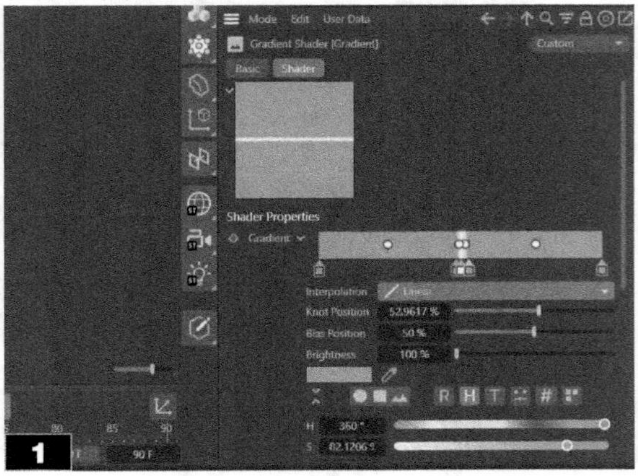

1

Displacement

I have activated the **Displacement** channel which differs from the **Bump** channel as it physically alters the object. The **Height** parameter determines the displacement height while the **Strength** parameter adjusts the maximum height defined by the **Height** parameter. If the **Type** is set to **Intensity**, displacement occurs in the positive direction. The black areas of the map do not displace the object, whereas the white areas generate maximum displacement. If the **Type** is set to **Intensity Centered**, displacement occurs in both positive and negative directions. A gray value of **50%** on the map does not displace the object. The white areas of the map cause maximum positive displacement while the black areas generate maximum negative displacement.

4. In the **Filter** shader settings, click the **Texture > Triangle** button and then choose **Gradient** from the popup. In the **Gradient** shader settings, load the **Pattern 6** preset and then change **Angle** to **45**.

5. In the **Filter** shader settings, change **Saturation** to **-100** and **Contrast** to **6**. Render the scene (see Figure 2). In the **Displacement** tab, change **Height** to **2**, select the **Sub Polygon Displacement** checkbox and then render the scene (see Figure 3).

WHAT JUST HAPPENED?
*By enabling the **Sub Polygon Displacement** option, you can generate intricate renders without needing to subdivide the geometry itself.*

6. Select the **Round Geometry** checkbox and then render the scene (see Figure 4).

WHAT JUST HAPPENED?
*When the **Round Geometry** checkbox is selected, an algorithm akin to that used by the **Subdivision Surface** object is employed to round the object prior to calculating sub-polygon displacement. This algorithm is necessary because normal Phong shading cannot be computed by the sub-polygon displacement feature.*

CREATING AN ABSTRACT MATERIAL - 3

In this tutorial, we will create an animated abstract material.

Summary	
Topics	Getting Started Creating the Material
Resources folder	**creating-materials**
Start file	**shadeGeo.c4d**
Final file	**abs3-finish.c4d**

Getting Started

Start Cinema 4D and open the **shadeGeo.c4d** file.

Creating the Material

Follow these steps:

1. Double-click in the **Material Manager** to create a new material. Rename the material as **matAbs3**. Apply the material to the **Geo-1** and **Geo-2** objects in the **Object Manager**. Select the **Luminance**, **Displacement**, and **Alpha** checkboxes in the **Attribute Manager > Basic** tab. Clear the **Color** checkbox.

2. In the **Alpha** tab, click the **Texture > Triangle** button and then choose **Noise** from the popup menu. Click the **Noise** button to open the **Noise** shader settings. Change **Noise** to **Cranal**, **Octaves** to **10**, and **Global Scale** to **1530**.

3. Change **Movement Z** to **0.001**, **Animation Speed** to **0.1**, **Brightness** to **3**, and **Contrast** to **94**. In the **Alpha** tab, select the **Invert** checkbox. Render the scene (see Figure 1).

WHAT JUST HAPPENED?
*To animate noise, you must assign a value to the **Animation Speed** parameter in the **Noise** settings. This value specifies the frequency at which the noise cycles per second. To adjust the noise's movement, you need to define a directional vector using the **Movement (XYZ)** parameters.*

4. Copy the texture from the **Alpha** tab and then paste it on the **Displacement** tab > **Texture** parameter. Select the **Sub Polygon Displacement** checkbox and then change **Height** to **15**. Also, select the **Round Geometry** checkbox. Render the scene (see Figure 2).

1

2

Rendering the animation

To render the animation, you need to specify a frame range in the **Render Settings** window > **Output** area using the **From** and **To** parameters. To save rendered animation to a file, select **Save** from the left pane of the **Render Setting** window. In the right pane, click the folder icon corresponding to the **File** parameter to open the **Save File** dialog box.

In this dialog box, navigate to the location where you want to save the file and then click **Save**. Select the file type from the **Format** drop-down list. To render a movie, you can choose **MP4** or **WMV** from the drop-down list. If you are rendering a still image and wants alpha channel in it, select the **Alpha Channel** checkbox. When selected, Cinema 4D calculates a pre-multiplied alpha channel that will be calculated during rendering.

WHAT IS PRE-MULTIPLIED ALPHA?
*There are two widely used alpha channel representations in computer graphics: **Straight** and **Pre-multiplied**. When an image employs straight alpha, the RGB components indicate the color of the pixels irrespective of their transparency, whereas pre-multiplied alpha manages opacity through multiplication. Pre-multiplied alpha is superior to straight alpha in accurately filtering images or compositing various layers.*

CREATING AN ABSTRACT MATERIAL - 4

In this tutorial, we will create an abstract material.

Summary	
Topics	Getting Started Creating the Material
Resources folder	**creating-materials**
Start file	**shadeGeo-1.c4d**
Final file	**abs4-finish.c4d**

Getting Started

Start Cinema 4D and open the **shadeGeo-1.c4d** file.

Creating the Material

Follow these steps:

1. Double-click in the **Material Manager** to create a new material. Rename the material as **matAbs4**. Apply the material to the **Geo-1** and **Geo-2** objects in the **Object Manager**.

2. In the **Attribute Manager** > **Color** tab, change **Color** to **HSV (33, 90, 74)**. Click **Texture** > **Triangle** button and then choose **Filter** from the popup menu. Click the **Filter** button to open the **Filter** shader settings. Then, in the **Filter** shader settings, click **Texture** > **Triangle** button and then load **IMG-06.JPG**. In the **Color** tab, change **Mix Mode** to **Multiply**.

3. Select the **Luminance** checkbox in the **Attribute Manager** > **Basic** tab. Copy the texture from the **Color** tab and then paste it on the **Luminance** tab > **Texture** parameter. Change **Color** to **HSV (33, 90, 74)** and **Mix Mode** to **Multiply**. Render the scene (see Figure 1).

4. Select the **Transparency** checkbox in the **Attribute Manager** > **Basic** tab. In the **Transparency** tab, change **Refraction Preset** to **Beer**.

5. Click the **Texture** > **Triangle** button and then choose **Noise** from the popup menu. Click the **Noise** button to open the **Noise** shader settings. Change **Noise** to **Luka**, **Octaves** to **6**, and **Global Scale** to **1569**. Change **Movement Z** to **0.001**, **Animation Speed** to **0.1**, **Brightness** to **3**, and **Contrast** to **94**. Change **Low Clip** to **7**, **High Clip** to **62**, and **Contrast** to **79**. Render the scene (see Figure 2).

6. Select the **Bump** checkbox in the **Attribute Manager** > **Basic** tab. Copy the texture from the **Color** tab and then paste it on the **Bump** tab > **Texture** parameter. Change **Strength** to **61**.

7. In the **Filter** shader settings, select the **Colorize** checkbox and then change **Brightness** to **-7** and **Contrast** to **16**. Render the scene (see Figure 3).

8. Select the **Displacement** checkbox in the **Attribute Manager** > **Basic** tab. Copy the texture from the **Transparency** tab and then paste it on the **Displacement** tab > **Texture** parameter. Select the **Sub Polygon Displacement** checkbox and then change **Subdivision Level** to **2**. Change **Height** to **12**.

9. In the **Reflectance** tab, change **Type** to **Beckmann**, **Attenuation** to **Average**, **Roughness** to **0**, **Reflection Strength** to **69**, and **Specular Strength** to **0**. In the **Layer Fresnel** area, change **Fresnel** to **Dielectric** and **Preset** to **Beer**. Render the scene (see Figure 4).

PRIMITIVE SPHERE

When adding a material to a primitive sphere, to visualize the displacement effect on the sphere, first select the sphere, then navigate to the ***Object*** *tab in the* ***Attribute Manager****, and clear the* ***Render Perfect*** *checkbox. A perfect sphere appears smooth and round and renders more quickly than a polygon sphere. Enable the* ***Render Perfect*** *checkbox when using the sphere as a foundation for other effects such as displacement or hair.*

CREATING AN ABSTRACT MATERIAL - 5

In this tutorial, we will create an abstract material.

Summary	
Topics	Getting Started Creating the Material
Resources folder	**creating-materials**
Start file	**shadeGeo-1.c4d**
Final file	**abs5-finish.c4d**

Getting Started

Start Cinema 4D and open the **shadeGeo-1.c4d** file.

Creating the Material

Follow these steps:

1. Double-click in the **Material Manager** to create a new material. Rename the material as **matAbs5**. Apply the material to the **Geo-1** and **Geo-2** objects in the **Object Manager**.
2. In the **Color** tab, click the **Texture > Triangle** button and then choose **Layer** from the popup menu. In the **Layer** shader settings, click **Folder** to create a new folder. Rename it as **Noise Folder**. Click **Shader** and then choose **Fresnel** from the popup. In the **Fresnel** shader settings, change **Value** of the first knob to **57**.
3. In the **Layer Shader** settings, click **Shader** and then choose **Noise** from the popup. In the **Noise** shader settings, change **Noise** to **Luka**, **Global Scale** to **1526**, **Movement Z** to **0.001**, **Animation Speed** to **0.1**, **Brightness** to **3**, and **Contrast** to **-48**. Change **Low Clip** to **23** and **High Clip** to **89**. Render the scene (see Figure 1).

4. In the **Layer** shader settings, change blending mode to **Screen** and strength to **25** for the **Noise** layer (see Figure 2). Render the scene (see Figure 3).

1

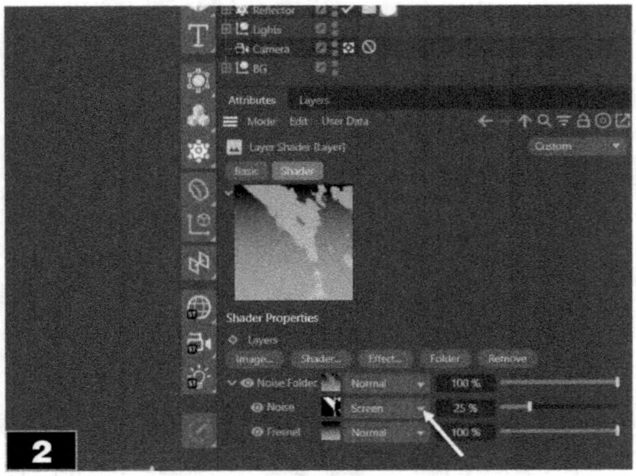

2

5. Click **Shader** and then choose **Noise** from the popup. In the **Noise** shader settings, swap **Color 1** with **Color 2**. Change **Noise** to **Nutous**, **Global Scale** to **1562**, **Movement Z** to **0.001**, **Animation Speed** to **0.1**, **Brightness** to **1**, and **Contrast** to **94**. Change **Low Clip** to **0**, **High Clip** to **38**, and **Contrast** to **76**.

6. In the **Layer** shader settings, change blending mode to **Overlay** and **Strength** to **25** for the **Noise** layer. Render the scene (see Figure 4).

3

4

7. Click **Effect** and then choose **Colorize** from the popup. Make sure the **Colorize** layer is at the top of the stack. Load the preset **Heat3** for the **Colorize** effect.

8. Select the **Luminance** checkbox in the **Attribute Manager** > **Basic** tab. Copy the texture from the **Color** tab and then paste it on the **Luminance** tab > **Texture** parameter. Render the scene (see Figure 5).

9. Select the **Transparency** checkbox in the **Attribute Manager** > **Basic** tab. Copy the texture from the **Color** tab and then paste it on the **Transparency** tab > **Texture** parameter. In the **Layer** shader settings, delete the **Colorize** layer. Render the scene (see Figure 6).

5

6

10. Select the **Glow** checkbox in the **Attribute Manager > Basic** tab. Clear the **Reflectance** checkbox. In the **Glow** tab, change **Inner Strength** to **200**, **Outer Strength** to **300**, **Radius** to **5**, **Random** to **78**, and **Frequency** to **5**. Render the scene (see Figure 7).

7

Glow

The **Glow** channel is utilized to impart a glow to pixels. However, the glow is not visible through reflections or transparent objects, and it does not function as a light source, therefore, it does not illuminate the scene or cast shadows. The maximum resolution that can be affected by the glow is **4000 x 4000** pixels. The **Inner Strength** and **Outer Strength** settings determine the intensity of the glow over the surface of the material and at the edges, respectively. The **Radius** setting specifies the distance that the glow can expand beyond the surface boundary. You can also adjust the intensity of the glow at each animation frame by defining a **Random** percentage. The **Frequency** setting determines the frequency at which the glow radius changes, in combination with the **Random** setting.

CREATING RUST MATERIAL

In this tutorial, we will create rust material.

Summary	
Topics	Getting Started Creating the Material
Resources folder	**creating-materials**
Start file	**shadeGeo.c4d**
Final file	**rust-finish.c4d**

Getting Started

Start Cinema 4D and open the **shadeGeo.c4d** file.

Creating the Material

Follow these steps:

1. Double-click in the **Material Manager** to create a new material. Rename the material as **matRust**. Apply the material to the **Geo-1** and **Geo-2** objects in the **Object Manager**.

2. In the **Color** tab, click **Texture > Triangle** button and then choose **Layer** from the popup menu. Click the **Layer** button to open the **Layer** shader settings.

3. In the **Layer** shader settings, click **Shader** and then choose **Fusion** from the popup. In the **Fusion** shader setting, click **Blend Channel > Triangle** button and then load the **rustPaint.jpg** using the **Load Image** option. Click **Base Channel > Triangle** button and then load the **rust.jpg** using the **Load Image** option.

4. Change **Mode** to **Darken** and then select the **Use Mask** checkbox. Click **Mask Channel > Triangle** button and then choose **Filter** from the popup. Then, in the **Filter** shader settings, click **Texture > Triangle** button and then load **scratchesMask.jpg**. Change **Contrast** to **72**. In the **Fusion** shader settings, select the **Invert Mask** checkbox. Render the scene (see Figure 1).

1

Fusion

The **Fusion** shader provides the ability to merge two textures using various blending modes commonly found in image editing software like Photoshop. You can control the intensity of the mix between the two textures by adjusting the opacity of the blend channel. Furthermore, the mask channel can be utilized to restrict the blend to specific areas. The **Base Channel** setting determines the texture for the bottom layer, while the **Blend Channel** setting specifies the top layer in the fusion.

5. In the **Layer** shader settings, click **Shader** and then choose **Noise** from the popup. In the **Noise** shader settings, change **Noise** to **Nutous**, **Octaves** to **6**, and **Global Scale** to **26**. Change **Contrast** to **48**, **Low Clip** to **0**, and **High Clip** to **30**.

6. Change **Color 1** to **HSV (31, 74, 85)** and **Color 2** to **HSV (31, 74, 30)**. In the **Layer** shader settings, change blending mode to **Multiply** and **Strength** to **30** for the **Noise** layer. Render the scene (see Figure 2).

7. Select the **Bump** checkbox in the **Attribute Manager > Basic** tab and clear the **Reflectance** checkbox. In the **Bump** tab, click **Texture > Triangle** button and then choose **Filter** from the popup menu. Copy the texture from the **Color** tab and then paste it on the **Filter** shader settings > **Texture** parameter.

8. In the **Filter** shader settings, select the **Colorize** checkbox and then change **Contrast** to **48**. In the **Bump** tab, change **Strength** to **40**. Render the scene (see Figure 3).

2

3

CREATING BROWN LEATHER MATERIAL

In this tutorial, we will create brown leather material.

Summary	
Topics	Getting Started Creating the Material
Resources folder	**creating-materials**
Start file	**shadeGeo.c4d**
Final file	**leather-finish.c4d**

Getting Started

Start Cinema 4D and open the **shadeGeo.c4d** file.

Creating the Material

Follow these steps:

1. Double-click in the **Material Manager** to create a new material. Rename the material as **matLeather**. Apply the material to the **Geo-1** and **Geo-2** objects in the **Object Manager**.

2. In the **Color** tab, click the **Texture > Triangle** button and then load the **brownLeather.jpg** using the **Load Image** option.

3. In the **Reflectance** tab, change **Type** to **Beckmann**, **Attenuation** to **Average**, **Roughness** to **10**, **Reflection Strength** to **23**, and **Specular Strength** to **0**. In the **Layer Fresnel** area, change **Fresnel** to **Dielectric** and **IOR** to **1.8**. Render the scene (see Figure 1).

4. Select the **Bump** checkbox in the **Attribute Manager > Basic** tab. In the **Bump** tab, click the **Texture > Triangle** button and then choose **Filter** from the popup menu. In the **Filter** shader settings, click **Texture > Triangle** button and then load the **brownLeather_bump.jpg** using the **Load Image** option. Now, change **Contrast** to **39**. In the **Bump** tab, change **Strength** to **27**. Render the scene (see Figure 2).

CREATING CONCRETE MATERIAL

In this tutorial, we will create concrete material.

Summary	
Topics	Getting Started Creating the Material
Resources folder	**creating-materials**
Start file	**shadeGeo.c4d**
Final file	**concrete-finish.c4d**

Getting Started

Start Cinema 4D and open the **shadeGeo.c4d** file.

Creating the Material

Follow these steps:

1. Double-click in the **Material Manager** to create a new material. Rename the material as **matConcrete**. Apply the material to the **Geo-1** and **Geo-2** objects in the **Object Manager**.

2. In the **Color** tab, click the **Texture > Triangle** button and then choose **Filter** from the popup menu. In the **Filter** shader settings, click **Texture > Triangle** button and then load the **concreteBare_Diffuse.jpg** using the **Load Image** option. Now, change **Contrast** to **8**.

3. In the **Color** tab, change **Mode** to **Oren-Nayar**, **Diffuse Falloff** to **-20**, and **Roughness** to **27**.

4. In the **Reflectance** channel, change **Type** to **Oren-Nayar (Diffuse)**. Change **Roughness** to **0**, **Reflection Strength** to **27**, and **Specular Strength** to **0**. In the **LAYER COLOR** area, click **Texture > Triangle** button and then load the **concreteBare_Reflection.jpg** using the **Load Image** option.

5. Select the **Normal** checkbox in the **Attribute Manager > Basic** tab. In the **Normal** tab, click **Texture > Triangle** button and then load the **concreteBare_Normal.jpg** using the **Load Image** option. Render the scene (see Figure 1).

6. Select the **Displacement** checkbox in the **Attribute Manager > Basic** tab. In the **Displacement** tab, click **Texture > Triangle** button and then load the **concreteBare_Displacement.jpg** using the **Load Image** option. Change **Strength** to **19** and **Height** to **2**. Also, select the **Sub Polygon Displacement** checkbox. Render the scene (see Figure 2).

1

2

CREATING RED BRICK MATERIAL

In this tutorial, we will create red brick material.

Summary	
Topics	Getting Started Creating the Material
Resources folder	**creating-materials**
Start file	**shadeGeo.c4d**
Final file	**brick-finish.c4d**

Getting Started

Start Cinema 4D and open the **shadeGeo.c4d** file.

Creating the Material

Follow these steps:

1. Double-click in the **Material Manager** to create a new material. Rename the material as **matBrick**. Apply the material to the **Geo-1** and **Geo-2** objects in the **Object Manager**. In the **Color** tab, click the **Texture > Triangle** button and then load the **redBrick.png** using the **Load Image** option. Change **Model** to **Oren-Nayar**, **Diffuse Falloff** to **-24**, and **Roughness** to **52**.

2. In the **Reflectance** tab, change **Type** to **Beckmann**, **Attenuation** to **Average**, **Roughness** to **0**, **Reflection Strength** to **20**, and **Specular Strength** to **0**.

3. In the **LAYER COLOR** area, click the **Texture > Triangle** button and then choose **Filter** from the popup menu. In the **Filter** shader settings, click **Texture > Triangle** button and then load the **redBrickGray.jpg** using the **Load Image** option. Now, change **Brightness** to **-39** and **Contrast** to **0**. Render the scene (see Figure 1).

4. Select the **Bump** checkbox in the **Attribute Manager > Basic** tab. In the **Bump** channel, click the **Texture > Triangle** button and then choose **Effects > Normalizer** from the popup menu. In the **Normalizer** shader settings, click **Texture > Triangle** button and then load the **redBrickGray.png** using the **Load Image** option. In the **Bump** tab, change **Strength** to **94**. Render the scene (see Figure 2).

1

2

CREATING LEATHER MATERIAL - 2

In this tutorial, we will create leather material.

Summary	
Topics	Getting Started Creating the Material

Summary	
Resources folder	**creating-materials**
Start file	**shadeGeo.c4d**
Final file	**leather2-finish.c4d**

Getting Started

Start Cinema 4D and open the **shadeGeo.c4d** file.

Creating the Material

Follow these steps:

1. Double-click in the **Material Manager** to create a new material. Rename the material as **matLeather2**. Apply the material to the **Geo-1** and **Geo-2** objects in the **Object Manager**.

2. In the **Color** tab, click the **Texture > Triangle** button and then load the **Leather_Texture.jpg** using the **Load Image** option.

3. Select the **Diffusion** checkbox in the **Attribute Manager > Basic** tab. In the **Diffusion** tab, click the **Texture > Triangle** button and then choose **Noise** from the popup menu. Click the **Noise** button to open the **Noise** shader settings. Change **Noise** to **Gaseous**, **Octaves** to **8**, and **Global Scale** to **1600**. Change **Brightness** to **42**, and **Contrast** to **4**.

4. In the **Diffusion** tab, change **Mix Mode** to **Multiply** and **Mix Strength** to **72** and also select the **Affect Reflection** checkbox. Render the scene (see Figure 1).

WHAT JUST HAPPENED?
*In the **Color** channel, I have multiplied the **Noise** shader with the color values but it only affects the color values. It does not affect channels such as **Reflectance**. You can use the **Diffusion** channel to give material a used look. Make sure that you select the **Affect Specular** and **Affect Reflection** checkboxes for the **Diffusion** channel.*

5. In the **Reflectance** tab, rename the **Default Specular** layer to **HighLights**. Change **Type** to **GGX**, **Attenuation** to **Average**, **Roughness** to **56**, **Reflection Strength** to **0**, and **Specular Strength** to **90**. In the **LAYER FRESNEL** area, change **Fresnel** to **Dielectric** and **IOR** to **1.3**.

6. In the **LAYER COLOR** area, change **Color** to **HSV (0, 39, 100)**. Create a new **GGX** layer and then rename it as **Reflections**. Change **Attenuation** to **Additive**, **Roughness** to **37**, **Reflection Strength** to **23**, and **Specular Strength** to **11**. In the **LAYER FRESNEL** area, change **Fresnel** to **Dielectric** and **IOR** to **1.3**. Render the scene (see Figure 2).

WHAT JUST HAPPENED?
I have also used two reflection layers for creating realistic diffuse reflection of the leather. The ***HighLights*** *layer controls the highlight properties whereas the* ***Reflections*** *layer controls the reflective properties.*

7. Select the **Bump** checkbox in the **Attribute Manager > Basic** tab. In the **Bump** tab, click the **Texture > Triangle** button and then choose **Noise** from the popup menu. Click the **Noise** button to open the **Noise** shader settings. Change **Noise** to **Gaseous**, **Octaves** to **8**, and **Global Scale** to **350**. In the **Bump** tab, change **Strength** to **16**. Render the scene (see Figure 3).

8. Select the **Normal** checkbox in the **Attribute Manager > Basic** tab. In the **Normal** tab, click the **Texture > Triangle** button and then choose **Effects > Normalizer** from the popup menu. In the **Normalizer** shader settings, click **Texture > Triangle** button and then load the **Leather_Texture.jpg** using the **Load Image** option. In the **Normalizer** shader settings, change **Filter** to **Sobel 4x** and **Strength** to **190**. Render the scene (see Figure 4).

CREATING CAR PAINT MATERIAL

In this tutorial, we will create car paint material.

Summary	
Topics	Getting Started Creating the Material
Resources folder	**creating-materials**
Start file	**shadeGeo.c4d**
Final file	**car-paint-finish.c4d**

Getting Started

Start Cinema 4D and open the **shadeGeo.c4d** file.

Creating the Material

Follow these steps:

1. Double-click in the **Material Manager** to create a new material. Rename the material as **matCarPaint**. Apply the material to the **Geo-1** and **Geo-2** objects in the **Object Manager**.

2. Clear all checkboxes except the **Reflectance** checkbox in the **Attribute Manager** > **Basic** tab. In the **Reflectance** tab, rename **Default Specular** layer to **Layer 1**. Change **Type** to **Lambertian (Diffuse)**, **Attenuation** to **Average**, **Reflection Strength** to **24**, and **Specular Strength** to **32**. In the **LAYER FRESNEL** area, change **Fresnel** to **Dielectric** and **IOR** to **2.3**.

3. In the **LAYER COLOR** area, change **Color** to **HSV (5, 93, 56)**. Render the scene (see Figure 1).

4. Add a new **Ward** reflectance layer and change blending mode to **Add** (see Figure 2). Change **Attenuation** to **Average**, **Roughness** to **64**, **Reflection Strength** to **22**, and **Specular Strength** to **22**. In the **Layer Fresnel** area, change **Fresnel** to **Dielectric** and **IOR** to **2.3**. Render the scene (see Figure 3).

5. In the **LAYER COLOR** area, change **Color** to **HSV (5, 93, 70)**. In the **LAYER MASK** area, click the **Texture** > **Triangle** button and then choose **Noise** from the popup menu. Click the **Noise** button to open the **Noise** shader settings. Change **Noise** to **Cell Voronoi** and **Global Scale** to **2**.

6. Add a new **Beckmann** reflectance layer. Change **Attenuation** to **Average**, **Roughness** to **0**, **Reflection Strength** to **100**, and **Specular Strength** to **0**. In the **LAYER FRESNEL** area, change **Fresnel** to **Dielectric** and **IOR** to **1.52**. Render the scene (see Figure 4).

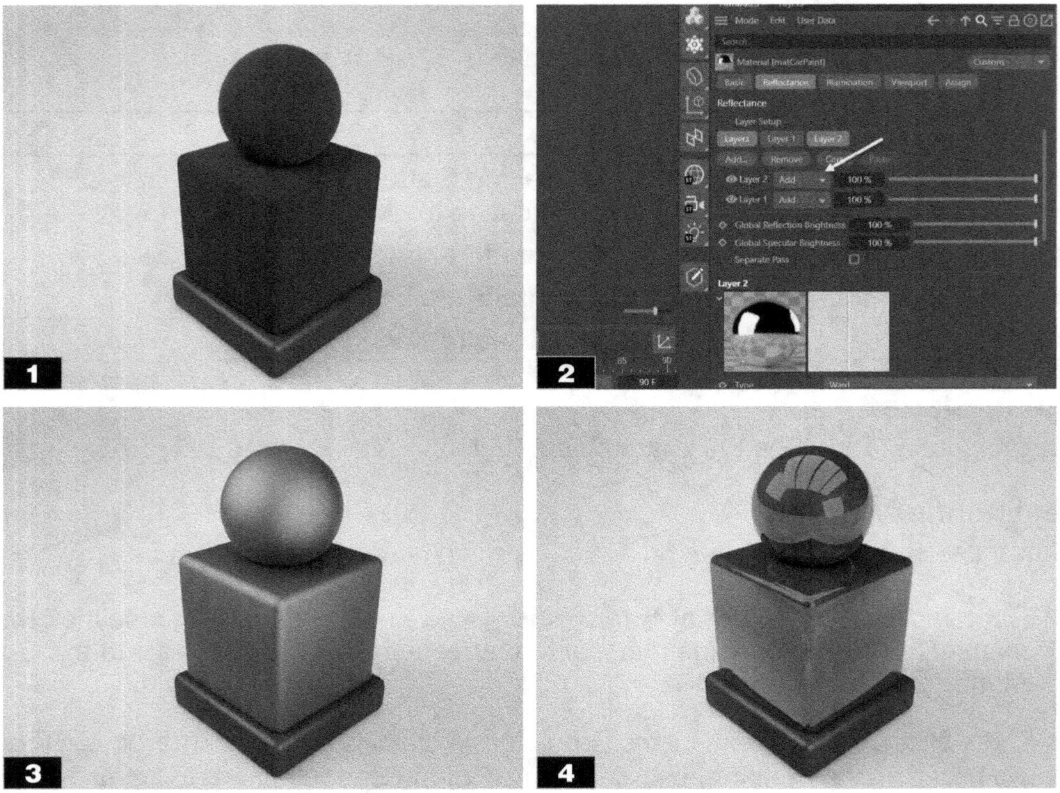

WHAT JUST HAPPENED?

*Typically, a car paint material is composed of three layers of reflection: base coat, metallic particles, and clear coat. To create a car paint material, this tutorial uses three reflectance layers. The first layer, **Lambertian (Diffuse)**, is used for smooth surfaces. For rough surfaces, the **Oren-Nayer (Diffuse)** type should be used. The **Roughness** parameter is only applicable to the **Oren-Nayer (Diffuse)** type.*

*The **LAYER COLOR** area has the **Color** parameter that sets the color for this layer. To reduce the contrast from center to edges, I have set the **IOR** to **2.3** for this layer. The second reflectance layer is masked with a noise shader to create a metallic particle effect, while the third reflectance layer simulates the clear coat effect. To achieve a perfect reflective surface, an **IOR** value of **1.52** is used.*

CREATING RUBBER MATERIAL

In this tutorial, we will create rubber material.

Summary	
Topics	Getting Started Creating the Material

Summary	
Resources folder	**creating-materials**
Start file	**shadeGeo.c4d**
Final file	**rubber-finish.c4d**

Getting Started

Start Cinema 4D and open the **shadeGeo.c4d** file.

Creating the Material

Follow these steps:

1. Double-click in the **Material Manager** to create a new material. Rename the material as **matRubber**. Apply the material to the **Geo-1** and **Geo-2** objects in the **Object Manager**. In the **Color** tab, change **Color** to **HSV (38, 2, 17)**. Change **Model** to **Oren-Nayar**, **Diffuse Falloff** to **30** and **Roughness** to **25**.

2. Select the **Normal** checkbox in the **Attribute Manager > Basic** tab. In the **Normal** tab, click the **Texture > Triangle** button and then choose **Effects > Normalizer** from the popup menu. In the **Normalizer** shader settings, click **Texture > Triangle** button and choose **Layer** from the popup menu.

3. In the **Layer** shader settings, click **Shader** and then choose **Surfaces > Tiles** from the popup menu. In the **Tiles** shader settings, change **Tiles Color 1** and **Tiles Color 2** to white. Change **Grout Width** to **9**, **Bevel Width** to **86**, and **Global Scale** to **8**. Render the scene (see Figure 1).

4. In the **Layer** shader settings, click **Effect** and then choose **Transform** from the popup menu. In the **Transform** shader settings, change **Angle** to **42**. In the **Normalizer** shader settings, change **Filter** to **Sobel 4x** and **Strength** to **242**. In the **Normal** tab, change **Strength** to **72**. Render the scene (see Figure 2).

1

2

5. In the **Reflectance** tab, rename **Default Specular** layer to **Layer 1**. Change **Type** to **Phong**, **Attenuation** to **Additive**, **Roughness** to **66**, **Reflection Strength** to **100**, and **Specular Strength** to **100**. In the **LAYER FRESNEL** area, change **Fresnel** to **Dielectric** and **IOR** to **1.52**. Change **Layer 1**'s strength to **12**. Render the scene (see Figure 3).

6. Create another **Phong** layer and set its blending mode to **Add**. Change **Attenuation** to **Average**, **Roughness** to **30**, **Reflection Strength** to **18**, and **Specular Strength** to **20**. In the **LAYER FRESNEL** area, change **Fresnel** to **Dielectric** and **IOR** to **2**. Change **Layer 1**'s strength to **10**. Change **Layer 2**'s strength to **13**. Render the scene (see Figure 4).

3

4

CREATING WOOD MATERIAL
In this tutorial, we will create wood material.

Summary	
Topics	Getting Started Creating the Material
Resources folder	**creating-materials**
Start file	**shadeGeo.c4d**
Final file	**wood-finish.c4d**

Getting Started
Start Cinema 4D and open the **shadeGeo.c4d** file.

Creating the Material
Follow these steps:

1. Double-click in the **Material Manager** to create a new material. Rename the material as **matWood**. Apply the material to the **Geo-1** and **Geo-2** objects in the **Object Manager**. In **Basic** tab, clear the **Color** checkbox.

2. In the **Reflectance** tab, change **Type** to **GGX** and **Attenuation** to **Average**. Expand the **Roughness** area and then click the **Texture > Triangle** button and then choose **Layer** from the popup menu.

3. In the **Layer** shader settings, click **Image** and then load the **scratch - 2.jpg**. Click **Shader** and then choose **Fresnel** from the popup menu. Change mode to **Multiply** and then change strength to **31**.

4. In the **Reflectance** tab, change **Roughness** to **20**, **Reflection Strength** to **100**, and **Specular Strength** to **5**. In the **LAYER COLOR** area, change **Brightness** to **59**. Render the scene (see Figure 1).

5. In **Basic** tab, select the **Color** checkbox. In the **Color** tab, click the **Texture > Triangle** button and then load the **woodCabinetDiff.png** using the **Load Image** option.

6. In the **Reflectance** tab, expand the **Bump Strength** area and then change **Mode** to **Custom Normal Map**. Click the **Custom Texture > Triangle** button and then choose **Effects > Normalizer** from the popup menu. In the **Normalizer** shader settings, click **Texture > Triangle** button and then load the **woodCabinetBump.png** using the **Load Image** option. In the **Normalizer** tab, change **Strength** to **250**. Render the scene (see Figure 2).

7. In the **Reflectance** tab, change **Bump Strength** to **90**. In the **LAYER COLOR** area, click the **Texture > Triangle** button and then choose **Layer** from the popup menu. In the **Layer** shader settings, click **Image** and then load the **woodCabinetGloss.png**.

8. Click **Shader** and then choose **Fresnel** from the popup menu. Change blending mode to **Lighten** and strength to **29**. Render the scene (see Figure 3).

9. In the **Reflectance** tab > **Layer FRESNEL** area, change **Fresnel** to **Dielectric** and **IOR** to **1.5**. Render the scene (see Figure 4).

3

4

CHAPTER 6: NODE-BASED MATERIALS

The **Node Editor** offers several modes based on the **Node** type. When you enable a **Node** material, for example, the **Material** mode is used. The **Scene** mode will be utilized if you enable the **Scene Manager**. In the **Material** mode, the **Node Editor** can be used to create materials for the **Standard** and **Physical** material systems.

The **Node Editor** always shows the **Node** Material that is presently selected. The general direction of data flow is always from left to right. Anything on the far right must always end in a **Material** node.

The **Node Editor** can be opened using the following methods:

- Double-clicking on the **Node** material.
- Navigating to the **Attribute Manager > Basic** tab of the **Node** material and then clicking on the **Node Editor** button.
- **RMB** clicking on the material node and then choosing **Open Material in the Node Editor** from the context menu. You can also press **Shift Alt F2** to execute this command.

This system integrates seamlessly with the existing material system and may be used to specify complex material properties that the old material system cannot create. Due to the fact that nodes are built on a physically-correct concept, you will observe while using the **Node Editor** that several material channels no longer exist. In this approach, diffuse shading is calculated using dispersed reflections using physically-based **BSDF** (Bidirectional Scattering Distribution Function) shading, which is equivalent to a physical material.

BSDF
*The term "**BSDF**" refers for "**Bidirectional Scattering Distribution Function**", a method that simulates the physically correct transmission and reflection behavior of surfaces, or physically accurate and realistic rendering of reflections and transparency.*

NODE EDITOR

Figure 1 shows the **Node Editor** interface.

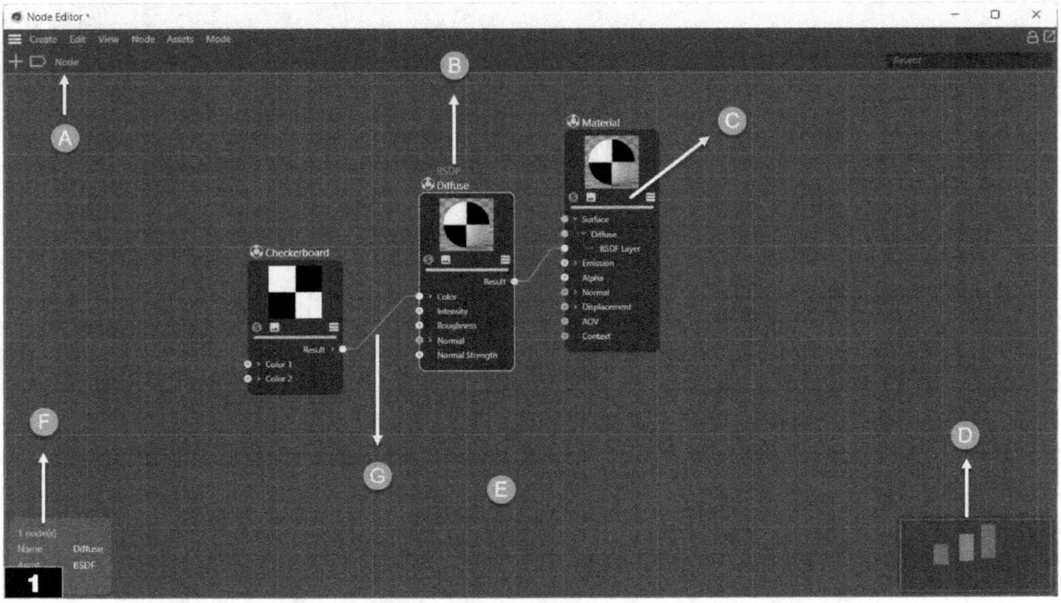

The following table summarizes these **Node Editor**'s interface elements:

Node Editor elements	
Label	**Name**
A	Node path
B	Node Name or custom name
C	Colored nodes (Basic tab)
D	Navigator
E	Node view
F	Info
G	Connection

NAVIGATING NODE EDITOR

To move in the **Node Editor**, press one of the following combinations and then drag the mouse: **MMB**, **1 LMB**, or **Alt MMB**. To zoom, press one of the following combinations and then drag the mouse: **Alt RMB** or **2 RMB**. To frame all or selected nodes, press **H** or **S**. These commands are also accessible from the **View** menu of the **Node Editor**.

TOUCHSCREENS
*If you have enabled **Touchscreen** in the **Preferences** window > **Input Devices** category, you can move vertically by scrolling the mouse wheel. To move horizontally, use **Shift** mouse wheel. Use **Ctrl** mouse wheel for zooming in or out.*

CREATING NODES

Drag a node from the **Node Commander** window to the **Node** view to create a new node that has no connections. The **C** hotkey can be used to invoke the **Node Commander** window. Ports will be linked immediately if you drag the node onto an existing node's input port. If you drag a node to a connection (a wire connecting two ports), it will be included in the connection if the port is compatible.

As an alternative, you can open the **Node Commander** window by choosing **Create > Add Nodes** from the **Node Editor** menubar, and then drag nodes from there. You can also double-click on the **Node** view or press the **Add Nodes** button under the menubar to activate this window. In either of the two approaches, when you drag a node over an input port and let go of the mouse button, a small menu will appear in case there are multiple output ports to choose from. From there, you can pick the output port of the start node that you want to link.

Nodes can be linked together using the connector icon which is accessible for virtually every input category within the **Attribute Manager**. To initiate the process, click on the connector icon to trigger a context menu. Next, choose the **Connect Node** option to view a list of all available nodes, then select the one you want (refer to Figure 2). You can also bring up the context menu by right-clicking on the connector symbol. Once you have selected a node, it will be generated and connected to the input right away.

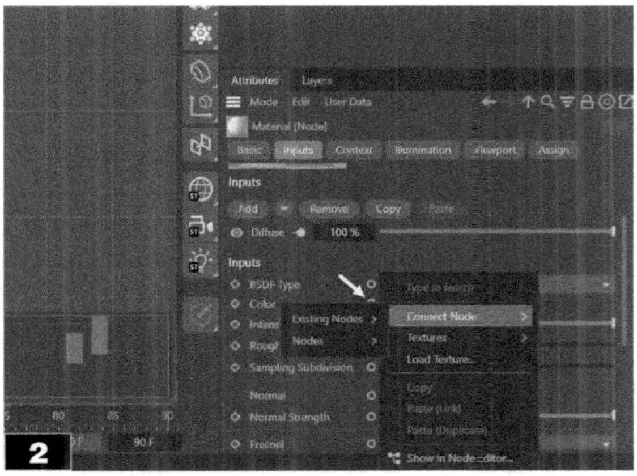

2

USING BITMAPS
*If you have a bitmap outside of Cinema 4D, you can simply drag it and drop it onto either the **Node** view or a port. This action will create an Image node that is automatically linked to the corresponding bitmap.*

CONNECTIONS
Cinema 4D provides feedback on whether a connection is feasible or not as you make connections. If you hover your cursor over the port that you intend to link, the prospective connection will be either bright (indicating that it is viable) or dark (indicating that it is not viable).

CONNECTIONS
It's important to note that not all output ports are compatible with all input ports, and therefore, incompatible nodes cannot be connected to each other.

MOVING NODES

To move nodes in the **Node Editor**, simply click on a node and drag it to the desired location. If you have selected multiple nodes, you can move them as a group. When you move the selected nodes towards the edges of the **Node** view, the view will automatically scroll in response.

CONNECTING NODES

To enable the transfer of data between nodes, they need to be linked together. To establish a connection, the output (typically located on the right side of the node) of one node must be linked to the input (usually located on the left side of the node) of another node. To create the connection, simply click once on the output node and then click once on the input node (or vice versa).

- You can also click and drag from the first port to the second and then release the mouse button.
- Alternatively, you can drop the connection onto the center of a node, which will prompt a list of all input and output ports to appear (refer to Figure 3), giving you the option to choose the appropriate port. If you drop the connection onto an empty space in the **Node Editor**, input/output ports can be created for groups (refer to Figure 4).

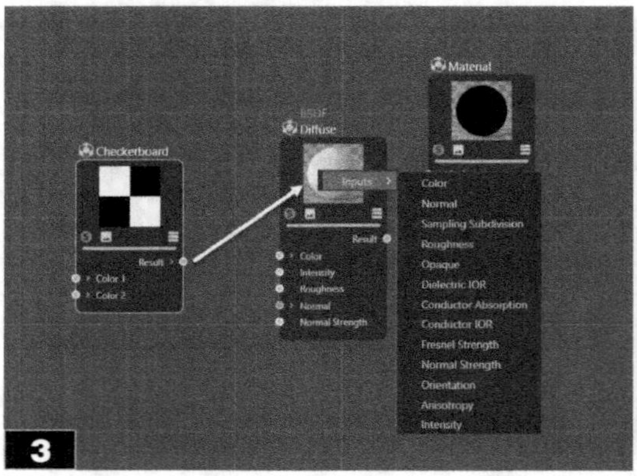

3

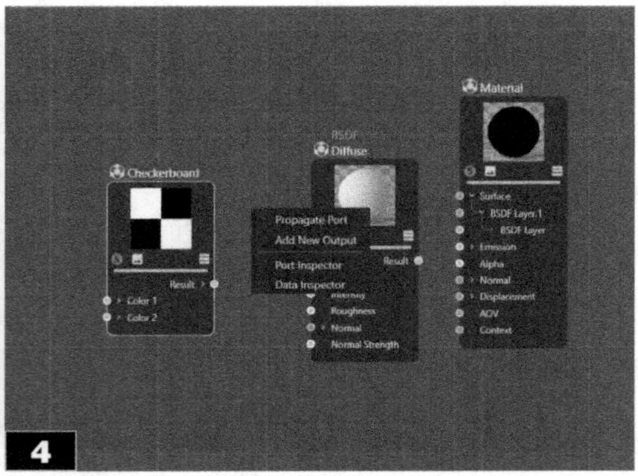

4

CONNECTION MODE
*Once you click on the first port that you wish to connect, you enter the connection mode. To exit this mode, simply press the **Esc** key.*

Updating a connection is also possible by dragging a node over an existing connector line. When the color of the line brightens (refer to Figure 5), it indicates that the node can be released to update the original connection (refer to Figure 6).

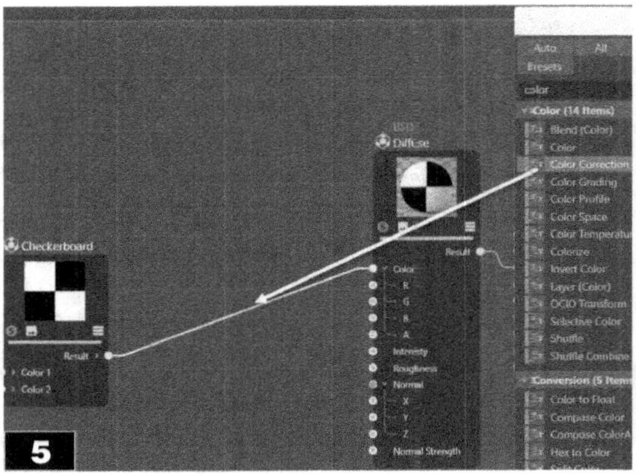

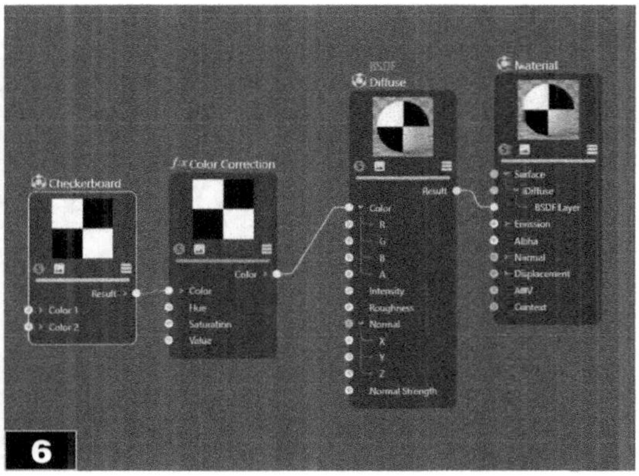

Optimizing Connections

As you build a more intricate node network, connector lines may cross over other nodes, which can make it harder to read. To enhance the clarity of the node network, you can use a detour point. To create a detour point, simply **Ctrl LMB** click on a connection (refer to Figures 7 and 8). To remove the detour point, select it and press **Del**. When you hover your cursor near a detour point, two port points will appear (refer to Figure 8), allowing you to drag a new connection by clicking on one of them.

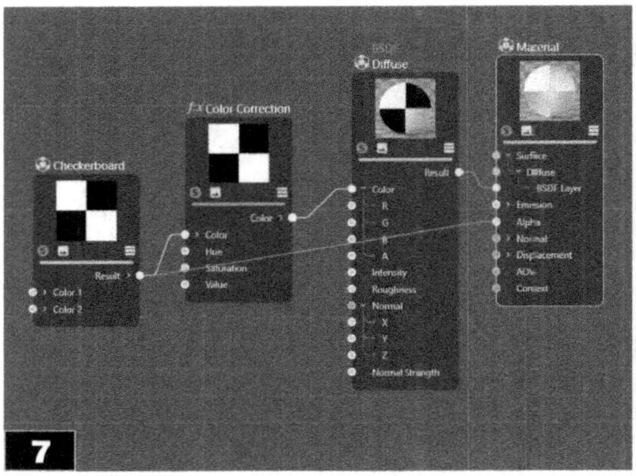

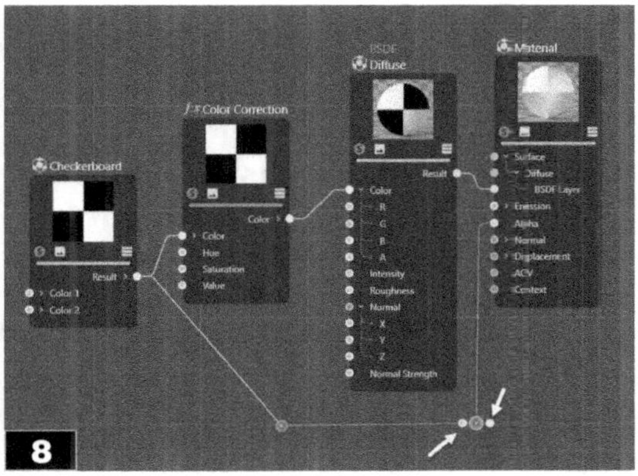

You can duplicate existing detour points by **Ctrl** dragging and dropping them to a new location in the **Node Editor**. Once placed outside of an existing connector line, the free-standing detour point can be connected to a node input, allowing it to be used for inputting a value (refer to Figures 9 and 10).

SELECTING/DELETING NODES

Nodes can be selected by either clicking on them individually or by dragging a rectangular selection around them. The **Shift** and **Ctrl** keys can be used to add or remove nodes from the selection, respectively. Additional editing commands are available in the **Edit** menu located in the **Node Editor** menu bar. To delete selected nodes or detour points, simply press either the **Backspace** or **Del** key.

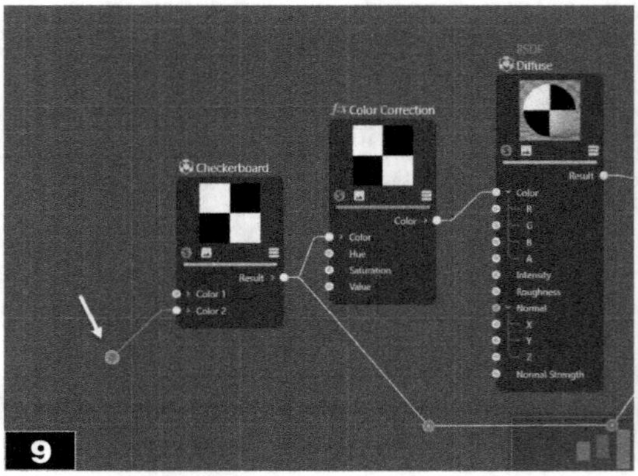

9

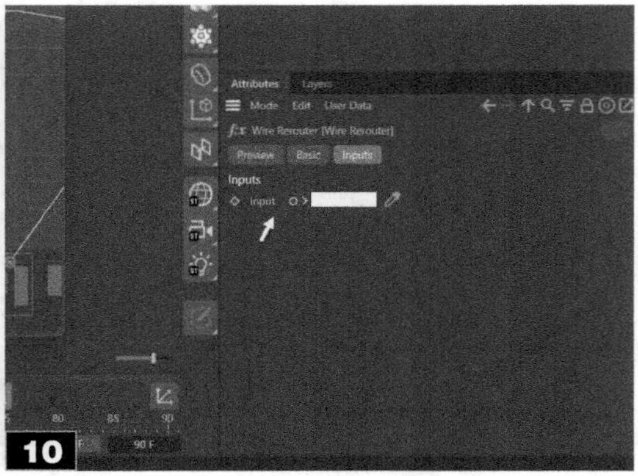

10

NODE EDITOR TITLE

At the top of the **Node Editor** view you will find the **Node Editor** title (see Figure 11). You will find the following items from left to right:

- **Add Nodes:** If you click on the **Add Nodes** button (represented by a plus symbol), it will open the **Node Commander** window. Alternatively, you can press the **C** key or double-click in the **Node** view to open the window as well.
- **Node Path:** The hierarchy tree is located next to the bookmark icon, which is currently being displayed in the **Node Editor**. The term **Scene Nodes** refers to the topmost layer of the hierarchy. If you are working on material nodes, the name of the respective material will be displayed in this area. When in the **Capsule** mode, the name of the **Asset Construction Node** being displayed will appear here. By clicking on the corresponding part of the **Node Path**, you can navigate to a higher level in the hierarchy. This follows the same principle as navigating through the hierarchy in the **Object Manager**. You can also click directly on the bookmark icon, which will open an input field for the search path.
- **Reveal:** Type in a series of characters in the **Reveal** field. Nodes that contain that specific series of characters in their name will be displayed more prominently by fading out all other nodes in the **Node Editor** (refer to Figure 12).

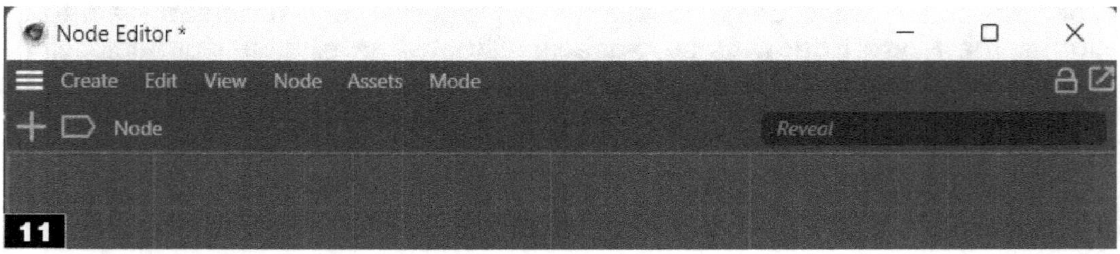

11

NAVIGATOR

The **Node Editor** view contains a navigator tool, located in the bottom-right corner (as shown in Figure 13). This tool is particularly helpful when working with complex node networks, as it enables quick navigation within the **Node** view. The navigator displays a light gray triangle indicating the currently visible section of the view. By clicking and dragging within the navigator, you can move the visible section of the **Node Editor** view.

The following nodes have a special display in the **Navigator**:

If you've customized the color of a node in the **Attribute Manager**'s **Basic** tab, those nodes will be displayed in the same color in the **Navigator** and labeled as **A** and **B** in Figure 13. Additionally, any selected nodes will appear selected in the **Navigator**, as labeled **D** in Figure 13. Group nodes will be shown with a diagonal element and labeled as **C** in Figure 13.

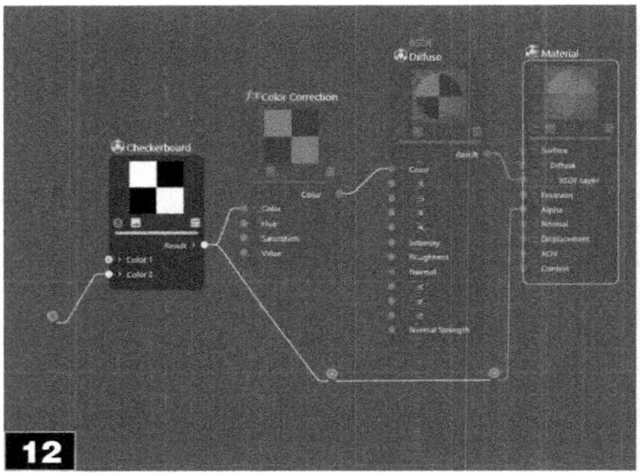

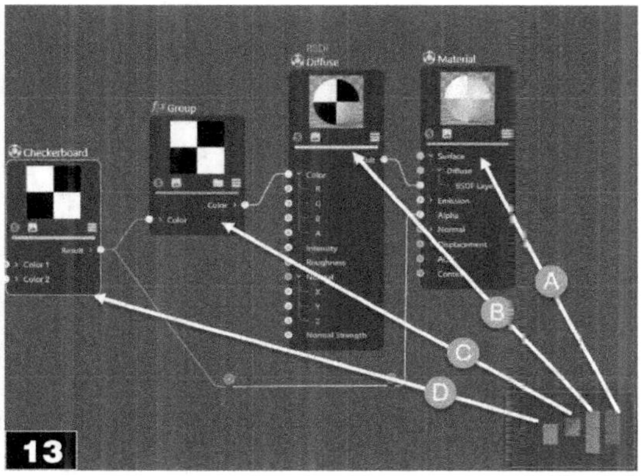

GETTING AROUND IN THE NODE EDITOR

Before we dive deep into the **Node Editor**, let's first learn some of the basics of the working with the **Node Editor**. Follow these steps:

1. Create a new scene in Cinema 4D and then choose **Create > Materials > New Node Material** from the **Material Manager** menubar (see Figure 14) or press **Ctrl Alt N**; a new node material with the name **Node** is created in the **Material Manager**. When you select the node in the **Material Manager**, its parameters will be displayed in the **Attribute Manager** (see Figure 15).

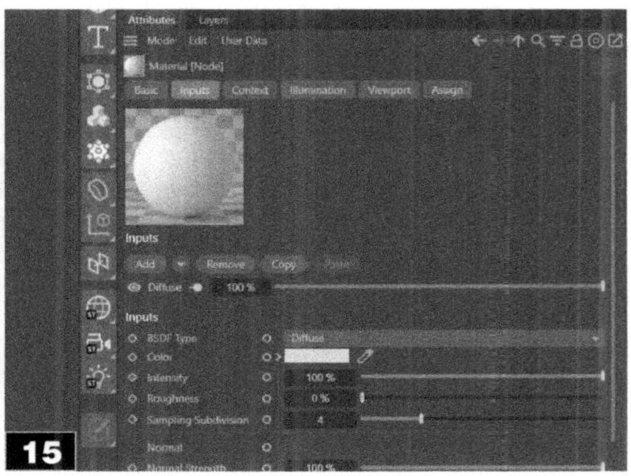

Materials

As shown in Figure 14, there are various ways to create materials in Cinema 4D. In the previous chapters, we have utilized the default material for this purpose, which is the **Standard** material. If you wish to change this default behavior, you can access the **Preferences** window and navigate to the **Material** category. From the right pane's **MATERIAL MANAGER** section, you can modify the default material by selecting a different option from the **Default Material** drop-down list, as illustrated in Figure 16.

To create a new default material, you can choose from several methods:

- Use the **New Default Material** command from the **Create** menu in the **Material Manager**, or use the shortcut **Ctrl N**.
- Double-click on an empty area of the **Material Manager**.
- Drag and drop a bitmap from the **Explorer/Finder** directly into the **Material Manager**.
- Drag and drop a color box or a color field from the **Color Chooser** into the **Material Manager**.

New PBR Material

The **New PBR Material** command in Cinema 4D functions similarly to the **New Default Material** command, with the difference being that it creates a physically accurate material. The new material is based solely on the active **Reflectance** material channel, which consists of two layers: a diffuse layer and a reflectance layer, as shown in Figure 17.

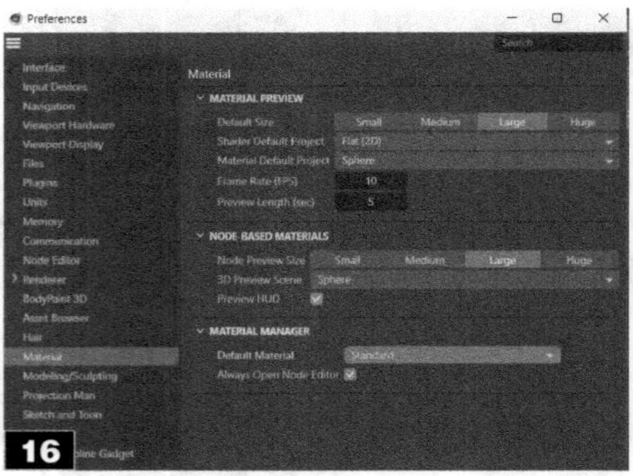
16

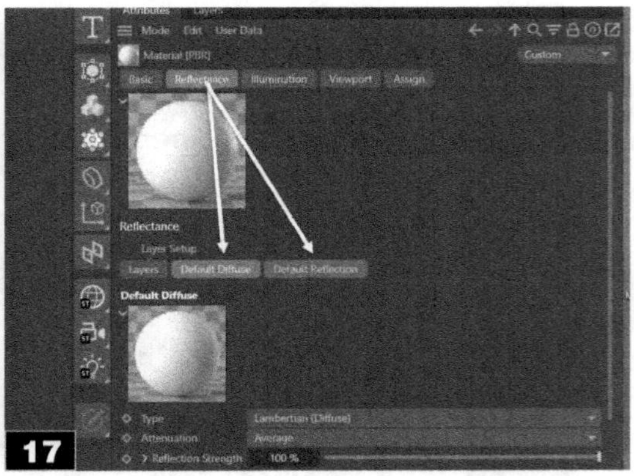
17

It is important to note that the **PBR** material system preset does not provide any additional features or functionality. It is simply a preset for creating a physically-based material with a diffuse layer and a reflectance layer. When using a **PBR** material, it is recommended to also use a **PBR** light to achieve the best results. Additionally, while **PBR** materials are compatible with all renderers, using them with older renderers may result in longer render times.

New Uber Material

The **New Uber Material** command in Cinema 4D creates a material that is node-based and easy to use. It has channels similar to those found in a **Standard** or **Physical** material. The settings of the **Uber** material can be modified in the **Attribute Manager** or by double-clicking on it in the **Material Manager** or **Material Editor** preview. The **Uber** material can also be configured directly in the **Node Editor**. It is considered a material asset, which is a saved and encapsulated arrangement of Node materials. These types of assets can be created and edited within the **Node Editor**.

Special Materials

To create special materials such as **Grass Material**, **Hair Material**, **PyroCluster Material**, **PyroCluster VolumeTracer Material**, **Shadow Catcher Material**, and **Sketch Material**, you can activate the corresponding function in Cinema 4D. Once activated, many of these materials are created automatically.

2. Double-click on the **Node** material swatch in the **Material Manager** or press **Shift Alt F2**. This action opens the **Node Editor** with two nodes displayed in the **Node Editor** view - **Diffuse** and **Material** (see Figure 18). The attributes of the selected nodes are displayed in the **Attribute Manager** (see Figure 19). Close the **Node Editor**.

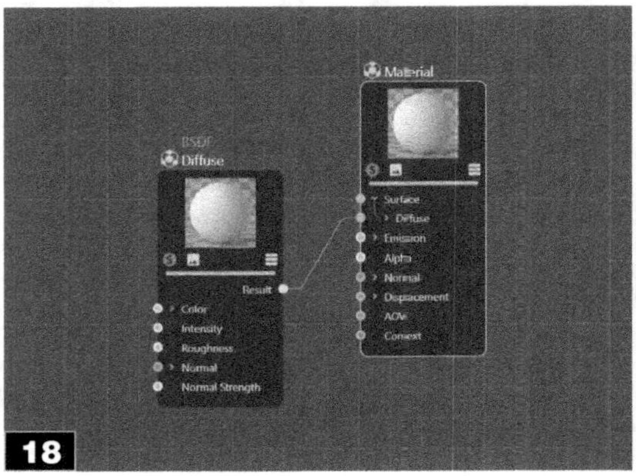

18

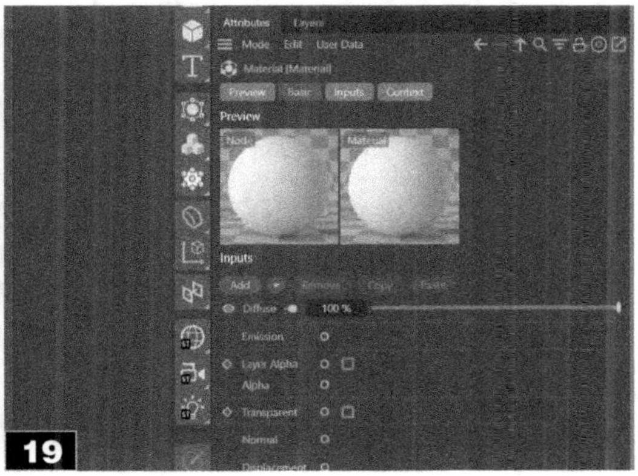

19

3. Choose **Create > Materials > New Uber Material** from the **Material Manager** menubar; a new material with the name **Uber** is created in the **Material Manager**.

4. **RMB** click on the **Uber** node and then choose **Edit** from the context menu to open the **Material Editor**. The **Uber** material can be edited in the **Node Editor** but you can also easily edit the material in the **Material Editor** or **Attribute Manager**.

5. Make sure the **Diffuse** channel is selected in the left pane and then in the right pane, click the **Color** connector and then choose **Connect Node > Nodes > Material Generator > Checkerboard** from the popup menu (see Figure 20); the **Checkerboard** node is connected to the **Color** parameter (see Figure 21).

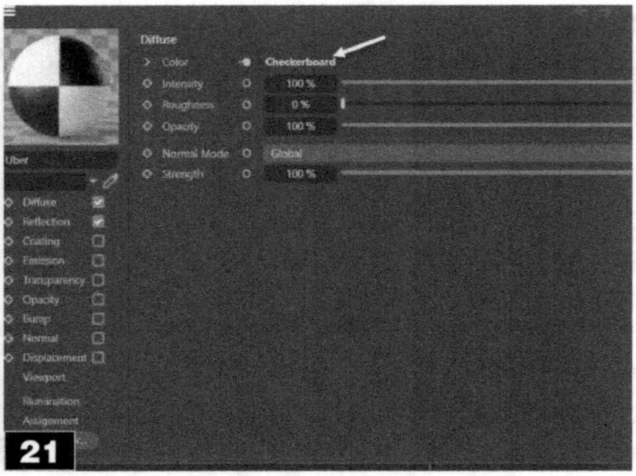

6. Click on **Checkerboard** to open the **Checkerboard** settings (see Figure 22). Select the **Diffuse** channel; notice the shape of the connector icon has changed (refer to Figure 21). Click on the icon; a popup menu will be displayed (see Figure 23). You can use the options available in the menu to farther edit the **Color** channel. For example, to replace the node, choose the **Replace Node** option, for deleting the node, choose the **Remove** option, and so on.

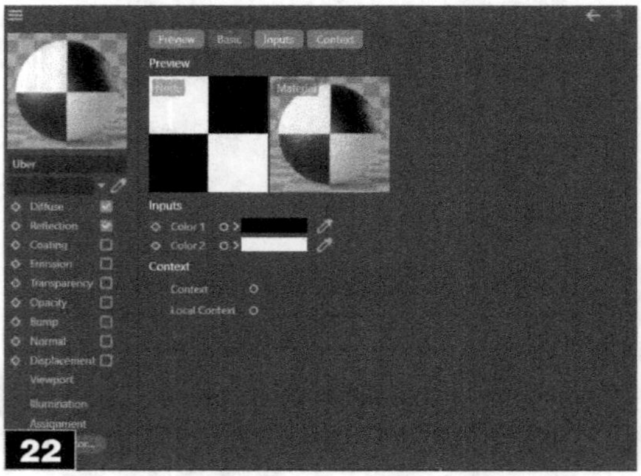

SHAPE OF THE CONNECTOR ICON
A connector icon can have three states: connected, muted, and disconnected. Figure 24 shows these states.

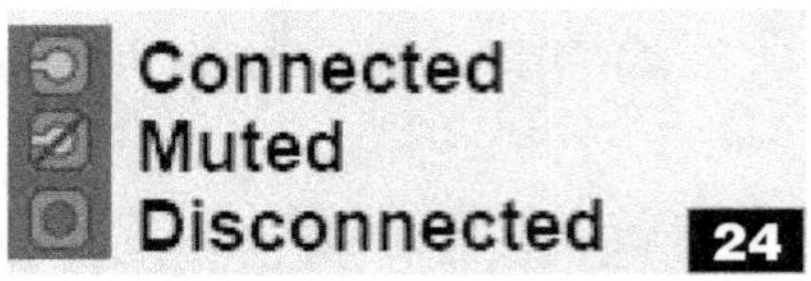

7. Click on the **Node Editor** button located at the bottom-left corner of the **Material Editor** to invoke the **Node Editor** (see Figure 25). Notice that the **Uber Material.1** and **Checkerboard** nodes are connected and displayed in the **Node** view. Close the **Node Editor** followed by the **Material Editor**.

8. Choose **Create > Node Material Presets** from the **Material Manager** menubar to display a list of materials available (see Figure 26). Select **Plastic** from the list to create a plastic material.

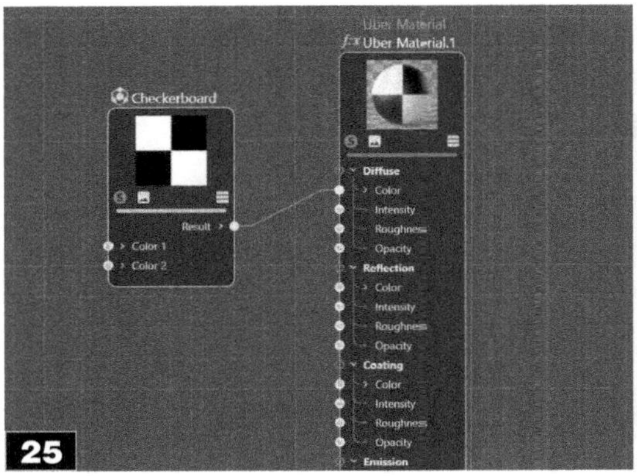

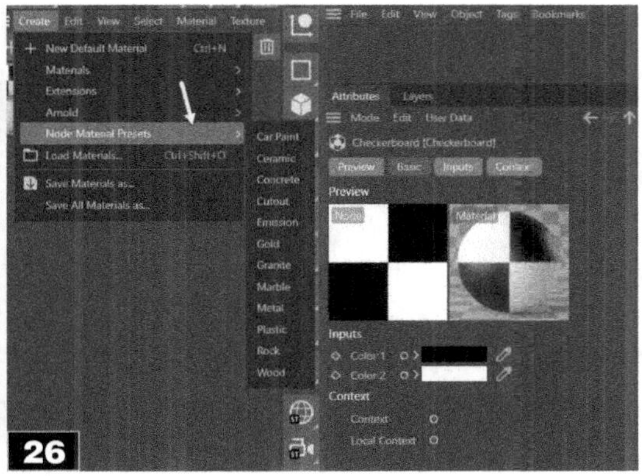

9. Close the current scene and start a new scene.

10. Create a new node material by pressing **Ctrl Alt N**. Double-click on the node in the **Material Manager** to open the **Node Editor**. Click on the empty area of the **Node** view to deselect all node. You can also choose **Edit > Deselect All** from the menubar or press **Ctrl Shift A**. All nodes can be selected using the **Ctrl A** hotkeys.

11. Select **Material** in the **Node** view; the **Material** node is highlighted with orange border in the **Node** view.

RENAMING NODES
*You can rename a node by first double-clicking on the name of node in the **Node** view and then typing a new name.*

12. **Alt RMB** drag to zoom in or out in the view. Then, **MMB** drag to pan the view and move the nodes outside the visible **Node** view. Select the **Diffuse** node and then press **S** to frame the node at the center of the **Node** view. Press **H** to frame both nodes.

13. Click on the **Material** node in the **Node** view; the information about the node is displayed in the **Info** area. Select the **Color** port of the **Diffuse** node in the view; its information will be displayed in the **Info** area.

The Info area

The **Info** area in Cinema 4D displays information related to nodes, connections, and ports.

For nodes:

- **Selection:** The number and type of selected elements. For example, Nodes: 1, and Ports: 2.
- **Name:** The name of the node as defined in the **Basic** tab.

- **Asset:** The non-modifiable asset name as it is defined internally.
- **Version:** The version of the asset, including date and time.
- **Asset ID/ID:** A unique ID for internal use.
- **Errors:** All errors will be displayed here.

Additional information for connections:

- **Selection:** The number of selected connections.
- **Port Type:** The input data type that a port accepts or the data type it itself puts out.
- **Connected Type:** The data type that flows through the connection.

Additional information for ports:

- **Port Value:** If a port has no connection, the value defined in the **Attribute Manager** will be displayed here.

14. Press **C** to open the **Node Commander** window.
15. Type **che** in the **Search** field to filter the nodes whose names contain the series of character **che**. Drag **Material Generator > Checkerboard** from the **Node Commander** to the **Node** view. Now, click drag the **Result** port of the **Checkerboard** node; a wire appears. Now, drop the wire on the **Color** port of the **Diffuse** node to make a connection (see Figure 27).
16. To delete the connection, drag and drop the wire on the empty area of the view. You can also delete the connection by first clicking on it and then pressing the **Delete** key. Another way to delete a connection is by double-clicking on the wire.
17. Delete the connection between the **Checkerboard** and **Diffuse** nodes. Click drag the **Result** port of the **Checkerboard** node and drop in the middle of the **Diffuse** node; a popup menu appears. Select **Inputs > Color** from the menu (see Figure 28) to make the connection.
18. Delete the **Checkerboard** node from the view. Then, drag **Checkerboard** from the **Nodes Commander** window and drop it on the **Color** port of the **Diffuse** node to make a connection.

CONNECTOR ICON
*You can also connect nodes using the **Attribute Manager**. Select the node in the **Node** view to display its attributes in the **Attribute Manager** and then use the connector icon of a parameter to connect a node to it.*

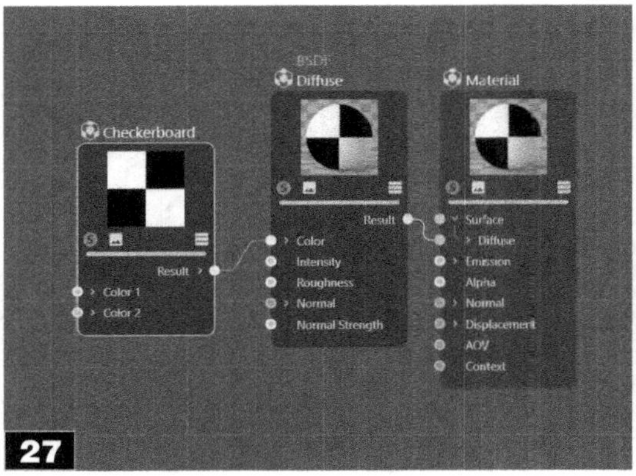

27

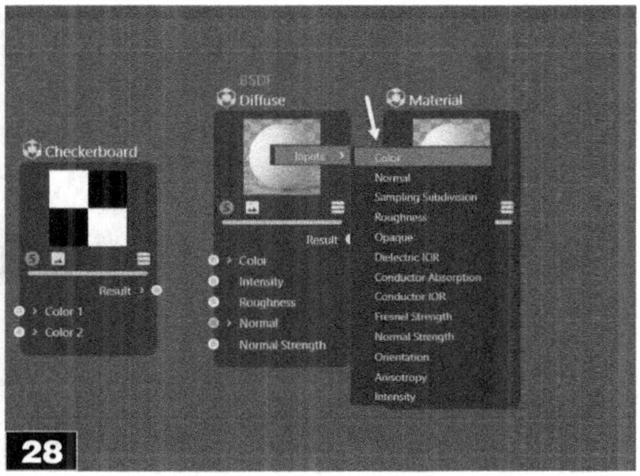

28

19. Create a **Cube** in the viewport and then assign the **Node** material from the **Material Manager** to the cube (see Figure 29).

20. In the **Node Editor**, drag **Color** > **Color** from the **Node Commander** window to the **Color 1** port of the **Checkerboard** port. In the **Attribute Manager** > **Inputs** tab, change **Input** to red. Figure 30 shows the result in the viewport.

29

30

21. In the **Node** view, click on the **Set Solo Node/Port** icon (marked as A in Figure 31) of the **Color** node to activate the solo mode for the **Color** node. Notice in viewport only red color is displayed on the cube (see Figure 32). Click on the icon again to clear the solo mode.

SOLO MODE AND OTHER OPTIONS
*You can also access the solo and other commands from the **Node** menu of the **Node Editor** menubar.*

22. Click on the **Preview** icon (marked B in Figure 31) to hide the preview of the **Color** node. Click again to show the preview.

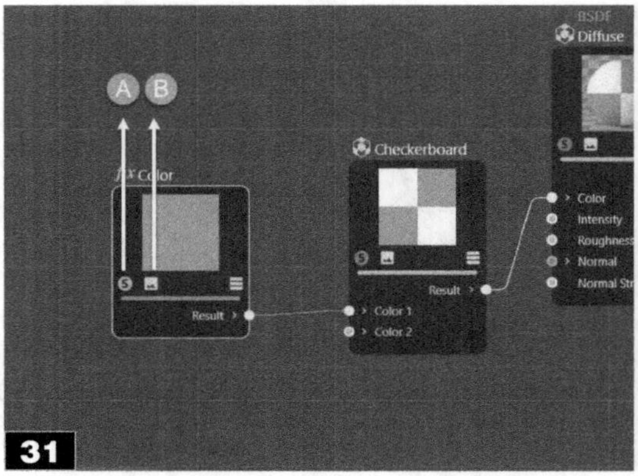

31

32

23. Select the **Color** node in the **Node** view and then in the **Basic** tab of the **Attribute Manager**, change **Color** to blue; the color is displayed in the preview area of the node as well as in the **Navigator** (see Figure 33).

Data types and color

In Figure 27, you can see that the **Diffuse** node has **Color** and **Normal** ports displayed in yellow and violet, respectively. These colors help identify the type of data associated with each port: yellow represents **Color** information, while violet represents **Normal** information. These colors can be used to identify the data type associated with the ports:

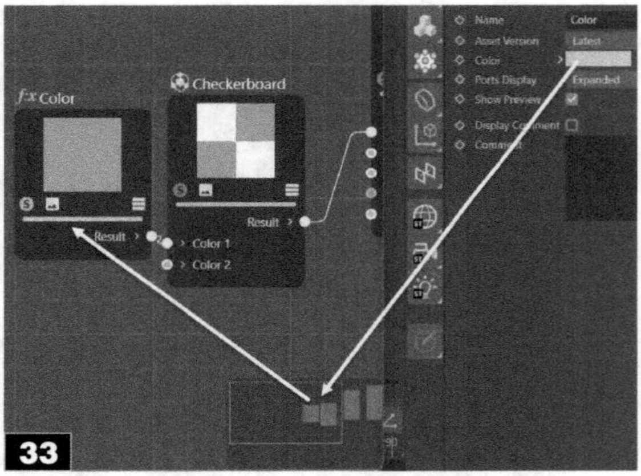

33

- **Dark gray:** Represents a container consists of various data types in a complex setting.
- **Light gray:** Represents a number integer or float value. This can be whole numbers (integers), percentages or a number with a comma value (float).
- **Yellow:** Represents color values (RGB vectors) or textures.
- **Blue:** Used for transferring data types such as **Matrix**, **Text**, **Boole**, **Array**.
- **Violet:** Represents vectors.
- **Green:** Reserved for **BSDF** layers for material nodes which can be used to define physical shading and reflectance information.

24. Select the **Color** node in the view and then choose **Edit > Duplicate** from the editor's menubar to create a copy of the node. Rename the node as **Color-2.** In the **Attribute Manager > Inputs** tab, change **Input** to green color. Then, connect **Color-2 > Result** to **Checkerboard > Color 2**.

25. Select the **Color** and **Color-2** nodes by drawing a rectangle around them and then choose **Create > Group Nodes** from the menubar (see Figure 34). Double-click on group's name and then type the new name as **color-group**. Similarly, rename the **Result** ports of the group as **Red** and **Green**, respectively (see Figure 35).

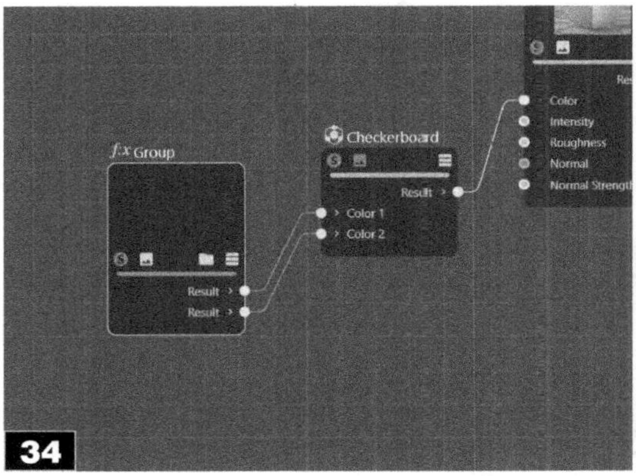

34

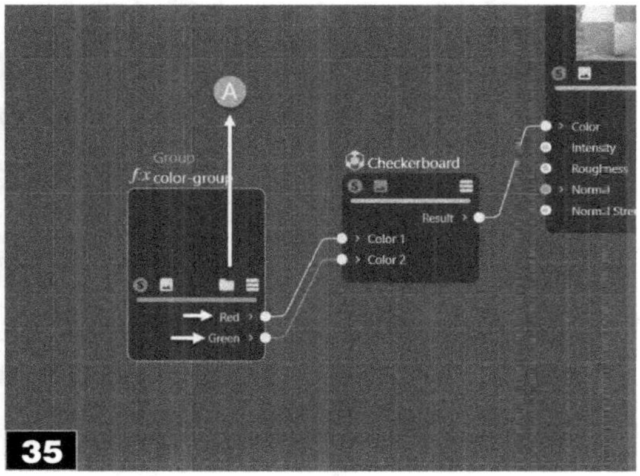

35

26. Click on the icon marked **A** in Figure 35 to expand the group (see Figure 36). **RMB** click on the empty area of the **Node** view and then choose **Add Input > Add New Input** from the context menu to add a new Input port (see Figure 37).

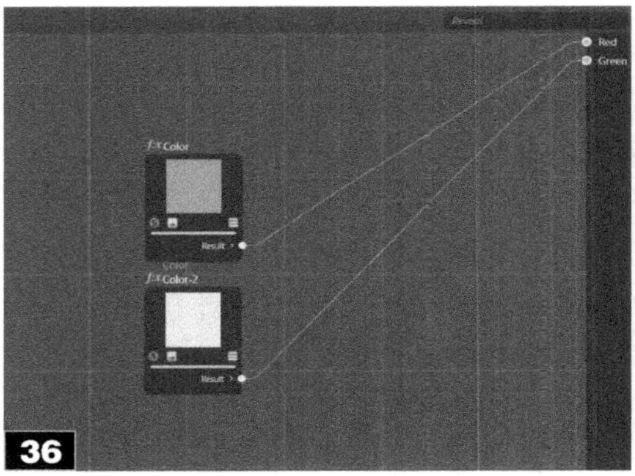

36

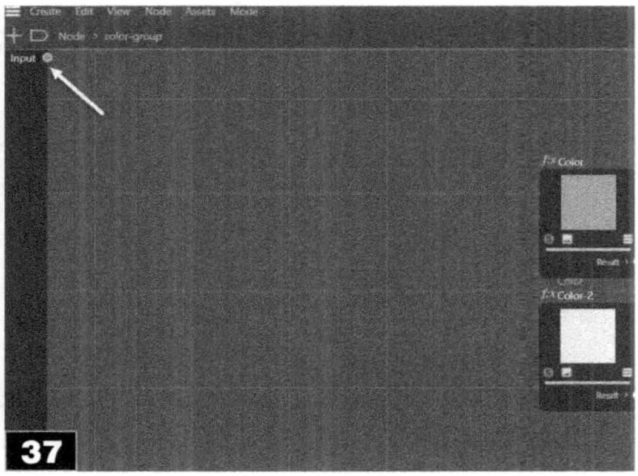

37

INPUT AND OUTPUT GROUP AREAS

*In Figures 36 and 37, vertical dark edges can be seen on both the left and right sides of the **Node** view. The **Red** and **Green** ports are located on the right edge. To connect ports with these edges, you can drag and drop a new connection into an empty space on the edges. This creates an inward or outward connection, which may not be useful for individual nodes, but can be used to create ports for groups when combining different groups together.*

27. Click on the **Node** icon (see Figure 38) in the **Node Editor** tile to switch back to the material nodes (see Figure 39). Notice in Figure 39 that the **Input** port is displayed on the **color-group** node that we created inside the group.

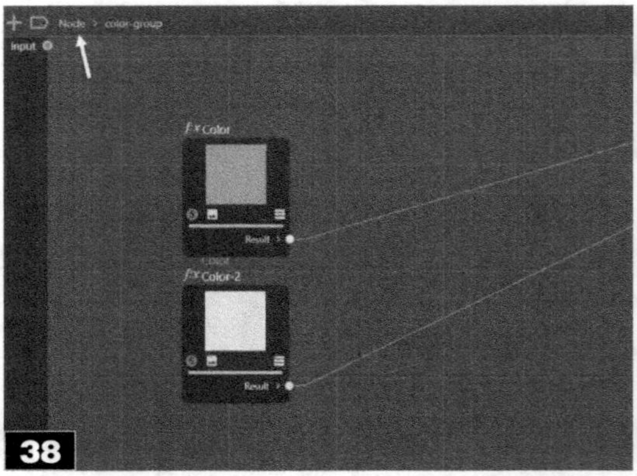

38

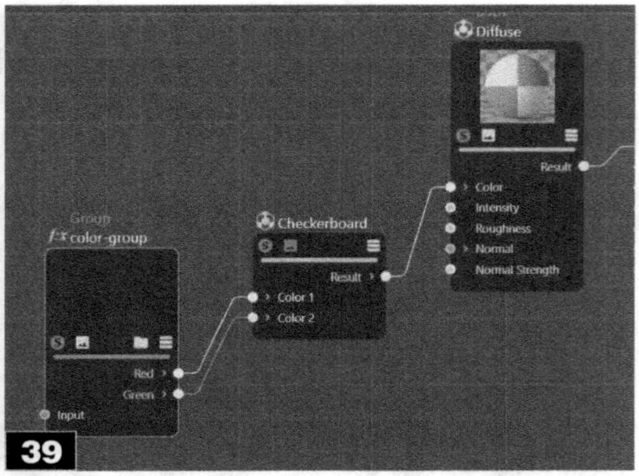

39

28. Select the **color-group** node and then choose **Create > Ungroup Nodes** from the editor's menubar or press **Shift G** to ungroup the nodes.

29. Drag **Node Commander** window > **Color** > **Color Correction** node to the wire connecting the **Color** and **Checkerboard** nodes and drop when the solid square icon is displayed with the mouse pointer; the **Color Correction** node appears in between the **Color** and **Checkerboard** nodes (see Figure 40).

30. In the **Attribute Manager > Inputs** tab, change **Hue** to **220**. Drag **Node Commander** window > **Color > Color Space** node to the wire connecting the **Color Correction** and **Checkerboard** nodes and drop when the solid square icon is displayed with the mouse pointer; the **RGB > RGB** node appears in between the **Color Correction** and **Checkerboard** nodes. In the **Attribute Manager** > **Inputs** tab, change **Output Color Space** to **HSV**.

31. Select the **Color Correction** and **RGB > HSV** nodes and then group them by choosing **Create > Group Nodes** from the menubar. Now, you if expand the node, you will notice that ports are now displayed in each dark edge in the view (see Figure 41).

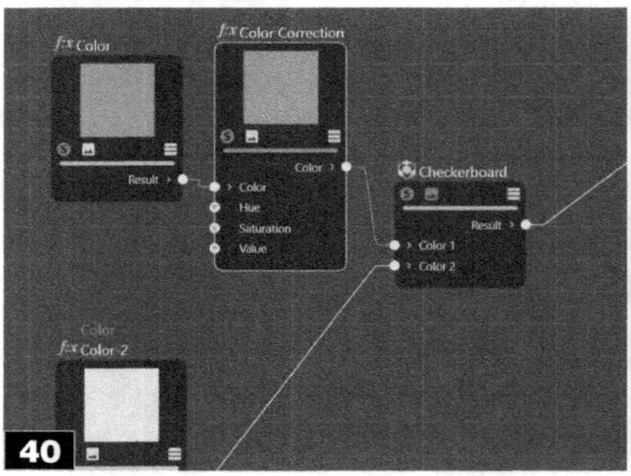

40

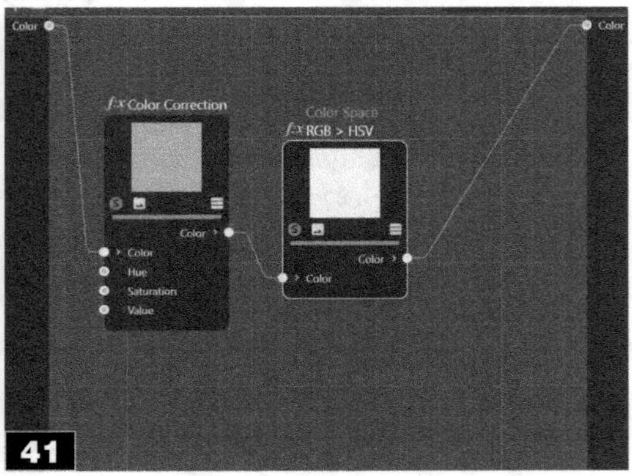

41

32. Switch back to the **Node** view and then ungroup the group we created in the last step group by pressing **Shift G**. Press **Shift L** to arrange all nodes. You can use the **L** key to arrange the selected nodes.

33. Enter **color** in the **Reveal** field; nodes whose names contain **color** will be displayed more prominently by fading all other nodes (see Figure 42). Click on the icon to clear the filter.

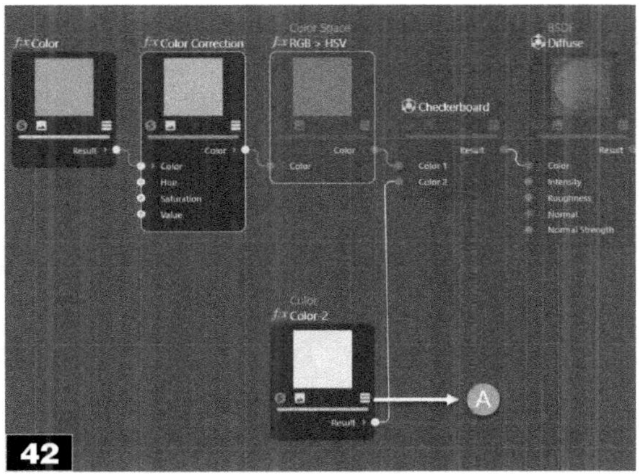

42

Icons at the top-right

There are two icons on the top-right corner of the **Node Editor**:

- **Lock Element:** The **Node** view shows the node network for the **Node** material currently selected in the **Material Manager**. Use this icon if you want to lock the node view to the currently selected material.
- **Undock a copy:** This icon can be used to open a new Node Editor, which can be useful when you want to view the node networks of two different materials or two different parts of the same material.

34. Select the **Checkerboard** node in the **Node** view and then **RMB** click. Then, choose **Select Connected Nodes** to select all nodes that are connected with the **Checkerboard** node. Likewise, you can select upstream and downstream nodes using the **Select Upstream Nodes** and **Select Downstream Nodes** commands.

SELECTING PORTS
*You can select ports using the **Shift** or **Ctrl** keys.*

35. Select a node and then **RMB** click. Then, choose **Hide All Ports** to hide all ports of the node. To just show the connected ports, choose the **Show Connected Ports** option. To hide all ports, choose the **Hide All Ports** option. You can also use the **Display** mode icons (labelled as **A** in Figure 42) to toggle the visibility of the ports.

36. Select all nodes except the **Material** node and then group the nodes. Then, expand the group. Select the **Intensity** port of the **Diffuse** node and then **RMB** click. Next, choose **Propagate Port** from the context menu to create two propagate ports (see Figure 43). These ports are denoted by a filled square icon. You can also drag ports to the left dark edge of the view to create propagated ports.

Propagate Ports

When you drag a wire from a port in the **Node** view, a menu will appear with the following options when you release the wire on an empty area:

- **Add New Input:** This option creates a round port that remains active even if the connection is deleted. The input port can be reconnected from the inside.
- **Propagate Port:** This option creates a square port that will be deleted if the connection is removed.
- **Post Inspector:** This option shows the values of simple data types.
- **Data Inspector:** This option displays a larger amount of data. When selected, a separate window opens displaying the data type and values present at the port.

37. Move one level up to the group node and notice the propagated nodes appear on the group node (see Figure 44).

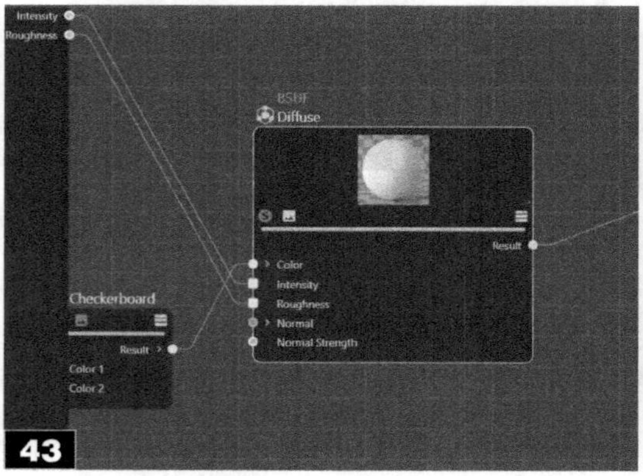

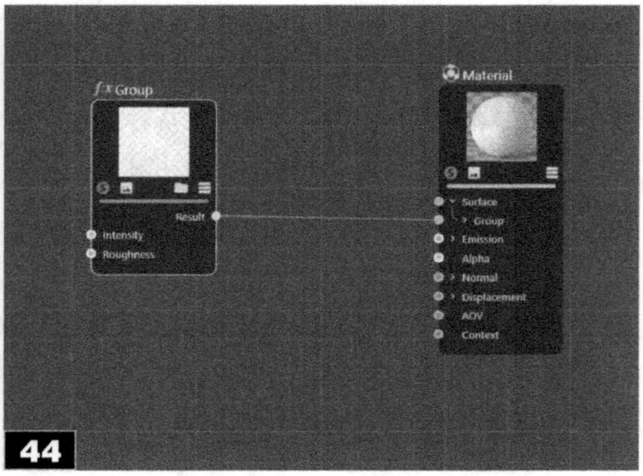

38. Close the Cinema 4D file.

NODE EDITOR MENUS

The **Node Editor** has a menubar that includes five different menus: **Create**, **Edit**, **View**, **Node**, **Node Commander window**, and **Mode**. However, it's important to keep in mind that depending on which **Node Editor** is being used, there may be different commands and options available.

A table has been provided below to summarize the various commands and options that can be found within the different menus.

Node Editor Menu Options		
Name	**Hotkey**	**Description**
Create menu		
Add Nodes	C	The **Node Commander** window can be opened using this particular command. By opening this window, you will have access to various nodes that you can use. The **Node Commander** has similar functionality to the asset list found in the **Content Browser**. To close the **Node Commander** window, you can either press the **Esc** key or click outside of the window. Additionally, you can press the **Tab** key to switch to the **Filter** field, and **Shift Tab** to switch back to the list.
Create Value Node from Clipboard		Using the **Copy Value** command allows you to copy a value to the clipboard. If you want to create a new **Value Node** with the same values as the one you just copied, you can use the **Create Value Node from Clipboard** command. This will ensure that the new **Value Node** has the correct values that were copied to the clipboard.
New Empty Group		This command creates an empty group within the current material. To view the contents of the group, click on the **Folder** icon (or double-click on the **Group** node) that is located on the node. By clicking on this icon, the node will expand and show its contents.
Group Nodes		This command allows you to select multiple nodes and group them together. These groups can be converted into assets that can be easily shared or reused in other projects.
Ungroup Nodes	**Shift+G**	This command allows you to ungroup a previously grouped set of nodes. This command will delete the group node, but maintain the connections between the nodes within the group. This can be useful when you want to edit individual nodes within a group or when you no longer need the group and want to simplify your material graph.
Edit menu		
Undo	Ctrl Z	You can use these commands to undo or redo changes that you have made in the **Material Editor**. However, it's important to note that these commands do not affect the movement or expansion of nodes within the editor. This is different from the **XPresso Editor**, where these commands also affect the movement and expansion of nodes.
Redo	Ctr Y	

Node Editor Menu Options		
Name	**Hotkey**	**Description**
Cut	Ctrl X	Use these commands for clipboard functions.
Copy	Ctrl C	
Paste	Ctrl V	
Duplicate		When you use this command in the **Material Editor**, it will create a duplicate copy of the selected nodes. However, this duplicate copy will not include any existing connections between the original nodes. Alternatively, you can **Ctrl** drag the node to create duplicates.
Delete	BS, Del	It deletes selected nodes.
Disconnect		This command removes all connections from a node.
Select All Nodes	Ctrl A	It selects all nodes.
Select Connected Nodes	UW	This command selects all nodes connected to the selected node.
Select Upstream Nodes		This command selects all the nodes that are upstream from the currently selected node. This means that it will select all nodes that are used as input for the selected node.
Select Downstream Nodes	Shift S	This command selects all the nodes that are downstream from the currently selected node. This means that it will select all nodes that are using the selected node's output as input.
Deselect All	Ctrl Shift A	It deselects all nodes.
Open in Material Editor		This commands opens the node in the **Material Editor**.
Select in Material Manager		It selects the corresponding material node in the **Material Manager**. This can be useful if you want to quickly locate and edit the material node that is associated with the selected node in the **Node** view.
Current Scene State to Classic		This command enables you to transform a **Scene** Node setup into a regular scene. The primary benefit of this conversion is that it grants access to the generated mesh, which can be further edited using standard Cinema 4D tools.
Node Editor Preferences		It opens the **Preferences** window with the **Node Editor** category selected in the left pane.
View menu		

Node Editor Menu Options		
Name	**Hotkey**	**Description**
Frame Selected	S	This command is useful when you want to bring nodes that are located outside of the current view in the **Node Editor** back into view. When you use this command, the view in the **Node Editor** will be scaled accordingly to ensure that all selected nodes are displayed within the editor's viewable area. Additionally, any ports on the selected nodes that are not currently connected to other nodes will be hidden.
Frame All	H	It shows all nodes in the **Node Editor**'s view. The view will be scaled accordingly.
Center Selected	Alt S	This command is useful when you want to view the selected nodes in the center of the **Node Editor**'s view without altering the zoom level. If you have multiple nodes selected, the center of all selected nodes will be positioned in the center of the viewable area.
Center All		It shows all nodes at the center of the view without changing the zoom factor.
Zoom In/Out	+/-	It enlarges or reduces the **Node Editor** view. However, using the mouse with the **2** key is faster than using these commands.
Zoom 100%		It sets the zoom to **100%**.
Show Grid		It hides or shows the grid in the **Node** view. However, this command does not affect the snapping.
Snap to Grid		It enables or disables the grid snapping. If enabled, node edges will snap to the grid lines.
Show Navigator		It toggles the visibility of the **Navigator**.
Show Info		It toggles the visibility of the **Info** area.
Step Up		This command is particularly useful when working with a group. Use it to move one level up in the hierarchy.
Arrange Selected Node	L	The nodes (selected/all) will be repositioned in a compact, organized manner, either horizontally or vertically. This arrangement makes it easier to understand the relationships between nodes, especially in complex node networks.
Arrange All Nodes	Shift+L	
Node menu		
Show Preview		These commands are used to show or hide a node's preview. You can control default behavior from the **Preferences** window > **Material** category **> NODE-BASED MATERIALS** section.
Hide Preview		

Node Editor Menu Options		
Name	**Hotkey**	**Description**
Hide all Ports/ Show All Ports		The **Hide all Ports** option hides the port area of the selected nodes. The **Show all Ports** command will make these ports visible again.
Show Connected Ports		This command is used to show only the ports that have connections for the selected node. All other ports will be hidden from view. To show all ports, execute the **Show all Ports** command.
Solo Node		This command allows you to solo the output of the selected node.
Start Node		When working with a complex node network, it can often consist of hundreds of nodes, making it difficult to make minor changes without having to navigate deeply into the network. To simplify this process, you can use the **Start Node** command to make one of the nodes the starting point for your modifications. When you execute this command, only the inputs for the selected node will be displayed in the **Attribute Manager**, making it easier to make changes without being overwhelmed by the entire network. The start node can be easily identified by its green boundary, which sets it apart from the other nodes in the network.
Asset menu		
Edit Asset		Executing this command will open a new **Node Editor** window, displaying the nodes that comprise the selected asset. This allows you to make edits to the asset and modify its behavior.
Save New Version		To edit existing assets, you can use this command to save any modifications you have made. This will open a dialog window similar to the one used for creating new assets, where you can specify a name, version, database, and category for the asset. When you save the modified asset using this command, the previous version of the asset will also be saved, allowing for versioning of assets.
Save as New Asset		When making changes to existing assets, it is possible to save the changes as a new asset without creating a new version of the original asset.
Convert To Asset		Node Commander window are often created from group nodes. When you execute this command on a selected group, the **Save Asset** window will be displayed allowing you to define various parameters such as the name, version, database, and category for the asset.

Node Editor Menu Options		
Name	**Hotkey**	**Description**
Edit Asset as Group		You can use this command to convert an asset to a group. When you run this command, the folder icon will be displayed again on the node.
Mode menu		
Scene		This mode works with the **Scene** nodes.
Material		This mode will be activated when a **Node** material is activated.
Capsule		If an element within the **Asset Construction Node**'s group is selected in the **Object Manager**, this mode will be activated automatically.

INDIVIDUAL NODE COMMANDER WINDOW

As mentioned earlier, assets in the **Node Editor** are accessed through the **Node Commander** window. The available assets are organized into various groups, and some of these groups are described below:

MATERIAL GENERATOR

The nodes in the **Generator** group are used to create patterns and color gradients. They are also used to create special shading effects. These nodes are discussed next:

Falloff

The **Falloff** node applies gradients to the front or backside of an object depending on the viewing angle. Its operation is similar to the combination of the standard **Falloff** shader and the **Fresnel** effect (see Figures 45 and 46). [**falloff.c4d**]

45

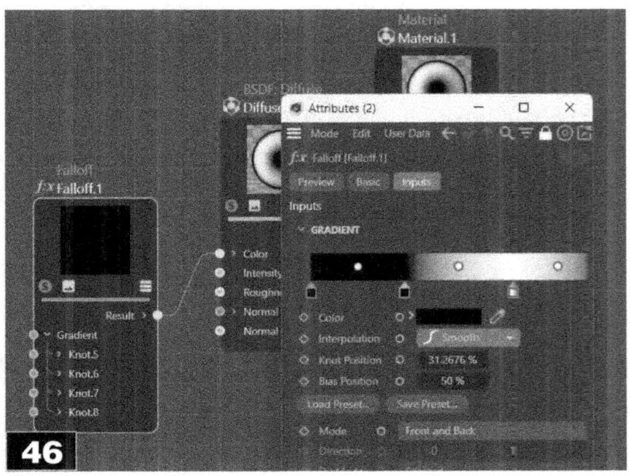

46

Ambient Occlusion

Ambient Occlusion is a method utilized to determine the level of exposure a specific sample point has to a virtual ambient light source that encompasses the entire scene. It can be utilized in two ways, either to compute diffuse lighting originating from an overcast sky or to improve contact shadows in indoor renderings. With this node, it is possible to determine the ambient occlusion.

It is also possible to reverse the direction in which the sampling is done. By doing this, the rays will be traced in the opposite direction of the surface normal, resulting in a darkening effect on the edges and corners. The **Invert Color** node can be utilized to create an approximation of the simple subsurface scattering effect.

Basic Noise

By using the **Basic Noise** node, you can generate a range of noise patterns in grayscale format with minimal parameters. The way this node operates is similar to that of the **Noise** shader in the **Standard** material system. If you require more sophisticated settings to create the desired noise effect, the **Noise** node can be utilized instead. Use the **Octaves** parameter to control the level of detail of the noise structure (see Figures 47 and 48). [**basic-noise.c4d**]

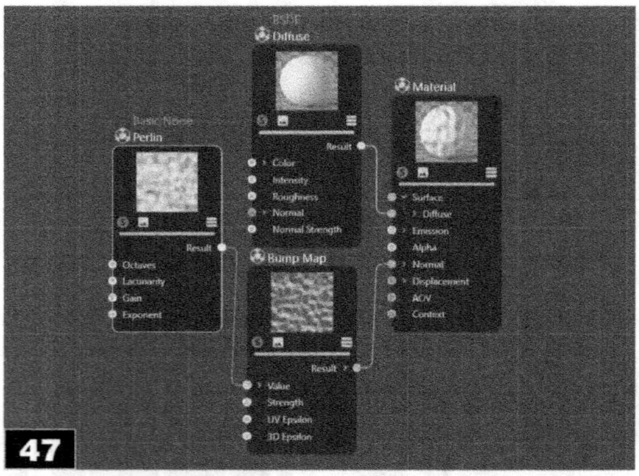

47

48

Basic Gradient

The **Basic Gradient** node operates similarly to the **Gradient** shader found in the **Standard** material system. However, what sets it apart is the inclusion of a percentage **Position** value, which enables the output of a color sample at any desired location (see Figures 49 and 50). [**basic-gradient.c4d**]

Image

The **Image** node is used to load bitmaps and videos into the **Node Editor** and output their color values.

> ***BITMAPS***
> *If you drag bitmaps from **Explorer/Finder** or **Content Browser** to the **Node Editor**, the **Image** node will be created automatically.*

49

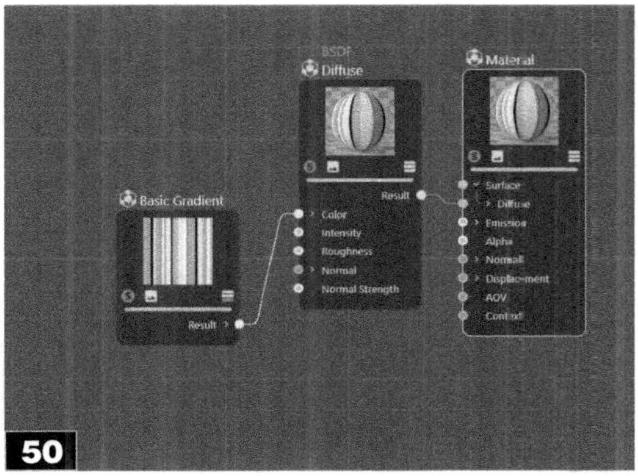

50

Color Key

The **Color Key** node is used to filter a color from the input and interpret as mask. This node is especially useful if the input has homogenous colors in the background (see Figures 51 and 52). [**color-key.c4d**]

51

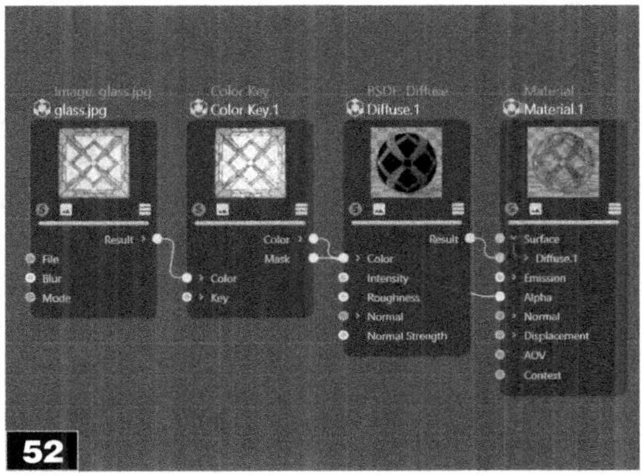

52

Thin Film

In nature, when light passes through a very thin layer of certain surfaces such as oil and soap, it refracts and bounces around, resulting in light interference. This interference, along with the presence of multiple wavelengths, causes certain wavelengths to cancel each other out (destructive interference) or enhance each other (constructive interference). As a result, depending on the thickness of the layer, the index of refraction, and the viewing angle, characteristic colors may appear on the surface. The **Thin Film** node is designed to replicate this effect in rendering.

Gradient

The **Gradient** node operates in a similar manner to the **Gradient** shader found in the **Standard** material system. It also includes a **Position** value, which allows the user to extract a color sample from any desired location and output it. However, in comparison to the **Basic Gradient** node, the **Gradient** node provides extra controls for both repetition and distortion.

Rock Surface

The **Rock Surface** node is a useful tool for generating typical rock structures, such as crystalline veins and oxidized effects. It achieves this by combining different noise patterns to replicate the typical colors and textures found in cliffs and stone surfaces (see Figures 53 and 54). [**rock-surface.c4d**]

53

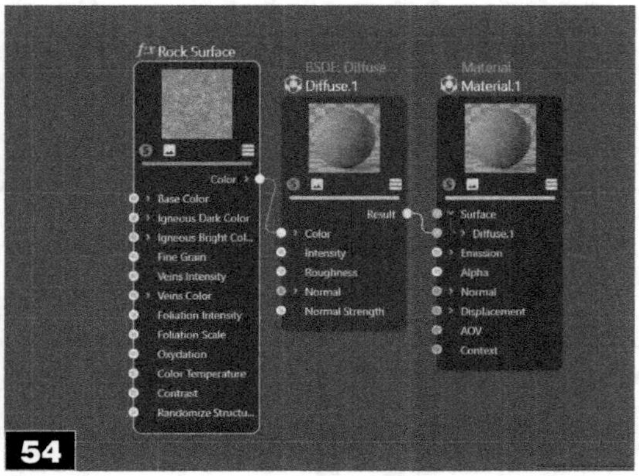

54

Flakes

The **Flakes** node is used to create tiny particles like the ones in the metallic car paint.

Fresnel Dielectric

The **Fresnel Dielectric** node is a tool that enables the creation of the fresnel effect, which is already included in the **BSDF** nodes that simulate conductive and dielectric materials. However, the **Fresnel Dielectric** node offers the additional capability of simulating color changes that are dependent on the angle of view. It generates a grayscale gradient output. The **Presets** drop-down list allows users to choose the refractive index of common dielectric materials, such as glass or water.

Fresnel Conductor

Similar to the **Fresnel Dielectric** node, the **Fresnel Conductor** node also produces the fresnel effect, but it is specifically designed for conductor materials. The Presets drop-down list can be utilized to choose from various presets.

Grid

The **Grid** node enables the creation of lines along the **X**, **Y**, and **Z** axes, with the ability to adjust their density and thickness individually in each direction. This node can produce uniformly spaced bands and grids. Users can also use index numbers to separate these elements from one another.

Hash

The **Hash** node is used to map data of any size to data of a fixed size. It generates pseudorandom colors, floats, and vectors based on both the **Seed** and **Salt** values. The **Seed** parameter value is employed for hash calculations, and the resulting values will remain the same for identical **Seed** values. However, the **Salt** parameter value further affects the **Seed** value, resulting in a different output even if the Seed value itself remains constant (see Figures 55 and 56). [**hash.c4d**]

55

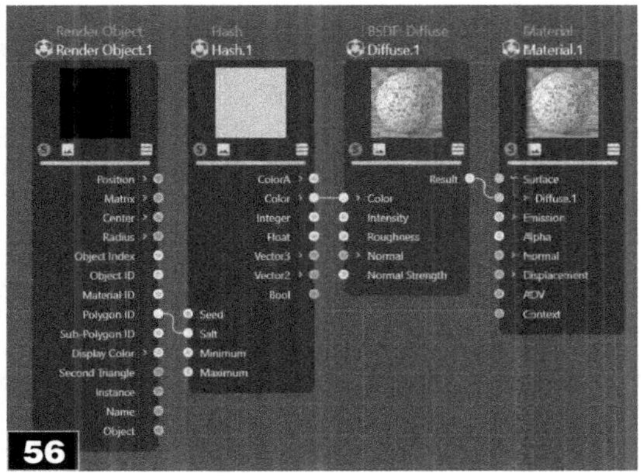

56

Wood

The **Wood** node is a tool used for generating colored wood grain patterns for planks or furniture. It enables the creation of complex color transitions and structures of wood grain, resulting in a more intricate and realistic output.

Edges Mask

The **Edges Mask** node is used to create masks that you can use to restrict properties to specific regions in the vicinity of edges. This functionality can be used to create a used or weathered look on objects with sharp edges.

Checkerboard

The **Checkerboard** node is used to create a continuous tile pattern using two input colors.

Complex Noise

The **Complex Noise** node operates similarly to the **Basic Noise** node and the **Noise** shader found in standard material systems. However, it provides additional options for defining the repetition behavior and orientation within the texture tiles. This allows for more control over the appearance of the generated noise pattern.

Scratches

The **Scratches** node is a tool used for generating scratches that are randomly placed, scaled, and rotated within a texture. These scratches are created in the form of black lines on a white background, with their placement being randomly determined.

Circle

The **Circle** node is used to create filled circle. The edge of the circle can be softened towards inside or outside. Follow these steps:

1. Open **shadeGeo.c4d**. Then, choose **Create > Materials > New Node Material** from the **Material Manager** menubar to create a new node material. Rename the material as **mat-circle**. Apply this material to the **Geo-1** and **Geo-2** objects.

2. Double-click on **mat-circle** to open the **Node Editor**. Add the **Node Commander** window> **Material Generator** > **Circle** node to the **Node** view. Connect **Circle > Result** to **Diffuse > Color**.

3. In the **Attribute Manager > Inputs** tab, change **Exterior** to red color and **Fill** to yellow color. Render the scene (see Figure 57).

WHAT JUST HAPPENED?
*In this case, the **Exterior** parameter is utilized to define the color of the background on which the circular shape is to be created. The **Fill** parameter is then utilized to determine the color used to fill the circle. When the **Scale** parameter is set to **50**, the circle only occupies half of the face of the cube as seen in Figure 57. However, by increasing the **Scale** parameter to **100**, the circle fills the entire face, as demonstrated in Figure 58. The Scale parameter functions to define the radius of the circle.*

57

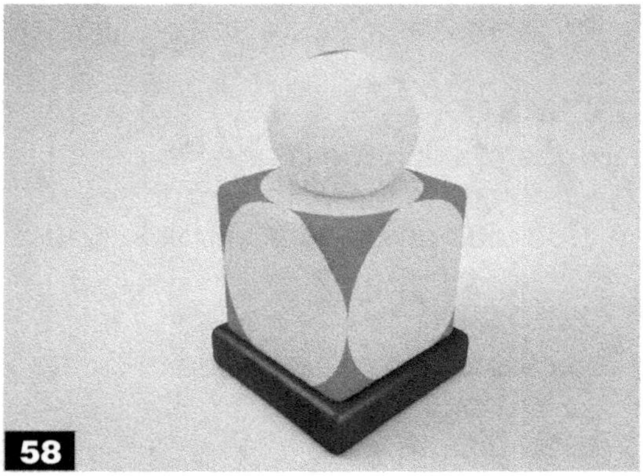
58

4. Change **Outer Softness** and **Inner Softness** to **15** and **35**, respectively to blur the outer edge and color filling, respectively. Render the scene (see Figure 59). Change **Outer Softness** and **Inner Softness** to **10** and **0**, respectively.

5. Add a **Basic Gradient** node by navigating to **Node Commander** window > **Material Generator**. Connect **Basic Gradient > Result** to **Circle > Scale**; notice in the **Circle** preview that the effect of the **Scale** parameter is maximum where gradient is white. Select **Basic Gradient** node and then in the **Attribute Manager > Inputs** tab, change the gradient as shown in Figure 60.

6. Render the scene (see Figure 61). Figure 62 shows the node network. [**circle.c4d**]

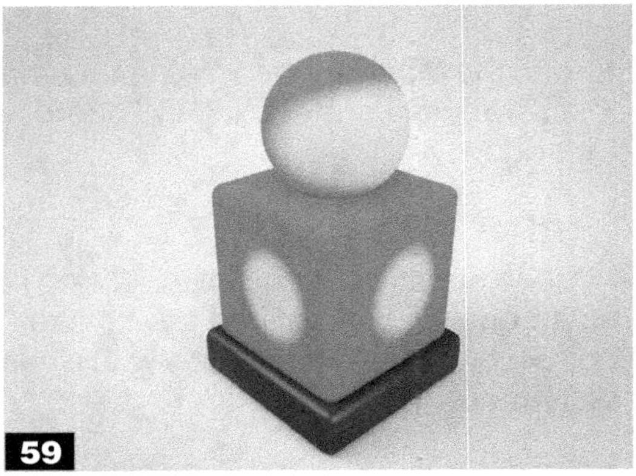

59

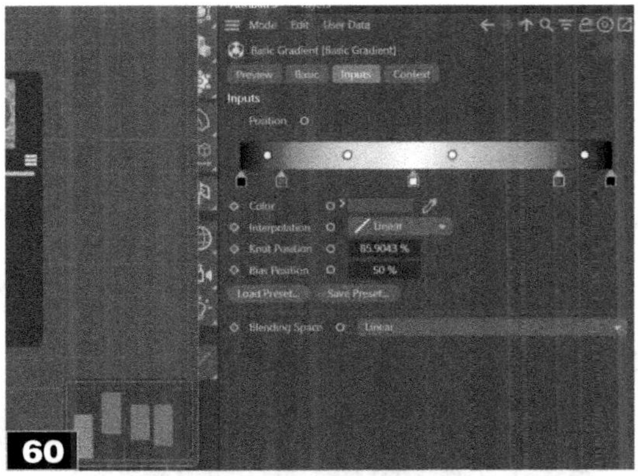

60

61

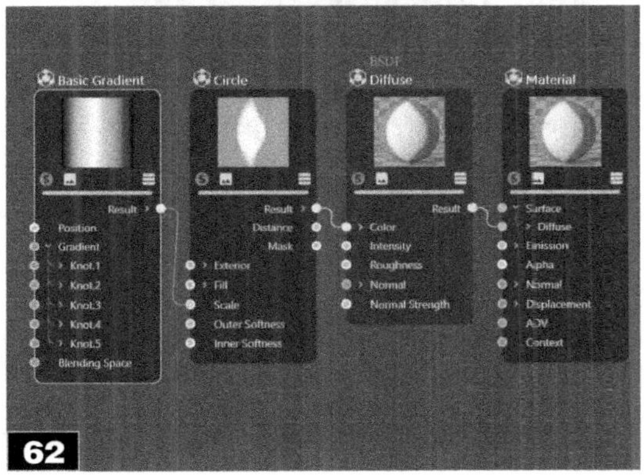

62

Landscape Mask

The **Landscape Mask** node enables the conversion of particular elevations and slopes of an object, such as a landscape, into grayscale values. The output of this node can then be used to mask these areas. This can be useful, for instance, in automatically creating a transition in material at a specific elevation on a terrain model, by utilizing the grayscale result from this node.

Line

The **Line** node allows for the creation of a line, where the start and end points can be specified, along with other attributes such as color, thickness, and blur. This node can be useful for adding scratches or patterns to an image or design.

Veins

The **Veins** node is a tool for producing a surface that looks finely grained or ridged. It achieves this by utilizing different noise structures to replicate the surface's appearance.

Metal Finish Surface

The **Metal Finish Surface** node enables the user to produce customary color gradations and designs seen on metallic surfaces, including imprints, grime, and marks.

Multi Shader

The **Multi Shader** node is intended to be utilized with the **MoGraph** module in Cinema 4D. It permits the user to alter the color of clones successively, either by their **UVW** coordinates or their initial color, by utilizing the **Multi Shader** node.

Trace Ray

To obtain information about the distance, position, and surface normals of a collision point, the **Trace Ray** node is used to trace a ray from an origin point defined by the user. The direction of the ray is also required for outputting the data. If the ray collides with a surface of an object, the node can generate the necessary data.

Patterns Generator

The **Pattern Generator** node creates geometric patterns using lines and circles, with the ability to scale, rotate, and repeat various primitives such as triangles, squares, circles, and stars. This allows for the creation of intricate patterns using the **Pattern Generator** node.

N-Gon

The **N-Gon** node is used to create a filled N-Gon. This node operates similarly to the **Circle** node, but includes an extra parameter called **Sides** that can be adjusted to specify the number of sides in the N-Gon. Higher values for **Sides** will produce a shape that closely resembles that of the **Circle** node.

Noise

The **Noise** node operates in a similar manner to the **Basic Noise** node and the **Noise Shader**, but it also provides extra options for specifying how the texture tiles repeat and their orientation.

Blackbody

In physics, a black body is an object that absorbs all incident electromagnetic radiation. The **Blackbody** node in Cinema 4D can be utilized to assign temperatures to actual colors. The node specifies a color alteration for specific temperatures, which is similar to heating a metal object. This generates colors ranging from red to yellow, white, and bright blue.

Spiral

To create a spiral shape using the **Spiral** node, you can fan out lines from the center point of the texture tile with a curved progression to achieve the desired effect. The number of arms that will be filled with the **Fill** color can be specified using the **Arms** parameter, while the **Scale** parameter controls the number of spiral arms.

A value of **0** will create curvature and cause the arms to run straight from the center outward, while negative values will invert the direction of the spiral.

Here are the steps you can follow:

1. Open **shadeGeo.c4d**. Then, choose **Create > Materials > New Node Material** from the **Material Manager** menubar to create a new node material. Rename the material as **mat-spiral**. Apply this material to the **Geo-1** and **Geo-2** objects.

2. Double-click on **mat-spiral** to open the **Node Editor**. Add a **Spiral** node by navigating to **Node Commander** window > **Material Generator**. Connect **Spiral > Result** to **Diffuse > Color**.

3. In the **Attribute Manager > Inputs** tab, change **Scale** to **120**, and **Arms** to **3**. Render the scene (see Figure 63).

WHAT NEXT?
*Next, let's randomize the arms using the **Noise** node.*

4. Add a **Noise** node by navigating to **Node Commander** window > **Material Generator**. Connect **Noise > Result** to **Spiral > Arms**. Render the scene (see Figure 64).

63

64

WHAT JUST HAPPENED?
*In Figure 64, the spiral produced is circular rather than having random arms. This is because the **Noise** node outputs values between **0** and **1**, and we need to remap these values to correspond with the desired range of arms. To achieve this and add variation to the arms, we can use the **Range Mapper** node.*

5. Navigate to **Node Commander** window > **Math > Range Mapper** and then drag **Range Mapper** onto the wire connecting the **Noise** and **Spiral** nodes to insert the **Range Mapper** node between them.

6. Select the **Range Mapper** node and then in the **Attribute Manager > Inputs** tab, change **Data Type** to **Float** and **Output Max** to **5**. Render the scene (see Figure 65). Figure 66 shows the node network. [**spiral.c4d**]

65

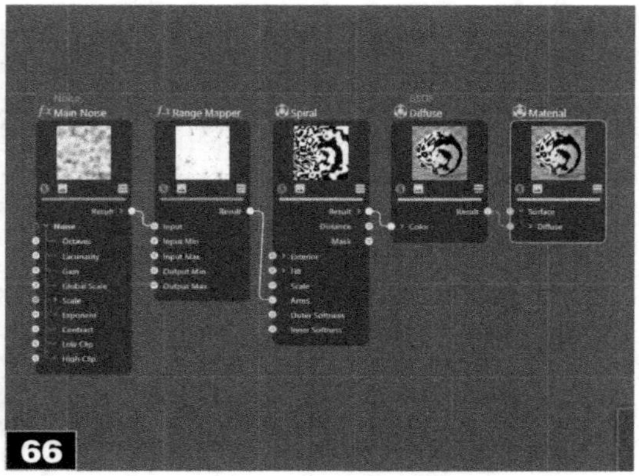

66

Star

The **Star** node produces star-shaped structures with customizable spikes whose length can be defined. By adjusting the **Spikes** parameter, you can determine how many spikes the star will have. The **Cutout** parameter can then be used to specify the distance from the center of the star to the tips of the spikes. As the **Cutout** value increases, the spikes become wider. When the node network depicted in Figure 67 is utilized, the outcome demonstrated in Figure 68 is produced. [**star.c4d**]

67

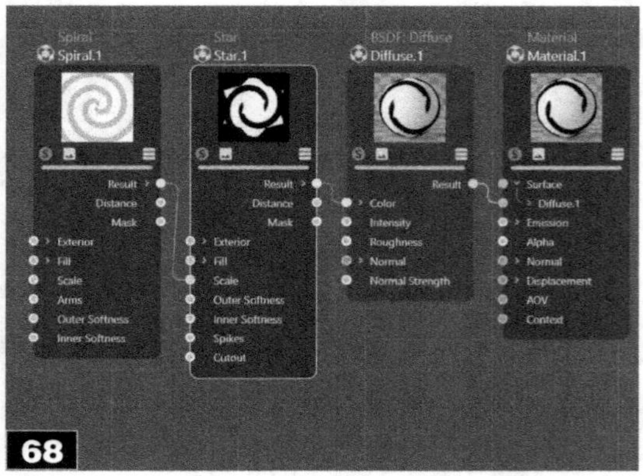

68

Trace Ray

The **Trace Ray** node has the ability to follow a path of light originating from a point specified by the user. When this ray of light hits an object's surface, information such as the distance to the collision point, the position, and the surface normals can be obtained and outputted. [**trace-ray.c4d**]

Voronoi Noise

The **Voronoi Noise** node is utilized for creating different voronoi patterns, which are akin to the MoGraph's **Voronoi Fracture** object that produces fragments. The generated pattern by this node resembles the one created by the **Noise** node.

Cells

To generate different shapes using the Voronoi pattern, the **Cells** node is used. However, it is restricted to creating structures solely on a two-dimensional plane.

Random

The **Random** node is comparable to the **Hash** node as it also creates random vectors, colors, and alpha values based on the **Seed** and **Salt** values. Moreover, the random values are recalculated for every modified animation time and calculated object surface point. When used as a surface color, every surface point is allotted a random color that varies along with the temporal data.

COLOR

The nodes in the **Color** group are used to modify input color values, adjust brightness, contrast, and gamma curves. The nodes in this category are discussed next:

Exposure

The **Exposure** node is used to regulate the brightness of the input data and balance the light and dark values. However, it should be noted that this node can produce a brightness value that exceeds **100%**. The **Exposure** parameter can be used to make the input either brighter or darker. Additionally, the **Offset** parameter adds to the **Exposure** value by including a specified offset value. Lastly, the **Gamma** parameter can be adjusted to modify the gamma curve and control the brightness of mostly mid-range colors.

The **Mask** tab contains settings that limit the influence of the node to particular color segments. This enables users to control the **Red**, **Green**, **Blue**, and **Alpha** sections of the color. The **Blend** parameter facilitates seamless blending between the original color and the modified color produced by the **Exposure** node. If you look at Figure 69, the outcome without the **Exposure** effect is visible. In contrast, Figure 70 displays the result of applying the **Exposure** effect. Figure 71 shows the node network. [**exposure.c4d**]

69

70

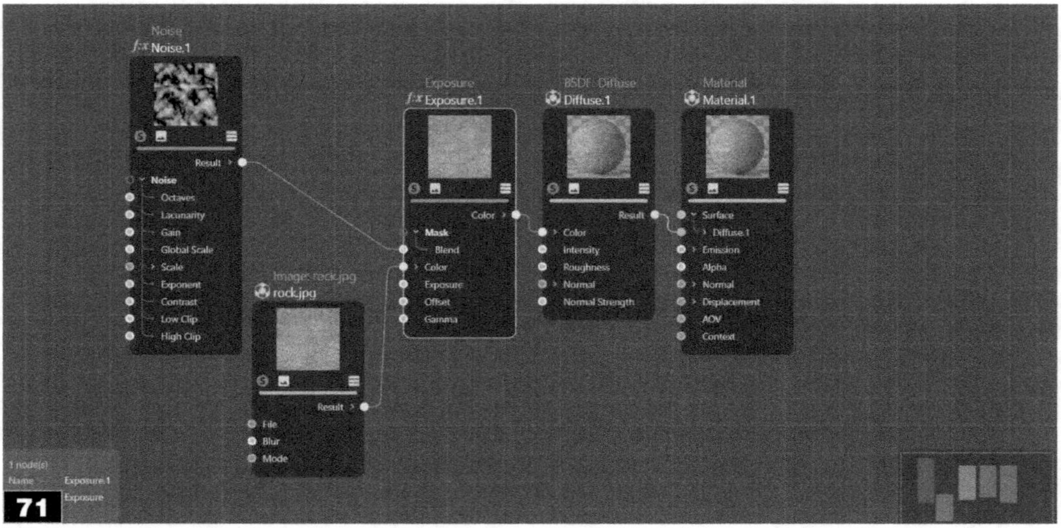

71

Bias/Gain

The **Bias/Gain** node adjusts color values based on their brightness. This means that it can brighten or darken colors with brightness that falls within the mid-range or at the extremes. The node decomposes the input colors into their red, green, and blue components and adjusts their intensity according to a range of values between **0%** and **100%**. This results in a recalculation of the **RGB** values.

When the **Bias** parameter is set to a value less than **0.5**, it decreases the intensity of colors that have mid-range brightness. Conversely, a value greater than **0.5** will increase the intensity of colors with mid-range brightness. A value of **0.5**, on the other hand, will have no impact on the colors. Similarly, the **Gain** parameter brightens all three color components, but it affects mid-range brightness to a lesser extent than the other brightness ranges. To view an example, see Figure 72 and the file **bias-gain.c4d**.

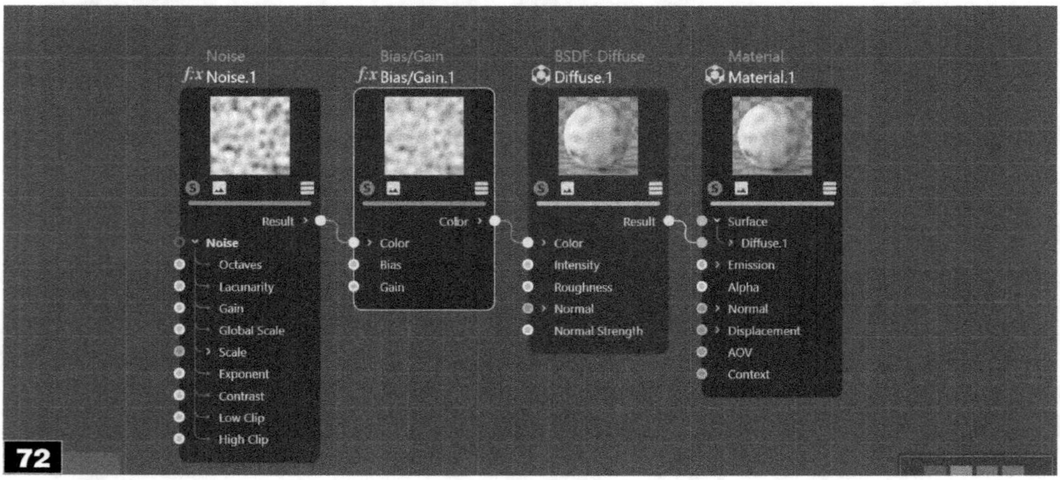

72

Image Processing

The **Image Processing** node provides several options to modify a linked bitmap, such as blurring it, adding a glow effect, changing its color, or adjusting its exposure and contrast.

Color Grading

By using the **Color Grading** node, you have access to an extensive range of features for color correction and saturation adjustments on textures. With this node, you can modify the hue, color, brightness, exposure, and other elements. To observe the effects of the node and view an example, refer to Figure 73 and the file **color-grading.c4d**.

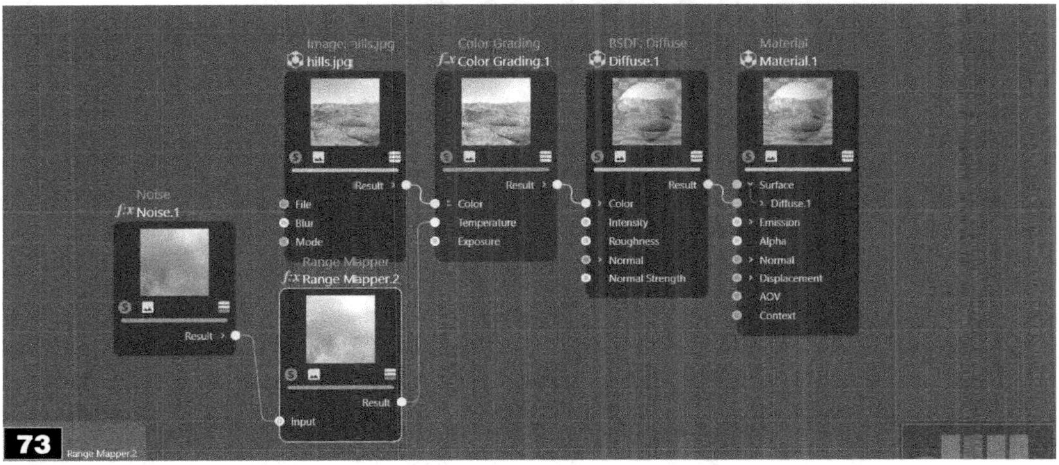

73

Layer

The **Layer** node has similarities to the **Layer** shader in the standard material system. It allows you to combine and blend multiple layers. The node considers the alpha channel of each layer when blending them together. To view an example of this node in action, see Figure 74 and the file **layer.c4d**.

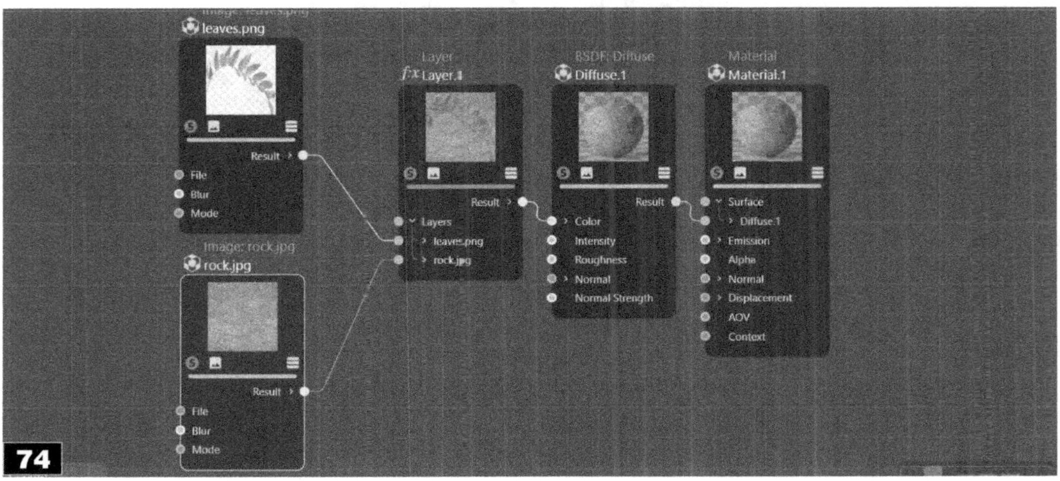

74

Shuffle

The **Shuffle** node is a tool that enables you to rearrange the red, green, blue, and alpha channels of an input color. It allows you to swap the **Color** and **Alpha** channels between one another. For a visual demonstration, please refer to Figure 75 and the file **shuffle.c4d**.

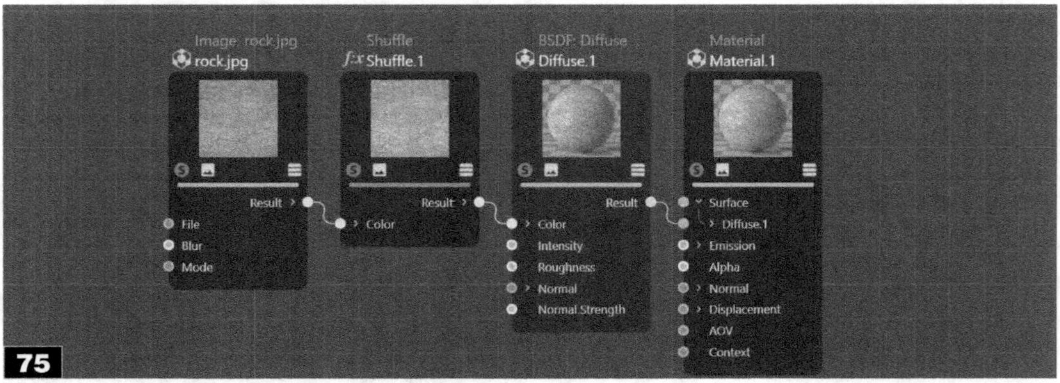

75

Shuffle Combine

With the **Shuffle Combine** node, you can combine the red, green, blue, and alpha components from two different color inputs into one single color output. This node rearranges the channels from both inputs to create a new color. To view an example of the **Shuffle Combine** node, refer to Figure 76 and the file **shuffle-combine.c4d**.

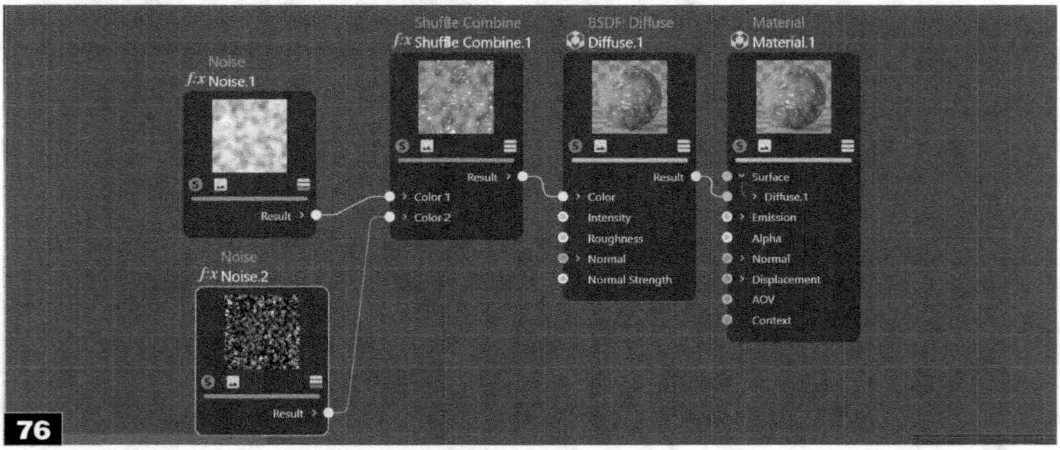

76

Color

The **Color** node is used to select a color value or alpha portion.

Invert Color

The **Invert Color** node is used to invert the color values of the input.

Color Correction

The **Color Correction** node serves the purpose of recoloring textures, even grayscale images. It allows you to replace the input color while preserving the original saturation and brightness. For an example of the **Color Correction** node in action, refer to Figure 77 and the file **color-correction.c4d**.

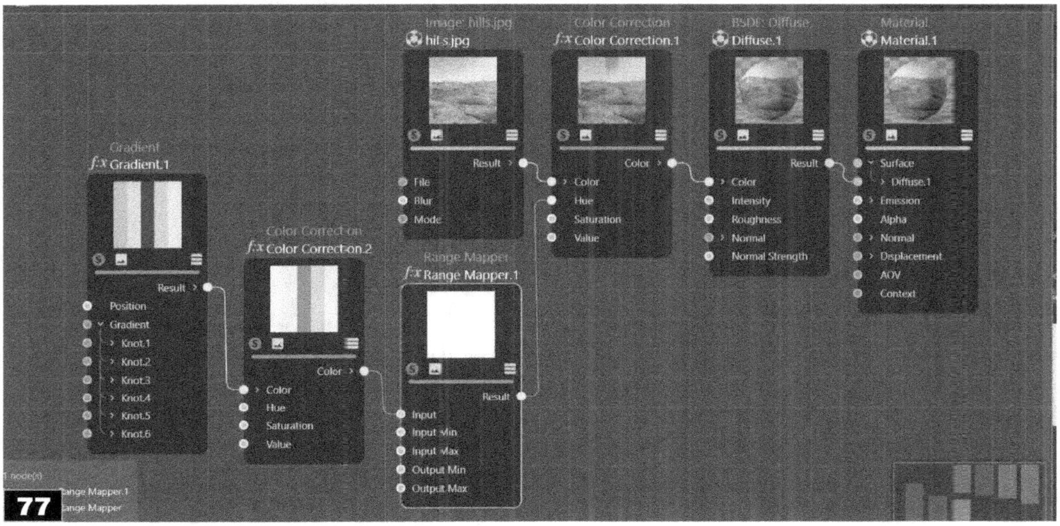

77

Color Profile

The **Color Profile** node enables you to convert a pre-defined color profile to another one. Cinema 4D typically employs a linear workflow to translate brightness values by default. To see how the **Color Profile** node works, you can check out Figure 78 and the file **color-profile.c4d**.

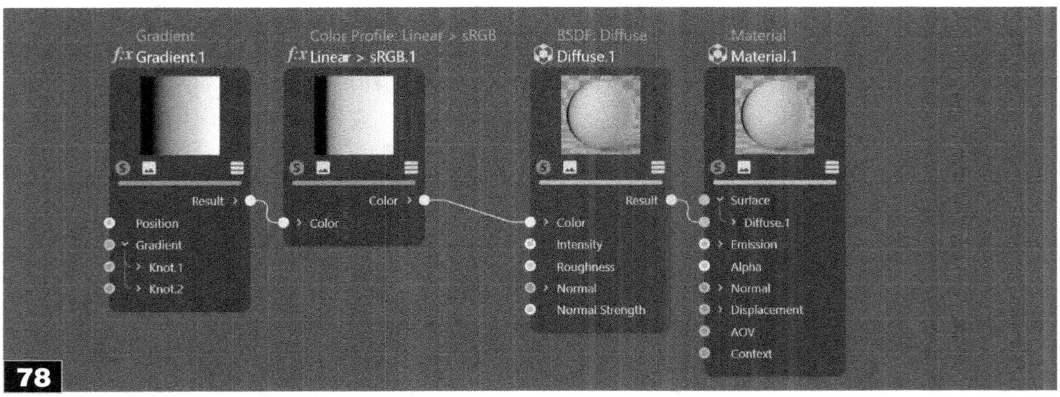

78

Color Space

The **Color Space** node allows you to convert a color space to another. This node supports several color spaces, including **RGB**, **HSV**, **HSL**, **XYZ**, and **CMY**. You can use this node to translate colors between these different spaces.

Color Temperature

The **Color Temperature** node can be utilized to make a color or texture look warmer. Although green and violet colors are not typically included in the typical range of color temperatures, you can use a separate Tint value to include these colors. If you want to see an example of how to use this node, take a look at the **temperature.c4d** file.

Colorize

The **Colorize** node is a useful tool for replacing colors in an image. It can be used to transfer brightness values to a gradient and define specific colors for the gradient. This node operates in a similar way to the **Colorizer** shader found in the standard material system. Additionally, the **Colorize** node can convert color images to grayscale. To see how it works, refer to the **colorize.c4d** file.

Contrast

The **Contrast** node is a tool used to adjust the level of contrast between the light and dark areas of an image. It can be used to make the transitions from light to dark more pronounced, or to soften them. Increasing contrast can cause loss of detail in lighter or darker regions, while decreasing contrast can make an image appear flat or washed out. You can see an example of this in the **contrast.c4d** file.

OCIO Transformation

The OpenColorIO (OCIO) provides guidelines for transforming different color spaces, and the **OCIO** node allows you to apply these guidelines to your own color values in a customized way.

Blend

The **Blend** node works similarly to the standard Layer shader. However, it differs from the Layer node in that it only allows for the mixing of two color layers with an optional mask. In contrast, the Layer node allows for the mixing of any number of color layers.

Premultiply

The **Premultiply** node adjusts the color values based on the transparency information provided in the alpha channel. The brightness information of the alpha channel is multiplied by the RGB values, which leads to the modification of the color values. If the input does not have an alpha channel, the color values remain the same. You can refer to **premultiply.c4d** for more information.

Selective Color

The **Selective Color** node allows you to adjust the hue, saturation, and brightness of predefined color ranges. If you have experience with editing photos in software such as Photoshop's RAW converter or Lightroom, you may already be familiar with this feature. By using this node, you can modify the hue, saturation, and luminance of colors within the Red, Orange, Yellow, Green, Aqua, Blue, Purple, and Magenta color groups. Refer to the **selective-color.c4d** file for further information.

Transform

The **Transform** node enables individual movement, rotation, or scaling of an input, and offers control over the repetition of colors or textures within the UV space. For more information, please refer to the **transform.c4d** file.

Un-premultiply

The **Un-premultiply** node is a reversal of the **Premultiply** node.

White Balance

Many light sources in nature emit light that is not perfectly white but slightly colored, resulting in white surfaces appearing tinted. This emitted color can appear to the human eye as yellow to orange, white, or blue, depending on the light source. To achieve the most accurate representation of surface colors when using colored lights, a white balance value can be used to correct any coloration in the rendered image. The **White Balance** node provides a means to set this value. For further details, please consult the **white-balance.c4d** file.

INFO

The nodes in the **Info** group are used to retrieve data from objects, tags, and scenes. These nodes are discussed next:

Camera

The **Camera** node provides access to the settings of the currently active render camera, including its position and focal length. By default, the **Camera** node corresponds to the active render camera in the scene. If there is no camera in the scene, the viewport camera is used instead.

Light

The **Light** node is designed to calculate diffuse and specular shading by utilizing the light sources present in the scene. However, it is important to note that the results of this node are a quick estimation and not physically accurate. Additionally, the **Light** node operates independently of the **BSDF** nodes in the scene.

MoGraph

When a material has been applied to a MoGraph clone, the **MoGraph** node can output several types of information regarding the clones, including their colors, internal index numbers, or UVW coordinates.

Render Object

The **Render Object** node gathers information about the object that is currently being rendered and to which the material has been applied. This node can provide details on the position and size of the object, as well as the ID of the polygon located at the current sample point.

Ray

By utilizing the **Ray** node, it is possible to retrieve information about the type of ray that is being used at the current sample position. This node can determine whether the ray is computing a shadow, creating a reflection, or being used for Global Illumination..

Scene

This **Scene** node lets you access information about the current scene available such as the render resolution, number of objects, or number of CPUs used.

Scene Object

The **Scene Object** node can be used to read out specific objects in the scene. You can, for example, retrieve information about the position, scale, or distance of a given object.

Vertex Color

If an object has a **Vertex Color** tag assigned to it, the **Vertex Color** node can be used to output the color values.

Vertex Map

If a **Vertex Map** tag is assigned to the object, the **Vertex Map** node can be used read out its color values.

Time

Whenever you want to make material properties or rendering dependent on the animation phase, the current time, or frame number within the animation can be valuable information. The **Time** node makes this and other information available.

SURFACE

The nodes in the **Surface** group are used to define individual properties of a given material such as the emission, reflectivity, normal orientation, and so on. Let's explore these nodes.

Material

The **Material** node is utilized to specify all of the relevant physical properties of a surface. It offers several input ports such as **Emission**, **Alpha**, **Normal**, **Displacement**, and **Context Only**, which can be used to define a material's properties, including its **BSDF** layers that define the shading and reflections of the surface. By combining all of a material's information, the **Material** node defines the surface of the object to which it has been applied. The **Result** output of this node is responsible for defining the final appearance of the object's surface.

BSDF

When a node material is created, the **BSDF** node is automatically added to the node network, which is responsible for defining the reflective properties of a surface. By default, this node calculates render-intensive indirect illumination through diffuse reflections, resulting in a highly realistic effect. However, this can often be too computationally expensive, particularly for interior scenes, and may not be practical within a reasonable time frame. To address this issue, you can enable the **Use Color Channel** checkbox for Node in **Project Settings** > **Nodes** tab > **MATERIAL NODES** section, which will configure the BSDF node to work with the **Global Illumination** effect. You can access **Project Settings** by pressing the keyboard shortcut **Ctrl D**.

Emission

The **Emission** node is utilized to specify the color and strength of a material's self-illumination characteristics. If a material is self-illuminating, it can also light up other surfaces that have a diffuse reflectance or a diffuse BSDF layer.

Displacement Map

The **Displacement Map** node is used to deform surfaces using a material. This node moves points on the surface.

Normal Map

The **Normal Map** node is used to prepare a normal map texture to be used with the **Normal** input of the **Material** node.

Bump Map

The **Bump Map** node allows for the simulation of minor surface irregularities and structures by affecting the surface normals. It uses grayscale values from a bump map to achieve this effect, and does not modify the geometry of the object. It should be noted that this node solely generates a shading effect and does not include information about the angles of the surface.

CONTEXT

The **Context** group of nodes is utilized for mapping color values onto the **UVW** texture space and modifying or creating **UV** coordinates. Additionally, **Texture** tags in the Object **Manager** can be used to adjust mapping through projection settings when applying node materials. Context group nodes allow for custom adjustments to be made to mapping for specific material elements. The majority of nodes in the node material system have separate inputs for both **Context** and **Local Context**.

CONTEXT INPUT
*The **Context** input pertains to all UV coordinates of the color inputs used for computing a node. If no additional changes are made, the **Texture** tag's projection feature will be used. Conversely, using the **Local Context** input will only modify the UV coordinates used by that particular node. In either case, the **Texture** tag has the last say and its **Offset** and **Length** settings can also be used to affect the projection of the material on a given surface.*

ORIGIN OF THE UV COORDINATES

*It is important to note that the UV coordinates for **Material** nodes have a different origin compared to the **Texture** tag. The **Material** node starts at (**0**, **0**) in the UV space at the bottom-left corner, while the **Texture** tag's origin is at the top-left corner of a texture tile due to its older implementation.*

The nodes in the **Context** group are discussed next.

Get Context

The **Get Context** node is used to read the context. It provides comprehensive access to data.

Override Context

The Override Context node is a useful tool for inserting a custom shading context anywhere in the node graph. It can be especially helpful when a node has multiple outputs and you want to preview multiple outputs simultaneously.

Projection

The Projection node is a useful tool for generating new UV coordinates that match different coordinate systems for materials. This node can be used to create projection coordinates for various materials.

Set Context

This node is opposite of the **Get Context** node.

Triplanar

The **Triplanar** node allows you to project up to six different shaders from different directions and blend them together. This can eliminate the need for unwrapping UV coordinates for complex objects.

UV Reprojection

The **UV Reprojection** node offers several projection types that can be used to warp UV coordinates and generate various patterns. The available modes include **Angular**, **Radial**, **Circular**, **Box**, **Star**, and **N-Angle**.

UV Transform

The **UV Transform** node is a useful tool for adjusting the placement, size, and rotation of UV coordinates within a texture projection. This node allows for easy repetition of UV coordinates as well.

UV Distorter

The **UV Distorter** node is a tool that can be used to modify the UV coordinates of a texture. It works by distorting the UV coordinates based on a specified **Direction** vector.

UVW Transform

Similar to the **UV Transform** node, this node allows for the translation, scaling, and rotation of UV coordinates. However, it generates a three-dimensional coordinate structure commonly used for volumetric materials, including an extra **W** component in addition to the regular **UV** coordinates.

Scatter

The **Scatter** node is useful for calculating the distribution, rotation, and scaling of UV tiles. It allows for the creation of UV tiles with variable positions, sizes, and rotations.

UTILITY

The nodes in **Utility** group are primarily used to create groups and get the information about rendering that can be displayed in the **Console**.

Debug

The **Debug** node can be used to output various information about a specific part of the rendering to the console.

Group

The **Group** node itself has no function, it is used as a container of other nodes that will be grouped.

Group (with Ports)

The **Group (with Ports)** node is a pre-made group node that comes with one input and one output. It can be used to connect the nodes within the group with other nodes and settings that are outside of the group. If needed, more inputs and outputs can be added to the node via the context menu.

Object Link

The **Object Link** node can be linked with any object in the scene whose link will then be made available at the output.

Variadic Count

You can use the **Variadic Count** node to determine the number of entries for variable inputs, such as the ports of a color gradient.

MATERIAL

The materials in the **Material** group are called **Node Materials**. You can also use these materials as nodes. The following material are available in this group: **Uber Material**, **Emission Material**, **Cutout Material**, **Car Paint Material**, **Concrete Material**, **Rock Material**, **Gold Material**, **Granite Material**, **Wood Material**, **Ceramic Material**, **Marble Material**, **Metal Material**, and **Plastic Material**.

WORKING WITH THE AMBIENT OCCLUSION NODE

This tutorial will demonstrate how to use the **Ambient Occlusion** node to detect the indentations on the surface of a **Landscape** object and make the material in those areas luminous. The process involves measuring the indentations and applying the appropriate materials to create the desired effect, as shown in Figure 1.

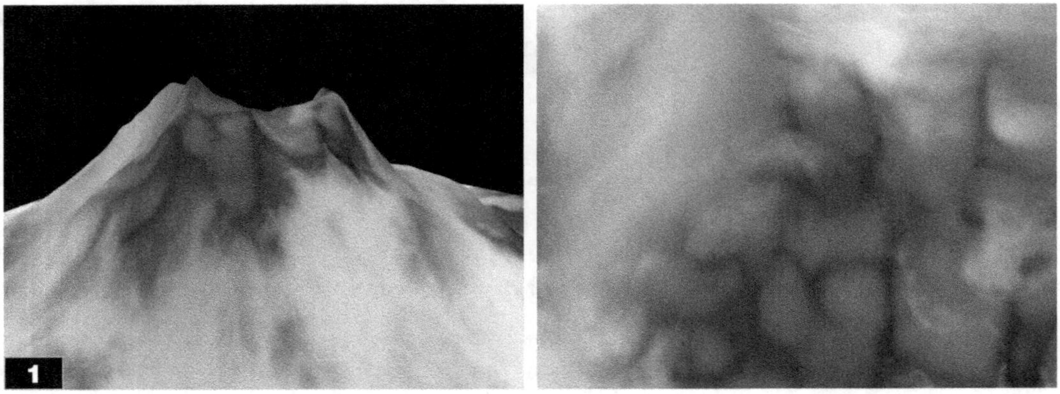

Summary	
Topics	Getting Started Working with the Node
Resources folder	**node-based-materials**
Start file	**ao-glow-start.c4d**
Final file	**ao-glow-finish.c4d**

Getting Started

Open **ao-glow-start.c4d**.

Working with the Node

Follow these steps:

1. Choose **Create > Materials > New Node Material** from the **Material Manager** menubar to create a new node material. Apply this material to the **Subdivision Surface** object. In the **Material Manager**, double-click on **Node** to open the **Node Editor**.

2. Select the **Diffuse** node and then in the **Attribute Manager > Inputs** tab, change **Color** to **HSV** (**0**, **38**, **2**). Add an **Ambient Occlusion** node by navigating to **Node Commander** window > **Material Generator**.

3. Connect **Ambient Occlusion > Occlusion** to **Material > Emission**. Select the **Ambient Occlusion** node and then in the **Attribute Manager > Inputs** tab, change **Max Ray Length** to **170** and **Accuracy** to **70**. Render the scene (see Figure 2).

4. Navigate to **Node Commander** window > **Color** > **Colorize** and then drag **Colorize** onto the wire connecting the **Ambient Occlusion** and **Material** nodes to insert the **Colorize** node between them. In the **Attribute Manager** > **Colorize** node > **Inputs** tab, click the **Load Preset** button and then select the **Heat 3** preset. Render the scene (see Figure 3).

2

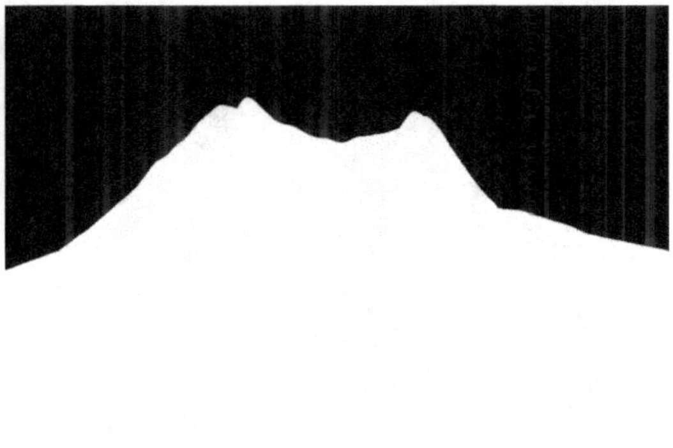

3

WHAT JUST HAPPENED?
*I have employed the **Colorize** node in this example to replace the colors produced by the **Ambient Occlusion** node. However, as depicted in Figure 3, the emission is not happening in the indentations. To solve this issue, we will invert the colors of the **Ambient Occlusion** node.*

5. Navigate to **Node Commander** window > **Color** > **Invert Color** and then drag **Invert Color** onto the wire connecting the **Ambient Occlusion** and **Colorize** nodes to insert the **Invert Color** node between them. Render the scene (see Figure 4).

WHAT NEXT?
Now, let's add some details to the shading.

6. Disconnect the **Colorize** and **Material** nodes. Add a **Noise** node by navigating to **Node Commander** window > **Material Generator**. In the **Attribute Manager** > **Noise** node > **Inputs** tab, change **Noise Type** to **Wavy Turbulence**, **Octave** to **8** and **Global Scale** to **300**. Also, change **Low Clip** to **29**.
7. Add an **Arithmetic** node by navigating to **Node Commander** window > **Math**. In the **Attribute Manager** > **Add** node > **Inputs** tab, change **Operation** to **Add** and **Data Type** to **Color**. Connect **Noise** > **Result** to **Add** > **Input 1**.
8. Connect **Colorize** > **Result** to **Add** > **Input 2**. Now, connect **Add** > **Result** to **Material** > **Emission**. Render the scene (see Figure 5). Figure 6 shows the node graph.

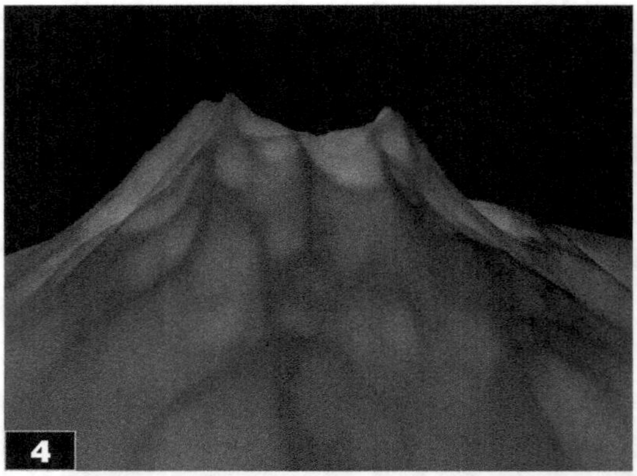

4

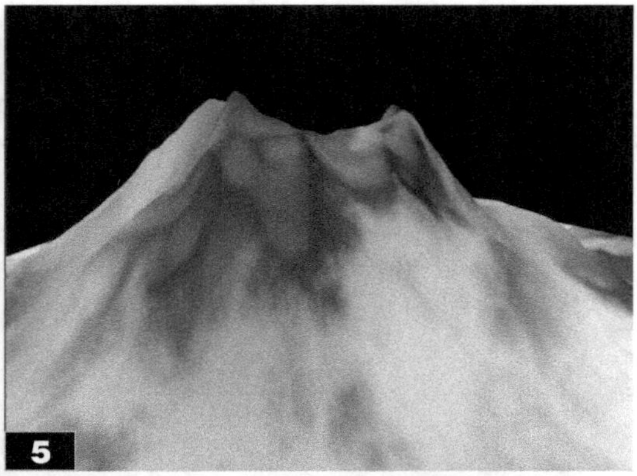

5

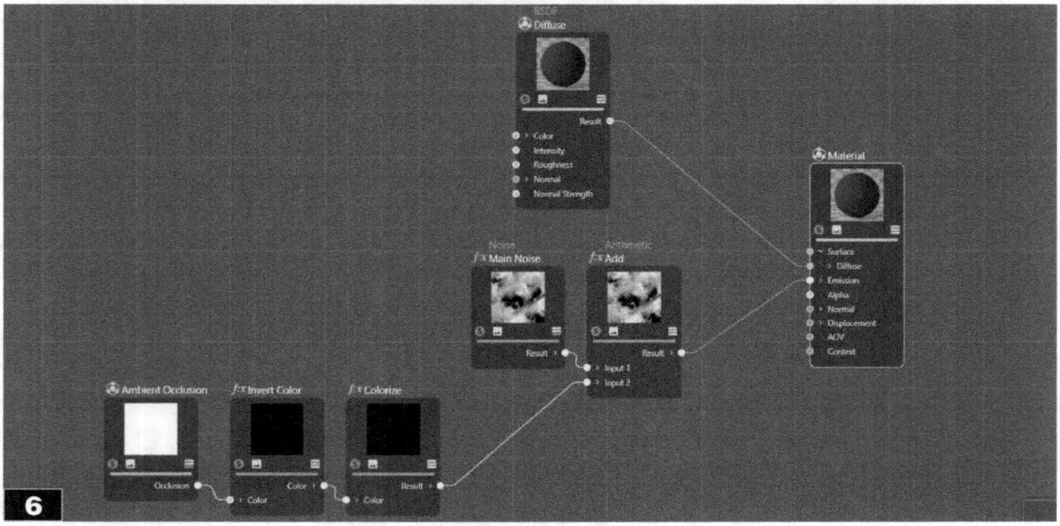

6

WORKING WITH THE BASIC GRADIENT NODE

In this tutorial, to shade clones of a **Cloner** object, we will use the **Basic Gradient** node to create a gradient.

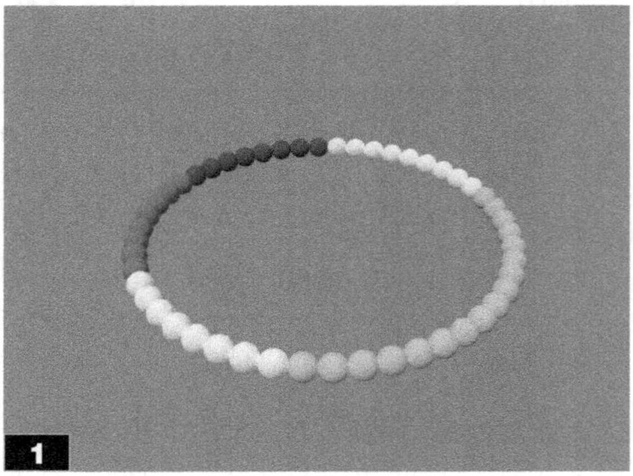

1

Then, we will use the **Render Object** node to read the index numbers of the clones and modify the color values along the progression of the gradient (see Figure 1).

Summary	
Topics	Getting Started Working with the Node
Resources folder	**node-based-materials**
Start file	**bgrad-start.c4d**
Final file	**bgrad-finish.c4d**

Getting Started

Open **bgrad-start.c4d**.

Working with the Node

Follow these steps:

1. Choose **Create > Materials > New Node Material** from the **Material Manager** menubar to create a new node material. Apply this material to the **Cloner** object. In the **Material Manager**, double-click on **Node** to open the **Node Editor**.

2. Add the **Basic Gradient** node by navigating to **Node Commander** window **> Material Generator**. In the **Attribute Manager > Basic Gradient** node > **Inputs** tab, click the **Load Preset** button and then select the **Pattern 3** preset.

3. Add the **Render Object** node by navigating to **Node Commander** window **> Info**. This node collects information about the object currently being calculated to which the material was assigned.

WHAT NEXT?
*The **Basic Gradient** node's **Position** input port requires values ranging from **0** to **1**, or alternatively from **0%** to **100%**. To ensure this range is met with **50** clones in the **Cloner** object, the value of the **Object Index** port in the **Render Object** should be divided by **50**.*

4. Add the **Arithmetic** node by navigating to **Node Commander** window **> Math**. In the **Attribute Manager > Add** node > **Inputs** tab, change **Operation** to **Divide**, **Data Type** to **Float**, and **Input 2** to **50**.

5. Connect **Render Object** > **Object Index** to **Divide > Input 1**. Connect **Divide > Result** to **Basic Gradient > Position**.

6. Connect **Basic Gradient > Result** to **Diffuse > Color**. Render the scene (see Figure 1), Figure 2 shows the node graph.

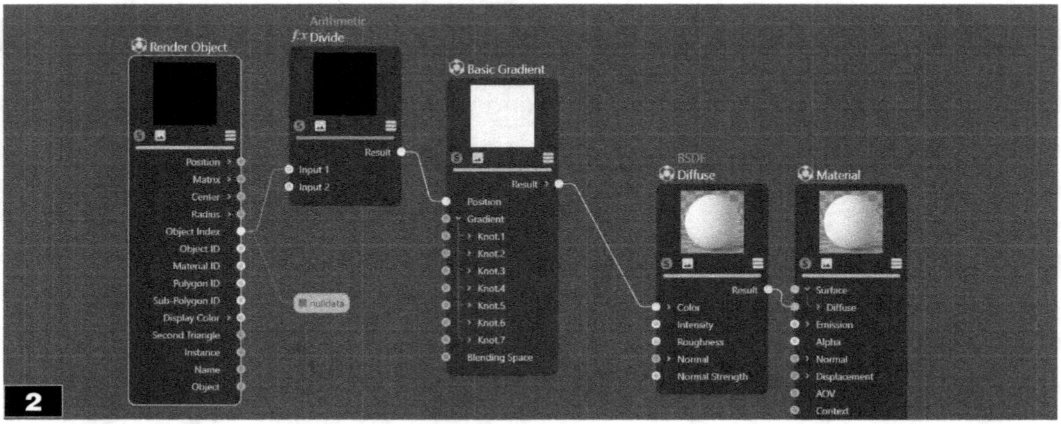

2

WORKING WITH THE THIN FILM NODE

The purpose of this tutorial is to demonstrate how to use the **Thin Film** node in order to simulate surfaces such as those found in oil or soap (see Figure 1).

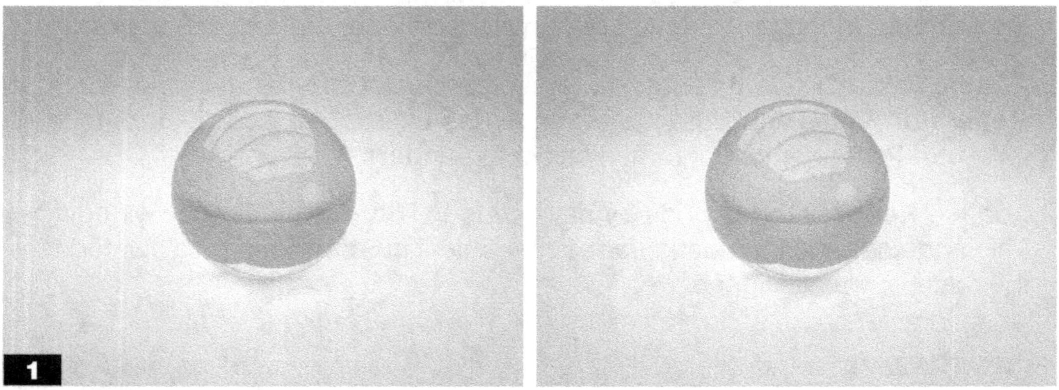
1

Summary	
Topics	Getting Started Working with the Node
Resources folder	**node-based-materials**
Start file	**thin-film-start.c4d**
Final file	**thin-film-finish.c4d**

Getting Started

Open **thin-film-start.c4d**.

Working with the Node

Follow these steps:

1. Choose **Create > Materials > New Node Material** from the **Material Manager** menubar to create a new node material. Apply this material to the **Sphere** object. In the **Material Manager**, double-click on **Node** to open the **Node Editor**.

2. In the **Attribute Manager > Material** node > **Inputs** tab, select the **Transparent** checkbox and then change **IOR** to **2**.

WHAT JUST HAPPENED?
*Here, I have selected the **Transparent** checkbox to get access to additional settings that we can use to define the transparency and refraction properties.*

3. Add the **Thin Film** node by navigating to **Node Commander** window > **Material Generator**. Connect **Thin Film > Result** to **Diffuse > Color**.

4. In the **Attribute Manager > Thin Film** node > **Inputs** tab, change **Thickness** to **300**, **IOR** to **2**, and **Spectral Samples** to **15**. Render the scene (see Figure 2).

Thickness and Spectral Samples

If you increase the value of the **Thickness** parameter, you will observe an increase in the number of spectral colors visible in the output. The quality of the render is controlled by the **Spectral Samples** parameter; using a very low value for this parameter will result in a monochrome output.

WHAT JUST HAPPENED?
As depicted in Figure 2, the output we obtained was completely transparent without any hint of the desired color. This occurred because we neglected to modify the transparency color of the material. To correct this, we will make the necessary changes.

5. In the **Attribute Manager > Material** node > **Inputs** tab, change **Transparency** to **HSV** (**0**, **0**, **72**). Render the scene (see Figure 3).

2

3

> **_WHAT NEXT?_**
> _Next, we will create variations in the film. To do so, we ill use a multiplied **Noise** node._

6. Add the **Noise** node by navigating to **Node Commander** window **>** **Material Generator**. In the **Attribute Manager** **>** **Noise** node > **Inputs** tab, change **Noise Type** to **Naki**.

7. Add the **Arithmetic** node by navigating to **Node Commander** window **>** **Math**. In the **Attribute Manager** **>** **Add** node > **Inputs** tab, change **Operation** to **Multiply** and **Input 2** to **20**.

8. Connect **Noise** **>** **Result** to **Multiply** **>** **Input 1**. Connect **Multiply** **>** **Result** to **Thin Film** **>** **Variation**. Render the scene. Figure 4 shows the node graph.

Variation

This parameter is used to create variations in the color patterns.

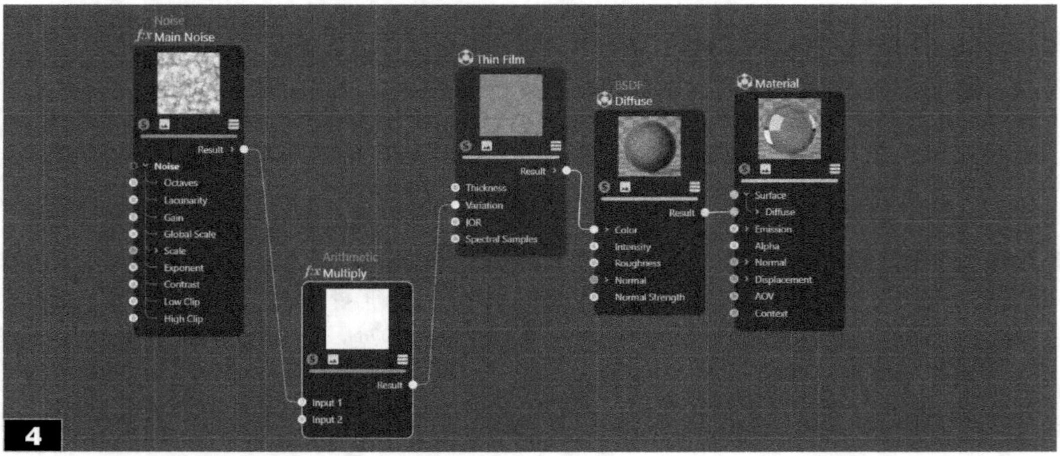

4

WORKING WITH THE GRADIENT NODE

This tutorial aims to demonstrate how to distort a gradient by utilizing the brightness values of another gradient.

Summary	
Topics	Getting Started Working with the Node
Resources folder	**node-based-materials**
Start file	**shadeGeo.c4d**
Final file	**grad-rot-finish.c4d**

Getting Started

Open **shadeGeo.c4d**.

Working with the Node

Follow these steps:

1. Choose **Create > Materials > New Node Material** from the **Material Manager** menubar to create a new node material. Apply this material to the **Geo-1** and **Geo-2** objects. In the **Material Manager**, double-click on **Node** to open the **Node Editor**.
2. Add a **Gradient** node by navigating to **Node Commander** window > **Material Generator**. In the **Attribute Manager > Gradient** node > **Inputs** tab, click the **Load Preset** button and then select the **Pattern 3** preset.
3. Connect **Gradient > Result** to **Diffuse > Color**. In the **Attribute Manager > Gradient** node > **Inputs** tab, select the **Distortion** checkbox in the **DISTORTION** section. Set, **Strength** to **70**. Render the scene (see Figure 1).
4. In the **PROJECTION** section, change **Local Rotation** to **90**. Render the scene (see Figure 2).

1

2

WHAT JUST HAPPENED?
*Upon selecting the **Distortion** checkbox, we gain access to both the **Strength** and **Color** settings. These settings enable us to create non-uniform color transitions within the gradient. The **Strength** setting serves as a multiplier for the intensity of color distortion within the gradient, which can also be reversed by specifying a negative value. Additionally, the **Color** setting allows us to specify which color components and brightness values should be multiplied by the **Strength** value.*

5. Add a **Basic Gradient** node by navigating to **Node Commander** window > **Material Generator**. Connect **Basic Gradient > Result** to **Gradient > Distortion > Color**. In the **Attribute Manager > Basic Gradient** node > **Inputs** tab, change the gradient, as shown in Figure 3. Render the scene (see Figure 4). Figure 5 shows the node graph.

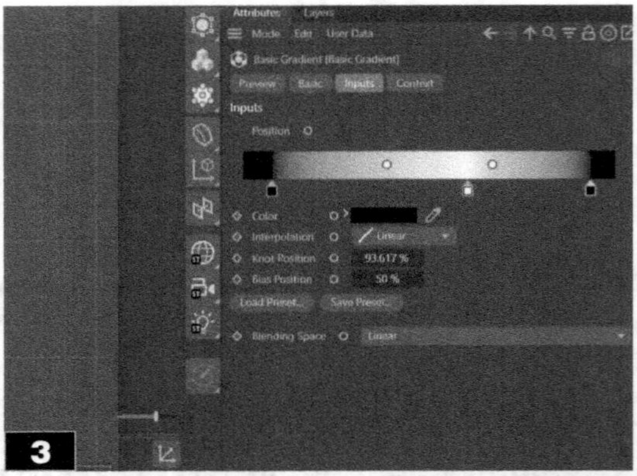

3

4

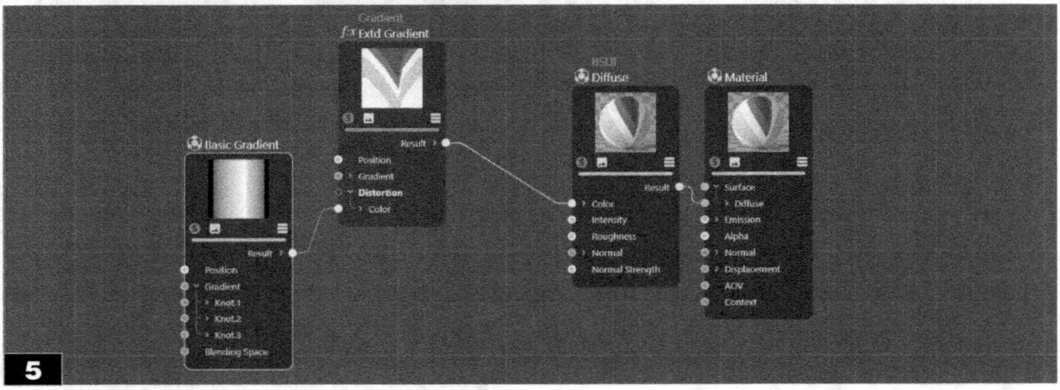

5

CREATING FLAKES USING THE FLAKES NODE

In this tutorial, we will create flakes on a surface using the **Flakes** node.

Summary	
Topics	Getting Started Working with the Node
Resources folder	**node-based-materials**
Start file	**shadeGeo.c4d**
Final file	**flakes-finish.c4d**

Getting Started

Open **shadeGeo.c4d**.

Working with the Node

Follow these steps:

1. Choose **Create** > **Materials** > **New Node Material** from the **Material Manager** menubar to create a new node material. Apply this material to the **Geo-1** and **Geo-2** objects. In the **Material Manager**, double-click on **Node** to open the **Node Editor**.

> **WHAT NEXT?**
> *The aim is to generate a metallic paint material with multiple layers. To accomplish this, we will incorporate three layers: a base layer, a layer for flakes, and a clear coat layer at the top.*

2. Rename **Diffuse** as **Base Coat**. Add the **BSDF** node by navigating to **Node Commander** window > **Surface**. Rename **Diffuse** as **Flakes**. Create another **BSDF** node and then rename it as **Clear Coat**.

3. In the **Attribute Manager > Material** node > **Inputs** tab, click the **Add** button to add a **BSDF** layer. Now, connect **Flakes > Result** to **BSDF Layer 2> BSDF Layer**. Similarly, create another layer and connect **Clear Coat** with it (see Figure 1).

4. In the **Attribute Manager > Base Coat** node > **Inputs** tab, change **Color** to **HSV** (**218**, **97**, **27**). In the **Attribute Manager > Flakes** node > **Inputs** tab, change **BSDF** type to **GGX**, **Fresnel** to **Dielectric**, and **Presets** to **PET**. In the **Attribute Manager > Clear Coat** node > **Inputs** tab, change **BSDF** type to **GGX**, **Fresnel** to **Dielectric**, and **Presets** to **PET**. Render the scene (see Figure 2).

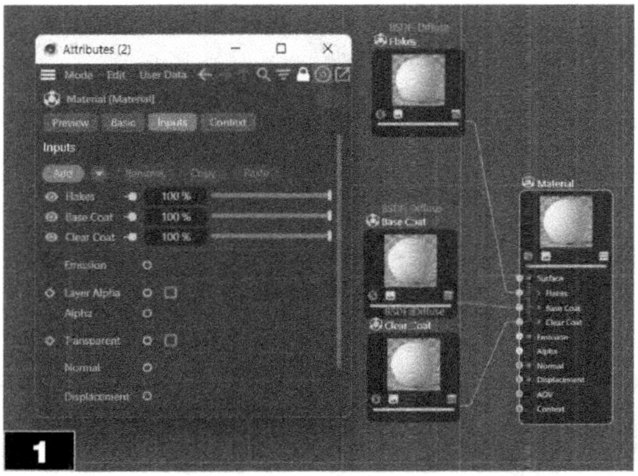

1

2

5. Add the **Flakes** node by navigating to **Node Commander** window > **Material Generator**. Connect **Flakes > Normal** to **Flakes > Normal**. Render the scene (see Figure 3). In the **Attribute Manager > Flakes** node > **Inputs** tab, change **Scale** to **0.05**, **Density** to **10**, and **Intensity** to **70**. Render the scene (see Figure 4).

> **WHAT JUST HAPPENED?**
> *The **Normal** port of the **Flakes** node generates a vector in the object axis system, based on the color values produced. In this instance, we aim to manipulate the normal direction utilizing the flakes effect, and thus, we have linked the **Normal** port of the Flakes node to the **BSDF** layer's **Normal** port.*

3

4

Scale, Density, and Intensity

The size of the flake structure can be controlled by adjusting the **Scale** parameter. Increasing this value will produce fewer, but larger flakes. In contrast, the **Density** parameter determines the size of each individual flake and the spacing between them. Finally, the Intensity parameter regulates the contrast of the flakes.

WHAT NEXT?
*Next, we will utilize the **Mask** output from the **Flakes** node to extract a mask and use it with the **Compose ColorA** node, which enables us to generate color for the flakes. The **Mask** output is a black and white mask for the flakes. The mask is white where flakes lie and black in-between.*

6. Add the **Compose ColorA** node by navigating to **Node Commander window > Conversion**. Connect **Flakes > Mask** to **Compose ColorA > Alpha**. Connect **Compose ColorA > Result** to **Flakes > Color**. In the **Attribute Manager > Compose ColorA** node > **Inputs** tab, change **RGB** to white. Render the scene (see Figure 5). Figure 6 shows the node graph.

5

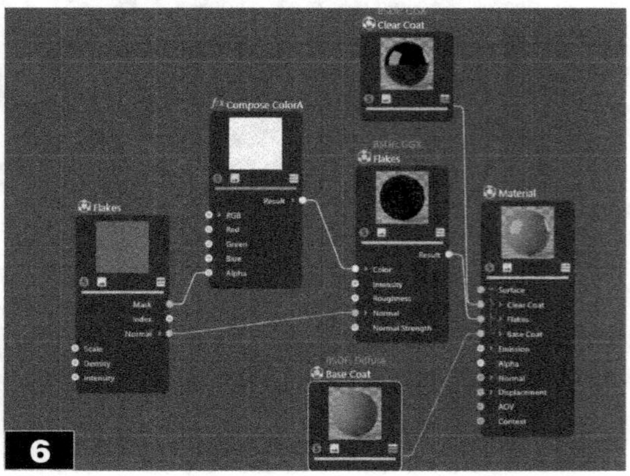

6

WORKING WITH THE GRID NODE

This tutorial will illustrate how to generate a grid pattern by utilizing the **Grid** node. The same grid pattern will also be employed for the **Displacement** map.

Summary	
Topics	Getting Started Working with the Node
Resources folder	**node-based-materials**
Start file	**shadeGeo.c4d**
Final file	**grid-finish.c4d**

Getting Started

Open **shadeGeo.c4d**.

Working with the Node

Follow these steps:

1. Choose **Create > Materials > New Node Material** from the **Material Manager** menubar to create a new node material. Apply this material to the **Geo-1** and **Geo-2** objects. In the **Material Manager**, double-click on **Node** to open the **Node Editor**.
2. Add the **Grid** node by navigating to **Node Commander** window > **Material Generator**. In the **Attribute Manager > Grid** node > **Inputs** tab, change **Thickness** to (**0.1**, **0.3**, and **0.1**), **Softness** to **0.05**, and **Frequency** to (**10**, **4**, **2**). Rename the node is **Grid.1**.
3. Create another **Grid** node and rename it as **Grid.2**. In the **Attribute Manager > Grid.2** node > **Inputs** tab, change **Thickness** to (**0.1**, **0.3**, and **0.1**), **Softness** to **0.05**, and **Frequency** to (**4**, **4**, **2**).

WHAT NEXT?
Our objective now is to alter the appearance of every other row of the grid pattern. To achieve this, we will apply a mask to a specific section of the ***Grid.2*** *output and subsequently merge it with the result of* ***Grid.1****.*

4. Add the **Compose ColorA** node by navigating to **Node Commander** window > **Conversion**. Connect **Grid.2 > Color** to **Compose ColorA > RGB**.
5. Add the **Modulo** node by navigating to **Node Commander** window > **Math**. Connect **Grid.2 > Index** to **Modulo > Value 1**. In the **Attribute Manager > Modulo** node > **Inputs** tab, change **Input 2** to **2**. Connect **Modulo > Result** to **Compose ColorA > Alpha**.

6. Add the **Layer** node by navigating to **Node Commander** window > **Color**. Connect **Compose ColorA** > **Result** to **Layer** > **Layer 1**. Connect **Grid.1** > **Color** to **Layer** > **Layer 2**.

7. Add the **Displacement** node by navigating to **Node Commander** window > **Surface**. Connect **Layer** > **Result** to **Displacement Map** > **Value**. In the **Attribute Manager** > **Displacement Map** node > **Inputs** tab, change **Strength** to **40**. Connect **Displacement Map** > **Result** to **Material** > **Displacement**. Render the scene (see Figure 1).

8. Add the **Invert Color** node by navigating to **Node Commander** window > **Color**. Connect **Layer** > **Result** to **Invert Color** > **Color**. Connect **Invert Color** > output **Color** to **Diffuse** > **Color**. Render the scene, see Figure 2. Figure 3 shows the node graph.

1

2

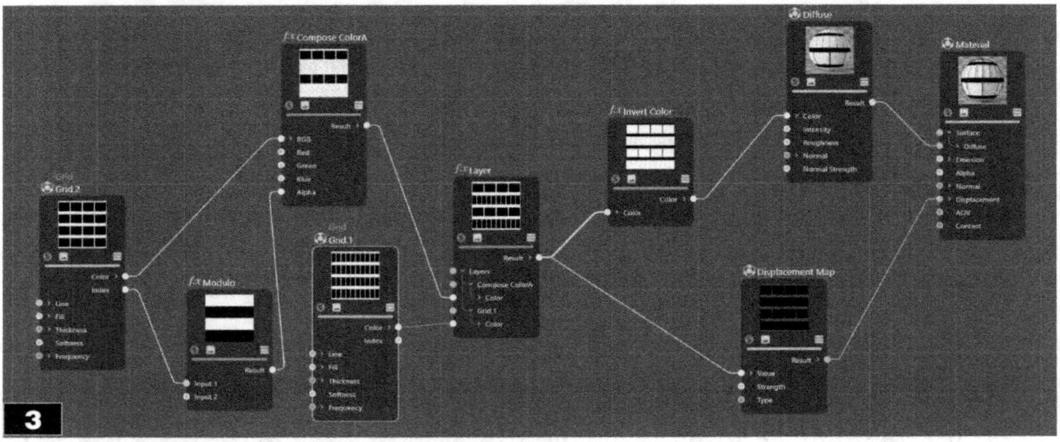

3

WORKING WITH THE SCRATCHES NODE

The goal of this tutorial is to produce scratch marks on a surface utilizing the **Scratches** node.

Summary	
Topics	Getting Started Working with the Node
Resources folder	**node-based-materials**
Start file	**shadeGeo.c4d**
Final file	**scratches-finish.c4d**

Getting Started

Open **shadeGeo.c4d**.

Working with the Node

Follow these steps:

1. Choose **Create > Materials > New Node Material** from the **Material Manager** menubar to create a new node material. Apply this material to the **Geo-1** and **Geo-2** objects. In the **Material Manager**, double-click on **Node** to open the **Node Editor**.

2. In the **Attribute Manager > Diffuse** node **> Inputs** tab, change **Color** to **HSV** (**234**, **93**, **93**). Rename the node as **Diffuse.1**.

3. Add a **BSDF** node by navigating to **Node Commander** window **> Surface**. Rename the node as **Diffuse.2**. Add another layer in the **Material** node and then connect it with **Diffuse.2 > Result**.

WHAT JUST HAPPENED?
An additional ***BSDF*** *layer has been incorporated in this step, which will be utilized to superimpose scratch marks on top of the original* ***BSDF*** *layer.*

4. Add the **Gradient** node by navigating to **Node Commander** window **> Material Generator**. In the **Attribute Manager > Gradient** node **> Inputs** tab, change the gradient as shown in Figure 1. In the **Attribute Manager > Gradient** node > **PROJECTION** area, change **Rotation** to **90**.

5. Add the **Scratches** node by navigating to **Node Commander** window **> Material Generator**. Connect **Gradient > Result** to **Scratches > Depth**. In the **Attribute Manager > Scratches** node **> Inputs** tab, change **Scale** to **32.15**, **Rotation** to **66**, **Layers** to **3**, **Frequency Step** to **0.75**, **Bend** to **60**, and **Thickness** to **60**.

WHAT JUST HAPPENED?

A gradient has been linked to the ***Depth*** *port in this step. This enables the user to control the intensity of the scratches by adjusting the* ***Depth*** *value. Raising the value will cause the scratches to appear darker. The* ***Scale*** *parameter is employed to regulate the size of the scratches. By default, the scratches will be generated perpendicular to the surface. However, this can be changed by adjusting the* ***Rotation*** *value to manipulate the orientation. The* ***Layers*** *parameter determines the number of layers of scratch marks to be superimposed. The* ***Frequency Step*** *value adjusts the scaling of each successive layer in comparison to the previous layer. The* ***Bend*** *parameter is used to add curvature to the scratches, while the* ***Thickness*** *parameter defines the maximum width of the scratches.*

WHAT NEXT?

In the following step, the ***Invert Color*** *node will be utilized to invert the output of the* ***Scratches*** *node. This operation will produce white scratches on a black background. The* ***Compose ColorA*** *node will then be used to extract the alpha information, which will allow the scratches information to be overlaid on the surface.*

6. Add the **Invert Color** node by navigating to **Node Commander** window > **Color**. Connect **Scratches** > **Result** to **Invert Color** > **Color**. Connect **Invert Color** > **Color** to **Diffuse.2** > **Color**. Render the scene (see Figure 2).

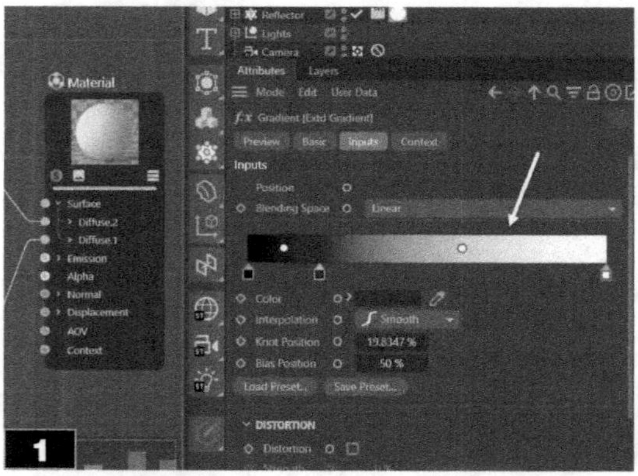

1

2

7. Navigate to **Node Commander** window > **Compose** > **Compose ColorA** and then drag **Compose ColorA** onto the wire connecting the **Invert Color** and **Diffuse.2** nodes to insert the **Compose ColorA** node between them.

8. Re-route the connection to the Alpha port of the **Compose ColorA** node. In the **Attribute Manager** > **Compose ColorA** node > **Inputs** tab, change **RGB** to white. Render the scene, see Figure 3.

9. Navigate to **Node Commander** window > **Math** > **Arithmetic** and then drag **Arithmetic** onto the wire connecting the **Gradient** and **Scratches** nodes.

10. In the **Attribute Manager** > **Arithmetic** node > **Inputs** tab > set **Result** to **Multiply**, **Data Type** to **Float**, and **Input 2** to **3**.

11. In the **Attribute Manager** > **Gradient** node > **Inputs** tab, change the gradient, as shown in Figure 4. Render the scene, see Figure 5.

3

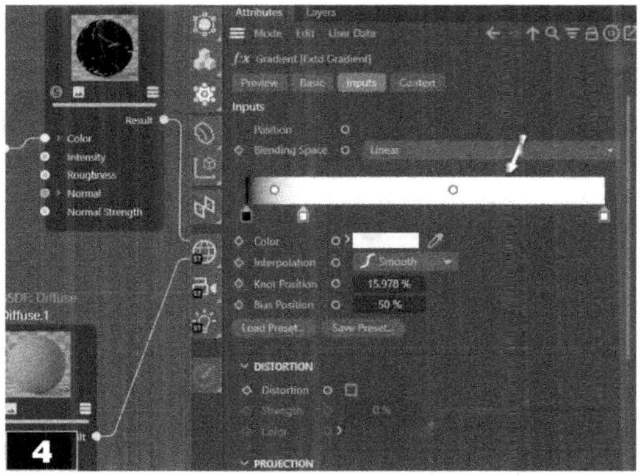

4

12. In the **Attribute Manager** > **Scratches** node > **Inputs** tab, change **Scale** to **5**, **Rotation** to **66**, **Density** to **100**, and **Thickness** to **79**. Render the scene (see Figure 6). Figure 7 shows the node graph.

5

6

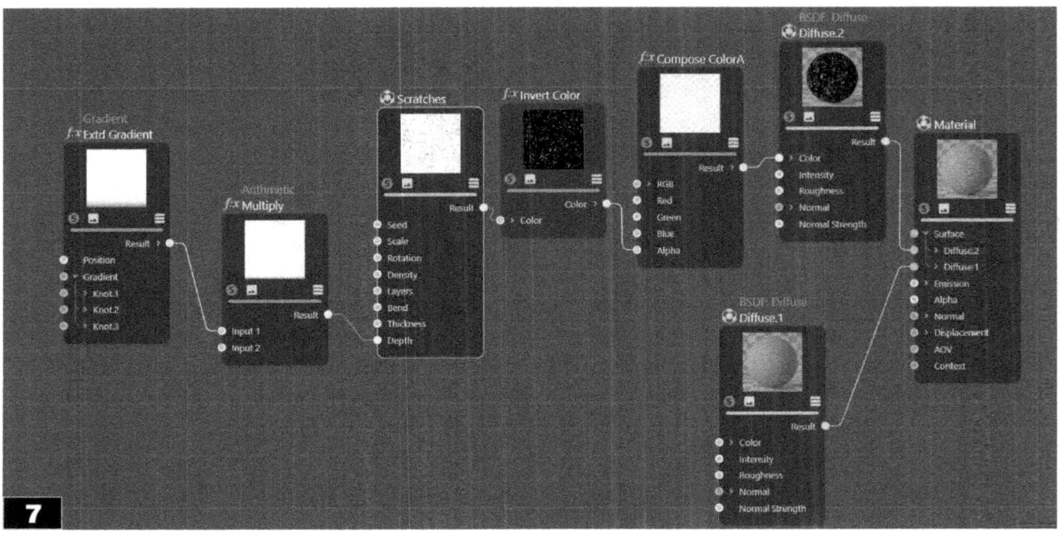

7

WORKING WITH THE BLACKBODY NODE

The tutorial will demonstrate the use of an **Ambient Occlusion** node to change the blackbody temperature.

Summary	
Topics	Getting Started Working with the Node
Resources folder	**node-based-materials**
Start file	**shadeGeo.c4d**
Final file	**blackbody-finish.c4d**

Getting Started

Open **shadeGeo.c4d**.

Working with the Node

Follow these steps:

1. Choose **Create** > **Materials** > **New Node Material** from the **Material Manager** menubar to create a new node material. Apply this material to the **Geo-1** and **Geo-2** objects. In the **Material Manager**, double-click on **Node** to open the **Node Editor**.

2. In the **Attribute Manager** > **Diffuse** node > **Inputs** tab, change **Color** to **HSV** (**0**, **0**, **9**). Add the **Ambient Occlusion** node by navigating to **Node Commander** window > **Material Generator**.

3. Add the **Range Mapper** node by navigating to **Node Commander** window > **Math**. Connect **Ambient Occlusion** > **Occlusion** to **Range Mapper** > **Input**. In the **Attribute Manager** > **Range Mapper** node > **Inputs** tab, change **Output Max** to **78**.

4. Add the **Blackbody** node by navigating to **Node Commander** window > **Material Generator**. Connect **Range Mapper** > **Result** to **Blackbody** > **Temperature**. Connect **Blackbody** > **Result** to **Material** > **Emission**. Render the scene (see Figure 1).

WHAT JUST HAPPENED?

In this process, we have redefined the output of ***Ambient Occlusion****, which is a float value ranging from* ***0*** *to* ***1****, and linked it to the* ***Temperature*** *parameter of the* ***Blackbody*** *node. The* ***Temperature*** *setting determines the temperature level at which the black body is heated. Then, we have linked the result of the* ***Blackbody*** *node to the* ***Emission*** *input of* ***Material****, which ensures that the emission characteristics of the material are controlled by the* ***Ambient Occlusion*** *node.*

WHAT NEXT?
*Next, we will use the **Invert** node to impact the region surrounding the objects, causing warmer colors to manifest in those particular areas.*

5. Navigate to **Node Commander** window > **Math** > **Arithmetic** and then drag **Arithmetic** onto the wire connecting the **Blackbody** and **Material** nodes. In the **Attribute Manager > Inputs** tab, select **Multiply** from the **Operation** drop-down list.

6. Add the **Invert** node by navigating to **Node Commander window > Math**. Connect **Ambient Occlusion** > **Occlusion** to **Invert > Value**. Connect **Invert > Result** to **Multiply** > **Input 2**. In the **Attribute Manager > Invert** node > **Inputs** tab, change **Data Type** to **Float**. Render the scene (see Figure 2). Figure 3 shows the node graph.

1

2

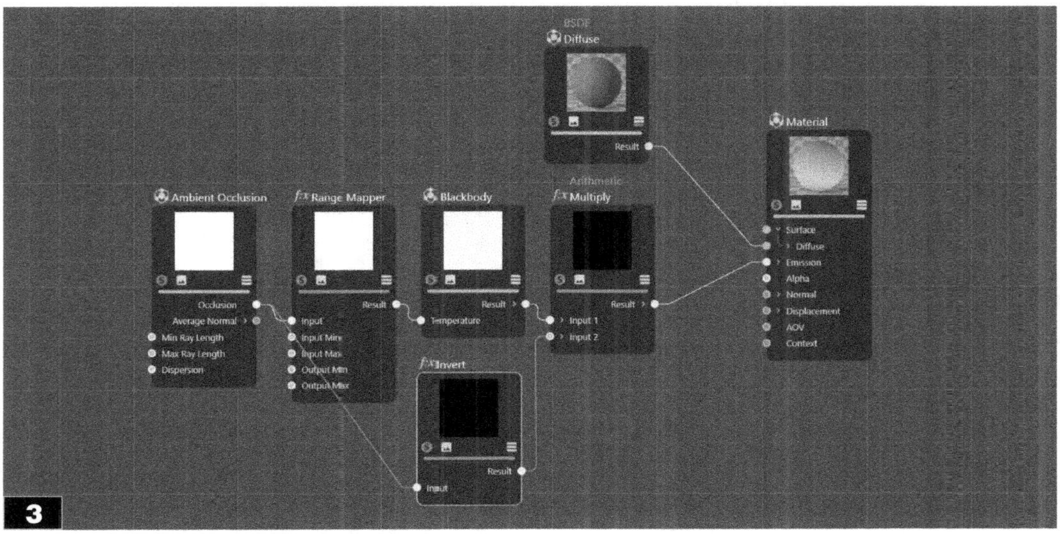

3

WORKING WITH THE LIGHT NODE

In this tutorial, we will employ the **Light** node to extract **Light Color** information, which we will then utilize to regulate the luminance effect of the material.

Summary	
Topics	Getting Started Working with the Node
Resources folder	**node-based-materials**
Start file	**shadeGeo.c4d**
Final file	**light-finish.c4d**

Getting Started

Open **shadeGeo.c4d**.

Working with the Node

Follow these steps:

1. Choose **Create > Materials > New Node Material** from the **Material Manager** menubar to create a new node material. Apply this material to the **Geo-1** and **Geo-2** objects. In the **Material Manager**, double-click on **Node** to open the **Node Editor**.

2. Add the **BSDF** node by navigating to **Node Commander window > Surface** and then connect it with the **Material** node using a new layer. Rename it as **Diffuse.2**. In the **Attribute Manager > Diffuse.2** node > **Inputs** tab, change **BSDF Type** to **GGX**, **Fresnel** to **Dielectric**, and **Intensity** to **40**.

3. Load the **glass.jpg** to the **Node Editor** and then add the **Veins** node by navigating to **Node Commander** window > **Material Generator**. In the **Attribute Manager > Veins** node > **Inputs** tab, change **Large Turbulence** to **30**, **Small Turbulence** to **5**, **Veins Gaps** to **26**, and **Contrast** to **20**.

4. Add the **Mix** node by navigating to **Node Commander** window **> Math**. Connect **Veins > Color** to **Mix > Input 1**. Connect **glass.jpg > Result** to **Mix > Input 2**.

WHAT JUST HAPPENED?
*I employed the **Mix** node to combine the output of the **glass.jpg** bitmap and the **Veins** node. The **Blend Factor** parameter allows for the interpolation between two values.*

WHAT NEXT?
*We will now utilize the output of the **Mix** node to influence the material's luminance characteristics by linking the node to the **Material > Emission** input. Following that, we will insert a **Light** node and apply its In **Shadow** input to produce shading through the use of shadows.*

5. In the **Attribute Manager > Mix** node > **Inputs** tab, change **Data Type** to **Color**. Connect **Mix > Result** to **Material > Emission**.

6. Add the **Light** node by navigating to **Node Commander** window > **Info**. Add the **Color to Float** node by navigating to **Node Commander** window > **Conversion**. Connect **Light > In Shadow** to **Color to Float > Color**.

WHY THE COLOR TO FLOAT NODE IS USED?
*As the **In Shadow** output of the **Light** node generates a boolean value while the **Blend Factor** input of the **Mix** node requires a float value, we must utilize the **Color to Float** node to convert the boolean value into a float value.*

7. In the **Attribute Manager > Color to Float** node > **Inputs** tab, change **Mode** to **Length**. Connect **Color to Float > Result** to **Mix > Blend**. Render the scene (see Figure 1).

WHAT JUST HAPPENED?
*Figure 1 illustrates that the impact of the **Mix** node is most apparent in the shadowed regions, but the effect is excessively strong. To mitigate this, we will introduce the **Reciprocal** node to diminish the intensity of the effect.*

8. Add the **Reciprocal** node by navigating to **Node Commander** window > **Math**. Connect **Color To Float > Result** to **Reciprocal > Input**. Connect **Reciprocal > Result** to **Mix > Blend Factor**. Render the scene, see Figure 2. Figure 3 shows the node graph.

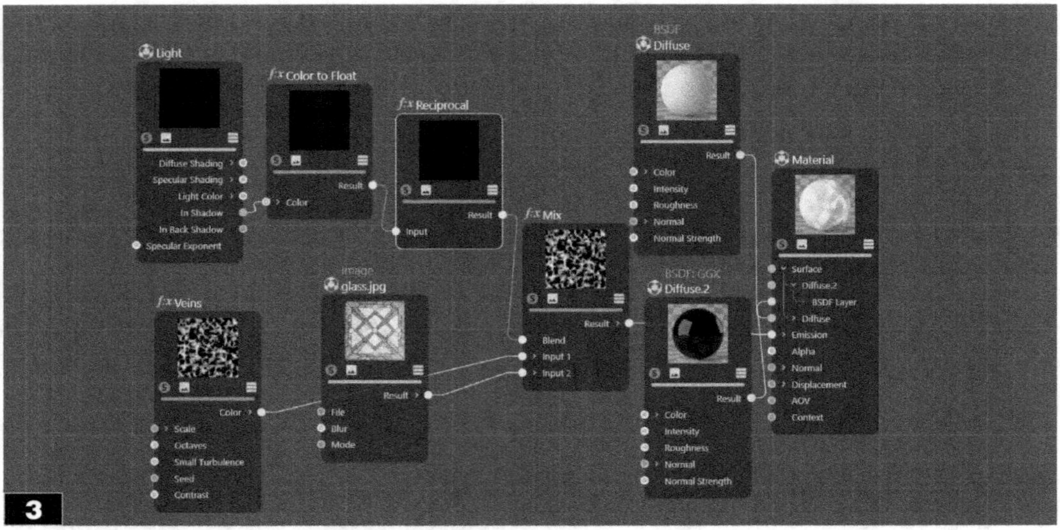

WORKING WITH THE QUANTIZE NODE

In this tutorial, we will use the **Quantize** node to reduce the number of colors using stepped values.

Summary	
Topics	Getting Started Working with the Node
Resources folder	**node-based-materials**
Start file	**shadeGeo.c4d**
Final file	**quantize-finish.c4d**

Getting Started

Open **shadeGeo.c4d**.

Working with the Node

Follow these steps:

1. Choose **Create > Materials > New Node Material** from the **Material Manager** menubar to create a new node material. Apply this material to the **Geo-1** and **Geo-2** objects. In the **Material Manager**, double-click on **Node** to open the **Node Editor**.
2. In the **Attribute Manager > Diffuse** node > **Inputs** tab, change **Fresnel** to **Dielectric**.
3. Add the **Noise** node by navigating to **Node Commander** window > **Material Generator**. In the **Attribute Manager > Noise** node > **Inputs** tab, change **Noise Type** to **Luka**, **Global Scale** to **2000**, **Low Clip** to **2**, and **High Clip** to **75**.

4. Add the **Quantize** node by navigating to **Node Commander** window **> Math**. Connect **Noise > Result** to **Quantize > Input**. In the **Attribute Manager > Quantize** node > **Inputs** tab, change **Steps** to **15**. Connect **Quantize.1 > Result** to **Diffuse.1 > Color**. Render the scene (see Figure 1).

5. Add the **UV Transform** node by navigating to **Node Commander** window **> Context**. Connect **UV Transform > Result** to **Noise > Context**. In the **Attribute Manager > UV Transform** node > **Inputs** tab, change **Local Repetitions** to **50** each. Render the scene (see Figure 2). Figure 3 shows the node graph.

1

2

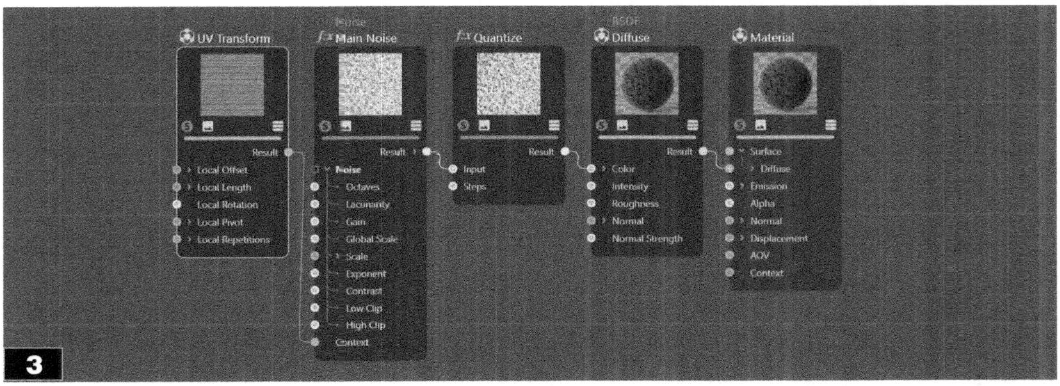

3

WORKING WITH THE OVERRIDE CONTEXT NODE

In this tutorial, we will use the **Override Shading Context** node to override context of sub-graph.

Summary	
Topics	Getting Started Working with the Node
Resources folder	**node-based-materials**

Summary	
Start file	**shadeGeo.c4d**
Final file	**override-finish.c4d**

Getting Started

Open **shadeGeo.c4d**.

Working with the Node

Follow these steps:

1. Choose **Create > Materials > New Node Material** from the **Material Manager** menubar to create a new node material. Apply this material to the **Geo-1** and **Geo-2** objects. In the **Material Manager**, double-click on **Node** to open the **Node Editor**.

2. Add the **Noise** node by navigating to **Node Commander** window > **Material Generator**. In the **Attribute Manager > Noise** node > **Inputs** tab, change **Noise Type** to **Voronoi 3**.

3. Add the **Override Shading Context** node by navigating to **Node Commander** window > **Context**.

4. Connect **Noise > Result** to **Override Shading Context > Color**. Connect **Override Shading Context > Result** to **Diffuse > Color**. Render the scene, see Figure 1.

5. Add the **UV Reprojection** node by navigating to **Node Commander** window > **Context**. Connect **UV Reprojection > Result** to **Override Shading Context > Context**.

6. In the **Attribute Manager > UV Reprojection** node > **Inputs** tab, change **Mode** to **Circular**. Render the scene, see Figure 2. Figure 3 shows the node graph.

1

2

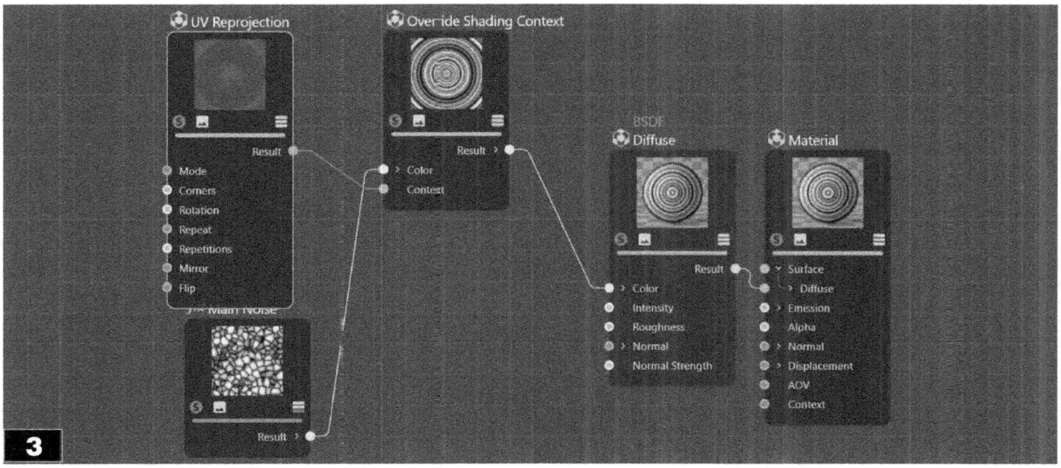

WORKING WITH THE PROJECTION NODE

In this tutorial, we will use the **Projection** node to alter the coordinate system.

Summary	
Topics	Getting Started Working with the Node
Resources folder	**node-based-materials**
Start file	**shadeGeo.c4d**
Final file	**projection-finish.c4d**

Getting Started

Open **shadeGeo.c4d**.

Working with the Node

Follow these steps:

1. Choose **Create** > **Materials** > **New Node Material** from the **Material Manager** menubar to create a new node material. Apply this material to the **Geo-1** and **Geo-2** objects. In the **Material Manager**, double-click on **Node** to open the **Node Editor**.

2. Add the **Grid** node by navigating to **Node Commander** window > **Material Generator**. In the **Attribute Manager** > **Grid** node > **Inputs** tab, change **Frequency** to (**2**, **4**, **2**). Connect **Grid** > **Color** to **Diffuse** > **Color**.

3. Add the **Projection** node by navigating to **Node Commander** window > **Context**. In the **Attribute Manager** > **Projection** node > **Inputs** tab, select the **Additional Transform** checkbox. Now, change **Rotation** to (**45**, **45**, **45**). Connect **Projection** > **Result** to **Grid** > **Context**. Render the scene (see Figure 1).

> **WHAT NEXT?**
> *Now, we will scale the UVs of the* ***Grid.1*** *node. To do so, we will use the* ***Scale*** *parameter of the* ***Projection*** *node. This parameter scales the texture file. The values are multipliers of the value of the* ***Reference Size*** *parameter. We will use a* ***Gradient*** *node to drive the* ***Scale*** *value.*

4. Add the **Gradient** node by navigating to **Node Commander** window **> Material Generator**. In the **Attribute Manager > Gradient** node > **Inputs** tab > **PROJECTION** section, change **Mode** to **Circular**.
5. Add the **Range Mapper** node by navigating to **Node Commander** window **> Math**. Connect **Gradient > Result** to **Range Mapper > Input**. In the **Attribute Manager > Range Mapper** node > **Inputs** tab, change **Data Type** to **Color**, and **Output Max** to **HSV** (**0**, **0**, **22**).
6. Connect **Range Mapper > Result** to **Projection > Scale**. Render the sene, see Figure 2. Figure 3 shows the node graph.

1

2

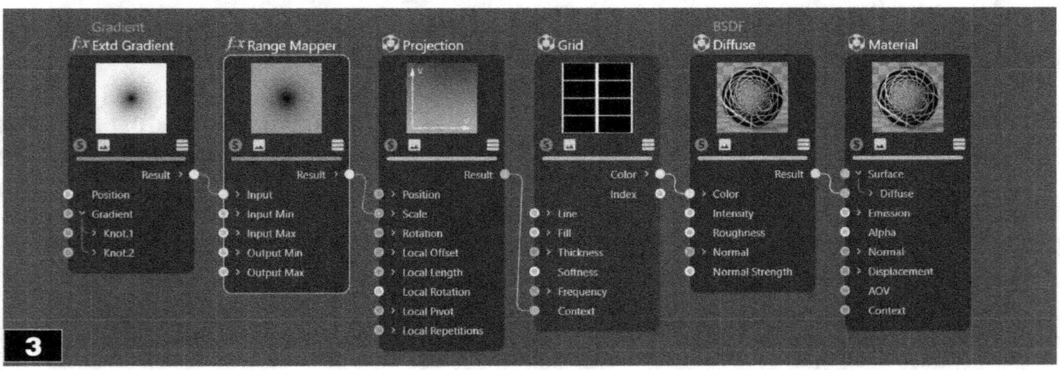

3

WORKING WITH THE SCATTER NODE

In this tutorial, we will use the **Scatter** node to scatter an image on a surface.

Summary	
Topics	Getting Started Working with the Node
Resources folder	**node-based-materials**
Start file	**shadeGeo.c4d**
Final file	**scatter-finish.c4d**

Getting Started

Open **shadeGeo.c4d**.

Working with the Node

Follow these steps:

1. Choose **Create > Materials > New Node Material** from the **Material Manager** menubar to create a new node material. Apply this material to the **Geo-1** and **Geo-2** objects. In the **Material Manager**, double-click on **Node** to open the **Node Editor**.
2. Load **Logo.png** and then connect its **Result** port with the **Diffuse > Color** port. Create a copy of **Logo.png** and rename it as **Logo-Alpha**.
3. Add the **Split Color** node by navigating to **Node Commander** window > **Color**. Connect **Logo-Alpha > Result** to **Split Color > Color**.
4. Add the **Scatter** node by navigating to **Node Commander** window > **Context**. Connect **Split Color > Alpha** to **Scatter > Shape**.
5. In the **Attribute Manager > Scatter** node > **Inputs** tab, change **Max Splat Count** to **50**, **Density** to **30**, and **Scale** to (**0.5**, **0.5**).
6. Connect **Scatter > Context** to **Logo.png > Context**. Render the scene, see Figure 1. Figure 2 shows the node graph.

1

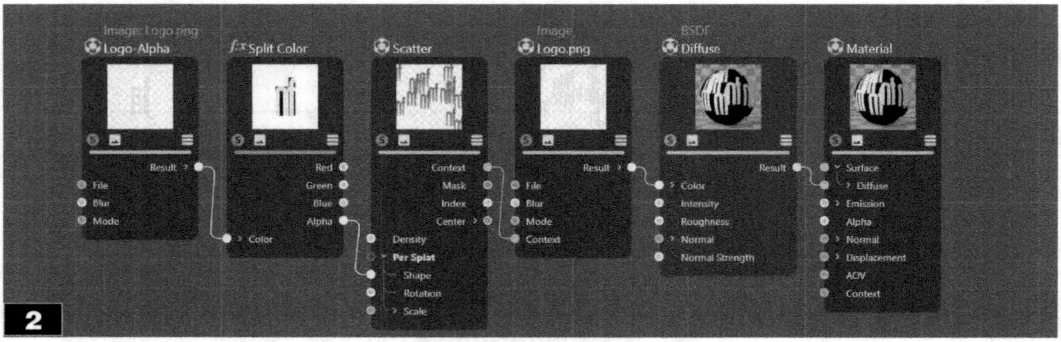

WORKING WITH THE UV DISTORTER NODE

This tutorial will demonstrate how to create distortion in the projection using the **UV Distorter** node.

Summary	
Topics	Getting Started Working with the Node
Resources folder	**node-based-materials**
Start file	**shadeGeo.c4d**
Final file	**distortion-finish.c4d**

Getting Started

Open **shadeGeo.c4d**.

Working with the Node

Follow these steps:

1. Choose **Create > Materials > New Node Material** from the **Material Manager** menubar to create a new node material. Apply this material to the **Geo-1** and **Geo-2** objects. In the **Material Manager**, double-click on **Node** to open the **Node Editor**.

2. Add the **Grid** node by navigating to **Node Commander** window > **Material Generator**. In the **Attribute Manager > Grid** node > **Inputs** tab, change **Frequency** to (**5**, **5**, **4**). Connect **Grid > Color** to **Diffuse > Color**.

3. Add the **UV Distorter** node by navigating to **Node Commander** window > **Context**. Connect **UV Distorter > Result** to **Grid > Context**.

WHAT NEXT?
*Next, we'll utilize the **Basic Gradient** nodes to control the distortion's direction, and the **Noise** node to control its strength. We can specify the direction using vectors,*

*where the **X** component determines the **U** direction, the **Y** component controls the **V** direction, and the **Z** component adjusts the **W** coordinates. The strength of the distortion can be adjusted using a multiplier value applied to the direction vectors.*

4. Add the **Basic Gradient** node by navigating to **Node Commander** window > **Material Generator**. Rename it as **Basic Gradient.1**. In the **Attribute Manager > Basic Gradient** node > **Inputs** tab, change the gradient, as shown in Figure 1.

5. Add the **Basic Gradient** node by navigating to **Node Commander** window > **Material Generator**. Rename it as **Basic Gradient.2**. Add the **Compose Color** node by navigating to **Node Commander** window > **Conversion**.

6. Connect **Basic Gradient.1** > **Result** to **Compose Color** > **Red**. Connect **Basic Gradient.2** > **Result** to **Compose Color.1** > **Green**. Connect **Compose Color** > **Result** to **UV Distorter** > **Direction**. Render the scene (see Figure 2).

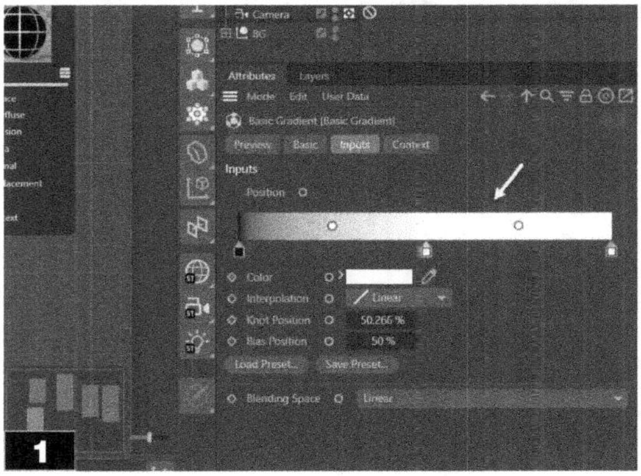

1

2

7. Add the **Noise** node by navigating to **Node Commander** window > **Generator**. In the **Attribute Manager** > **Noise** node > **Inputs** tab, change **Noise Type** to **Box**. Connect **Noise** > **Result** to **UV Distorter** > **Strength**. Render the scene (see Figure 3). Change **Noise Type** to **Dents**. Render the scene (see Figure 4). Figure 5 shows the node network.

3

4

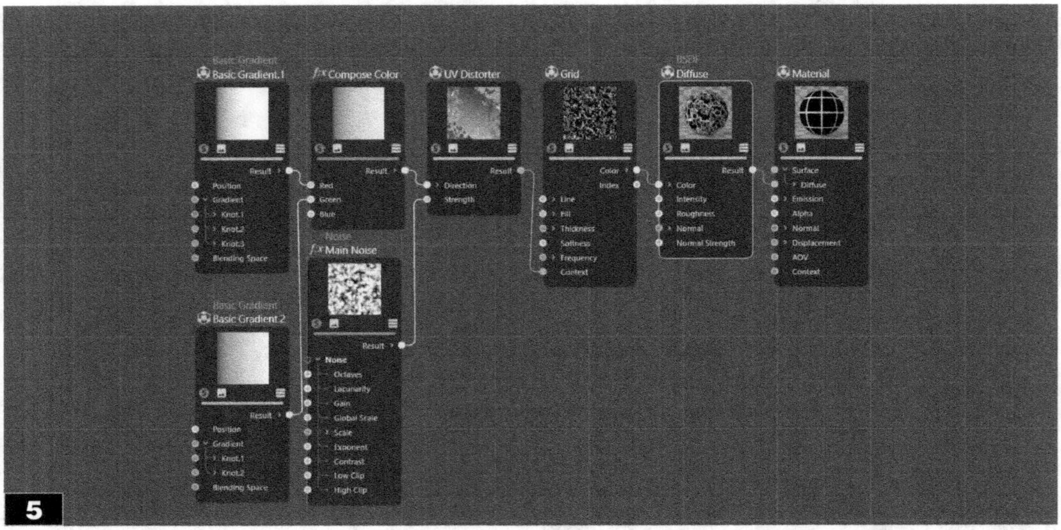
Basic Gradient
Basic Gradient.1
Result
Position
Gradient
Knot.1
Knot.2
Knot.3
Blending Space
Compose Color
Result
Red
Green
Blue
UV Distorter
Result
Direction
Strength
Grid
Color
Index
Line
Fill
Thickness
Softness
Frequency
Context
BSDF
Diffuse
Result
Color
Intensity
Roughness
Normal
Normal Strength
Material
Surface
Diffuse
Emission
Alpha
Normal
Displacement
AOV
Context
Noise
Main Noise
Result
Noise
Octaves
Lacunarity
Gain
Global Scale
Scale
Exponent
Contrast
Low Clip
High Clip
Basic Gradient
Basic Gradient.2
Result
Position
Gradient
Knot.1
Knot.2
Blending Space
5

CHAPTER 7: LIGHTING

To create realistic visualizations in Cinema 4D, it's crucial to excel in the skill of lighting. Lighting has a significant impact on the overall visual outcome as it determines the world around us. Observing real-world lighting is the key to emulating realistic light effects. The lights that are added to a scene illuminate other objects present within the scene, and the objects' appearance is influenced by the material used, which determines their color and texture.

LIGHT OBJECTS

Cinema 4D utilizes a default light, known as auto light, to light up the scene when you create a new one. If you introduce a **Light** object into the scene, the auto light will be disabled. In case you turn off any lights during the animation, Cinema 4D's auto light will be activated automatically unless you choose to disable the **Auto Light** feature. You can find this option under the **Options** category within the **Render Settings** window.

DEFAULT LIGHTING
If you want to modify the default lighting configuration for upcoming new scenes, you can accomplish this by constructing a new scene that has the lights that you prefer for the default lighting. Afterward, save this scene as ***new.c4d*** *within the Cinema 4D folder located in your Cinema 4D directory. This default lighting setup will then be implemented automatically every time you initiate a new Cinema 4D scene.*

DEFAULT SCENE
In addition to saving light objects, you can also store environment properties like ***Sky, Floor, Environment****, and others. To achieve this, create a scene and select* ***Window > Customization > Save As Default Scene*** *from the main menu.*

To create lights in Cinema 4D, click on the desired light object in the **Objects** palette > **Light** command group. You can also access these objects from the **Create > VIRTUAL SET > Light** menu. These light objects are discussed next.

DISPLAYING LIGHTS IN THE VIEWPORT
*To preview lights within the viewport, you can activate the **Gouraud Shading** option in the **Display** menu of the editor view.*

To generate a **Light** object, you can either select **Light** from the **Objects** palette or go to **Create > VIRTUAL SET > Light > Light** in the main menu. The **Light** object will appear in the scene. Once you select the **Light** object, its properties will appear in the **Attribute Manager** under various tabs, which are discussed below:

GENERAL TAB

The **Color** parameter is used to adjust the color of the light. Figure 1 displays the outcome when the **Color** is set to **HSV** (**56**, **65**, **100**). If you prefer to adjust the light's color via the color temperature, select the **Use Temperature** checkbox and enter the desired color temperature in the **Color Temperature** parameter. Figure 2 displays two renders, one at a **Color Temperature** of **4000** on the left, and another at **7000** on the right. [**lights.c4d**]

The **Intensity** parameter governs the overall luminosity of the light source. Not only can this parameter be used to increase the scene's brightness, but it can also be utilized to generate negative lighting by setting a negative value. When a negative value is set, the light's color becomes crucial as it will not be incorporated into the scene when the negative light source is in effect. This feature allows you to create artificial shadows and darken specific areas of your scene. Values greater than **100%** can be entered into the **Intensity** field. Figure 3 displays renders obtained when the **Intensity** is set to **25**, **50**, and **75**.

3

The options in the **Type** drop-down list allow you to select the type of the light:

- **Omni:** This type works like a real-world light bulb — casting light in all directions. If you place the **Omni** light at the center of the scene, it will illuminate the scene evenly in all directions (see Figure 1).
- **Spot:** This type of lights cast their rays in just one direction, which is along the Z axis by default (see Figure 4).
- **Infinite:** This light type simulates distant light sources such as Sun (see Figure 5).

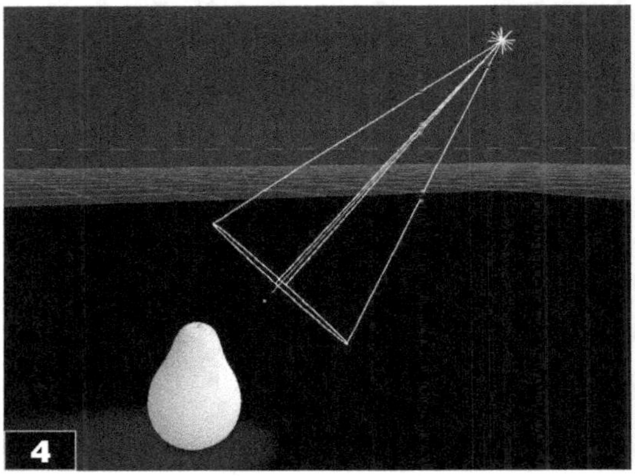
4

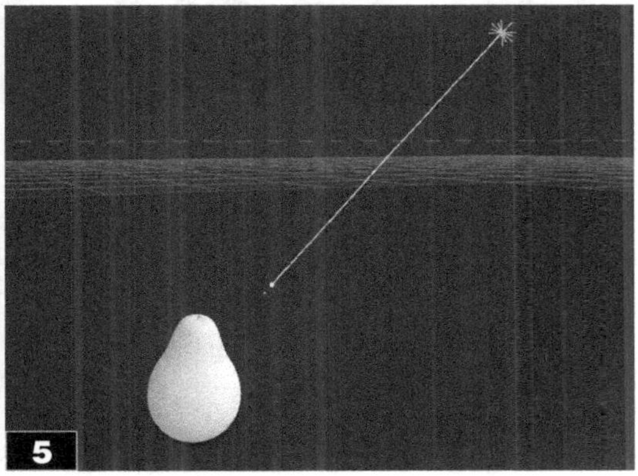
5

- **Area:** This type of light source expands light rays from all points on its surface outwards in all directions (see Figure 6).
- **Square Spot:** See **Spot**. This type projects a square cone of light (see Figure 7).
- **Parallel:** This type resembles the **Infinite** light. Unlike the **Infinite** light source however, the **Parallel** light has an origin and simulates a large, single axis wall of light.
- **Parallel Spot:** This light type resembles the regular spotlight but do not have light cone to define falloff or distance. Instead, light rays are cast along cylinders (see Figure 8).
- **Square Parallel Spot:** See **Parallel** Spot. In this type, light rays are cast along bars (see Figure 9).

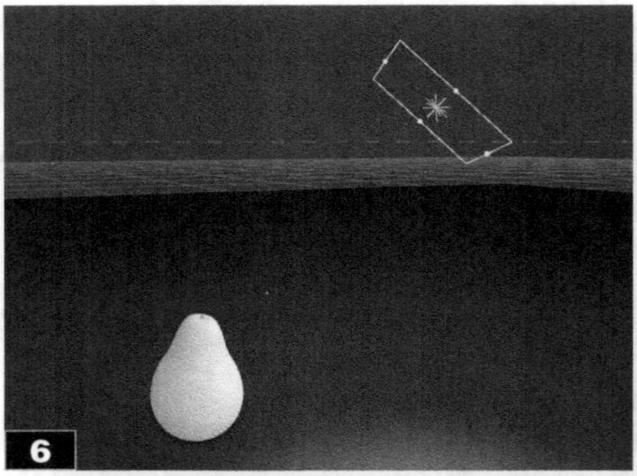
6

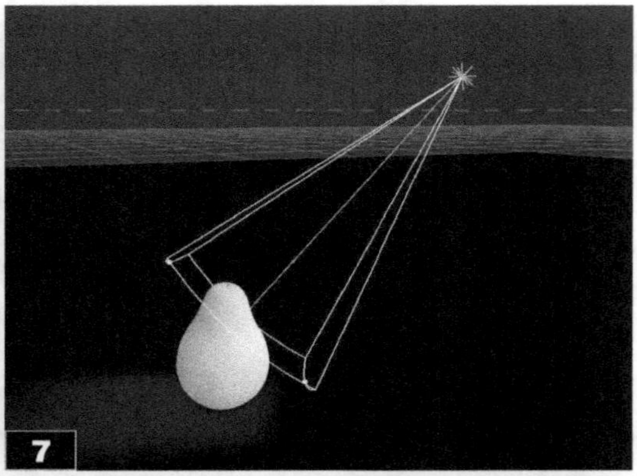
7

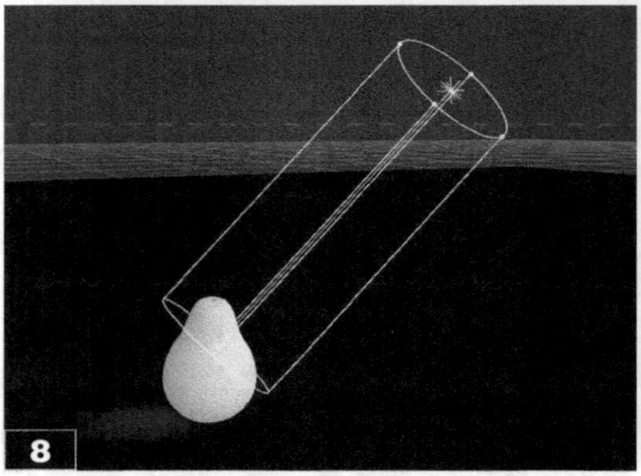
8

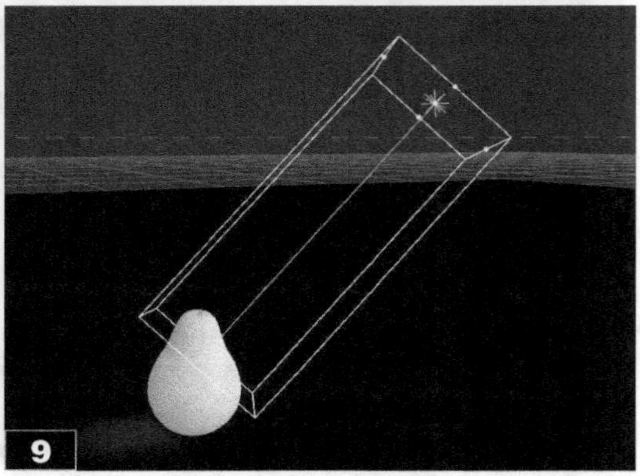
9

The options in the **Shadow** drop-down list are utilized to determine the type of shadow produced by a light source. Select **None** if you want the light to produce no shadows. The **Shadow** drop-down list's clone can also be found in the **Shadow** tab, which will be covered later in the **Shadow Tab** section.

The options in the **Visible Light** drop-down list enable you to specify the visibility of the light in your scene. You can use these options to create a light effect in a smoky room, for instance.

This effect is similar to fog, which does not diminish the light but adds to its brightness. With these options, you can produce effects like headlights, twinkling lights, laser beams, and more. In Cinema 4D, all light sources can be made visible.

When you set **Visible Light** to **Visible** (as seen in Figure 10), the light source will generate visible light that passes through all objects in the scene. For instance, a visible light can be placed at the center of a planet's sphere to simulate an atmosphere. Visible light can be used to create various effects such as nebula clouds, smoke, comet tails, fire, flames, and more. [**light-visible.c4d**]

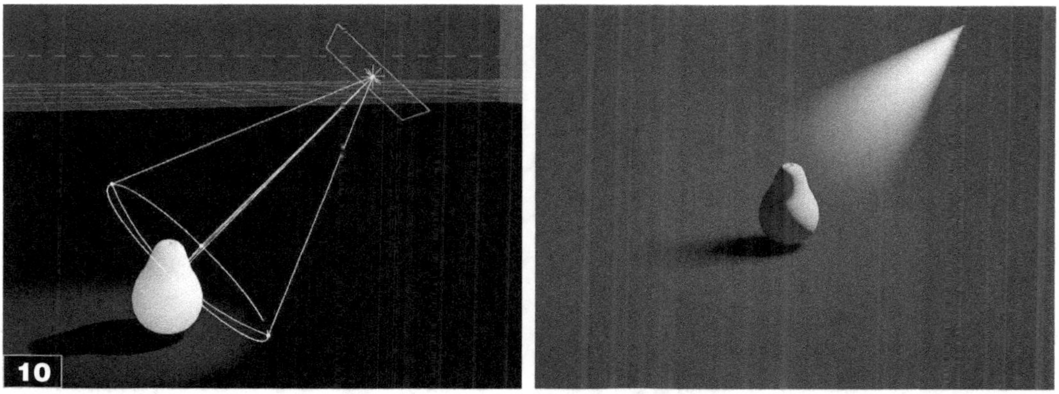

10

As mentioned earlier, **Visible** light passes through objects without creating any shadows in its beam. If you want a **Visible** light source to cast shadows, you can use the **Volumetric** option (as shown in Figure 11). [**light-visible-1.c4d**]The **Inverse Volumetric** option can be used to invert this effect (as shown in Figure 12). This option can be useful in logo design, where you can place the light source behind the logo, creating the impression that the light is emanating from the logo itself.

11

12

To view only the visible light and/or its lens effects without the light source illuminating objects, you can select the **No Illumination** checkbox. On the other hand, the **Show Illumination** checkbox is enabled by default, which displays a wireframe approximation of the light's illumination in the viewports. For example, in the left image of Figure 10, the white wireframe of the spot light is visible due to the **Show Illumination** checkbox being enabled.

Under normal circumstances, the brightness of a surface depends on the angle at which the light ray hits it. If the angle between the ray and a tangent to the surface is greater, then the surface will be illuminated more by the light. However, when the **Ambient Illumination** checkbox is turned on, this rule is disregarded, and the angle becomes irrelevant. Instead, all surfaces are illuminated with the same intensity by the light rays, and only the material's color is considered in the lighting calculations. This results in a much flatter appearance.

Figure 13 depicts the render with the **Ambient Illumination** checkbox turned off and on. [**ambient-illumination.c4d**]

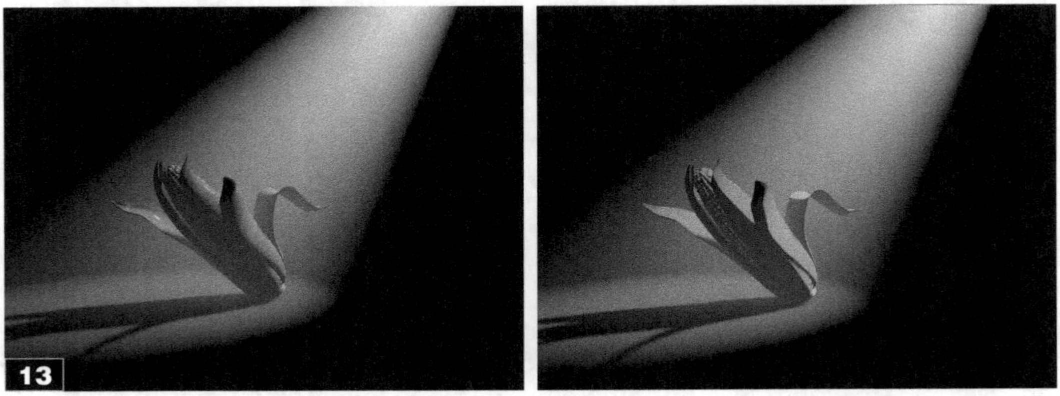

The image on the right demonstrates the effect of enabling the **Ambient Illumination** checkbox with falloff. This technique can be used to brighten certain areas of a scene, similar to how negative lighting can be used to darken and shade specific areas.

To get an idea of what the **Visible** light would look like in the actual scene, you can check the **Show Visible Light** checkbox. This will display an approximation of the **Visible** light in the viewports, which can be adjusted using interactive handles. Figure 14 provides a comparison with and without the **Show Visible Light** checkbox enabled.

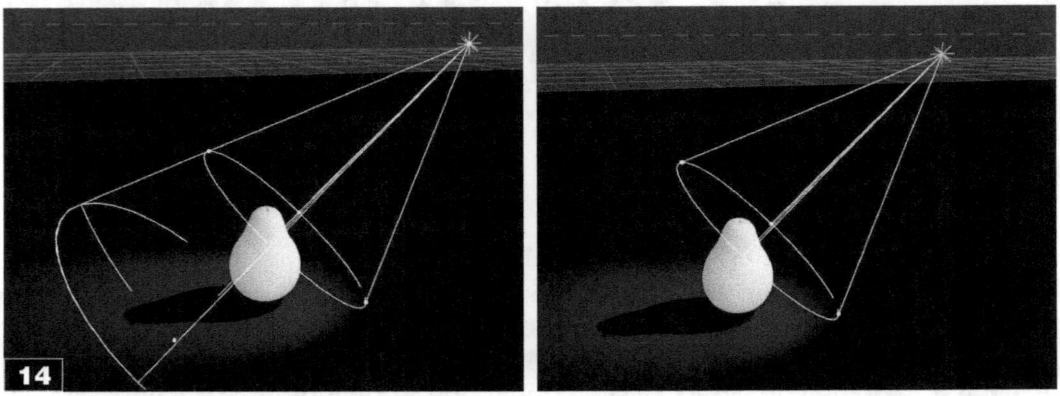

If you disable the **Diffuse** checkbox, the light source ignores the color of the object it is illuminating. The images in Figure 15 illustrate the difference between having the **Diffuse** checkbox enabled and disabled. Similarly, if you disable the **Specular** checkbox, the light source won't produce any specular highlights. The images in Figure 16 demonstrate the effect of having the **Specular** checkbox enabled and disabled.

Enabling the **Show Clipping** checkbox displays an approximate representation of the light's clipping range in the viewports, which can be adjusted interactively using the wireframe handles.

15

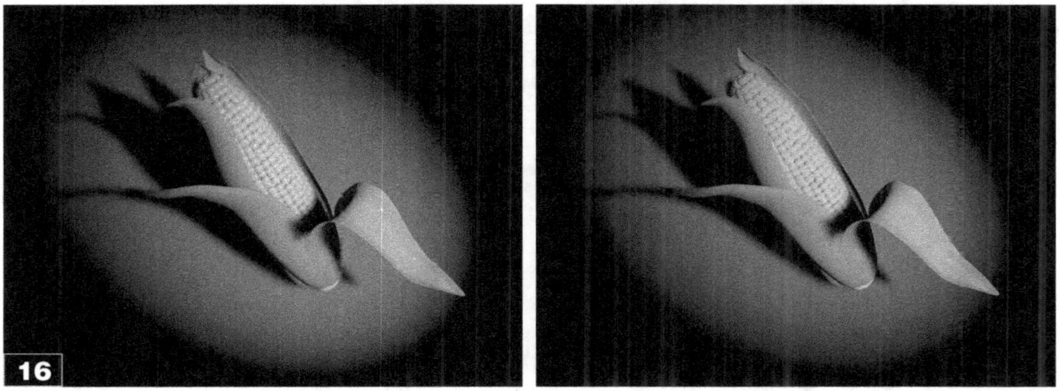

16

By selecting the **Separate Pass** checkbox, Cinema 4D generates different layers (diffuse, specular, and shadow) for the light source during rendering. Clearing the **GI Illumination** checkbox means that the light source won't be used in **Global Illumination** (GI) calculations. The objects in the scene will still be affected by the light sources, but they won't reflect light onto any other objects. When exporting the scene to an external application for compositing, it's recommended to select the **Export to Compositing** checkbox to include the light source in the exported file.

DETAILS TAB

Enabling the **Use Inner** checkbox provides you the option to create a brightness falloff at the edge of a light. This feature is dependent on the values of the **Inner Angle** and **Inner Radius** parameters, which vary depending on the type of light used. For a standard **Spot** light, the **Inner Angle** parameter is adjusted, whereas for a **Parallel Spot** light, the **Inner Radius** parameter is adjusted.

Within the region defined by the **Inner Angle** parameter, the light's intensity remains at **100%**. However, the luminosity value of the light decreases from **100%** to **0%** from the **Inner Angle** to the **Outer Angle** parameter. Figure 17 illustrates the resulting output that occurs when the **Inner Angle** is set to **50** and the **Outer Angle** is set to **80**.

If the **Use Inner** checkbox is disabled, the light's luminosity within its cone will be at **100%**, resulting in a sharp cone of light (as shown in Figure 18). However, by setting the **Inner Angle** parameter to **0**, you can create a soft transition from the center of the light to its edge.

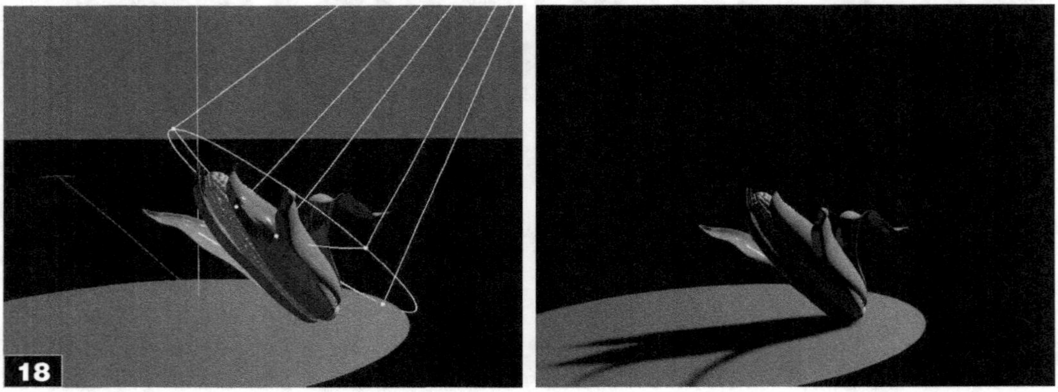

By adjusting the **Aspect Ratio** parameter, you can modify the shape of the light's cone by stretching or shearing it. For example, setting the value of this parameter to **2** will increase the height of the light cone to twice its width, while reducing it to **0.5** will make the light cone half as tall as it is wide. Figure 19 shows the shape of the light cone, where three different **Aspect Ratio** values of **1**, **0.5**, and **2** have been utilized.

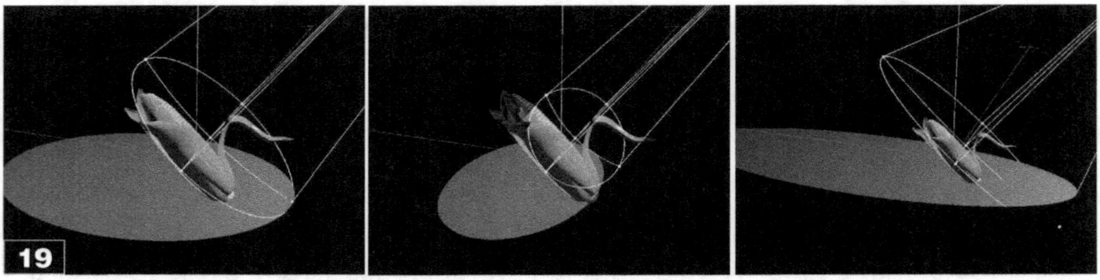

When falloff is not used, the brightness of a light source on an object is not influenced by the distance between the object and the light source. Instead, it depends on the angle of incidence, which is the angle at which the light rays hit the object. At **90** degrees, the object is illuminated with the light's maximum intensity, considering any falloff that is applied. As the angle decreases, the strength of the illumination also decreases, resulting in a gradual transition between the lit and shadowed areas of the surface. The **Contrast** parameter controls the sharpness of this transition from the illuminated area to the shadowed area. Figure 20 shows a rendered image, wherein the **Contrast** values have been set to **0**, **50**, and **100**. [**contrast.c4d**]

20

Enabling the **Shadow Caster** checkbox will allow a light to cast shadows without adding any illumination to the scene. This feature can be used to fix shadows in a scene. In Figure 21, the scene is illuminated by four lights, all casting shadows. [**shadow-caster.c4d**] In contrast, Figure 22 shows the scene with shadows disabled for all lights except the top light. For the top light, the **Shadow Caster** checkbox is enabled. [**shadow-caster-1.c4d]**

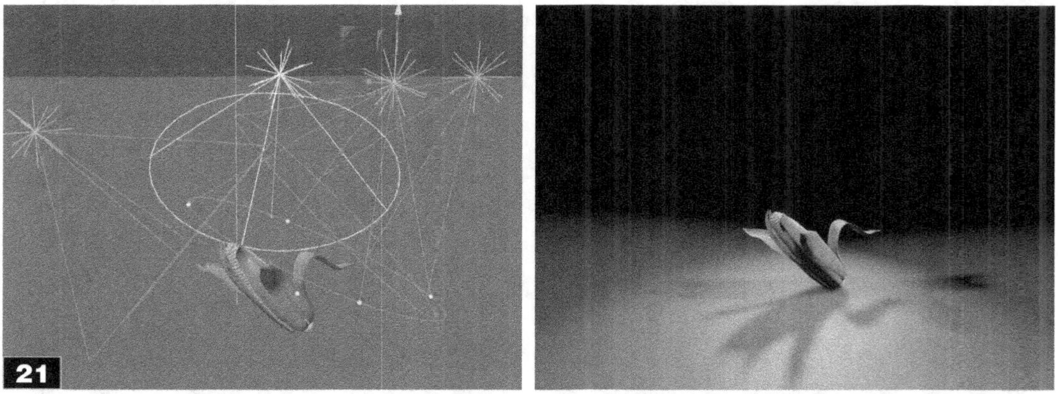

21

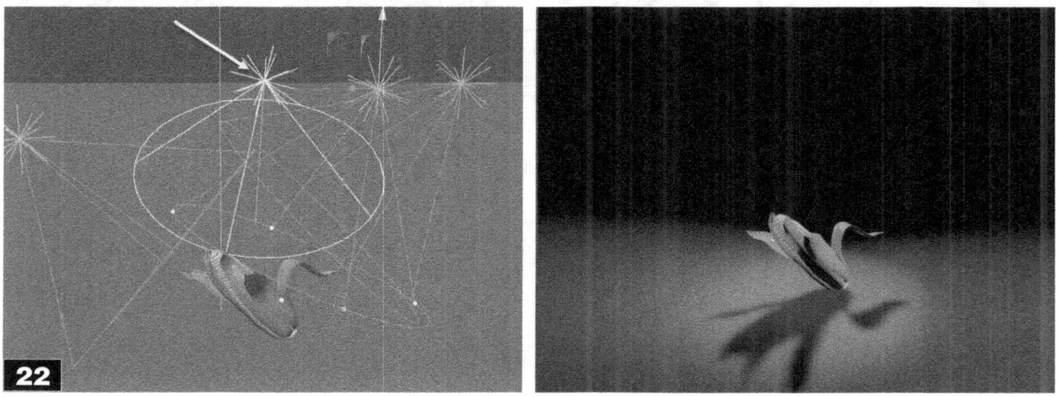

22

Without falloff, the illumination of the environment by a light source is uniform and linear. However, in reality, light is absorbed as it travels and its brightness decreases with distance.

The **Falloff** drop-down list provides several falloff functions that you can use to simulate falloff in Cinema 4D. Figures 23 (scene), 24 (**Falloff**: **Inverse Square (Physically Accurate)**, **Radius/Decay**: **70**), 25 (**Falloff**: **Linear**, **Inner Radius**: **35**, **Radius/Decay**: **135**), and 26 (**Falloff**: **Inverse Square Clamped**, **Radius/Decay**: **150**) show the effect of falloff functions. [**falloff.c4**]

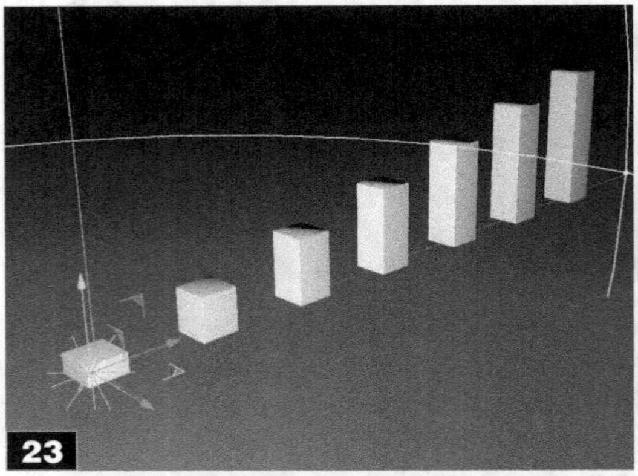
23

24

25

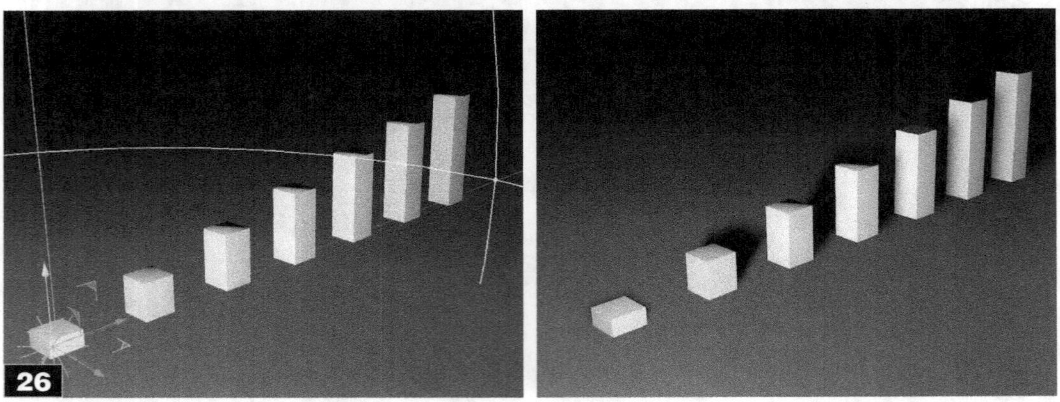
26

When using the **Inner Radius** parameter, the brightness of the light remains constant within the defined boundary. However, outside this boundary, the falloff starts to occur. The **Colored Edge Falloff** option works together with the **Use Gradient** option, and their effect can be seen in Figures 27 and 28. [**falloff-2.c4d**]

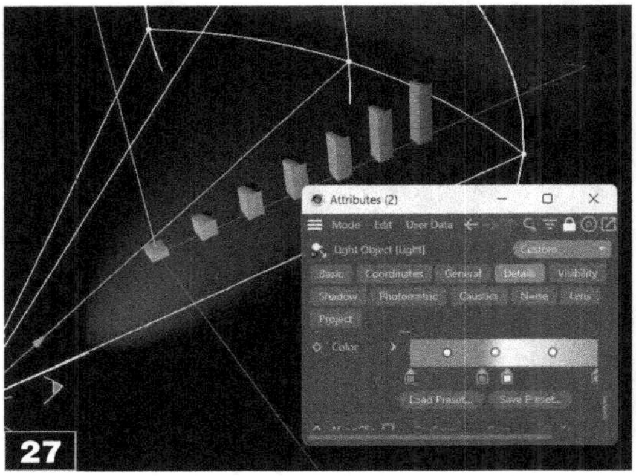

27

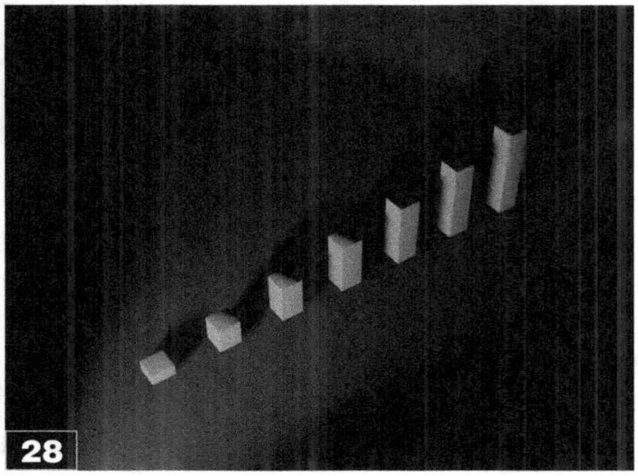
28

Enabling the **Z Direction Only** checkbox will restrict the light emission to the positive Z-direction of the light source. Figure 29 displays a scene illuminated by an area light, and the right image showcases the effect of enabling the **Z Direction Only** checkbox. [**z-direction-only.c4d**]

29

The **Near Clip** and **Far Clip** checkboxes allow you to limit the area where the light illuminates. The **Near Clip** checkbox restricts the illumination in a radial way for **Omni** lights and linearly for all other types of lights. You can use these checkboxes to start the illumination from a specific distance from the origin.

Figure 30 demonstrates the effect of using the **Near Clip** checkbox. Additionally, you can adjust the clipping range by manipulating the wireframe handles in the viewport. [**clipping.c4d**]

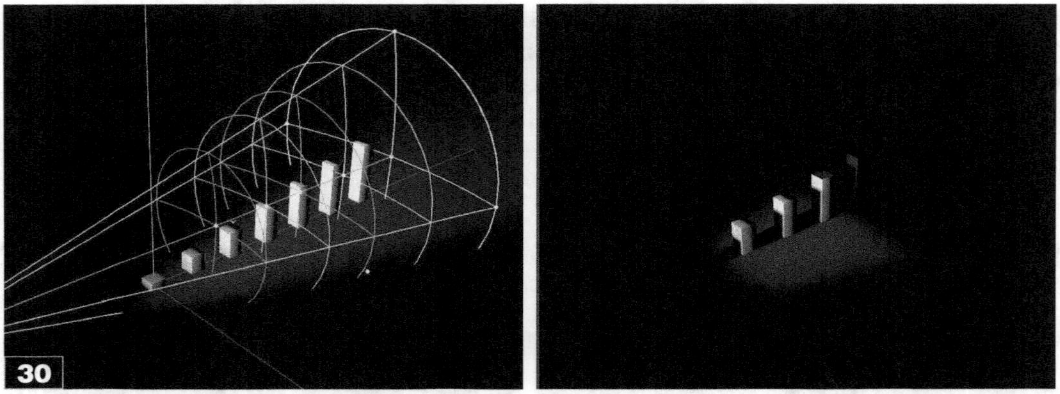

30

The **Area Shape** drop-down list provides options to set the shape of an area light. Area lights offer realistic lighting and shadows when used with area shadows, but rendering area lights with area shadows takes longer. Area lights can be given any shape and can be made visible in both the viewport and the final render. When a shape is selected from the **Area Shape** drop-down list, corresponding parameters (**Size X**, **Size Y**, and **Size Z**) are revealed to set the size of the area.

The images in Figure 31 show the **Disc** (left), **Rectangle** (center), and **Line** (right) shapes. The images in Figure 32 show the **Sphere** (left), **Cylinder** (center), and **Cylinder (Perpendicular)** (right) shapes, respectively. The images in Figure 33 show the **Cube** and **Hemisphere** shapes.

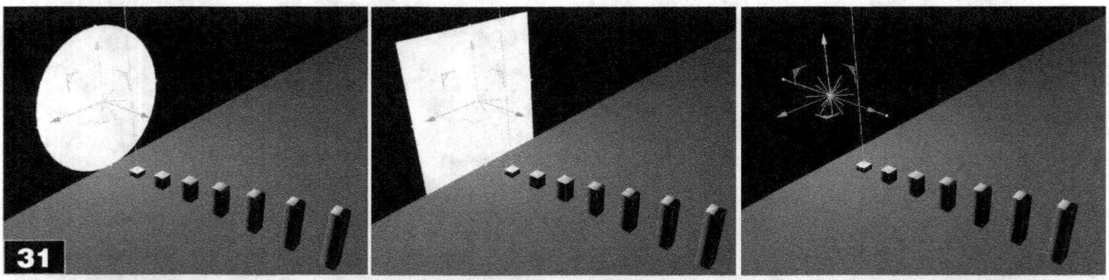

31

32

You can select the **Object/Spline** option if you want to use any polygonal object or spline for the shape of the light. Simply drag the object to **Object** field in the **Attribute Manager**.

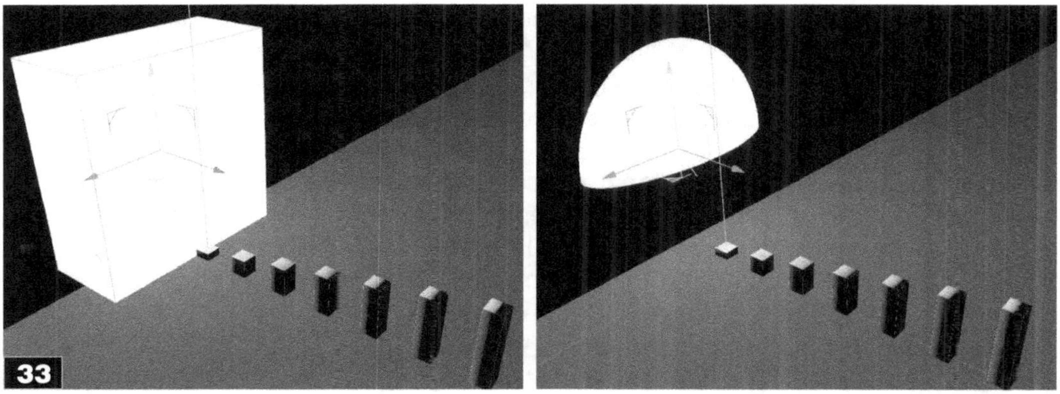
33

The **Falloff Angle** parameter is used to control the illumination of a **Disc** or **Rectangle** area light. By adjusting this parameter, you can decrease the amount of light emitted from the edges. The smaller the value of **Falloff Angle**, the more light will be reduced from the edges. Figure 34 displays the output of **Falloff Angle** set to **0** (left) and **180** (right). On the other hand, Figure 35 shows the result of **Falloff Angle** set to **150** (left) and **120** (right). [**falloff-angle.c4d**]

34

35

In some cases, the structure of the area light can be seen in specular highlights, causing the output to look like the object is being lit by multiple light sources. To fix this issue, you can increase the value of the **Samples** parameter. This will help to even out the light dispersion and create a smoother, more natural appearance.

Enabling the **Add Grain (Slow)** option can also address the issue of uneven light dispersion discussed earlier. This option uses a grainy rendering method to remove visible light source structures. However, to avoid an excessively grainy output, the **Samples** value should be set high enough. Keep in mind that selecting this option will significantly increase the render time compared to a normal render.

If you want to include the light source in the rendering, you can select the **Show in Render** checkbox. The light source will be displayed in white, depending on its intensity. However, note that line and spline object shapes cannot be rendered. To display the light shape as a luminous surface in the viewport without rendering, you can select the **Show as Solid in Viewport** checkbox.

If you enable the **Show in Specular** checkbox, the light shape will appear as a specular highlight in reflective materials. The **Show in Reflection** checkbox is used to reflect the area light in another object, but this is not possible for **Line** and **Spline** object shapes. However, if the roughness of the material is set to greater than **0**, these shapes can also be reflected.

You can adjust the brightness of a visible area light or its reflection in another object using the **Visibility Multiplier** parameter. However, this parameter is only accessible if you choose to select the **Show in Render** or **Show in Reflection** checkboxes.

VISIBILITY TAB

By default, the **Use Falloff** checkbox is enabled which provides access to the **Falloff** parameter. This parameter is used to regulate the decrease in density of the light and is set to a default of **100%** for axial falloff of the visible light. The images in Figure 36 demonstrate the rendered output with **Falloff** values set to **0** and **100**. [**falloff-3.c4d**]

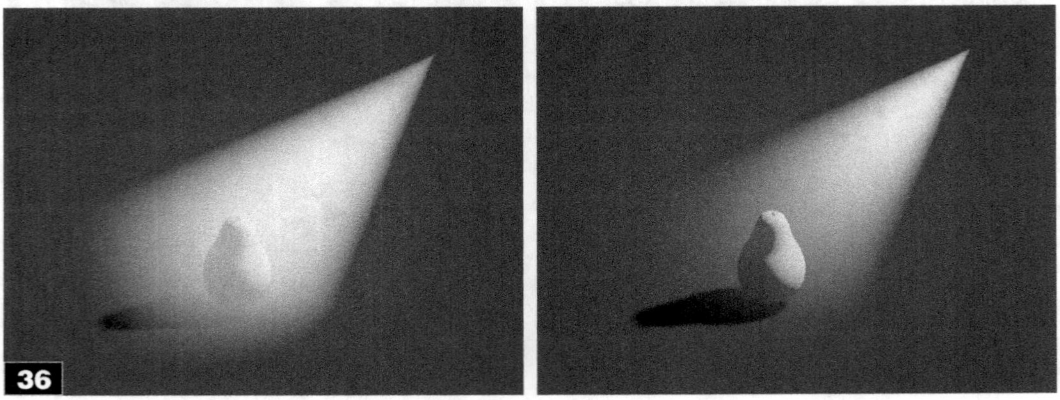

36

The **Use Edge Falloff** and **Edge Falloff** parameters are specific to **Spot** lights. The **Edge Falloff** parameter determines the rate at which the light's intensity decreases towards the edge of the cone of light. The images in Figure 37 illustrate the rendering with **Edge Falloff** set to **0** (left), **50** (center), and **100** (right).

When using **Spot** lights, the **Colored Edge Falloff** checkbox is only applicable if the **Use Edge Falloff** checkbox is checked. Activating **Colored Edge Falloff** will result in the inner color spreading outward from the inner angle to meet the outer color. Figure 38 displays the rendering with and without **Use Edge Falloff** enabled, where the **Edge Falloff** parameter was set to **50%**. [**colored-edge-falloff.c4d**]

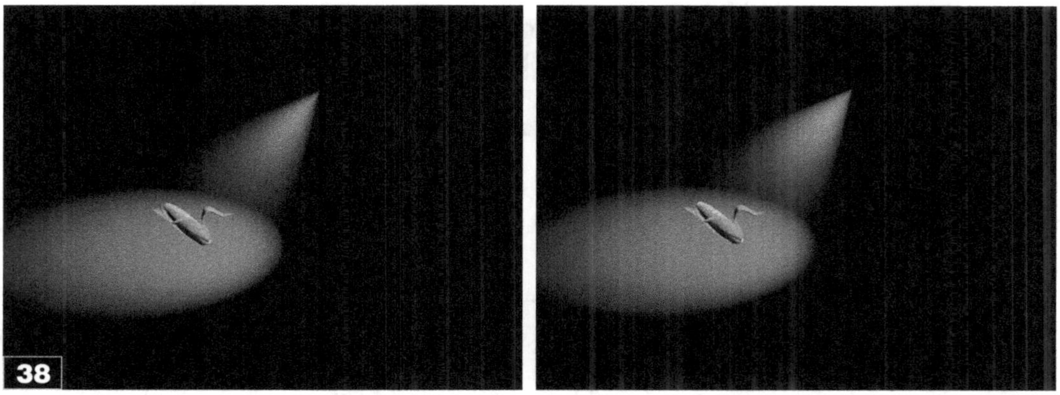

The density of the visible light can be controlled by adjusting the **Inner Distance** parameter. When a value is set for this parameter, the density of the visible light remains constant at **100%** below that distance. Beyond this distance, the light starts to decrease gradually until it reaches **0%** at the Outer Distance value.

Open **colored-edge-falloff.c4d** and experiment with these parameters. The **Relative Scale** parameter works in conjunction with **Omni** lights. You can use this parameter to scale the **Outer Distance** value.

The **Sample Distance** parameter is responsible for controlling the level of detail in the volumetric shadow produced by the visible light. A smaller value will result in a higher level of detail, but it will take longer to render. This parameter is measured in world units and determines how the shadows within a visible light will be sampled.

The **Sample Distance** parameter is typically set to a value between **$1/10^{th}$** to **$1/1000^{th}$** of the radius of the light source. Increasing the value can lead to faster renders, but it can also result in artifacts. The images in Figure 39 demonstrate the difference between **Sample Distance** values of **8** (left) and **20** (right). [**sample-distance.c4d**]

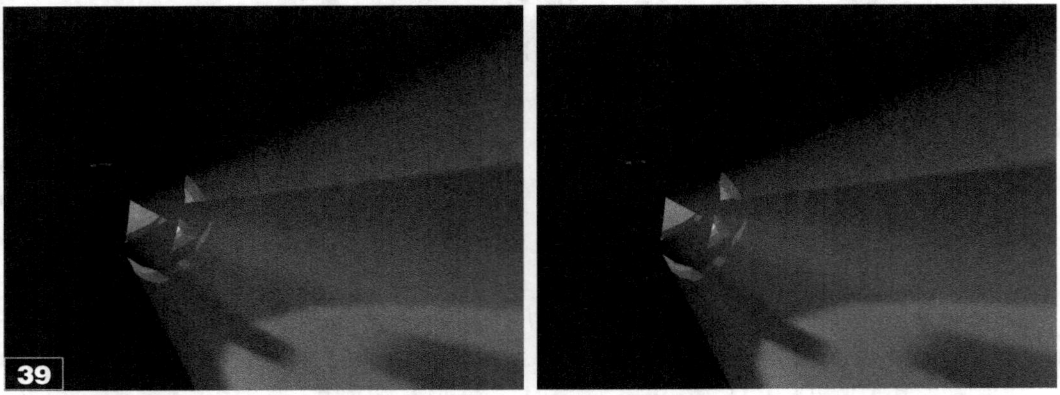

39

The **Brightness** parameter adjusts the intensity of the visible light source, while the **Dust** parameter adjusts its darkness. To see the full effect of the **Dust** parameter, you may need to lower the value of the **Brightness** parameter. When you set a value greater than **0** for the **Dust** parameter, it subtracts from the brightness rather than adding to it. The **Dithering** parameter adds irregularities to the visible light, which can be used to eliminate undesired banding or contouring in the visible light source.

You can use the **Color** parameter to create color and brightness gradients in the visible light. The images in Figure 40 shows the color gradient generated using the **Omni** and **Spot** lights. [**color-gradient.c4d**]

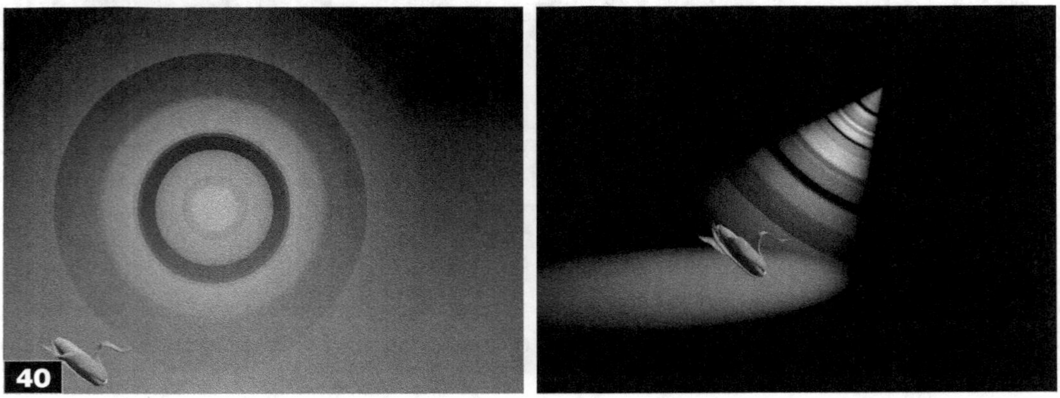

40

INTENSITY
*The gradient's brightness, which is the visible light's intensity, is also impacted by the **Intensity** parameter located in the **Details** tab.*

> **GRADIENT**
> *The gradient defined in the **Details** tab may not be applied if the **Use Gradient** checkbox is not selected.*

By enabling the **Additive** checkbox, you can combine the light beam with other light sources using additive mixing. The **Adapt Brightness** checkbox can be selected to prevent over-exposure of the light beam. The brightness of the light is reduced automatically until the over-exposure effect is no longer visible.

SHADOW TAB

From this tab, you have the option to choose different types of shadows. These types can be selected from the **Shadow** drop-down list.

Shadow Maps (Soft)

In the physical world, objects are illuminated by multiple light sources resulting in a gradual shift of light to shadow. To replicate this effect in Cinema 4D, one can use the **Shadow Maps (Soft)** shadow type.

41

This shadow type is computed very fast and produces natural looking shadows (see Figure 41). [**shadow-map-soft.c4d**]

> **SOFT SHADOW MAP**
> *A soft shadow map is a grayscale representation of the scene as seen from the perspective of the light source. This map includes all the objects illuminated by the light source. While rendering, the renderer determines which objects will be cast shadows.*

> **MEMORY CONSUMPTION**
> *The **Shadow Maps (Soft)** shadow type may require a significant amount of additional memory depending on the size of the map. Therefore, it is important to exercise caution when choosing this type and setting the map size.*

The **Density** parameter controls the opacity of the shadows in Cinema 4D. A value of **0%** makes the shadow completely transparent, while a value of **100%** makes it fully opaque. The parameter can be adjusted to any value between these two extremes to create varying degrees of transparency. Figure 42 illustrates the difference in the shadow when the **Density** parameter is set to **50** (left) and **80** (right).

You can adjust the color of shadows to create contrast between light and shade, as real-world shadows are not completely black. The **Transparency** checkbox can be selected to ensure that shadow maps take into account transparency and alpha channels. Figure 43 demonstrates the difference in results when the **Transparency** checkbox is disabled and enabled. [**transparency.c4d**]

42

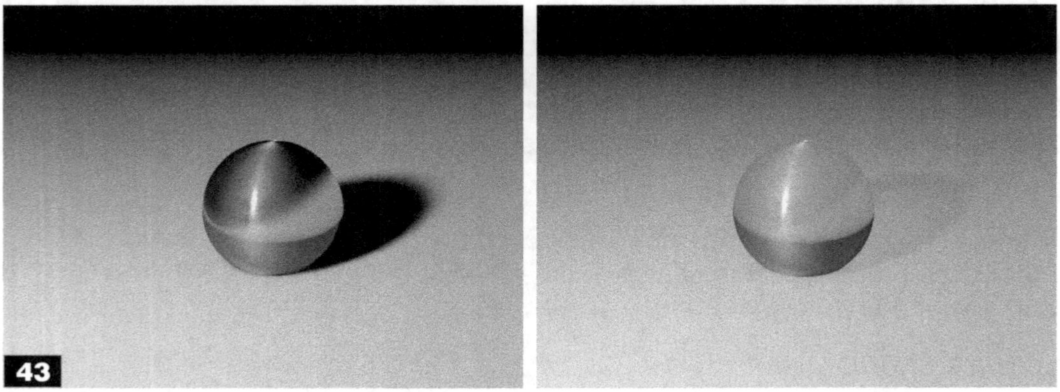

43

To apply the clipping settings from the **Details** tab to shadow casting, select the **Clipping Influence** checkbox. The **Shadow Map** drop-down list is only accessible when the **Shadow Maps (Soft)** shadow type is selected. The default size for the shadow map is **250 x 250**, but it can be increased substantially. To achieve sharp and well-defined shadows, the map size should be increased. However, if you want smoother shadow edges, the **Sample Radius** parameter should be increased instead. Keep in mind that both of these options will increase rendering time.

> ***MAP SIZE***
> *Instead of using a larger **Shadow Map** size, you can achieve a similar soft edge effect by doubling the value of the **Sample Radius** parameter.*

You can specify the size of the map manually by using the **Resolution X** and **Resolution Y** parameters. The **Memory Usage** label displays the maximum memory used for the shadow map. You can use this information to estimate how much memory will be needed for the shadow maps. The **Sample Radius** parameter defines the shadow map accuracy. The higher the value you specify, the more accurate the shadows will be, and the longer it will take to render them.

> **_RENDER TIME VS MEMORY_**
> *If you have a small shadow map, you can choose to sacrifice memory usage for faster rendering by setting a high value for the* ***Sample Radius*** *parameter.*

When creating animations, shadows can sometimes flicker and not move smoothly due to the fixed resolution of the shadow maps. To address this problem, the resolution of the map needs to be reduced. However, this will result in sharper edges, which will require a larger **Sample Radius** value to compensate for.

Using the **Sampling Radius Boost** parameter can help avoid setting the **Sample Radius** value too high, which can cause problems. This feature parameter the **Sample Radius** value and scatters the samples randomly, instead of using a stepping effect. This creates noise, which is less noticeable in animations. The **Absolute Bias** parameter is there for compatibility reasons, and it's recommended to keep it selected.

The **Bias (Abs)** parameter can be utilized to alter the location of the shadow. When you focus on small objects in the scene, the distance between the object and shadow becomes more visible. This can be resolved by decreasing the value of the **Bias (Abs)** parameter. If you choose to enable the **Outline Shadow** checkbox, Cinema 4D will display a thin outline of the shadow instead of the complete shadow, as shown in Figure 44.

44

When using an **Omni** light in a scene, six shadow maps must be generated in total, which can lead to artifacts in the shadows. To mitigate this, you can select the **Shadow Cone** option, which generates a single shadow map and limits shadows to a cone, resulting in faster rendering. The **Angle** parameter is used to set the vertex angle of the shadow cone, and selecting the **Soft Cone** checkbox gives the cone a softer edge.

45

Raytraced (Hard)

The **Raytraced (Hard)** type is especially useful for creating technical illustrations that require hard-edged shadows, as shown in Figure 45. However, this type requires a large number of additional rays to be computed, which can significantly increase the render time.

Area

To render using the **Area** shadow type, more time is needed than other types. Hence, it's best to use this type only when you have enough time for rendering. While soft shadows generated by the **Shadow Maps (Soft)** shadow type appear more realistic than hard shadows, they do not exactly mimic real-world conditions because the soft edge has a consistent width. In reality, as an object gets closer to a surface, the soft edge becomes sharper. The **Area** shadows reproduce this effect in Cinema 4D resulting in more natural shadows, as shown in Figure 46.

46

The area shadows are controlled by the **Accuracy**, **Minimum Samples**, and **Maximum Samples** parameters. The area shadows are calculated using samples, the more samples you use, the less grainy the rendering will be, and the longer they will take to render.

The **Minimum Samples** and **Maximum Samples** parameters allow you to specify samples for the area light. The **Accuracy** parameter controls how and how many samples will be allotted in order to achieve the best result. In the most critical areas, the value of the **Maximum Samples** parameter may be set to its highest value.

Follow the steps given next to optimize area lights:

- Find out critical areas in your scene where you see grain.
- Set the **Minimum Samples** and **Maximum Samples** parameters to the same value and render the critical regions using the **Render Region** tool.
- Increase the value of the **Minimum Samples** and **Maximum Samples** parameters equally until you achieve a good result.
- Lower **Minimum Samples** to **25%** of the **Maximum Samples** value and set **Accuracy** to **50%**.
- Raise the **Accuracy** setting until you have a result you are happy with.

AREA SHADOWS

*Increasing any of the values (**Accuracy, Minimum Samples**, or **Maximum Samples**) will result in an increase in render time. However, if you set the **Minimum Samples** and **Maximum Samples** to the same value, then changing the **Accuracy** value will not have any impact on the render. Generally, increasing the values of **Maximum Samples** and **Accuracy** can improve quality, but even if you set the **Accuracy** value to **100%**, the quality will not improve if you have specified a very low value for the **Maximum Samples** parameter.*

PYROCLUSTER CLOUDS
If you attempt to use area shadows with ***PyroCluster*** *clouds, the feature will not work. Cinema 4D will render the clouds with hard shadows instead of area shadows.*

ANTI-ALIASING
By setting ***Anti-Aliasing*** *to* ***Best*** *in the* ***Render Settings*** *window, you can decrease the graininess present in shadows. Additionally, you can utilize the* ***Compositing*** *tag to adjust the anti-aliasing settings on a per-object basis, which allows you to override the global anti-aliasing settings.*

Render time

Here are some points to consider regarding render time:

- Soft shadows are faster to calculate than hard shadows, which in turn are faster than area shadows.
- If you choose to make a light visible in the render, it will only add a small amount of render time.
- The **Sample Distance** parameter in volumetric lights can substantially increase render time.
- The **Noise** function increases render time, with hard and soft turbulence types taking longer than the basic noise type.
- The wavy turbulence function takes approximately double the time to render compared to the basic noise function.
- Using a high **Sample Radius** value can increase render time.
- While area lights do add to the render time, they are less processor-intensive than volumetric lights.

PHOTOMETRIC TAB

The **Photometric** tab's parameters enable the use of **IES** (Illuminating Engineering Society) format within Cinema 4D scenes. This format allows light sources to behave in a realistic manner. IES Photometric files are files with the **.ies** extension that contain information about light for use in architectural programs that simulate light. These files are available online and are in plain text (**ASCII**) format.

To generate an IES light, follow these steps:

1. Create a **Light** object and navigate to the **Attribute Manager > General** tab.
2. Change the **Type** to **IES**.
3. Position the light within the scene to your desired alignment. The z-axis determines the direction of the light's emission.

4. Load the **.ies** file by adjusting the **Photometric** tab > **Filename** parameter. You can also drag **.ies** files from the **Content Browser** to the **Filename** field.

IES FILE
*The **Filename** field indicates the path of the IES file, but the IES data itself is included in the Cinema 4D scene file. Therefore, if you need to distribute the file, you do not have to include the IES file with it.*

To modify the brightness of the **IES** light, the **Intensity** parameter can be utilized. This parameter determines the maximum intensity of the light. The **Units** drop-down list presents various unit options (such as **Candela**, **Lumen**, and **Lux**) that can be assigned to the light. By default, the **Photometric Data** checkbox is enabled, allowing Cinema 4D to assess the IES data. However, if this checkbox is unselected, the light source will revert to an **Omni** light source, permitting the adjustment of **Lumen** or **Candela** intensity.

The **Photometric Data** checkbox allows you to turn on or off the calculation of IES data. If this option is disabled, the light source will return to being an **Omni** light source that can be adjusted in terms of **Lumen** or **Candela** intensity. The **Information** section provides information stored within the **IES** file, such as the manufacturer's name and catalog number. If no data is saved with the file, these fields will remain blank.

NOISE TAB

The **Noise** tab provides options that enable the creation of effects such as animated fog and Sun flares, bypassing the need to use the computationally expensive volume shaders. However, utilizing the **Noise** feature can increase render times as it is slower to calculate.

In the natural world, objects are not uniformly illuminated on their surfaces. The presence of dust or small particles in the environment causes irregularities in the illumination. To replicate this effect in Cinema 4D, the Illumination option in the **Noise** drop-down list can be used to add these irregularities to the light source (as shown in Figure 47).

47

Additionally, the noise type can be selected from the **Type** drop-down list, which includes options such as **Soft Turbulence**, **Noise**, **Hard Turbulence**, and **Wavy Turbulence** (as shown in Figure 48). [**noise.c4d**]

The **Octaves** parameter is used with turbulence types to determine the coarseness of the noise. Increasing the value of this parameter will result in a rougher texture. Figure 49 illustrates the outcome of setting **Octaves** to **1** (left) and **5** (right), respectively.

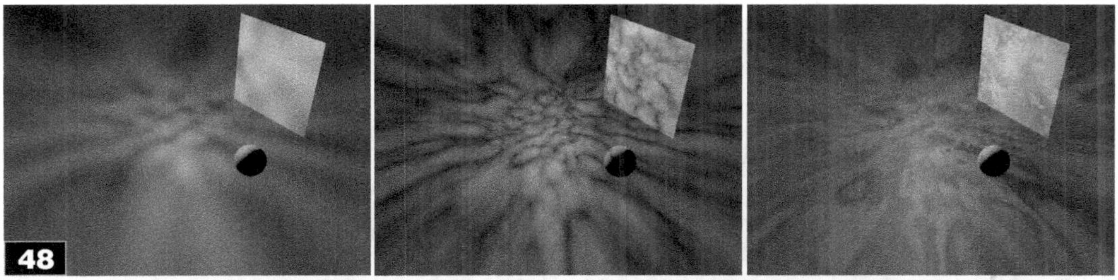

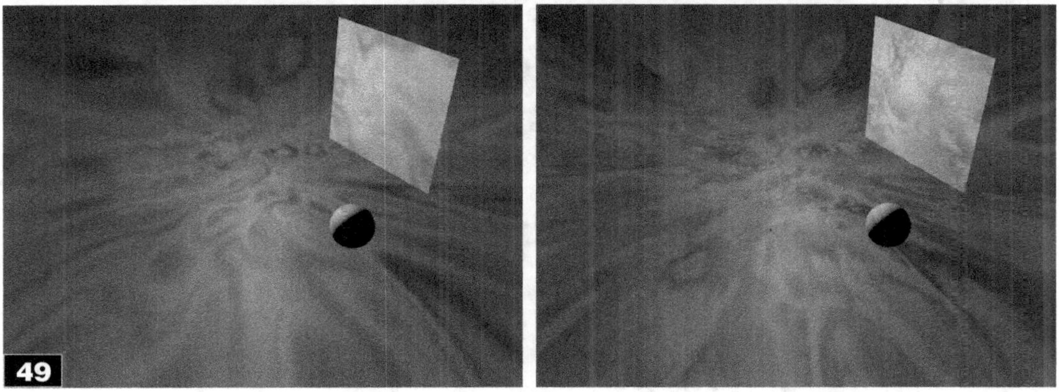

The **Velocity** parameter is used to adjust the speed of the irregularities. The **Brightness** and **Contrast** parameters are used to increase the overall brightness of the noise and control its contrast. Lowering the contrast value will reduce the contrast of the noise while increasing it will enhance the contrast.

The movement of dust and particles in nature is caused by natural forces and is not affected by the movement of the light source. However, in Cinema 4D, you have the option to move these irregularities along with the light source by enabling the **Local** checkbox. It is important to note that leaving this checkbox disabled will create a more natural appearance in your scene.

The **Visibility Scale** parameter is used to change the size of the irregularities in the **X**, **Y**, and **Z** directions relative to the scene's coordinates. If the noise effect is too strong, decreasing these values may help. The **Illumination Scale** parameter determines the size of the noise on illuminated objects. Lower values produce coarse noise while larger values create finer noise. The **Wind** parameter applies a wind effect to the noise, making it seem like it's being blown away by the wind. The **Wind Velocity** parameter controls the strength of the wind effect, and these parameters work together to make the animation more realistic.

LENS TAB

The **Lens** tab options are designed to mimic real-world camera effects. The way to utilize these options is to choose the **No Illumination** checkbox located in the **General** tab. This will enable you to use the light object solely for producing visible light without actually illuminating objects. Afterwards, you can use the light for lens effects. However, in real-world scenarios, cameramen typically avoid such effects as they can become distracting for the viewer.

To become familiar with the options in the **Lens** tab, it is recommended to experiment with them. However, it is important to keep in mind that these effects can become distracting in real-world photography. Also, it's worth noting that lens effects cannot be displayed in **QuickTime VR** panoramas. Some examples of lens effects available in Cinema 4D are shown in Figures 50 (**Wideangle**, **Artifact**, and **Sun 1**) and 51 (**Blue1**, **Candle**, and **Zoom**).

50

51

PROJECT TAB

The **Project** tab contains settings that are used to determine which objects in the scene will be impacted by the light. To specify that the light should affect only certain objects, choose the **Include** mode and drag the desired objects from the **Object Manager** to the **Objects** list in the **Project** tab. On the other hand, if you want to turn off the light for certain objects, choose the **Exclude** mode and then add those objects to the **Objects** list. As you add objects to the **Objects** list, you will see five icons appear next to the object's label, as shown in Figure 52.

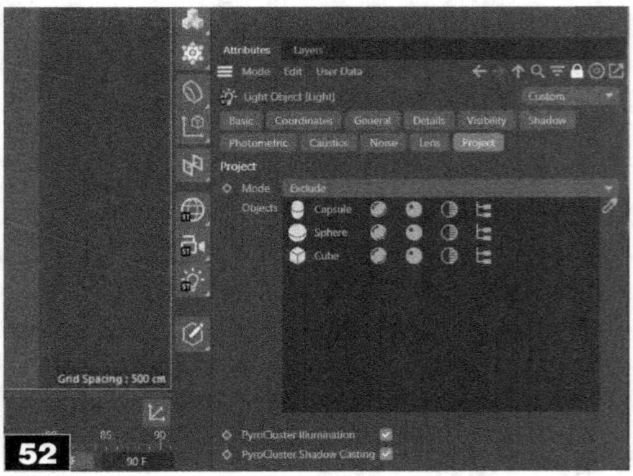

52

These icons can be clicked to enable or disable illumination, specularity, and shadows for the object. The icons, from left to right, are **Object**, **Illumination**, **Specularity**, **Shadows**, and **Include Entire Hierarchy**. Clicking the **Include Entire Hierarchy** icon will ensure that the object's children are also affected by inclusion or exclusion.

The **PyroCluster Illumination** and **PyroCluster Shadow Casting** checkboxes determine if a light source should cast shadows on smoke or steam or if it should illuminate them.

TUTORIALS

CREATING A 3-POINT LIGHTING SETUP

This tutorial will involve creating a 3-point light setup using **Area** lights and rendering the resulting scene, as shown in Figure 1.

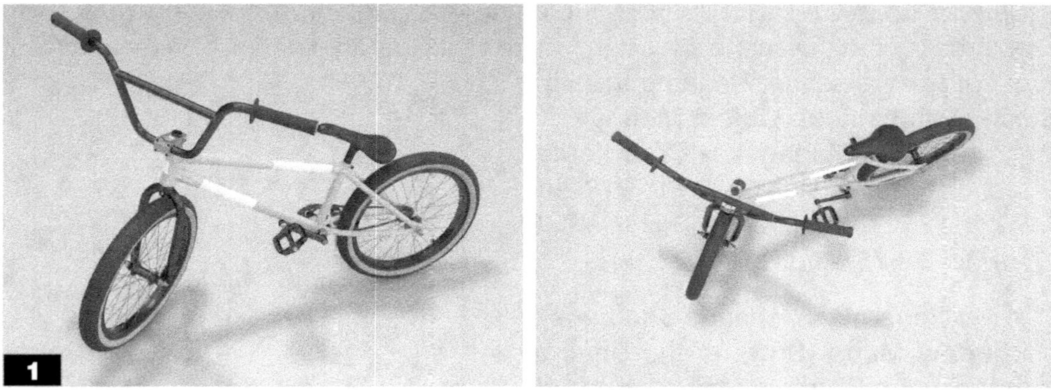

1

Summary	
Topics	Getting Started Creating Setup
Resources folder	**lighting**
Start file	**3point-start.c4d**
Final file	**3point-finish.c4d**

Getting Started

Open **3point-start.c4d**.

Creating Setup

Let's first start by assigning a material to the **Floor** object. Follow the steps given next:

1. Double-click on the **Material Manager** to create a new material and assign it the **Floor** object in the **Object Manager**. Rename material as **mat-floor**. In the **Color** channel of the material, change **Color > V** value to **75**.

WHAT FLOOR OBJECT DOES?
*The **Floor** object generates a floor on the **XZ** plane. It can be rendered as if it extends to infinity and can also be used to create skies. It is not limited to creating only floors and can be duplicated and transformed to create multiple layers for clouds or other effects.*

HOW 3-POINT LIGHTING WORKS?
A 3-Point lighting setup is composed of three lights: the main light (also called key light), fill light, and back light (also known as rim light). The main light is the most intense light in the scene and its direction and intensity determines the shadows' appearance. The fill light illuminates areas that are not directly lit by the main light. The back light is used to enhance the silhouette of an object, usually when rendering a single object. The fill and back lights do not produce shadows or affect the material's specular component.

2. Choose **Create > VIRTUAL SET > Light > Area Light** from the main menu to create an area light in the scene. This light will work as key light and will be the main source of light in the scene. Rename this light as **key-light** in the **Object Manager**. In the **Attribute Manager > Coordinates** tab, change **P.X** to **-165**, **P.Y** to **818**, and **P.Z** to **-26**. Then, change **R.H** to **-82.8**, **R.P** to **-78.75**, and **R.B** to **0**.

3. In the **General** tab, change **Shadows** to **Shadow Maps (Soft)**. In the **Shadow** tab, change **Shadow Map** to **500x500**. Render the scene (see Figure 2).

2

WHAT JUST HAPPENED?
*I have adjusted the shadow map resolution to **500x500**, which is higher than the default resolution of **250x250**. Increasing the resolution will result in smoother shadows, but will also increase rendering time. To further improve the smoothness of the shadow edges, you can use the **Sample Radius** parameter, but this will also increase rendering time.*

RESOLUTION
*To achieve soft edges in shadows, you don't necessarily need to increase the resolution. You can achieve the desired effect by increasing the value of the **Sample Radius** parameter instead.*

4. Create another light in the scene and then rename it as **fill-light**. In the **Attribute Manager > Coordinates** tab, change **P.X** to **409**, **P.Y** to **644**, and **P.Z** to **-281**. Then, change **R.H** to **59.445**, **R.P** to **-46.431**, and **R.B** to **0**. In the **General** tab, clear the **Specular** checkbox.

WHAT JUST HAPPENED?
*When the **Specular** checkbox is disabled, it means that the light will not contribute to the specular highlights of the material.*

5. Create another light in the scene and then rename it as **back-light**. In the **Attribute Manager** > **Coordinates** tab, change **P.X** to **676**, **P.Y** to **799**, and **P.Z** to **1035**. Then, change **R.H** to **146.578**, **R.P** to **-34.814**, and **R.B** to **0**. In the **General** tab, clear the **Specular** checkbox. Render the scene (see Figure 3).

6. In the **General** tab, turn off the **Specular** checkbox. Drag **Floor** from the **Object Manager** to the **Objects** field of the **Project** tab. Render the scene (see Figure 4).

3

4

WHAT JUST HAPPENED?
*In this case, I have chosen to prevent the back-light from illuminating the **Floor** object, so I have set the **Mode** to **Exclude** and added the **Floor** object to the list of excluded objects. By default, the **Mode** is set to **Exclude**, but if you want a light to only illuminate specific objects, you can change the **Mode** to **Include** and add those objects to the **Objects** field in the **Project** tab by dragging them from the **Object Manager**. If you want to include or exclude an object and its children from the light, you can use the fourth icon.*

7. Choose **Create** > **VIRTUAL SET** > **Environment** > **Sky** from the main menu to add a **Sky** object to the scene. **RMB** click on **Sky** in the **Object Manager** and then choose **Render Tags** > **Compositing** from the context menu. Make sure the tag is selected in the **Object Manager** and then in the **Attribute Manager** > **Tag** tab, clear all checkboxes except the **Seen by Rays**, **Seen by GI**, **Seen by Reflection**, and **Seen by AO** checkboxes.

WHAT PURPOSE DOES THE COMPOSITING TAG SERVE?
*The **Compositing** tag provides multiple options that impact the rendering process. It enables you to restrict specific operations for objects, like casting and receiving shadows. In this case, the **Sky** object will only be visible to rays, global illumination, reflection, and ambient occlusion.*

8. Assign the **Sunny Marketplace 01** material (search it in the **Content Browser**) to the **Sky** object.

WHAT IS THE REASON FOR APPLYING THIS MATERIAL?
The material used here has an HDR image, which is ideal for achieving realistic reflections in the scene. HDR images have a higher color depth of ***32-bit*** *compared to regular* ***8-bit*** *images. Assigning this material to the* ***Sky*** *object ensures that objects in the scene will have reflections from the HDR image. Cinema 4D offers a range of HDR images that are accessible in the* ***Content Browser*** *at* ***Template & Presets > Lighting > HDRI****.*

9. Open the **Render Settings** window and then add the **Global Illumination** effect. Render the scene. You will notice that scene is bright (see Figure 5), we need to reduce the intensity of the lights to get the desired effect.

10. Change intensity of **key-light**, **fill-light**, and **back-light** to **70**, **60**, and **60** respectively. Render the scene (see Figure 6).

5

6

11. Select **mat-floor** in the **Material Manager** and then in the **Attribute Manager > Basic** tab, select the **Diffusion** checkbox. In the **Diffusion** tab, click **Texture > Triangle** button and then choose **Effects > Ambient Occlusion** from the popup. Click on the **Ambient Occlusion** button to open the shader settings. Change **Maximum Ray Length** to **200**, **Accuracy** to **100**, and **Maximum Samples** to **128**. Render the scene (see Figure 7). Figure 8 shows the lights in the scene.

7

8

WHAT AMBIENT OCCLUSION EFFECT DOES?
*The **Ambient Occlusion** shader is a quick substitute for **Global Illumination**, although it has some constraints. It assesses the exposure of each individual surface point and colors it accordingly. It darkens areas like corners, holes, and objects that are closer to each other. By using it in the **Diffusion** channel, we can darken the areas where the tires touch the floor.*

CREATING A PRODUCT VISUALIZATION RENDER

The purpose of this tutorial is to demonstrate how to use **Area** and **Spot** lights to render a bike on a dark background. The final result can be seen in Figure 1.

1

Summary	
Topics	Getting Started Creating Render Post-Production
Resources folder	**lighting**
Start file	**bike-start.c4d**
Final file	**bike-finish.c4d**

Getting Started

Open **bike-start.c4d**.

Creating Render

We will begin by creating a material for the floor. Here are the steps you need to follow:

1. Create a new material and assign it to the floor in the **Object Manager**. Rename material as **floor-mat**. In the **Color** tab, change color to **HSV** (**0**, **0**, **6**). In the **Reflectance** tab, change **Type** to **GGX**, **Attenuation** to **Average**, **Roughness** to **10** **Reflection Strength** to **100**, **Specular Strength** to **0**, and **Brightness** to **60**.

2. Create a new camera and adjust its angle of view. **RMB** click on **Camera** in the **Object Manager** and then choose **Rigging Tags** > **Protection** from the popup.

WHAT JUST HAPPENED?
In this case, the camera has been assigned a ***Protection*** *tag, which serves to prevent any unintended modification of the camera's attributes.*

3. Create a new spot light, rename it as **Main Light** and then in the **General** tab, change **Type** to **Square Spot**. Make sure **Main Light** is selected and then choose **Cameras** > **CAMERA** > **Use Camera** > **Selected Object as Camera** from **MEV** menu. Now, using the navigation tools place the light as shown in Figure 2 and also adjust outer angle of the light in the view interactively or using the **Outer Angle** parameter in the **Details** tab.

WHAT JUST HAPPENED?
Selecting the ***Selected Object as Camera*** *option allows you to view the scene from the position of the selected object (in this case, the* ***Main Light****), which can be helpful for precise placement of the light in the scene.*

4. Switch back to **Camera** view and then in **Render Settings** make sure the **Physical Test** preset is active. Render the scene see Figure 3.

WHAT NEXT?
Next, we'll create a light that will provide frontal illumination for the bike.

5. Create an area light and then position it, as shown in Figure 4. Rename the light as **Fill Light**. In the **General** tab, change **Intensity** to **3** and in the **Details** tab, select the **Z Direction Only** checkbox. Switch to camera view and render the scene (see Figure 5).

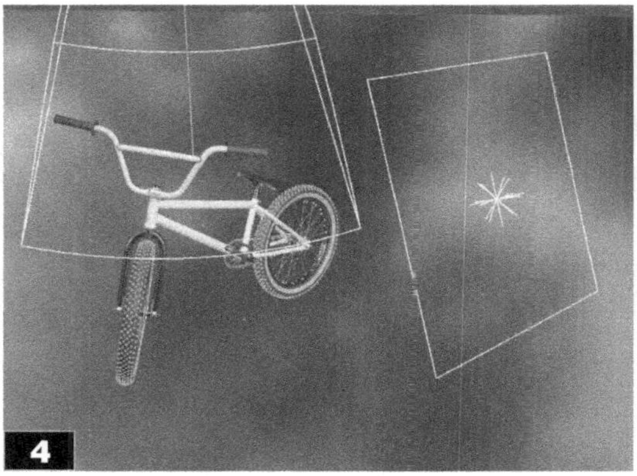

4

5

6. Create a new **Spot** light and aim it at the seat of the bike (see Figure 6). In the **Attribute Manager > General** tab, change **Intensity** to **500** and clear the **Diffuse** checkbox. Switch to the **Project** tab and then drag **Sport Bike > Saddle** from the **Object Manager** to **Objects** field. Also, change **Mode** to **Include**. Render the scene (see Figure 7).

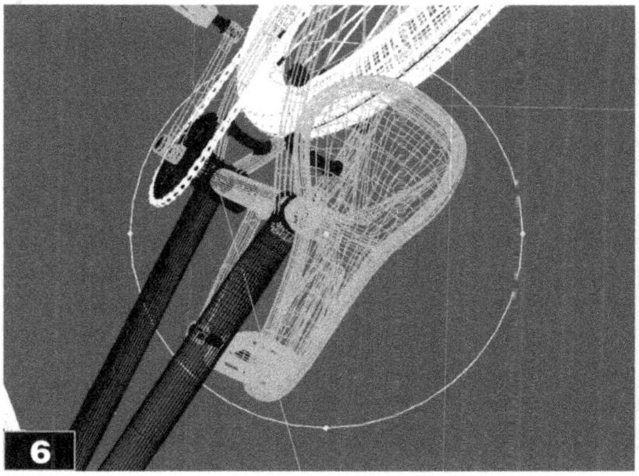

6

7

WHAT JUST HAPPENED?
In this step, the seat of the bike has been added to the ***Project*** *tab to ensure that the* ***Spot*** *light only illuminates the seat and doesn't affect the* ***Diffuse*** *component. Adding this light will create a rim highlight on the seat.*

7. Create another **Spot** light and this time focus it on the **Handle Bar** object (see Figure 8). Switch to the **Project** tab and then drag **Sport Bike > Handle Bar** from the **Object Manager** to **Objects** field. Also, change **Mode** to **Include**. Change spot light's **Intensity** parameter to **250**. Render the scene (see Figure 9).

WHAT NEXT?
Let's proceed by adding a ***Sky*** *object to the current scene.*

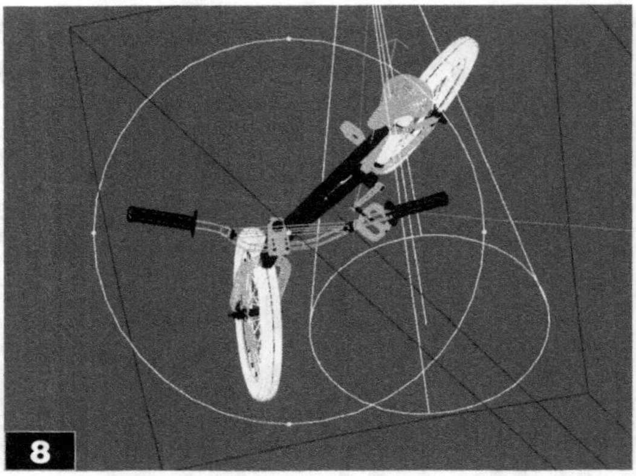

8. Press **Shift F8** to open the **Content Browser**. In the browser, choose **Presets > Templates & Presets > Lighting > HDRI** and double-click on **Photo Studio** swatch to add it to the **Material Manager**.

9. Create a **Sky** object and then apply the **Photo Studio** material to the **Sky** object. Add a **Compositing** tag to the **Sky** object. Make sure tag is selected in the **Object Manager** and then in the **Attribute Manager** > **Tag** tab, clear all checkboxes except **Seen by Rays**, **Seen by GI**, **Seen by Reflection**, and **Seen by AO** checkboxes.

10. Select **floor-mat** in the **Material Manager** and then in the **Attribute Manager > Basic** tab, select the **Diffusion** checkbox. In the **Diffusion** tab, click **Texture > Triangle** button and then choose **Effects > Ambient Occlusion** from the popup. Click on the **Ambient Occlusion** button to open the shader settings. Change **Maximum Ray Length** to **200**.

11. Add a **Compositing** tag to the **Sport Bike** object and then in the **Attribute Manager** > **Object Buffer** tab, select the first **Enable** checkbox and make sure if **Buffer** is set to **1**.

12. Switch to the **Render Settings** window. Ensure that **PhysicalFinal** preset is active. **RMB** click on the **Multi-Pass** checkbox in the left pane of the window. Choose **Object Buffer** from the popup. Also, select the **Multi-Pass** checkbox.

13. In the left pane, select the **Save** checkbox and select this option. In the **Regular Image** section of the right pane, choose a location and set file name to **bikeRender**. Change **Format** to **PNG** and **Depth** to **16 Bit/Channel**. Also, use the same settings in the **Multi-Pass Image** section. In the left pane, select the **Anti-Aliasing** and then on the right pane select the **Consider Multi-Passes** checkbox.

WHAT CONSIDER MULTI-PASSES CHECKBOX DOES?
*Enabling this checkbox ensures that multi passes and **Alpha** channels remain unaffected by any quality issues that may arise during rendering. Such issues typically occur when an object is rendered against a black background or is situated behind a thin, transparent surface.*

14. Render the scene (see Figure 10). Notice that the **Floor** object is getting affected by the HDR illumination. Next, we will fix it.

15. Select the **Compositing** tag of the **Sky** object and then switch to the **Exclusion** tab in the **Attribute Manager**. Drag **Floor** from the **Object Manager** to this tab. Make sure **Mode** is change to **Exclude**. Render the scene (see Figure 11); after completion of the rendering process, you will get two PNG files namely, **bikeRender.png** and **bikeRender_object_1.png**. These files contains the regular image and the multi-pass image, respectively.

10

11

Post Production

Follow the steps given next:

1. Start **Photoshop** and then open two PNG files. In the **bikeRender_object_1.png** file, press **Ctrl A** to select the whole image and hen press **Ctrl C**. Switch to the **bikeRender.png** file. Switch to the **Channels** panel, click the **Create new channel** icon at the bottom of the panel and then press **Ctrl V** to paste the image from the clipboard (see Figure 12). Now, turn of the **Alpha 1** channel and turn on the **RGB** channels.

WHAT NEXT?
*The image **bikeRender.png** shows a horizon line that needs to be corrected.*

2. Switch to the **Layers** panel and then press **Ctrl D** to clear the selection. Make sure the **Background** layer is selected and then press **Ctrl J** to duplicate the layer. Switch to the **Channels** panel and **Ctrl** click on the **Alpha 1** layer swatch to load the selection. Press **Ctrl Shift I** to invert the selection.

3. Switch back to the **Layers** panel and click on the **Add layer mask** icon at the bottom of the panel to add a mask. Change blending mode to **Overlay** and **Opacity** to **60**. Notice that now the horizon line has disappeared (see Figure 13). Press **Ctrl E** to merge the layers and rename it as **Base**. Save the file as **bikeRender.psd**.

12

13

4. Duplicate **Base** and rename it as **Clarity**. Choose **Filter > Camera Raw Filter** from the menubar and then change **Clarity** to **15** (see Figure 14). Click **OK**.

5. Duplicate the **Clarity** layer and rename it as **High Pass**. Choose **Filter > Other > High Pass** from the menubar to open the **High Pass** dialog box. In this dialog box, change **Radius** to **2** and click **OK**. Change **Blending Mode** to **Overlay** and **Opacity** to **50** (see Figure 15).

14

15

WHAT CLARITY AND HIGH PASS DO?
To enhance the clarity of the image and make it appear sharper without adding actual sharpness, you can use the ***Clarity*** *filter which adds midtones contrast. Additionally, the* ***High Pass*** *filter can be used to restore highlights and edges in the image. The* ***Radius*** *parameter determines the number of pixels on both sides of the edge that will be considered as part of the edge. For instance, a value of* ***1*** *pixel would only include a single pixel on each side of the edge.*

6. Click **Create new fill or adjustment layer** and choose **Color Lookup** from the popup. In the **Properties** panel, change **3DLUT File** to **Fuji F125 Kodak 2393**. Change **Opacity** to **35** (see Figure 16).

7. Now, apply a curve adjustment (see Figure 17). Save the PSD file.

16

17

RENDERING AN INTERIOR SCENE

In this tutorial, we will go through the process of rendering an interior scene, as shown in Figure 1.

1

Summary	
Topics	Getting Started Specifying Settings for Test Rendering Illuminating the Scene Specifying Settings for Final Rendering
Resources folder	**lighting**
Start file	**int-start.c4d**
Final file	**int-finish.c4d**

Getting Started

To begin, open the file **int-start.c4d**. One of the important materials used in the scene is called **mat-curtain** which is applied to the curtains. Because the curtains will be illuminated from outside the room, we need a specific material to achieve this effect.

I used the **Backlight** shader to make the material for the curtains, which I connected to the **Luminance** channel (refer to Figure 2). The texture bitmap is linked to the **Transparency** channel's **Texture** attribute with a brightness level of **54** (refer to Figure 3). I made these modifications to produce a particular look for the curtains when they're lit from outside the room.

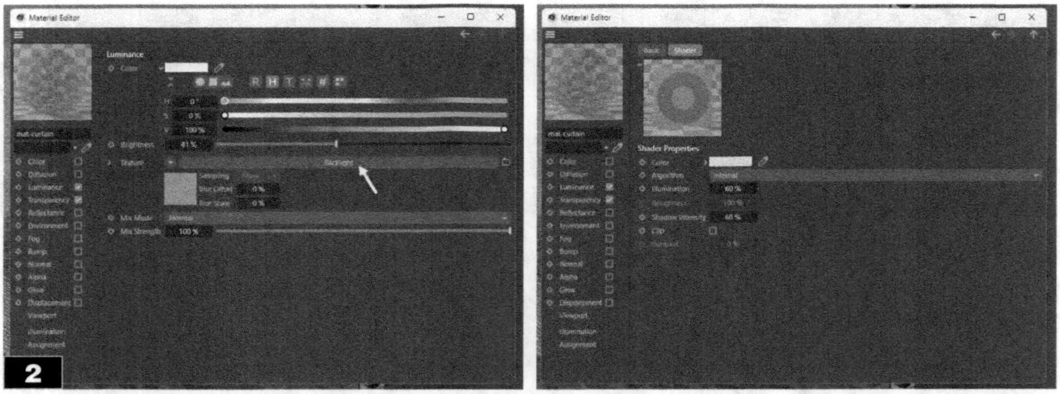

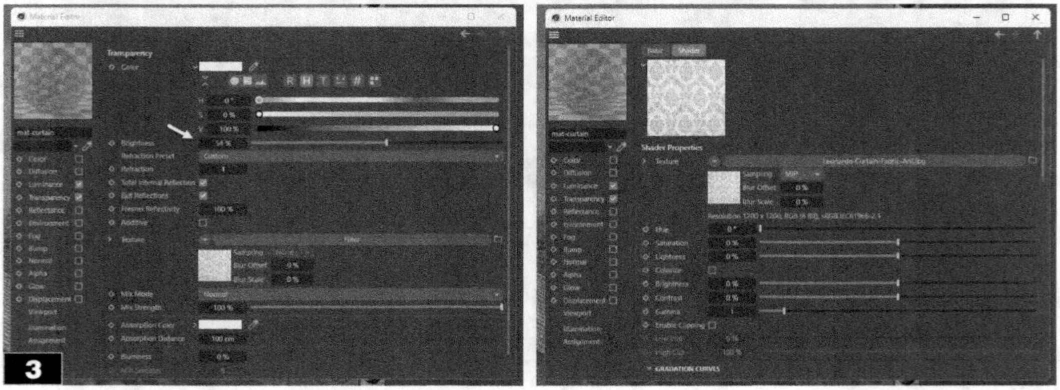

The **Backlight** shader is capable of collecting light from the back side of an object. However, it only works with actual lights and cannot be used with polygon lights. Typically, this shader is utilized in conjunction with the **Luminance** channel.

Specifying Settings for Test Rendering

Follow these steps:

1. Press **Ctrl B** to open the **Render Settings** window. Select **Physical** from the **Renderer** drop-down list. Select **Physical** from the left pane. In the right pane, make sure the **Sampler** is set to **Adaptive**. Change **Sampling Subdivisions** to **0**, **Blurriness Subdivision (Max)** to **0**, **Shadow Subdivision (Max)** to **1**, **Ambient Occlusion Subdivision (Max)** to **1**, and **Subsurface Scattering Subdivision (Max)** to **0**. Rename **My Render Settings** to **Test**.

2. Click on the **Effect** button and then choose **Global Illumination** from the popup menu. Select **Global Illumination** from the left pane and then in the **General** tab of the right pane, change **Primary Method** to **Irradiance Cache**, **Secondary Method** to **None**, and **Samples** to **Low**.

3. In the **Irradiance Cache** tab, change **Record Density** to **Low**. Save the scene as **int-start-01.c4d**.

Illuminating the Scene

To begin, we will create a simulation of sunlight using three Infinite Light objects: **Sun**, **Sun Diffuse**, and **Sun Beam**. The primary light source will be the **Sun** light, which will emit warm colors. The angle of the shadows cast by the **Sun** can be adjusted using the **Infinite Angle** parameter, with a value of **0** resulting in hard shadows. The **Sun Diffuse** light will provide soft illumination by using a larger value for the **Infinite Angle** parameter. Finally, the **Sun Beam** light will be used to create the effect of sunlight entering through the window. Follow the steps below to create this effect.

1. Create an **Infinite Light** and then rename it as **Sun**. In the **Attribute Manager > Coordinates** tab, change **P.X**, **P.Y**, and **P.Z** to **420**, **585**, and **1272**, respectively. Change **R.H**, **R.P**, and **R.B** to **180**, **-26**, and **0**, respectively (see Figure 4). Render the scene (see Figure 5).

4

5

2. In the **General** tab, change **Color** to HSV (**26**, **24**, **100**) and **Shadow** to **Area**. Render the scene (see Figure 6). In the **Details** tab, change **Infinite Angle** to **0.38** and then render the scene (see Figure 7).

WHAT JUST HAPPENED?
*The **AB** comparison shown in Figure 8 highlights the effect of the **Infinite Angle** parameter, resulting in more natural and softer shadow edges.*

6

7

3. In the **Render Settings** window, disable **Global Illumination** for the time being so that we get faster test renders while we are placing the direct light sources. In the **Object Manager**, create a copy of **Sun** and rename the new object as **Sun Diffuse**. In the **Attribute Manager > General** tab, select the **Use Temperature** checkbox and then change **Color Temperature** to **5536**. In the **Details** tab, change **Infinite Angle** to **6.5** and then render the scene (see Figure 9).

8

9

WHAT JUST HAPPENED?
By increasing the value of the ***Infinite Angle*** *parameter, I have adjusted the angle of the shadow to create a more realistic soft shadow with smoother edges (as shown in Figure 9).*

4. In the **Object Manager**, create a copy of **Sun Diffuse** and rename the new object as **Sun Beam**. In the **Attribute Manager > General** tab, change **Color Temperature** to **5532** and **Type** to **Square Parallel Spot**. In the **Details** tab, change **Outer Radius** to **160**.

5. In the **General** tab, select the **No Illumination** checkbox and then change **Visible Light** to **Volumetric**. In the **Visibility** tab, change **Brightness** to **126**. Align the light, as shown in Figure 10 and then render the scene (see Figure 11).

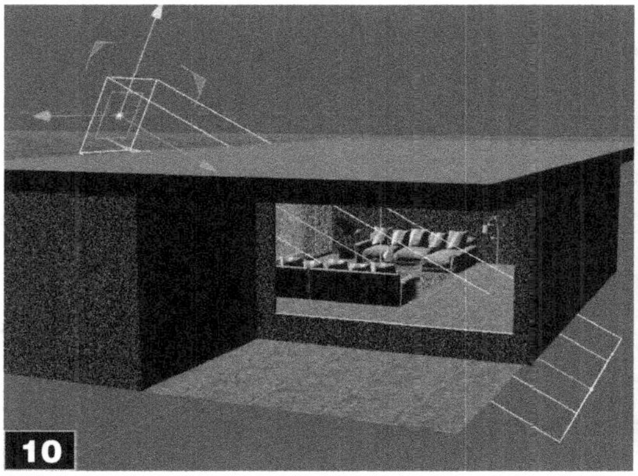

10

11

WHAT JUST HAPPENED?
*I utilized the **Sun Beam** light to imitate the sunlight rays entering the room. Furthermore, I disabled the Illumination option by selecting the **No Illumination** checkbox in the **General** tab. This setting will enable the light to only cast rays and not produce any illumination on the scene.*

WHAT NEXT?
*Our next step involves creating the simulation of daylight by adding an **Area** light.*

6. Create an **Area** light and then rename it as **Day Light**. In the **Attribute Manager > Coordinates** tab, change **P.X**, **P.Y**, and **P.Z** to **407**, **213**, and **535**, respectively. Change **R.H**, **R.P**, and **R.B** to **0**, **180**, and **0**, respectively. In the **Details** tab, select the **Z Direction Only** checkbox. Also, change **Size X** and **Size Y** to **360** and **287**, respectively (see Figure 12).
7. In the **General** tab, select the **Use Temperature** checkbox and then change **Color Temperature** to **6800**. Also, change **Shadow** to **Area**. Render the scene (see Figure 13).

12

13

WHAT JUST HAPPENED?
The ***Day Light*** *was utilized to simulate the daylight entering the room, while the other lights were employed to simulate the scattering of skylight and room light in the scene.*

8. Create a **Light** object and then rename the light as **Bounce Light**. In the **Attribute Manager > Details** tab, change **Falloff** to **Inverse Square (Physically Accurate)** and **Radius/Decay** to **386**. Now, align the light, as shown in Figure 14.

9. In the **General** tab, select the **Use Temperature** checkbox and then change **Color Temperature** to **4958**. Change **Intensity** to **65** and then render the scene (see Figure 15). Now, in the **Render Settings** window, enable **Global Illumination**. Then, render the scene (see Figure 16).

14

15

WHAT JUST HAPPENED?
I utilized the ***Bounce Light*** *to mimic the way light bounces around the room, which can help to break up any uniformity caused by the* ***Global Illumination*** *used in the scene. However, some adjustments to the parameters are necessary in order to achieve an even distribution of light.*

10. Select **Day Light** in the **Object Manager** and then in the **Attribute Manager > General** tab, change **Intensity** to **55**. Similarly, change **Intensity** to **20** for the **Bounce Light**. Render the scene (see Figure 17).

16

17

11. In the **Render Settings** window, select **Global Illumination** from the left pane of the window and then in the right pane > **General** tab, change **Secondary Method** to **Light Mapping**. In the **Light Mapping** tab, change **Path Count (x1000)** to **2000** and **Sample Size** to **0.02**. Render the scene (see Figure 18).

HOW TO FINE TUNE RENDER?
To adjust the lighting results precisely, you can isolate each light and render the scene to observe the effect of each light individually. This way, you can analyze and adjust the impact of each light on the scene. The images in Figures 19 through 23 illustrate the separate output of the ***Sun, Sun Diffuse, Sun Beam, Day Light****, and* ***Bounce Light****.*

18

19

20

21

12. Disable all lights in the scene. Create an **Area** light and then rename it as **SkyLight-01**. In the **Attribute Manager** > **Coordinates** tab, change **P.X**, **P.Y**, and **P.Z** to **-761**, **237**, and **577**, respectively. Change **R.H**, **R.P**, and **R.B** to **0**, **180**, and **0**, respectively. In the **Details** tab, change **Size X** and **Size Y** to **469** and **341**, respectively, (see Figure 24). Also, select the **Z Direction Only** checkbox.

13. In the **General** tab, change **Intensity** to **40**. Select the **Use Temperature** checkbox and then change **Color Temperature** to **7516**. Next, change **Shadow** to **Area**. Render the scene (see Figure 25).

22

23

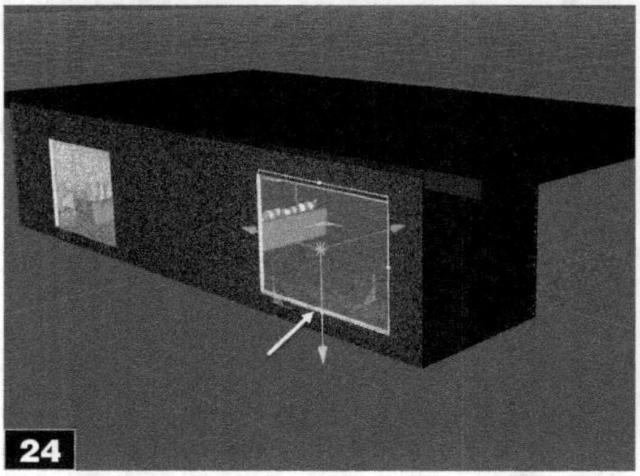

24

25

14. Create a copy of **SkyLight-01** and then rename it as **SkyLight-02**. In the **Attribute Manager > Coordinates** tab, change **P.X**, **P.Y**, and **P.Z** to **-574**, **237**, and **-263**, respectively. Change **R.H**, **R.P**, and **R.B** to **90**, **180**, and **0**, respectively. In the **Details** tab, change **Size X** and **Size Y** to **585** and **282**, respectively, (see Figure 26). In the **General** tab, change **Intensity** to **20**. Render the scene (see Figure 27).

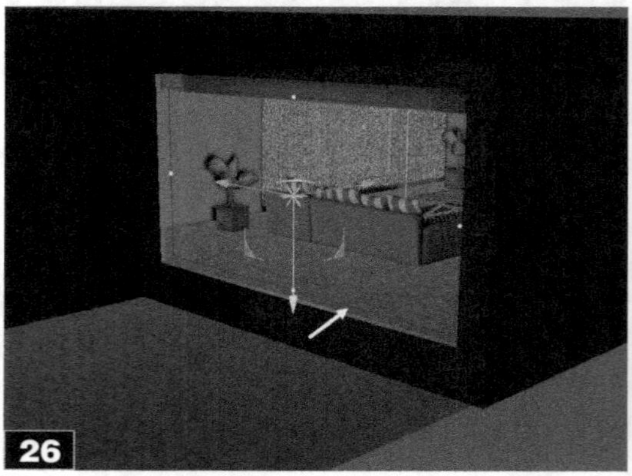

26

27

15. Enable all lights in the scene and then render it (see Figure 28).

Specifying Settings for Final Rendering

Follow these steps:

1. Open the **Render Settings** window. Select **Physical** from the left pane. In the right pane, change **Shading Subdivisions (Min)** to **1**, **Shading Subdivisions (Max)** to **4**, **Shadow Subdivision (Max)** to **2**, and **Ambient Subdivision (Max)** to **2**.

2. Select **Global Illumination** from the left pane and then in the **General** tab of the right pane, **Samples** to **Medium**. In the **Irradiance Cache** tab, change **Record Density** to **Medium** and **Smoothing** to **50**. In the **Light Mapping** tab, change **Path Count (x1000)** to **5000** and **Sample Size** to **0.01**. Select the **Show Preview Paths** checkbox and then select the **Prefilter** checkbox. Change **Prefilter Samples** to **8**.

3. Click the **Effect** button and then choose **Ambient Occlusion** from the flyout. Select the **Ambient Occlusion** option and then in the **Basic** tab of the right pane, change **Maximum Ray Length** to **150**. Render the scene (see Figure 29).

28

29

This page is intentionally left blank

Index

www.ingramcontent.com/pod-product-compliance
Lightning Source LLC
LaVergne TN
LVHW080029210926
848481LV00011B/3139
* 9 7 9 8 2 1 5 5 2 2 5 1 6 *